THE INSIDERS' GUIDE
TO
North Carolina's
CENTRAL COAST
& NEW BERN

THE INSIDERS' GUIDE®

TO

North Carolina's
CENTRAL COAST
& NEW BERN

by
Janis Williams
and
Claire Doyle

Insiders' Publishing Inc.
By The Sea Publications, Inc.

Co-published and marketed by:
By The Sea Publications Inc.
Hanover Center P.O. Box 5386
Wilmington, NC 28403
(910) 763-8464

Co-published and distributed by:
Insiders' Publishing Inc.
The Waterfront • Suite 12
P.O. Box 2057
Manteo, NC 27954
(919) 473-6100

•

SIXTH EDITION
1st printing

•

Copyright ©1997
by By The Sea Publications Inc.

•

Printed in the United States of America

•

Publications from The Insiders' Guide® series
are available at special discounts for bulk
purchases for sales promotions, premiums
or fundraisings. Special editions, including
personalized covers, can be created in large
quantities for special needs. For more
information, please write to Insiders'
Publishing Inc., P.O. Box 2057, Manteo, NC
27954 or call (919) 473-6100 x 233.

ISBN 1-57380-021-X

By The Sea Publications Incorporated

President/Publisher
Jay Tervo

Sales and Marketing
Deborah Dunn

Administrative Manager
Gerry Tyhacz

Creative Consultant
Ashley Ware

Insiders' Publishing Inc.

Publisher/Editor-in-Chief
Beth P. Storie

President/General Manager
Michael McOwen

Affiliate Sales and Training Director
Rosanne Cheeseman

Partner Services Director
Giles MacMillan

Sales and Marketing Director
Jennifer Risko

Creative Services Director
Mike Lay

Online Services Director
David Haynes

Managing Editor
Theresa Shea Chavez

Fulfillment Director
Gina Twiford

Project Editor
Molly Perkins

Project Artist
Elaine Fogarty

Special thanks to NC Travel and
Tourism for providing
cover photographs.

Preface

Welcome to the sixth edition of *The Insiders' Guide® to North Carolina's Central Coast and New Bern*. The purpose of this book is to give you an Insider's knowledge of this beautiful coastal region. Use this guide like a road map and keep it handy. If you are a newcomer, you'll learn much by reading our Area Overviews and Getting Around chapters. If you've been around awhile, you're sure to enjoy our short features (we call them close-ups) and tips, and you might learn something you didn't know before. Keep this guide handy for all your visiting relatives and friends.

This book is divided into two major parts. The first section covers the beautiful Crystal Coast, which includes all of Carteret County and Swansboro. The name Crystal Coast was given to the Carteret County sea towns several years ago by the Carteret County Chamber of Commerce. It was hoped the name would attract visitors to the county's crystal waters and brilliant beaches — and it has. This book's name is North Carolina's Central Coast because that name is more recognizable nationally from a marketing standpoint, even though Crystal Coast is the Insiders' moniker of choice. The second major part of this book addresses the historic city of New Bern. Best known as the site of Tryon Palace, the city offers much to delight visitors and guests. It is the second-oldest town in North Carolina and is rich with history.

Besides the Crystal Coast and New Bern, you'll also discover information about our neighboring city of Havelock, home to Marine Corps Air Station Cherry Point and the Naval Aviation Depot. Havelock is Craven County's largest city and is continually growing. Following Havelock, we tell you about quaint Oriental, the sailing capital of North Carolina. This charming riverside village is quiet and slow-paced and just the place to help you forget your cares and focus on — well, perhaps, nothing at all, except the beauty of Oriental. In the last section, we offer daytrip itineraries for a few favorite getaway spots such as Ocracoke Island, Wilmington and Belhaven.

We've packed this book with chapters and sections that cover just about every topic you can imagine: History, Restaurants, Accommodations, Weekly and Long-term Cottage Rentals, Shopping, Nightlife, Annual Events, Camping, Fishing, Boating and more. We tell you about places to launch and store your boat, have a picnic, get a surf report, rent a boat, go for a hike and play a round of golf. There are also chapters on Schools and Child Care, Worship, Commerce and Industry, and Sports, Fitness and Parks. You'll find information about buying a home or land to build on. For some of our readers, the best parts of this book are the sections on Kidstuff — indispensable information for parents whose kids are on vacation too.

Please be assured that the businesses featured here are chosen from the many as being the best in the area. We decide which businesses to include based on their quality, their uniqueness or their popularity.

Our general maps will help you see the overall picture. These are site detailed and should be used in conjunction with your regular road map. We also offer the following invaluable hints for getting around by car — U.S. Highway 70 takes on a different name in each town it passes through: Main Street in Havelock; Arendell Street in Morehead City; and Cedar and Live Oak streets in Beaufort. N.C. Highway 58 takes on a new name in each of the beach towns it passes through: Fort Macon Road east or west in Atlantic Beach; Salter Path Road between Atlantic Beach and Indian Beach; and Emerald Drive in Emerald Isle.

From a map, the entire area might seem to be little more than a highway. However, North Carolina's Crystal Coast and New Bern have much to offer visitors and residents. If you are visiting, don't expect to see everything in one trip. If you have relocated to the area, we urge you to spend occasional weekends exploring the many treasures that surround you.

The Crystal Coast, New Bern, Havelock and Oriental are within the 919 telephone area code. Dial 910 to reach Swansboro and Wilmington. All telephone numbers in this book are in the 919 area code unless otherwise noted. Milepost numbers are given to help locate places on Bogue Banks.

We've written about many, many of the wonderful sights, sounds and tastes of the Crystal Coast and its environs. We've done our best to ensure that all the information is accurate. However, we know room for improvement always exists. Let us know what you think so that future editions can accommodate your ideas and suggestions. Write to us in care of By The Sea Publications Inc., Hanover Center, Box 5386, Wilmington, North Carolina 28403. Or visit us online and make your comments there: www.insiders.com/explore.

Our hope is that the coast's lure and its varied pleasures will please you as much as they do us and other Insiders. We trust this book will guide you well and that you will enjoy exploring, revisiting or living along North Carolina's Crystal Coast and in New Bern.

About the Authors

Janis Williams moved to Carteret County 18 years ago to publish an entertainment magazine, *The Maritimes*, with a friend. To their surprise, it worked, and they eventually learned how to do it. She worked as managing editor for eight years, sold it, went sailing, then returned for a romp in the retail clothing business. For six years she learned how that was done and, realizing that it wasn't the 1980s anymore, she closed the store and returned to editing. Since 1995, she has worked as editor of *Coaster Magazine* where she keeps up with the Crystal Coast all year.

Winters, whenever possible, Janis works with her husband in the Florida Keys and Bahamas managing the galley aboard their charter sailboat, *Good Fortune*. Summers, she's aboard for those gorgeous sunset sails out of Beaufort. At all other times, she is down by the sound throwing sticks for her golden retriever.

Claire Doyle is a relative newcomer to Carteret County. She and her husband and bull dogs, Spike and Rocky, purchased a home here in 1993. They became permanent year-rounders in 1995, and all four plan on staying forever. Before discovering the charms of the Crystal Coast, for 16 years Claire was a writer, editor and manager of federal government publications. In the 1970s and 1980s, she produced and marketed articles and newsletters for political organizations, healthcare consulting firms and the cable television franchise industry. She also did brief stints as a government auditor, manager of a printing business and as a program administrator for a suburban county in Maryland. Today she lives contentedly at the seashore and edits the newsletter for the Carteret County Master Gardener Volunteers.

Walking hand in hand along the beach is a great way to end a day along the Crystal Coast.

Acknowledgments

The most enjoyable thing about updating this book is the warm winter visits with those of you who are too busy with the Crystal Coast to slow down in the summers, and I really enjoyed that warmth this winter. You're showing good training, after three years of this, in pointing out all that I should see and things I should include. Ron, I really appreciate your taking up the slack lines at home, not to mention keeping the boat in the slip this year. Jay, your access and humor are always the right medicine for the moment and, as always, I appreciate your friendship but, this year, I was also grateful for your 800 number.

— Janis

This sixth edition is the first Insiders' Guide® that I have had the pleasure to work on. I owe a lot to many people — the dozens who were patient with me as I learned along the way, and the many staff of Carteret and Craven counties and Cherry Point Marine Corps Air Station who answered my questions and were kind enough to provide me with information. A healthy helping of my gratitude goes to my deserving family: Larry, my husband, who has done all manner of Insider-related chores to help me out; my son, Michael, who said "Go for it, Mom!"; and my soon-to-be daughter-in-law, Aimee DeBone, who encouraged me to apply for the job as writer for the Insiders' Guide.

I should also like to acknowledge Jay Tervo, publisher of this book and my boss, and Molly Perkins, my editor in Manteo. Both have been gracious, patient and encouraging. And last, but by no means least, acknowledgement is due my co-author, Janis, who taught me some tricks that saved the day for me more than once.

—Claire

If You Think All Checking Accounts Are Alike, Look Again.

And Again.

(Wachovia also offers you a no-annual-fee Visa® or MasterCard.®)

And Again.

(Reduced loan rates.)

And Again.

(A standard safe deposit box at no charge.)

And Again.

(No-fee traveler's checks and much more.)

Wachovia Crown Account.

Take a good look at your checkbook. Is it giving you everything you want from your bank? Well, when you open a Crown Account at Wachovia, you'll get interest checking plus ten extra services, including specially designed checks, a consolidated banking summary and a gold Banking Card with Visa Check – all at no extra charge. And all it takes is $2,500 in savings or $10,000 in Wachovia CDs, a Cash Investment Account,℠ Premiere Money Market Account, BankLine® or Equity BankLine. The Crown Account from Wachovia. You'll never look at your checkbook the same way again. For more information, stop by your local Wachovia branch. Or call 1-800-922-4684.

Table of Contents

Directory of Maps

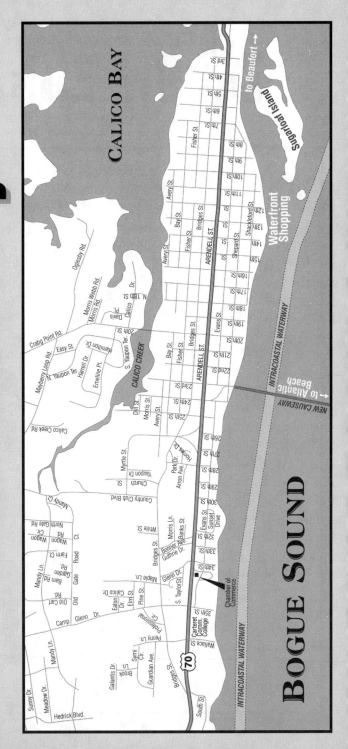

Down East

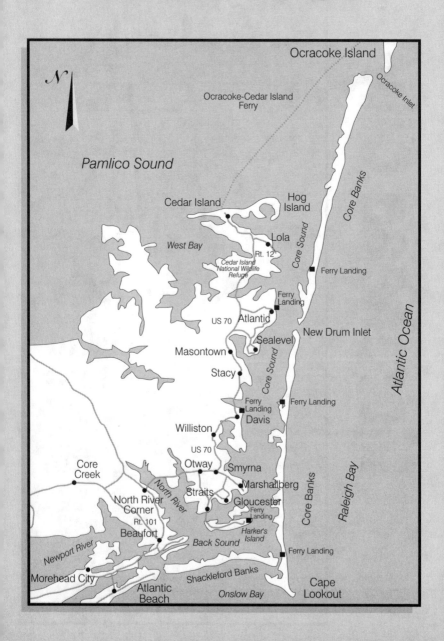

Downtown
Beaufort

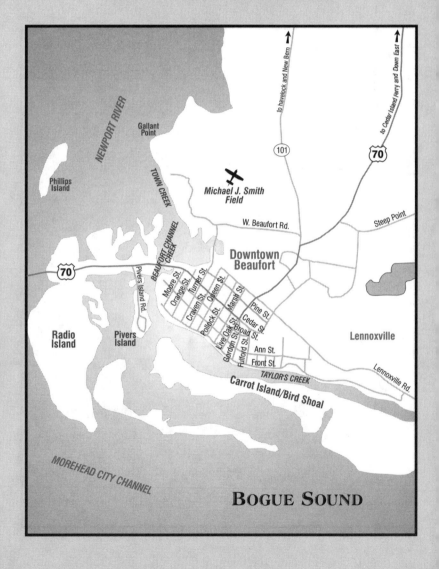

New Bern

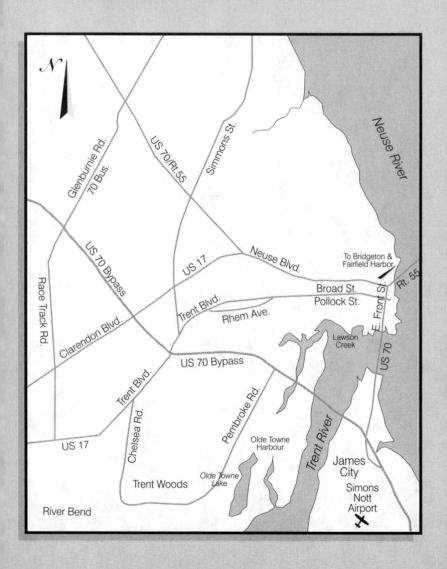

New Bern
HISTORICAL DISTRICT

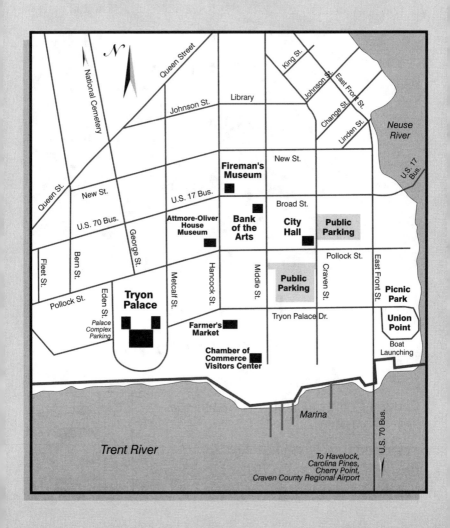

663 businesses
working together
to help make
a great place even better

Carteret County
CHAMBER
OF COMMERCE

Let us know
how we can help you.

Carteret County Chamber of Commerce
801 Arendell Street
Morehead City, North Carolina 28557
Ph. (919)726-6350 Fax (919) 726-3505
email: cart.coc@coastalnet.com

Getting Around

Whether by land, sea or air, more and more people are coming year round to visit or relocate to the Crystal Coast. Getting to the area is half the fun by sea or air, but 95 percent of the millions who visit our shores annually arrive by land.

By Land

If you're coming to the area from the north or south, Interstate 95 or U.S. Highway 17 will take you to either U.S. Highway 70 and on to Morehead City or to N.C. Highway 58, which leads straight to Emerald Isle. From the west, Interstate 40 will also take you to U.S. 70, which leads directly to Morehead City. From the east, travelers who will persevere to see the southernmost of North Carolina's Outer Banks must reserve space for the 2¼-hour ferry ride from Ocracoke to Cedar Island. At the ferry landing, N.C. Highway 12 continues a short distance to intersect with U.S. 70 W. at the town of Atlantic, the highway's point of origin. (Interestingly enough, U.S. 70 ends in Los Angeles.) From here, it's an astonishing ride through lowland fields of junkus and spartina marsh grasses and Down East fishing villages to Beaufort and the Crystal Coast or on to Havelock and New Bern.

Between Morehead City and Emerald Isle or Swansboro, the main thoroughfare is N.C. Highway 24. This partially five-lane highway offers lovely views of Bogue Sound as you cross its bridges at Broad Creek and Gales Creek. Work in progress to complete the five-laning of N.C. 24 between U.S. 70 at Morehead City and N.C. 58 at the Cameron Langston Bridge to Emerald Isle. The first 2.5-mile portion of the project from Morehead City

is scheduled for completion by spring 1997 when the final phase, between Broad Creek and N.C. 58, will be in progress. Those of you who question why highway projects always occur during the seasons of highest traffic may be interested to know that it's not solely for the inconvenience involved. It seems that the optimum temperature for working with asphalt is 275 degrees, and transporting it during cooler months causes it to chill quickly. So, prepare for a slowdown on N.C. 24 near N.C. 58 as the 1997 temperatures are rising.

On the island of Bogue Banks, N.C. 58 runs parallel to the beach for more than 20 miles from Atlantic Beach west to Emerald Isle. Milepost markers along the way make it easy to locate anything. Mile 1 (MP 1) begins at Fort Macon State Park on the east end of the island.

Bus and Taxi Service

Daily bus service by **Carolina Trailways**, 726-3029, arrives in Morehead City at 105 N. 13th Street. Connections to Morehead City from all directions are made in Raleigh.

Several cab and limousine companies service the area.

A-1 Yellow Cab Co., 728-3483, services Atlantic Beach, Beaufort and Morehead City.

Crystal Coast Cab, 728-5365, offers service to Atlantic Beach, Beaufort, Down East, Morehead City and Newport.

Yellow Cab Co., 726-3125, provides service to Atlantic Beach, Beaufort and Morehead City.

Emerald Isle Taxi, 393-8866, offers service to Swansboro, Emerald Isle and Cape Carteret.

Presidential Limousine Service, 726-8109, offers car and driver service anywhere within the tri-county area.

Car Rentals

This area has very few car rental establishments. More rental options exist in New Bern or a nearby larger area. In Carteret County, try the **Michael J. Smith Airfield**, Beaufort Airport, 728-1777. In Morehead City, rental cars are offered by **Merritt-Williams Ford,** Highway 70 W., 247-2131, and **Enterprise Rent-A-Car**, Highway 70 W., 240-0218.

By Air

Passenger airline service is available at several airports convenient to the coastal area. You can reach New Bern by commercial carrier, or you can fly into New Bern or Beaufort by private plane. Flights directly to the Crystal Coast are accommodated at the area's only airport in Beaufort.

Michael J. Smith Airport
N.C. 101, Beaufort
• 728-1777

The Crystal Coast's only airport offers only chartered or private aircraft service. It has no landing fee but charges for overnight storage of aircraft. Rental cars, an airport courtesy car and taxi service are available. Beaufort Aviation is the fixed-base operator and handles all fueling, rentals, flight instruction, charters and sightseeing flights. The airport was named for Capt. Michael J. Smith, a Beaufort native who died aboard the space shuttle *Challenger*.

Craven County Regional Airport
U.S. 70, New Bern • 638-8591

Craven Regional is the nearest commercial service airport to Morehead City. Daily flights by USAir Express take passengers to the large hub airport of Charlotte. Charter services are available with Carolina Air, 633-1400. Car rental agencies are based at the airport and limousine services to Havelock and the Crystal Coast are wise to the arrival schedule for passengers' convenience.

Albert Ellis Airport
N.C. 111, Jacksonville • (910) 324-1100

Commercial air service to the Crystal Coast is available from the Albert Ellis Airport located 20 miles west of Jacksonville off U.S. Highway 258 toward Richlands. It is the closest airport to Camp Lejeune, the U.S. Marine Corps Base at Jacksonville. The airport offers commuter service of USAir, Henson and ASA Delta to Charlotte and Atlanta hubs. Car rental and taxi services are at the airport.

Raleigh-Durham International Airport
Aviation Parkway • 840-2123

Raleigh-Durham (RDU) is the major international airport serving North Carolina from the Research Triangle Park area. RDU is a three-hour drive from the Crystal Coast. The airport is a major hub for domestic and international travelers and is served by all major and several feeder carriers. Commercial feeder services to New Bern are presently available only from Charlotte; commercial service to Jacksonville is available from RDU. Car rental services are at the airport.

By Sea

The Intracoastal Waterway (ICW) provides access by water to the Crystal Coast via Morehead City, Beaufort, Swansboro and Emerald Isle. To reach New Bern by water, slip into Pamlico Sound and head up the Neuse River. Beaufort is a favorite stop for boaters on the north-south ICW run in the spring and fall each year. Transient dockage at either the Beaufort Town Docks or Town Creek Marina is hospitable, and anchorage is plentiful in the town's harbor of refuge north of the Grayden Paul drawbridge or in the designated anchorage off the town's waterfront. See our Marinas chapter for details.

By Ferry

A number of state-owned and private ferries serve the Crystal Coast, offering visitors and residents a timesaving and enjoyable transportation alternative via inland sounds and rivers.

FYI

Unless otherwise noted, the area code for all phone numbers in this guide is 919.

State Ferries

The state's ferries operate under the administration of the North Carolina Department of Transportation (NCDOT) and are large, seaworthy vessels.

Three ferries connect Ocracoke Island with other parts of North Carolina. The **Cedar Island-Ocracoke Toll Ferry** is the state's most popular ferry and carries passengers and vehicles between the Crystal Coast and Ocracoke Island. This ferry is popular with people coming to the Crystal Coast from the north or with people leaving the mainland to travel to the Outer Banks. The **Ocracoke-Hatteras Inlet Free Ferry** connects Ocracoke with Hatteras Island and the Outer Banks. The **Ocracoke-Swan Quarter Toll Ferry** crosses the Pamlico sound to connect the island with Swan Quarter.

The **Cherry Branch-Minnesott Ferry** carries passengers and vehicles and is a good connection between the Crystal Coast and Oriental. The **Hammocks Beach State Park Ferry** connects passengers only with Bear Island.

Regardless of the ferry you choose, you can almost always be assured of a calm crossing with plenty of time to look around. All ferry schedules and tolls are subject to change without notice, and ferries do not operate in rough weather. For more information about state-owned ferry crossings, contact the N.C. Department of Transportation Ferry Division, (800) BY-FERRY. Information about state ferries can also be obtained by tuning to New Bern's radio station 1610 AM. No reservations are required if you are traveling as a pedestrian or with a bicycle. Following is a list of state-operated ferry schedules and fares.

Cedar Island - Ocracoke Toll Ferry

The Cedar Island-Ocracoke Ferry Service carries passengers and their vehicles between the Crystal Coast and Ocracoke Island. The Cedar Island terminal is a little more than 30 miles east of Beaufort, but allow at least an hour and a half for the trip. Reservations must be claimed 30 minutes before departure time or they will be cancelled. Call the ferry terminals at Cedar Island, 225-3551, or Ocracoke, 928-3841, for reservations and to verify times.

2¼ hours crossing - 50 car limit
Reservations Recommended
Summer Schedule, May 22 - Oct. 1

Depart Cedar Island	Depart Ocracoke
7 AM	7 AM
8:15 AM	9:30 AM
9:30 AM	10 AM*
Noon	10:45 AM
1 PM *	Noon
1:15 PM	3 PM
3 PM	4:15 PM*
6 PM	6 PM
8:30 PM	8:30 PM

*Additional departures Memorial Day through Labor Day.

Nov.1 - April 2, April 17 - May 7

7 AM	7 AM
10 AM	10 AM
1 PM	1 PM
4 PM	4 PM

April 3 - April 16, May 8 - May 21, Oct. 2 - Oct. 31

7 AM	7 AM
9:30 AM	9:30 AM
Noon	Noon
3 PM	3 PM
6 PM	6 PM
8:30 PM	8:30 PM

Fares (One Way)
Pedestrian, $1
Bicycle Rider, $2
Motorcycles, $10
Vehicle and/or combination less than 20 feet, $10
Vehicle and/or combination 20 feet to 40 feet, $20
Vehicle and/or combination up to 55 feet, $30.

Ocracoke - Swan Quarter Toll Ferry

For departures from Ocracoke, call 928-3841; from Swan Quarter, call 926-1111.

2½ hours crossing - 28 car limit
Reservations Recommended
Year-round Schedule

Depart Ocracoke	Depart Swan Quarter
6:30 AM	7 AM*
12:30 PM	9:30 AM
4 PM*	4 PM

*Additional departures Memorial Day through Labor Day.

Fares are the same as those for the Cedar Island - Ocracoke Toll Ferry.

Ocracoke - Hatteras Inlet Free Ferry

40 minute crossing - 30 car limit
No Reservations Accepted
Summer Schedule, May 1 - Oct. 31

Depart Ocracoke	Depart Hatteras
5 AM	5 AM
6 AM	6 AM
7 AM	7 AM
8 AM	
Every 30 minutes:	Every 30 minutes:
8:30 AM-6:30 PM	7:30 AM-6:30 PM
7 PM	7 PM
8 PM	8 PM
9 PM	9 PM
10 PM	10 PM
11 PM	Midnight

Winter Schedule, Nov. 1 - April 30
Leaves Ocracoke every hour from 5 AM through 11 PM.
Leaves Hatteras every hour from 5 AM through 10 PM and at midnight.

INSIDERS' TIP

Crystal Coast beaches face south rather than east from the southern point of Core Banks at Cape Lookout to the west end of Bogue Banks. Therefore, the sun rises and sets on the ocean here, and the north wind calms the sea close to the beaches. The only other East Coast beaches with this orientation are those along Brunswick County at the south end of Wilmington and those on Long Island, New York.

Cherry Branch - Minnesott Beach Free Ferry

The Cherry Branch-Minnesott Beach Ferry is essential for commuters from Oriental who must travel with their cars across the Neuse River to work in Havelock and surrounding areas. On the Crystal Coast side, the Cherry Branch terminal is off N.C. Highway 101, about 5 miles south of Havelock. Signs along the highway give directions to the terminal. This ferry takes you on an interesting exploration north to Oriental and is an especially nice route to Belhaven.

20 minute crossing - 30 car limit
No Reservations Accepted
Year-round Schedule

Dep. Cherry Br.	Dep. Minnesott Beach
Every 30 minutes:	Every 30 minutes:
5:45 AM-12:15 PM	6:15 AM -12:15 PM
Every 30 minutes:	Every 30 minutes:
1:15 PM-6:45 PM	1:15 PM-6:15 PM
Every hour:	Every hour:
6:45 PM-12:45 AM	6:15 PM-1:15 AM

Hammocks Beach State Park Ferry

The seasonal, "people only — no cars" ferry at Hammocks Beach State Park provides transportation from the park headquarters terminal to Bear Island. The ferry terminal is off N.C. 24 2 miles west of Swansboro at the end of State Road 1511. If you are visiting Bear Island between Memorial Day and Labor Day, get to the ferry landing early to avoid long waiting lines. Pets are not allowed on the ferry, and alcoholic beverages are prohibited in the park (see our Attractions chapter). Call Hammocks Beach, (910) 326-4881, to verify times.

25-minute crossing - No vehicles
No Reservations Accepted
Operates seasonally
Memorial Day - Labor Day

Monday - Tuesday
Every hour on the hour from 9:30 AM - 4:30 PM
Wednesday - Sunday
Every half-hour from 9:30 AM - 4:30 PM
May and September
Wednesday - Sunday
Every hour on the half-hour from 9:30 AM - 4:30 PM

April and October
Friday - Sunday
Every hour on the half-hour from 9:30 AM - 4:30 PM

Fares (Round trip)
Adult, $2
Children ages 4-12, $1
Younger than 4, Free

Private Ferries

A number of privately owned vessels also stand ready to carry passengers to popular destinations along the Crystal Coast. Of course, you always have the options of hiring a luxurious sailboat complete with crew and catered meals or renting a small motorboat to do your own navigating. Whatever your choice, there is a lot to explore.

Along with state-owned ferries and private charters, the National Park Service (NPS) authorizes specified concessionaires to operate under NPS guidelines for carrying passengers and/or vehicles to the uninhabited Cape Lookout National Seashore (see our Attractions chapter). The seashore is a 56-mile stretch of barrier islands made up of North Core Banks, home of Portsmouth Village; South Core Banks, home of Cape Lookout Lighthouse; and Shackleford Banks, home to wild ponies.

The NPS allows two privately owned ferries to carry passengers and vehicles to North and South Core Banks and Portsmouth Village (see descriptions below). These small ferries operate out of the Down East communities of Davis and Atlantic and don't have all the extras you will find on the state ferries. They do have medium-size, seaworthy vessels equipped to carry one or two vehicles, a few passengers and some equipment. They normally operate from April to December, although schedules and fees vary. Most concessionaires require reservations, so it is best to call ahead to see what schedule the ferry is operating on, to check current fares and to see if there is room aboard for you. Each concessionaire can provide information on cabins and camping (see the Accommodations and Camping chapters). Federal regulations prohibit pets on any of these ferries and on the islands of the national seashore.

Alger Willis Fishing Camps Inc.
142 Willis Rd., Davis • 729-2791

Operating out of the Down East community of Davis off U.S. 70 E., ferry service to fishing camps carries passengers, vehicles and all-terrain vehicles to the northern end of South Core Banks four times a day, April until December. Fares are $13 round trip per adult and about $65 round trip for a standard-size vehicle. Cabins, delivered supplies (ice, groceries, bait, etc.) and island transportation can be arranged at the office. For more information about the fishing camps, see our Accommodations chapter.

Morris Marina Kabin Kamps and Ferry Service Inc.
Morris Marina Rd., Atlantic • 225-4261

Operating out of the Down East community of Atlantic off N.C. 12, this ferry service transports passengers, vehicles and all terrain-vehicles to Portsmouth or to the south end of North Core Banks at Drum Inlet three times a day from mid-March through early December. Transportation costs are $13 round trip per person and around $65 round trip for a vehicle. Island transportation and supplies (ice, groceries, etc.) may be arranged. See our Accommodations chapter for cabin rental information.

A few other passenger ferries are permitted by the NPS to transport island hoppers to Cape Lookout, Portsmouth Village and Shackleford Banks. Most of these can also be hired for service to other areas or just for a cruise around the harbor. Charter and rental boats are available for getting around the area's waterways (see the Fishing, Boating Watersports and Beach Access chapter). The concessionaires with the NPS are listed below in alphabetical order. Keep in mind, however, that there are other privately run services.

Barrier Island Transportation Co. Inc.
P.O. Box 400, Harkers Island • 728-3908, (800) 423-8739

Barrier Island provides passenger ferry and water taxi service to Shackleford Banks and the Cape Lookout Lighthouse area. No vehicles are accommodated. Fares are $12 round trip per person, $6 for passengers younger than age 6 and $15 for overnight campers. Group rates are offered. Once at the lighthouse, visitors can take the quarter-mile boardwalk to the ocean or hitch a ride on the jitney at a cost of $3 to the beach, $8 to Cape Point. On a hot July day, the jitney is definitely worth the money. The ferry leaves from the Harkers Island Fishing Center on Harkers Island between Easter and Thanksgiving. Call for departure times and to make reservations.

Outer Banks Ferry Service
328 Front St., Beaufort • 728-4129

The Outer Banks Ferry Service, owned and operated by Perry Barrow, offers transportation to Carrot Island, Shackleford Banks and Cape Lookout. The service runs on schedule during summer months and by reservation year round. The ferry office is open from 9 AM to 5 PM. Group rates are available.

Sand Dollar Ferry Service
Harkers Island • 728-6181

This ferry service departs by reservation from Barbour's Harbor Marina on Harkers Island to Shackleford Banks and the Cape Lookout Lighthouse area. Round-trip fare per adult is $12; for children younger than 6, it's $6. Beach transportation at the Cape may be arranged.

Island Ferry Service
300 Front St., Beaufort • 728-6888

In spring and summer, Capt. Ronnie Lewis leaves every 30 minutes between 9 AM and 5 PM for Shackleford Banks and Carrot Island. Island Ferry Service is at the end of Orange Street behind Harpoon Willie's Restaurant. During late fall and the winter months, service is on demand. Guided tours of Shackleford Banks are offered by reservation as is transportation to Cape Lookout.

INSIDERS' TIP

The gulls that follow the Cedar Island Ferry always expect a handout. They'll almost eat from your hand. Ferry officials ask that you only feed them off the back of the ferry.

Be prepared for weather changes when boating on the Crystal Coast.

Once You're Here

When you get to the Crystal Coast, you'll find that a car is almost essential. There isn't a public transportation service here, and a look at the map will show you that most communities are far enough apart to make a car the best way to get around.

If you've brought your bicycle, there are some marked bike routes. But remember you're in a tourist area, and vehicle traffic is often heavy. Beaufort has a 6-mile marked bike route; a routing guide is available at the Safrit Historical Center on Turner Street. Biking in residential developments on Bogue Banks and in Morehead City neighborhoods is safe and pleasant. The Atlantic Beach Causeway has biking and walking paths that link Atlantic Beach with Morehead City in relative safety. A 26-mile bicycle touring route is marked in and around Swansboro.

Now, about the roads within the area.

U.S. Highway 70 is generally very easy to drive from New Bern through Havelock and on to Morehead City, Beaufort and Down East. From Beaufort east, however, U.S. 70 is a two-lane highway that winds through marshes and between canals, but the road is adequately wide and always in excellent repair. An important detail to remember about U.S. 70 is that it has many names as it traverses Carteret County. In Morehead City, it's Arendell Street, the main street through town. It's also the Morehead-Beaufort Causeway. In Beaufort, it's called Cedar Street until it takes a left turn and becomes Live Oak Street. And by any name, it's always heavily trafficked in the Beaufort area.

Upon arrival in the Crystal Coast area, stop at one of the **Carteret County Tourism Development Bureau's Visitors Centers**. In Morehead City it's at 3409 Arendell Street next to North Carolina's Institute of Marine Sciences; in Cape Carteret it's on Highway 58 at the Cameron Langston Bridge to Emerald Isle. These centers are chock-a-block full of information brochures and local and area maps, including street maps. Friendly staff will answer your questions and help you find your way. The North Carolina Ferry Division welcomes Crystal Coast visitors at its center at the Cedar Island Ferry terminal.

As you will find, there is much to see and do on the Crystal Coast. It's also a beautiful destination for doing nothing at all. Whatever you choose, you have an enviable exploration ahead of you.

We support the community with no strings attached. (Or wires, for that matter.)

Whether we're running ads in a publication like this one, sponsoring local events, or providing cellular phones for emergencies, 360° Communications is proud to support the communities it serves.

Cellular, Paging, Long Distance Right Down The Street.

Call 1-800-409-4343 for details.
Quality Customer Service

Area Overviews

North Carolina's Central Coast, or as we call it, the Crystal Coast, is such a diverse and dynamic place that just one overall introduction to the entire area wouldn't do it justice. Each of our geographic areas — Bogue Banks, Beaufort, Morehead City, Swansboro, Down East and western Carteret County — is unique in its own way, so we have divided this chapter into sections that give a brief introduction to our geographic areas. We hope this will help you get to know the area and find your way around.

You'll learn more about the area as you go through this book. There is a lot to enjoy on the Crystal Coast, so take your time and explore. We'll still be here!

Bogue Banks

Bogue Banks is the narrow island almost parallel to Morehead City and N.C. Highway 24. It begins on the east at Fort Macon in the town of Atlantic Beach and stretches to Emerald Isle on the west. The 30-mile-long island is connected to the mainland by a high-rise bridge at each end. Because the island attracts visitors and summer residents, there are many second homes, condominiums and hotels on the island.

N.C. Highway 58 extends the length of the island. Along the way it is marked with mileposts (MP). The MP series begins with mile 1 at the east end of the island and continues along the road to mile 21 on the west end. Throughout this book we have given the MP as part of the address for places on Bogue Banks.

The great majority of Bogue Banks development, both business and residential, is along N.C. 58. A ride from one end to the other on N.C. 58 and down a few of the side streets can give you a quick overview of the island communities and what is offered. From several points along the road you can see the sound and the ocean at the same time.

Bogue Banks embraces five townships that tend to blend together. Atlantic Beach is at the far east end of the island and borders the town of Pine Knoll Shores. Indian Beach surrounds

Photo: Scott Taylor

By land, air or sea, any approach to Beaufort is a good one.

the small unincorporated community of Salter Path, and Emerald Isle is at the far west end of the island. Each town has its own personality and points of interest. Checking our maps might help you get an overall picture of how these towns combine into Bogue Banks.

As N.C. Highway 58 passes through the different communities, it often takes on a new name. In Atlantic Beach, it is called Fort Macon Road. East Fort Macon Road is the strip between the old fort and the main intersection in town. West Fort Macon Road is the strip between that intersection and the western edge of town. The longest stretch of the highway is called Salter Path Road: It stretches from Atlantic Beach through Pine Knoll Shores, Indian Beach and Salter Path. In Emerald Isle, the highway is called Emerald Drive. It really isn't as confusing as it sounds — it's just one road with lots of names.

Atlantic Beach

A pavilion built on the beach in 1887 gave birth to Atlantic Beach. That one-story building had a refreshment stand and areas for changing clothes. The popularity of surf bathing was growing, and guests at the Atlantic Hotel in Morehead City (which stood at the site of today's Rike Jefferson Motor Lodge) were taken to the sound side of Atlantic Beach by sailboat. The guests then walked across the island to the pavilion, which faced the ocean.

Later a large two-story pavilion was built on the island, and a boardwalk was built from the dock to the pavilion. Supplies were carted over the sand dunes by ox cart. In 1916 the first pavilion and 100 acres were bought by Von Bedsworth, and the 100-room Atlantic View Beach Hotel was built. The hotel later burned. By 1928 a group of county citizens

had built a toll bridge from Morehead City to today's Atlantic Beach and constructed a beach resort complete with a dining area, bathhouses and a pavilion. Just a short year later, the entire complex was destroyed by fire. A New York bank took possession of the property, and a new hotel was built. In 1936 the bridge was sold to the state, which dropped the toll charges. In 1945 Morehead City resident Alfred Cooper bought the property, and in 1953 a drawbridge replaced the old bridge. In the late 1980s, the drawbridge was replaced by the current high-rise bridge.

Today, Atlantic Beach has a year-round population of about 3,000 that swells to about 35,000 during the summer. The waterfront area known as The Circle, found at the southernmost end of the Atlantic Beach Causeway, underwent a face-lift in 1996 and now sports new pavements, parking and landscaping.

Pine Knoll Shores

Incorporated in 1973, Pine Knoll Shores is in the center of Bogue Banks. The heirs of Theodore Roosevelt developed this planned community that is called one of the state's most ecologically sensitive communities. The town's 1,400 residents share their community with the N.C. Aquarium, Theodore Roosevelt Natural Area and the Bogue Banks Public Library.

The N.C. Aquarium at Pine Knoll Shores is one of the state's three aquariums. It offers educational exhibits, displays and a meeting area for civic and special-interest groups. The Theodore Roosevelt Natural Area is a 265-acre maritime forest owned and protected by the state. It surrounds the N.C. Aquarium and is one of the few remaining maritime forests on North Carolina's barrier islands. (See our Attractions chapter for more about these sites.)

Pine Knoll Shores officials stress the importance of protecting existing maritime forests in the town and enforce regulations that restrict the amount of maritime forest acreage

Wave Away The World

At Atlantic Beach you can hide away on beaches that are intimate and peaceful... leave the hurried world behind and spend your vacation days stretching endlessly in time.

A Place At The Beach, Sands Villa Resort and SeaSpray offer oceanfront condominiums with full amenities. Relax in our indoor/outdoor pools and whirlpools or perfect your tennis game on our lighted courts. We'll be happy to arrange tee-times for golfers on any of our 12 nearby courses or arrange charter boats for off-shore angling.

For a day off the beach, our surrounding historic town offers quaint and inviting shopping and antique treasures.

The Sands Kids Club keeps kids busy flying kites, treasure hunting, building sand castles and trips to the Aquarium. We even have a summer baby sitting service for kids aged 2-10 when parents want their own fun.

Visit us soon. We promise you'll leave with some sand in your shoes and plenty of memories that will make you want to return for more. For reservations, brochures and information on our condominium sales call **1-800-334-2667** ext. 34.

**Sands
Oceanfront
Resorts**

Local: **919-247-2636** Ft. Macon Rd. Atlantic Beach, N.C. 28512 Fax: 919-247-1067

http://www.nccoast.com/cry/acc/cot/sands/sands.htm

Photo: NC Travel and Tourism

Mending nets is a regular part of the workday for many Down East residents.

that can be cleared for development. The town itself owns significant forest tracts.

A historic marker stands at the corner of N.C. 58 and Roosevelt Boulevard noting the area of the first landing of Europeans on the North Carolina coast. Giovanni da Verrazzano, a Florentine navigator in the service of France, explored the state's coast from Cape Fear north to Kitty Hawk in 1524. His voyage along the coast marked the first recorded European contact with what is now North Carolina.

Indian Beach

Indian Beach is a resort and residential town near the center of Bogue Banks. Incorporated in 1973, the town offers residents and visitors a fishing pier and wide, beautiful beaches for sunbathing, surf fishing and watersports. Quite a few condominiums, camping areas and restaurants are in this area and are profiled in various chapters within the Crystal Coast section.

The town surrounds the unincorporated community of Salter Path, creating an east Indian Beach and a west Indian Beach.

Salter Path

Much of Salter Path's quaintness was lost when modern development began moving in. Now the community's modest homes seem crowded together. But the character of the community can still be seen in the close family ties, the fishing boats beside the homes and the fish nets being mended in the yards.

In the late 1890s the first families to settle in Salter Path came over from Diamond City, which at the time was the largest community on Shackleford Banks, a 9-mile-long island that is now part of Cape Lookout National Seashore. Diamond City was a whaling community, and a large hill in the center of town was used as a lookout. Once a whale was spotted, the men would jump into boats and row after the whale and, if successful, harpoon and kill the creature.

By 1897 about 500 people lived in Diamond City and had erected stores, a school, a post office and church buildings. Two hard storms in the late 1890s convinced many Diamond City residents it was time to leave the island. Houses

were cut into sections, tied to skiffs and floated or sailed across the water. Once at the new homesites, the houses were reconstructed. Many settled on Harkers Island, in the Shackleford Street area of Morehead City or in Salter Path.

Legend has it that the name Salter Path originated with Joshua Salter, a Broad Creek resident who often came by boat from the mainland to the beach to fish and hunt. He made a path from the sound area where he anchored his boat to the oceanfront. Folks called the walkway Salter's Path, and the name stuck.

Many locals credit the early residents of Salter Path with bringing shrimp into the culinary limelight. These plentiful creatures were once considered only a menace by fishermen.

After local residents began to eat them, the seafood soon became a marketable item throughout the county and all coastal areas.

Emerald Isle

Stories say this end of the island was originally home to nomadic Indians and whalers. It is also said that about 15 families, perhaps from Diamond City, came here in 1893 and settled at Middletown, a small section of the island that is now part of Emerald Isle.

Other than those small groups, Emerald Isle was largely unsettled until the 1950s. Several years after Atlantic Beach was developed as a seashore resort, a Philadel-

---

INSIDERS' TIP

Average annual air and water temperatures along North Carolina's Crystal Coast:

January	— Low 32	High 53	Water 50
April	— Low 48	High 75	Water 59
July	— Low 69	High 88	Water 78
October	— Low 51	High 75	Water 70

Photo: Scott Taylor

Crystal Coast waters provide peaceful getaways for quiet fishing and wildlife watching.

phia man named Henry K. Fort bought the land that now makes up most of Emerald Isle and about 500 more acres on the mainland in what is today the town of Cape Carteret. Fort planned to tie the two areas together with a bridge and develop a large resort. When support for constructing a bridge could not be raised from the state or county, he abandoned the project. A ferry was later operated in the area where he had hoped to put a bridge. The ferry carried motorists and pedestrians between the beach and mainland and landed on the beach near Bogue Inlet Pier, which was the first recreational spot at the island's west end.

Today, a modern high-rise bridge provides access from the mainland to Emerald Isle and the western end of Bogue Banks. The Cameron Langston Bridge spans the Atlantic Intracoastal Waterway and from the top provides a great view of area land formations, the waterway and Bogue Banks.

Emerald Isle has a year-round population of 2,434 and a seasonal population of 16,000. The town's $1.4 million municipal complex and community center offers large meeting rooms, a full basketball court and a gym area (see the Sports, Fitness and Parks chapter). The town's residential and business sections line Emerald Drive (N.C. 58). Several new housing sections have been developed west of the high-rise bridge in the section surrounding the Coast Guard Station.

In 1995, *Business North Carolina* magazine placed Emerald Isle as number seven in the "Top Ten Tarheel Towns Overall."

Beaufort

Beaufort is a small seaport brimming with charm and history. Once you walk along the wooden boardwalk and quiet tree-lined streets, hear the tolling church bells and smell the salt air, you will come to understand the special feeling Beaufort gives.

Beaufort is the third-oldest town in North

INSIDERS' TIP

Stop by the Crystal Coast Visitors Center, 3409 Arendell Street (U.S. Highway 70 E.), Morehead City, to pick up free street maps of Morehead, Beaufort, Swansboro, Atlantic Beach, Newport and many of the area's other towns.

Carolina and was named for Henry Somerset, the Duke of Beaufort. The town was surveyed in 1713, nearly 20 years before George Washington's birth. Beaufort was incorporated in 1722 and has been the seat of Carteret County since that time. The English influence is apparent in the architecture and, more noticeably, in the street names: Ann and Queen, for Queen Anne; Craven, for the Earl of Craven; Orange, for William the Prince of Orange; Moore, for Col. Maurice Moore; and Pollock, for the governor at the time of the survey.

Beaufort offers a glimpse at a relatively unspoiled part of North Carolina's coastal history. The town has made great strides in the restoration of many of its oldest structures. Much of that can be credited to the Beaufort Historical Association, which was organized in 1960 to celebrate the town's 250th anniversary. The association commemorates Beaufort's historic homes with special plaques. To be plaqued, a home must be at least 80 years old and have retained its historic and architectural integrity. The first home plaqued

was the Duncan House, c. 1790, at 105 Front Street. Through the years the Beaufort Historical Association has moved old structures threatened with demolition to an area on Turner Street. For more information about the Beaufort Historic Site, see the Attractions chapter.

The town's designated historic district is between Gallant's Channel and the east side of Pollock Street and between Taylor's Creek and the south side of Broad Street. (Gallant's Channel flows under the drawbridge and Taylor's Creek is the body of water faced by the boardwalk.) The one-block area of the county courthouse is also included in the historic district.

Beaufort's historic houses and sites each have their own story to tell. Many structures and areas are listed on the National Register of Historic Places. The house with the most lively history is the Hammock House of 1698, which is considered Beaufort's oldest standing house. It once stood so close to the water that visitors could tie a skiff to the front porch. Through the years, dredging changed the creek's course, and now the house stands one block back from the creek. The house later served as an "ordinary" (an inn), and Blackbeard, the fiercest of all pirates, was a regular guest. Legend has it that Blackbeard hung one of his wives from a live oak in the front yard, and neighbors can still hear her screams on moonlit nights. The house was used as accommodations by the Union Army during the Civil War and is now privately owned.

The Old Burying Ground on Ann Street is an interesting place to wander and look at grave markers and the messages they bear. Deeded to the town in 1731, the Old Burying Ground was declared full in 1825, and the General Assembly said no more burials would be allowed. The town was ordered to lay out a new graveyard, but the townspeople did not support the act and continued to bury their loved ones in the Old Burying Ground until the early 1900s. The north corner of the graveyard is the oldest section.

Many interesting graves are in the grounds, and tours are often given by the Beaufort Historical Association. Those buried here include Capt. Josiah Pender, whose men took Fort Macon in 1861; James W. Hunt, who had the distinction of marrying, making his will and dying the same day; Esther Cooke, mother of Capt. James W. Cooke, who once commanded the Ironclad *Albemarle*; the Dill child, who was buried in a glass-top casket; the common grave of the *Crissie Wright* crew, who froze to death when the ship wrecked on Shackleford Banks in 1886; and the child who died aboard a ship and was brought to Beaufort in a keg of rum for burial — in the keg.

With the town's waterfront revitalization project in the late 1970s, Beaufort took a new direction. The renovation involved tearing down many old waterfront structures not considered salvageable and building the existing wooden boardwalk, docks and facilities. Businesses were encouraged to stay or move to the downtown waterfront. Soon word of the new old town spread, and it hasn't been the same since. What was once a coastal hideaway is now a favorite spot for visitors traveling by car or boat.

As you enter Beaufort from the west, you will cross the Grayden M. Paul Bridge. The bridge's namesake was a lively 96-year-old historian, best known for his songs, poems and tales about Beaufort and Carteret County. He lived on Front Street with his wife, Mary Clark, until his death in the summer of 1994.

Drawbridges in coastal areas are slowly becoming things of the past as more and more towns are choosing to replace these romantic bridges with concrete high-rises. And that's the case for this old landmark. Because of increased traffic, plans are in the works to replace the drawbridge in the next few years. The only sticking point is where to locate the new high-rise bridge.

Beaufort is home to a number of attractions, including the North Carolina Maritime Museum and Watercraft Center and the Rachel Carson Component of the North Carolina National Estuarine Research Reserve.

Beaufort's Nearby Communities

Lennoxville is the community closest to Beaufort. The area begins at the east end of Front Street and continues to the east end of Lennoxville Road. This is primarily a residential area with the exception of Beaufort Fisheries and Atlantic Veneer (see the Commerce and Industry chapter). At one time, there were several tomato canneries in the community. Lennoxville is surrounded by water: Taylor's Creek on the south and North River on the north. New developments continue to spring up along the forested waterfront areas of Lennoxville.

INSIDERS' TIP

Out of the eight types of sea turtles found in the Indian, Pacific and Atlantic oceans, five kinds are found off the coast of North Carolina: Leatherback, Atlantic Ridley, Greeen Turtle, Hawksbill and Loggerhead.

North River is a small community that lies to the north of Beaufort on Merrimon Road. The community can be reached by traveling east on U.S. Highway 70 out of Beaufort and continuing straight at East Carteret High School. (A right turn at the school would take you to the Down East area.) Baseball pitcher Brien Taylor put the community of North River on the map in 1991 when, as a high school senior, he signed a $1.55 million contract with the New York Yankees.

The **South River** community actually lies to the north of the North River community. Named for the body of water it nestles beside, South River is primarily a fishing-based community. Many of this community's early residents came from Lukens. Today much of the land is owned by recreational hunters and businesses, and there are several private airstrips in the area. Many artifacts and Indian pottery pieces have been found in the South River area.

The community of **Merrimon** lies to the west of South River. This rural area borders the Neuse River and Adams Creek, which is a stretch of the scenic Intracoastal Waterway. The seaport of Oriental is just across the Neuse River and, on most days, is visible.

In recent years a few neighborhood developments have sprung up around South River, Merrimon and the Intracoastal Waterway. Sportsman's Village, Jonaquin's Landing and Indian Summer Estates offer waterfront and mainland lots.

Morehead City

Morehead City is the county's largest city. A look into the history of the city starts with an early land prospector from Virginia by the name of John Shackleford. In 1714 Shackleford saw a future for the area and purchased 170 acres at the mouth of the Newport River, stretching from Bogue Sound on the south to Calico Creek on the north.

The land became known as Shepard's Point after it was purchased in 1723 by David Shepard. The community grew but was not incorporated until 1861.

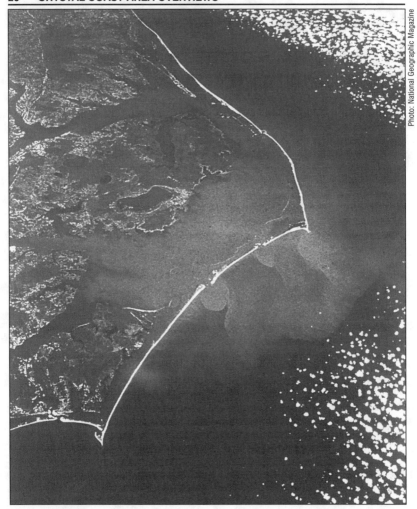

Photo: National Geographic Magazine

The Crystal Coast forms the southern part of North Carolina's Outer Banks.

In 1852 the state decided to extend a railroad line to connect Raleigh with the coast, and several towns vied to be the end location since it would bring growth to their communities. For a while it was considered inevitable that the line would end in Beaufort. To make a bid for the rail business, a new town named Carolina City was formed by the Carolina City Company. The company purchased 1,000 acres at the western end of the Shepard's Point land, and Carolina City lots went on sale in 1855.

John Motley Morehead, who was elected governor of the state in 1840 and again in 1842, came to the coast in 1856 when he was put in charge of extending the railroad to the coast. He began to buy land in what is now, appropriately, Morehead City. In 1857 he began selling lots at public auction.

In May 1858 Morehead described the area: "The City of Morehead is situated on a beautiful neck of land or dry plain, almost entirely surrounded by salt water; its climate salubrious;

its sea breezes and sea bathing delightful; its drinking water good and its fine chalybeate spring, strongly impregnated with sulfur, will make it a pleasant watering place . . . ."

The sale of the land was successful, Morehead was successful in his bid for the end of the railroad and Morehead City was incorporated. When the N.C. Legislature authorized the incorporation of the town, surveyors laid out the streets and named the primary ones after men who had been influential in the settlement of the area — Fisher, Arendell, Bridges, Evans, Shackleford and Shepard.

At that time, the only roads entering the county were sandy, narrow lanes, so most of the influential visitors arrived by rail, steamer or sailboat.

One of the first commercial buildings in Morehead City was the Macon Hotel at the corner of Arendell and Ninth streets. Constructed in 1860, this three-story building was a landmark for 80-some years.

The town was started just in time to be taken over by the Union forces when they at-tacked Fort Macon on April 26, 1862, thus ending for a time any significant development. Even after the end of the War Between the States, Morehead City was not able to get its commercial life active again until about 1880 when the shipping industry began to bring business to town. In the early 1880s a new Atlantic Hotel was built in Morehead City, replacing the old Atlantic Hotel that had been destroyed by a hurricane. Located where the Rike Jefferson Motor Lodge now stands, the Atlantic Hotel had 233 rooms and claimed to have the largest ballroom in the South. It drew the cream of the state's society to the coast until it was destroyed by fire in 1933.

In 1911 the city began a road improvement program to alternately pave the way and keep up with the town's slow but steady growth.

Crab Point is one area that grew as a result of road improvement. Crab Point is what Moreheaders call that part of the city that is east of Country Club Road and north of the 20th Street Bridge over Calico Creek. The area got its name because when tides came in crabs got trapped on the shoreline, making them an easy catch. In the early days Crab Point served as a port and had windmills for grinding grain and generating power for lumber companies. A private cemetery in the area has graves dating back to the early 1700s.

Today Morehead City continues to grow and to offer many services to residents and visitors. The town has recently incorporated several tracts along its western border and the North Carolina Department of Transportation is planning to make major road improvements along Highway 70/Arendell Street within the next five to six years.

The most visible changes taking place in town are along the waterfront. Morehead City's leaders have provided for a major face-lift that includes wide sidewalks, new docks, bathroom facilities and parks.

Swansboro

Swansboro, in Onslow County, can be reached by taking either N.C. 58 (from Bogue Banks) or N.C. 24 (from Morehead City). From its origins as the site of an Algonquian Indian village at the mouth of the White Oak River to its current status as the "Friendly City by the Sea," Swansboro is a lovely place to visit because of its relatively mild climate and its friendly residents.

The town's history began about 1730, when Jonathan and Grace Green moved from Falmouth, Massachusetts, to the mouth of the White Oak River. With them, and owning half of their property, was Jonathan Green's brother, Isaac. They lived there about five years until Jonathan Green died at the early age of 35. His widow married Theophilus Weeks, who had moved with his family from Falmouth to settle on Hadnot Creek a few miles up the White Oak River.

After their marriage, the Weekses moved into the Green family home on the Onslow County side of the White Oak River. Theophilus soon purchased the interest of Isaac Green to become sole owner of the large plantation. Weeks first farmed, then opened a tavern and was appointed inspector of exports at the thriving port. In 1771, he started a town on that portion of his plantation called Weeks Wharf, selling 48 numbered lots recorded as being "in the plan of a town laid out by Theophilus Weeks," thus earning him the title of founder of the town.

Originally called Week's Point, the New-Town-upon-Bogue was established by law in 1783. The General Assembly named the town Swannsborough, in honor of Samuel Swann, former speaker of the N.C. House of Representatives and longtime Onslow County representative.

Another name that became well-known in Swansboro (the later spelling of the town's name) was that of Otway Burns. During the War of 1812, this native son became a privateer with his schooner, the *Snapdragon*. His participation during this "Second War of Independence" was acclaimed as an act of bravery and patriotism. After the war, he returned to the trade of ship building and was later appointed keeper of the lighthouse at Portsmouth where he died in 1850. He is buried in Beaufort's Old Burying Ground.

Swansboro's port continued to prosper, particularly because of the nearby pine forests that produced the lumber, tar, pitch and other naval items shipped through the port. It continued to prosper until the end of the War Between the States. Then, gradually, the town came to support itself with farming and fishing.

The town is water-oriented, situated on the Intracoastal Waterway and along the mouth of the White Oak River, with the Atlantic Ocean easily accessible through Bogue Inlet. A good many fishing boats call Swansboro home port, and many residents keep sportfishing boats at marinas in Swansboro or Cedar Point.

The town's historic commission supervises the restoration of many of the town's oldest structures. Several of these fine structures now house businesses, while others remain private residences.

Down East

Down East is the area that stretches from the North River on the east side of Beaufort to Cedar Island. This beautiful part of Carteret County contains marshes, canals and undis-

turbed places, particularly as you get closer to Cedar Island.

In the past the livelihood of the Down East people depended on the water. Today some people still rely on the water for work, but many people work in Beaufort or Morehead City or travel to the Marine Corps Air Station Cherry Point in Havelock. Still that tie and love for the water is obvious by the number of boats, fish houses and seafood businesses.

There are no incorporated towns Down East, so it is governed by the county. Activities center around the schools, churches, volunteer fire and rescue squads, post offices and local stores. Most of the communities lie along U.S. 70, the main road running through Down East. The history of this area is rich and could fill volumes. We'll just give you a very brief overview and invite you to explore it on your own.

After leaving Beaufort on U.S. 70, **Bettie** is the first Down East community you reach. It lies between the North River Bridge and the Ward's Creek Bridge. The next community is **Otway**, named for famous privateer Otway Burns, who is buried in Beaufort's Old Burying Ground.

As you turn off U.S. 70 onto Harkers Island Road, **Straits** is the community you see embracing the road to Harkers Island. It is also the name of the body of water that lies between the Straits community and the island. The spelling of Straits is shown on early maps as "Straights." Later cartographers probably noticed the name was not applicable to a water course and changed the spelling to Straits, meaning narrows. Years ago Straits was a farm community, and a substantial amount of cotton was grown here. Straits United Methodist Church, c. 1778, was the first Methodist Church built east of Beaufort.

Originally called Craney Island, **Harkers Island** once was the home of a thriving band of Tuscarora Indians. By the turn of the 20th century, all that remained of the native Indian settlement was a huge mound of sea shells at the east end of the island, now called Shell Point. Folks say the Indians were attempting to build a shell walkway through the water to Core Banks. Standing at Shell Point today, you can see the Cape Lookout Lighthouse and nearby islands.

In 1730 George Pollock sold the island to Ebenezer Harker of Boston, Massachusetts, who began living on the island. Later he divided the island among his three sons, and the divisions he used, "eastard," "westard" and "center," have remained unofficial dividers ever since. The Harker heirs did not part with their land for years, so the island population remained sparse. By 1895 fewer than 30 families lived there. The population grew when folks from the Shackleford Banks community of Diamond City left because of the devastation of hurricanes. Some loaded homes on boats and brought them to this safer ground. With this new surge in population, schools, churches and businesses sprang up. Still, the island was isolated. Ferry operations to the mainland began in 1926, with the ferry leaving from the west end of the island and docking in the Gloucester community. A bridge to the island was built in 1941. The island is home to the Core Sound Waterfowl Museum and the Cape Lookout National Park Service Office. See the Attractions chapter for more information about this fascinating place.

As you return from Harkers Island and re-enter U.S. 70, **Smyrna** is the next Down East community. It was named in 1785 from a deed that conveyed 100 acres from Joseph Davis to Seth Williston. The land was on Smunar Creek, and the spelling was later changed to Smyrna.

Off U.S. 70 on Marshallberg Road, Deep Hole Point was the first name for **Marshallberg**. Folks say that clay was dug from the area and used to fill ramparts and cover easements at Fort Macon, leaving a large hole, thus the name. It was later renamed for Matt Marshall, who ran the mailboat from Beaufort. Marshallberg lies on a peninsula formed by Sleepy Creek and Core Sound.

Graham Academy was established in Marshallberg by W.Q.A. Graham in 1880 at the head of Sleepy Creek. Curriculum prepared students for college, and students who did not live in town stayed in the school's dormitories. Monthly board was about $5.50 per student, and the school's attendance in 1892 was 126. The Academy was destroyed by fire in 1910.

Gloucester was named in the early 1900s by Capt. Joseph Pigott for the Massachusetts town that he loved. A ferry once ran between Gloucester and Harkers Island.

Williston was named for John Williston who was one of the area's first settlers. The community has long been nicknamed "Beantown," though why is still a point of confusion. Some say it was because of the large amount of beans that were grown in the community, and others say it was because residents had a reputation for loving beans. Williston United Methodist Church was built in 1883.

Davis was settled by William T. Davis in the 1700s and was a farming village. People worked the water and the land to make a living. Farm crops, such as cotton and sweet potatoes, were taken by sailboat to Virginia to be sold or traded for needed items (flour, sugar, cloth, etc.). Davis residents were known as "Onion Eaters," either because of the number of green onions grown in the community or because Davis Shore people simply liked onions. An Army camp was opened in Davis during World War II, and some of the old camp buildings remain along the water's edge.

Stacy is really made up of two, even smaller, communities: Masontown and Piney Point. The post office was opened in 1885. Stacy Freewill Baptist Church is more than 100 years old.

Originally called Wit, **Sea Level** is still the fishing community it has always been. In 1706 Capt. John Nelson was granted about 650 acres by the King of England, and that land is today's Sea Level. Sailors' Snug Harbor, the oldest charitable trust in America, opened a facility for retired merchant marines there in 1976. The original facility of its type opened in 1833 on Staten Island. Sea Level Extended Care Facility is a nursing home on Nelson's Bay. A satellite clinic of Carteret General Hospital now operates alongside the nursing home.

U.S. 70 ends in the township of **Atlantic**. This community was settled in the 1740s and was originally called Hunting Quarters. The first post office opened in 1880, and the name was changed to Atlantic. The community's nickname is Per, and old timers refer to their home as Per Atlantic. In the 1930s progress arrived in the form of paved roads. Atlantic is home to two of the East Coast's largest seafood dealers, Luther Smith & Son Seafood Company and Clayton Fulcher Seafood Company.

N.C. Highway 12 takes travelers to **Cedar Island** and beyond to the North Carolina State ferry landing. Cedar Island was known by that name until two post offices were established in the early 1900s. Then the east end of the island became known as Lola and the west end as Roe, each with its own post office and school. In the 1960s, the two post offices closed and a new one was opened. The whole island became known as Cedar Island again.

Locals still use the old names, and some homes on the island date back to the 1880s.

Newport/
Western Carteret County

Newport is known as "the town with old-fashioned courtesy." When traveling from New Bern to Carteret County on U.S. 70, it is the first incorporated town you pass. *Business North Carolina* magazine ranked Newport 10th in the "Top Tarheel Towns Overall."

The town continues to grow along with Marine Corps Air Station Cherry Point in Havelock. The last census showed a population of 2,569, meaning the town grew by 1,000 people in the past 10 years.

Chartered in 1866, Newport was first supported by logging, farming and fishing. Today, many residents work at Cherry Point. Newport is home to a development park on U.S. 70 and the National Oceanic and Atmospheric Administration Weather Forecast Office that offers state-of-the-art weather tracking and forecasting. Operated as part of the National Weather Service, this facility includes a Doppler weather radar system with advanced weather capabilities.

Newport offers many quiet residential areas, a school, stores, a town hall and a public library. Newport is home to the popular Newport Pig Cooking Contest each April. The town has a strong volunteer fire department and rescue squad.

Northeast of Newport is the community of **Mill Creek**. This is mainly a farming community, including a large blueberry farm, that can be reached from Newport or N.C. 101 out of Beaufort.

N.C. 24 traces the waterfront west along Bogue Sound from Morehead City to Onslow County. The highway passes through several communities, then across the White Oak River into Onslow County and the town of Swansboro.

From Cape Carteret N.C. 58 goes west through the Croatan National Forest through several old settlements including **Peletier**, the **Hadnot Creek** community and **Kuhn's Corner** and then into Jones County. If you turn east on N.C. 58 from Cape Carteret, you'll cross a high-rise bridge and enter the beach town of Emerald Isle.

Cedar Point is the westernmost incorporated town in Carteret County and the westernmost point of the county. The town was established in 1713 but not incorporated until 1988.

Cape Carteret is one of the few planned communities in Carteret County. It was chartered in 1959, and the late W.B. McLean began the development of the town. The first homes were built on the Bogue Sound waterfront near the foot of what is now the B. Cameron Langston Bridge, the high-rise bridge built in 1971 to replace the ferry. The town grew slowly and today is complete with stores, a town hall, fire and rescue departments and a school.

Bogue was incorporated in a special election held in September 1995. With about 200 registered voters, the town's new commissioners and mayor are now busy putting together policies and regulations. Bogue is home to the U.S. Marine Corps Auxiliary Landing Field.

Several communities dot the western part of the county. **Ocean** is an old community and was once a small thriving village with one of the county's first post offices. **Broad Creek** is another old-timer, once made up almost exclusively of commercial fishermen and their families. Some of these fishermen came to the area as long as 100 years ago; others came from Diamond City on Shackleford Banks after the horrible hurricanes forced them to vacate. Today, there is a school and lots of new residential development.

Kuhn's Corner marks the intersection of N.C. 24 that leads to **Stella**, which was once a thriving community with stores, a couple of mills, a good many farmhouses and even a couple of huge plantation houses.

CLAWSON'S

SINCE
1905

Restaurant & Pub

...a history of good foods on the Beaufort waterfront!

Open All Year Round...
All Day Long!

Join us for Casual Dinning in Mr. Clawson's 1905 Grocery Store. We feature Seafood, Ribs and Steaks, Salads and Dinner size Spuds as well as a variety of Sandwiches and Specialties at Lunch.

Enjoy one of your favorites from our extensive beer, wine and mixed drink selection while surrounded by memorabilia from Beaufort's Historic past.

Friday Night *JAZZ*

429 Front St. Beaufort, NC
919-728-2133

Restaurants

Seafood is the featured entree in most Crystal Coast restaurants. In all coastal Carolina areas, deep frying used to be the most common way to prepare seafood, but today restaurant guests have a choice of many preparation options — some exclusive to individual restaurants. On the Crystal Coast, where we used to have cooks, we now have a bank of talented chefs.

In the older restaurants where traditions reign, fried hush puppies continue to be a local favorite and are often used as a means of rating restaurants. Hush puppies are made with cornmeal, flour, eggs and sugar. Some folks add some chopped onion; others add sweet milk. Once blended, the mixture is dropped by the spoonful into hot fat and fried to a golden brown. Old-timers say the name derived from cooks, who, while preparing meals, tossed bits of fried batter to yapping dogs in an effort to quiet them.

Most natives were raised on conch and clam chowders, and even the newest eateries include them among their soups and appetizers. Local conch chowder is made with whelk. To easily remove the meat from whelks and clams, locals recommend freezing the shell; the frozen meat is then easily pulled from the shell, and juices are saved. Traditional chowder is made with chopped meat, water, butter, salt, pepper and diced potatoes. For a different flavor, you might also add squash, onions and other spices.

Collards are a traditional mainstay in the diet of most locals, especially those living Down East. A "mess" of collards cooking in the kitchen creates an unforgettable aroma that you either love or hate. Collards are leafy green vegetables that grow almost year round in this area. Most locals say the best way to cook collards is with a streak-of-lean salt pork or some fatback added to the pot. Top it off with a few new red potatoes and some cornmeal dumplings. Cornmeal dumplings are unique to eastern North Carolina and are basically made by shaping cornmeal, water and salt into small patties and dropping them into the collard pot for about 15 minutes.

There is nothing like a traditional Down East clam bake — you won't find eating like this on any restaurant menu. But you can sometimes luck out and catch a school or fire department holding a fund-raising clam bake. If that happens, drop all your plans and head on over for some real good food. It is said that the idea for the clam bake came from the Native Americans, who taught early residents to cook clams, fish and corn in the steam of hot stones. Today, there are businesses that have large steamers for hire. Modern-day clam bakes usually offer clams, chicken, sweet potatoes, white potatoes, onions, carrots, corn and sometimes a few shrimp. They are all steamed together in a net bag or cheesecloth and served with melted butter. This is not the time for table manners, so use your fingers!

Peelers, pickers, jimmies, white bellies, hens, steamers, paper shells or soft-shells — no matter what you call them, they're still crabs. Learning the difference between the names and the stages of a crab's life is the hard part. Knowing when crabs are ready to shed and are marketable as soft-shells is important to the livelihood of many Crystal Coast fishermen. Understanding the process a crab goes through to become a soft-shell is an art as well as a science.

A peeler is a crab that will, if all goes well, become a soft crab within 72 hours. They are carefully handled and put in vats where they can go through this molting process. Jimmies are the large male crabs that measure 6 inches from upper shell tip to tip, and steamers or pickers are just regular crabs. The sure way to tell if a crab is a peeler is by the pinkish-red ring on the outer tip of the flipper or back fin. Those that complete the molting process are sold live or dressed. Many are packed with damp sea grass, refrigerated and shipped live to restaurants as far away as New York. Most are sold dressed because live soft-shells are delicate to handle and have a life of only about three days. Locals consider soft-shell crabs a delicacy, and favorite ways to prepare them include lightly frying them in batter or sauteing them in butter and wine. There is nothing better, or stranger looking, than a soft-shell crab sandwich.

Shrimp burgers, another very popular local seafood treat, are little more than fried shrimp on a hamburger bun with slaw and special sauce. Each restaurant has its own sauce, which is the secret to a great shrimp burger. Some places have come up with variations (oyster burgers, clam burgers), but it's all basically put together the same way. Oh, what a wonderful lunch it makes.

Within the past three years, an interesting trend has been impacting Crystal Coast dining. A respectable population of culinary talent is flourishing in our haven of fabulous seafood. On the Morehead City waterfront alone, three new gourmet-quality restaurants reflect the demand of increasingly upscale appetites. Openings around Morehead and in Beaufort, new menus and redecorated restaurants from Atlantic Beach to Emerald Isle tell us that our tastes are changing. Our dining choices certainly are.

Great numbers of fast-food and chain restaurants are also convenient on the Crystal Coast. Most of these restaurants are concentrated on U.S. Highway 70, the main artery through the area. You'll find Burger King, Hardee's, McDonald's, Bojangles, Pizza Inn, Shoney's, Taco Bell, KFC, Wendy's, Golden Corral and many more. This guide does not review chain restaurants, under the assumption that you are already familiar with their fare.

Planning and Pricing

When planning your lunch or dinner outing, we recommend you call ahead to verify the information offered in the following restaurant profiles and to check the hours or seating availability. While we intend to reflect each restaurant as accurately as possible, menu modifications do occur. Some area restaurants close during slow winter months, and some that remain open may limit menu items to ensure freshness.

Mixed drinks are available in restaurants and lounges in all towns throughout the Crystal Coast except Newport. Mixed drinks are not served in the Down East area or any other unincorporated area except in the Bogue Banks community of Salter Path. Most restaurants do serve wine and domestic and imported beers, and some allow brown-bagging.

Some restaurants in the area also offer special discounts to early diners, and many have discounts for senior citizens and children's dinner menu items.

Because of the large number of restaurants on the Crystal Coast and the limited space in this chapter, we have referred you to restaurants that continue to be favorites. There are certainly more restaurants — check the local phone book and newspaper advertisements if you need other suggestions. We have designed these descriptions in hopes of making your selection easier, but we know you will want to try several of the establishments in town to get a full taste of local fare. Restaurants are arranged alphabetically according to their location. We have given the milepost (MP) number for those

FYI

Unless otherwise noted, the area code for all phone numbers in this guide is 919.

INSIDERS' TIP

If you come across a school or fire department holding a fundraising clam bake, drop all your plans and head on over for some real good food. Clam bakes offer clams, chicken, sweet potatoes, white potatoes, onions, carrots, corn and sometimes a few shrimp — all steamed together in a net bag or cheesecloth and served with melted butter. This is not the time for table manners, so use your fingers!

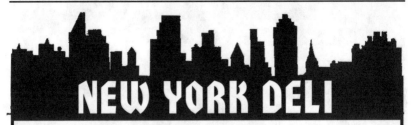
on N.C. Highway 58 on Bogue Banks to help you find them more easily.

Price Code

We have arranged a price code to give you a general idea of the cost of a dinner for two, including appetizers, entrees, desserts and coffee. Because entrees come in a wide range of prices, the code we used reflects an average meal, not the most expensive item or the least expensive item. For restaurants that do not serve dinner, the price code reflects the cost of lunch fare. These codes do not include gratuity or the state's 6 percent sales tax. Most of the dinner establishments listed honor all major credit cards and take reservations, but we'll let you know of the ones that don't. The price code is as follows:

$	Less than $20
$$	$21 to $35
$$$	$36 to $50
$$$$	More than $50

Bogue Banks

Atlantic Beach

Channel Marker Restaurant & Lounge
$$$ • Atlantic Beach Causeway • 247-2344

Channel Marker specializes in grilled fish and aged beef. Overlooking Bogue Sound, the restaurant offers waterfront dining during dinner hours and has all ABC permits. House specialties include grilled fish, land and sea combinations, seafood platters, steak-and-shrimp kebabs and broiled lobster tails. A grilled or broiled fish special is offered each night, and the chef also prepares cold-plate entrees, grilled chicken breasts and stuffed flounder. Desserts include French silk, lime and lemon pies and Bananas Foster. The dock in front of the restaurant is available for those arriving by boat, and the adjoining lounge (see our Nightlife chapter) has all permits and a

Crystal Coast salty oysters are the best.

good selection of wines and beers. The restaurant can accommodate groups of up to 100.

Franco's

$$$ • MP 2, Fort Macon Rd. • 240-3141

The parking lot is typically full here on summer nights, indicating the numbers of diners who enjoy the authentic Neapolitan cuisine of chef-owner Franco Licciardi. Freshly made pastas, baked bread and house specialties — such as Paglia E Fieno with homemade Italian sausages, chicken and mushrooms in a rich sauce served with just-made spinach fettuccine — may tell you why. Franco's gets rave reviews every year from those who have discovered the restaurant. Dinner only is served.

Harper's Oceanfront Dining at the Jolly Knave

$$ • Oceanfront, Atlantic Beach Cir. • 726-8222

The Jolly Knave offers casual indoor and outdoor oceanfront dining. Voted by locals as providing the "Best Oceanview on the Island," the outdoor third-floor deck is a great place to dine and enjoy the view of the Atlantic, the beach and, on clear days, the Cape Lookout light. Appetizers include potato skins, wings,

shrimp, beef ribs and oyster cocktails. They offer all kinds of sandwiches (club, barbecue, chicken breast), burgers and salads. Dinner entrees include seafood (try the combination platter, broiled or fried), steak, pasta, barbecue beef ribs and daily specials — often fresh fish caught by the owner. The chef also makes pizza, fajitas, soups and cold plates, and a children's menu is offered. This establishment has all ABC permits (for lounge information, see our Nightlife chapter).

Kelli's

$$$ • Atlantic Beach Causeway • 247-1094

Kelli's is known for its Angus beef and great seafood. Appetizers include crab-stuffed mushrooms and chicken fingers. Entrees feature rib eye steaks, prime rib, stuffed flounder and shrimp, lobster, chicken and all kinds of seafood, broiled, grilled, fried or panned in butter. There are a variety of land and sea combination platters available. All entrees come with a garden or spinach salad, baked potato, fries or wild rice and rolls. A fresh fish special is featured each night. Guests can park cars in front or dock boats at the lounge deck. Patrons often enjoy a drink in the lounge or on the deck before or after dinner (see our Nightlife chapter).

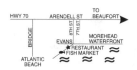

Mar Y Cielo
$$$ • MP 4, Holiday Inn Oceanfront • 726-2544

The newly remodeled dining area at the Holiday Inn Oceanfront is a window on sea and sky, an appropriate setting for lovely service at breakfast, lunch or for a special dinner. A daily breakfast buffet is spread, and specialty breakfast preparations, including fluffy Belgian waffles, are also prepared. Lunch choices include a broad selection of salads and sandwiches, soups and daily specials. Dinner entrees take advantage of the local seafood catch as well as fine cuts of beef and house preparations of chicken and seafood with a touch of the Caribbean.

New York Deli
$ • Crow's Nest Shopping Center, Atlantic Beach Causeway • 726-0111

This is the place for authentic deli food, and it is wonderful. We recommend the authentic South Philadelphia cheesesteak — heck, order two cheesesteaks, and we'll join you. They serve overstuffed sandwiches, subs, great kraut, chili dogs, homemade soups, salads and pasta. They also have one of the area's best selections of imported beers and wines. Deli meats and cheeses are also available for you to take home and create your own feast. New York Deli offers take-out or eat-in service, catering, party trays, gift baskets and a retail wine shop.

No Name Grill & Lounge
$$ • MP 3, Atlantic Station Shopping Center • 240-2224

No Name Grill & Lounge at Atlantic Station Shopping Center offers many of the same great tastes as its sister restaurant in Beaufort. In addition to Greek salads and excellent pizza, the beach restaurant serves a worldwise entree selection that includes pastas, kebabs, stir-fries and crowd-pleasing steaks, prime rib and seafood. Sandwiches are served during year-round dinner and summer lunch hours. They serve a terrific Greek salad at No Name, loaded with feta cheese and served

Coffee, Culture and Coastal Carpentry

It's hard to remember how days got started in this area before espresso, although those innocent days are not so far in the past. Regulars at local coffeehouses get a jumpstart with a straight espresso or a gentle latte before work, during work, at lunch or mid-afternoon. It may not be the entire coastal population that is affected (percentages

are impossible to estimate largely because the regulars are so regular) but it's enough people to support four espresso bars, each with other business components such as restaurants, delis, gourmet foods or hardware on the side.

"A cafe latte with a shake of cinnamon here in a hurry, please. May I have it to go? G'morning. This is an emergency." The steamed milk explodes through a shot of espresso until an uncappable head forms, cinnamon is sprinkled, bills are passed and the customer is off. What's this all about?

In the short version, basically, it's demand and supply. The eyes of the Crystal Coast and New Bern have been opened. Like windowshades.

". . . just a quick espresso, please . . ."

Stay on the page, and we'll get to the beginning. The first stop is the point of origin, the common Italian corner espresso bar, for a basic two-ounce espresso which is concentrated coffee valued for its richness, strength and ability to be fulfilling in small quantities. Add steamed milk and it's a cappuccino.

". . . Another cappuccino, please. What time is it?"

Espresso arrived in New Bern from Italy via Seattle, then found its way to the Crystal Coast. It was a fast trip.

By 1994 the Trent River Coffee Company in New Bern was nurturing a clientele that touched base each morning for a kick into the day. Morehead City's Gourmet Galley remodelled to add an espresso bar to it's gourmet food repertoire, while in Beaufort espresso machines were espressing at lunch, dinner and Sunday brunch at Beaufort Grocery Company and Clawson's 1905. Art and culture follow espresso, and in New Bern, alternative theater productions are as

Espresso starts the day at Fishtowne Java in Beaufort.

routinely served as the lattes. By 1996, the Blue Moon Espresso Bar and Cafe opened in Beaufort with espresso from early morning through mid-afternoon plus breakfast breads and pastries, lunch sandwiches, salads and soups. Clawson's 1905 expanded and added an espresso bar for Joe on the Go and a comfortable sitting area for sipping with CNN. Culture followed closely with the Down East FolkArts Society concert performances at both Clawson's 1905 and Trent River Coffee Company.

And last winter, coffee followed culture to Williams Hardware in Morehead City
— continued on next page

where, from dawn to dusk, carpenters hardly ever left the store without a rasberry hazelnut latte, or just a fast espresso, from the espresso cart that came to a stop between the paint and drill bits.

"I need an espresso and give me three lattes for the crew. And a bag of number two nails."

The hardware espresso cart is now steaming among the grocery shoppers at Pak-A-Sak. Hardware has its limits and Rome wasn't built in a day. But, only three years ago it was hard to find an interesting cup of coffee on the Crystal Coast.

---

with a loaf of garlic bread. For dessert, baklava is always our choice.

Skipper's Cove Restaurant and Lounge
$$ • MP 2 • 726-3023

Skipper's Cove is a popular restaurant that offers an extensive buffet and live entertainment. The restaurant's famous all-you-can-eat buffet is served every night in season until 10 PM. It features all types of seafood — shrimp, fish, clams, crabs, scallops, oysters and more — along with beef, chicken, ham, pasta, barbecue, soups, salads, vegetables and breads. Homemade salad dressings and tempting desserts round out the delicious fare. Skipper's Cove offers banquet facilities. Entertainment varies and includes a house band that plays beach, country and Top 40 music for evenings of dining and dancing (see our Nightlife chapter).

Pine Knoll Shores

Clamdigger Restaurant
$$ • MP 8¼, Ramada Inn • 247-4155

Open for breakfast, lunch and dinner, the Clamdigger in the Ramada Inn is a favorite of locals as well as visitors. You'll find fluffy omelets for breakfast and delicious sandwiches like soft-shell crab, shrimp scampi melt, roast beef or a classic club for lunch. Dinner entrees include steaks and all kinds of seafood. The Clamdigger features authentic Mexican cuisine every Friday at lunch. There is a special every evening — oysters on Monday, rib eye steak on Tuesday, seafood combination on Wednesday, shrimp on Thursday, flounder on Friday, lobster and shrimp on Saturday and steak and shrimp on Sunday. Locals have the schedule memorized.

Paradise Restaurant
$$$ • MP 4, Sheraton Resort • 240-1155

Overlooking the ocean on Atlantic Beach at the Sheraton Resort, this restaurant serves breakfast, lunch and dinner daily. It spreads a gorgeous seafood buffet on Friday evenings, a prime rib buffet on Saturday and an exquisite Sunday brunch buffet. The à la carte dinner selections are varied among seafood, poultry, beef and veal specialties served with salad, baked potato or rice. They include tempting selections such as shrimp Rockefeller stuffed with spinach and tossed with a Parmesan cream sauce, or smoked salmon and baked bay scallops with a pepper vodka sauce served with pasta. The Sunday brunch buffet includes carved top-round roast, ham, omelets or eggs to order, salads, cheeses, soups, chicken and seafood entrees, pasta and an array of desserts. Early Islander dinner specials are available until 6:30 P.M. each night. Paradise Restaurant has all ABC permits.

Tradewinds
$$$ • MP 5½, Royal Pavillion Resort • 726-5188

Tradewinds at the Royal Pavillion Resort serves breakfast, lunch and dinner daily in season and from midweek through the weekend in winter. The louvered privacy and soft decor of the dining room is an appropriate setting for the numerous house specialties that make generous use of fresh fruits and vegetables. Dinner entrees include seafood favorites like stuffed flounder and grilled or blackened fresh filets, prime cuts of beef, veal, pasta and chicken along with soups and salads. Try the Jack Daniels rib eye, veal Saltimbocca with prosciutto or one of the announced seafood specialities. Tradewinds offers banquet and meeting facilities. The Passport Lounge is a comfortable respite at the resort. Late fall and winter have brought special evening events like dinner theater productions and theme menus to the Tradewinds.

Indian Beach/Salter Path

Big Oak Drive In
$ • MP 10½ • 247-2588

Turn on the blinker and stop the car. Big Oak has the Best Shrimp Burger on the Crystal Coast — that's according to the results of an Insiders' poll. While others serve a good shrimp burger, Big Oak serves a great one. They've been at it for 20 years in Salter Path where the locals remember shrimp were first actually eaten and harvested commercially. Other goodies you'll find include chicken and barbecue sandwiches, burgers, hot dogs, pizza and even BLTs. Big Oak has plates of barbecue, fried chicken, chicken salad and shrimp as well as mighty good french fries, onion rings and slaw. But it's that shrimp burger that will keep you coming back!

Crab Shack
$$ • MP 10½, On Bogue Sound • 247-3444

Tucked back off the main road, the Crab Shack offers excellent seafood and a wonderful view of Bogue Sound — the restaurant actually hangs over the water. This is one of the our favorite places for steamed crabs in addition to shrimp, crab cakes and crab legs. Yum! The restaurant has an extensive seafood menu and will fry, grill, pan in butter or broil your choice. For the landlubber, there is rib eye, chicken and hamburger steak. The Crab Shack serves wine, beer and has setups for those wishing to brown-bag their favorite beverage. The outside deck is a great place to relax.

Frank and Clara's Restaurant & Lounge
$$$ • MP 11 • 247-2788

Frank and Clara's is a local favorite and is very popular with visitors too. The restaurant serves a variety of dinner choices that include seafood and steaks. Insider favorites are jumbo shrimp stuffed with crabmeat, chargrilled rib eyes or filets, and flounder stuffed with your choice of crab and shrimp or scallops and oysters. Each meal is prepared to order. Dinner entrees come with either a salad topped with homemade dressings or a cup of clam chowder, choice of potato, rice or cole slaw and hush puppies or rolls. There are special entrees for senior citizens and children. During summer months, lunch is served by popular demand. Beside the Salter Path Post Office, the restaurant has all ABC permits. Frank and Clara's has a lot of repeat business. If there is a wait, the upstairs lounge is a comfortable spot for refreshment.

Frost Seafood House and Oyster Bar
$$ • MP 10 • 247-3202

In the heart of Salter Path, Frost's serves all kinds of seafood "Salter Path style" and has an oyster bar. The restaurant serves dinner nightly, weekends in winter, and all three meals in the summer, including all-you-can-eat breakfast specials. Frost's also offers steak, chicken, barbecue, lobster and fresh vegetables. Favorites include shrimp scampi, popcorn shrimp and snow crab legs. Frost's prepares seafood from old family recipes and has the best hush puppies around. The restaurant has facilities to accommodate private parties and offers a takeout service. During the summer, a line of hungry people forms, so we suggest you go early. Frost Seafood Market is also the place to get fresh local seafood to prepare at home.

Plum Tree Deli
$$ • MP 9, 1401 Salter Path Rd. • 808-3404

Good eating at the beach keeps satisfied customers driving to Salter Path to the Plum Tree. Sandwiches and salads can be prepared from early morning (for picnics), or deli meats, cheeses and salads are available by the pound. Lunch at the Plum Tree is a real treat. We recommend the magnificent crab-cake

INSIDERS' TIP

The Crystal Coast offers great "secret" fishing spots, like the back side of Shackleford Banks and the jetty at Fort Macon.

sandwich made with a sautéed, lump crabmeat cake served on a croissant with a spicy dressing, provolone, lettuce and tomato. Plum Tree serves by candlelight in the evenings with preparations from menus announced each week. Presentations are beautiful, and entrees are just right for the season. We particularly enjoyed the mushroom-stuffed meat loaf, especially when served with garlic mashed potatoes. Call for reservations, and don't expect to sit in the smoking area — there isn't one.

Emerald Isle

Bushwackers Restaurant
$$$ • 100 Bogue Inlet Dr. • 354-6300

Bushwackers, at Bogue Inlet Pier, is known for its fun wait staff, spectacular oceanfront view and adventurous decor. It is a favorite dinner spot for fresh seafood prepared in a variety of ways including grilled, blackened, broiled and steamed. There are also steaks and inventive pastas, and Bushwackers is a great place for ribs. The appetizer menu is extensive, including gator bites and calamari. We love the blooming onion and the stuffed clams. Entrees feature fresh seafood just off the boat, chargrilled Angus steaks, prime rib and more. Try the rock 'n' roll cheesecake for dessert. The Safari Lounge is a great place to meet friends and make new ones. Bushwackers has all ABC permits and serves beer and wine. Come enjoy an island dining adventure.

Cafe 58
$$$ • 8802-5 Reed St. • 354-4058

If you'd like to impress someone with your knowledge of good food, take them for lunch or dinner to Cafe 58 across from Emerald Plantation. There are no disappointments here. The chef is a pro, the ownership is the same as Westside Cafe in Morehead City and the harmony works for the discerning diner. With the light decor, pleasant patio for drinks, modern jazz and food to match, you may just want to move in. Don't hesitate to try a gourmet pizza for lunch. Fresh fish dinner entrees are grilled, sautéed, poached or steamed with a selection of perfect sauces. All menu items are available for take-out convenience in case you'd like to move your feast to the beach.

RuckerJohns
$$ • Emerald Plantation Shopping Center • 354-2413

RuckerJohns, in its new location in Emerald Plantation, offers all in-house preparations from a great menu for the entire family. Dinner entrees, prepared to order, include fresh seafood, pasta, barbecue shrimp, beef ribs, steaks, chicken and pork chops. Favorite appetizers include fried calamari, shrimp cooked in beer, hot crab dip and chicken wings. For lunch, try the grilled Cajun chicken salad, the spinach salad with hot bacon, coastal pasta salad, any of the juicy burgers or a creative sandwich. RuckerJohns has all ABC permits and also has a location in Wilmington. RuckerJohns' lounge (see our Nightlife chapter) is a cozy gathering place enjoyed by the local population, especially on winter nights when there's a crackling fire in the fireplace.

Beaufort

Beaufort Grocery Co.
$$$$ • 117 Queen St. • 728-3899

Beaufort Grocery Company represents a standard of excellence recognized by all other local restaurants. Chef Charles Park offers fine cuisine in a restored town grocery store that's a see-and-be-seen location. Everything served is exquisite, and the service is professional and friendly. The lunch menu includes creative salads (try the smoked-fish option), soups and sandwiches. Favorites are the gougeres (herb pastries stuffed with crab, shrimp, chicken or egg salads), smoked turkey, a country ham and cheese sandwich on sourdough or chicken salad with apples on a croissant. Dinner starts with such creative appetizers as Oriental pork ribs marinated in dried

fruit, fabulous Carolina crab cakes, or the fisherman's soup filled with shrimp, scallops, clams, fish and vegetables. For your entree, we suggest fresh grouper encrusted with crabmeat and asparagus, grilled turkey steak served with corn salsa or the filet mignon. The dinner menu features fresh seafood, choice steaks, chicken, duck and lamb. Early diner specials are also offered. Top your meal off with raspberry cheesecake or any other dessert. Entrees are served with a salad, fresh vegetables and delicious breads. Beaufort Grocery Co. offers a wonderful Sunday brunch, a take-out menu and a full delicatessen with meats, cheeses, homemade salads and breads. There is a small bar area, and the restaurant has all ABC permits. Private catered dining facilities are next door at 115 Queen Street.

Blue Moon Espresso Bar & Cafe
$ • 119 Queen St. • 504-3036

In its newly remodeled location, the Blue Moon is a favorite stop to start the day with fresh breads, bagels and pastries and a caffe of choice. Specials for bigger appetites are announced each morning by the kitchen. Lunch sandwiches, soups and salads include a choice of fresh breads. You can't go wrong with any sandwich, and they'll make them to go if you have plans on the water. Be sure to try a homemade dessert with your espresso.

Clawson's 1905 Restaurant
$$ • 429 Front St. • 728-2133

Clawson's 1905 has a masterful atmosphere and is a favorite destination throughout the day, throughout the year. An architectural focal point in the middle of downtown, the newly remodeled Clawson's 1905 is housed in what was Clawson's General Store back in the early 1900s. The clientele is greeted with options to step up for a cup of joe at the Fishtowne Java coffee bar, to shop the general store shelves for a T-shirt

Photo: Scott Taylor

Some beach goers never use towels or coolers.

or a cigar, to proceed to a comfortable chair and catch up with the world according to CNN, to move on to the rear for the best beer selection in town, or to be seated upstairs or down for lunch or dinner. There are lots of choices, and it's a choice spot. Lunch favorites are the Dirigible, a hearty baked potato stuffed with seafood, vegetables or meats, and a long list of generous sandwiches and burgers. Dinner entrees always include fresh seafood prepared with style, zesty ribs, steaks, chicken and pasta. Private banquet facilities are available and, from fall through spring, Down East FolkArts Society concerts are performed here. Clawson's gets crowded during the summer months, but it's worth the wait.

Finz Grill & Eatery
$$ • 330 Front St. • 728-7459

Finz is the perfect place to relax, enjoy good food and visit with friends in a casual atmosphere. Guests are seated inside or on the back porch over Taylor's Creek. The lunch menu offers sandwiches, subs, burgers, soups (try the wonderful gumbo or black bean) and fresh fried fish baskets. Dinner over the water focuses on seafood, especially the fresh fish catch that can be grilled, blackened or fried. Steaks and pasta dishes are also options. Finz is proud of offering seafood caught by local fishermen, many of whom are friends and customers. Finz has great desserts and all ABC permits.

Front Street Grill
$$$$ • 419 Front St. • 728-3118

This new American bistro focuses on seafood, grilled meats, pasta and other creative entrees for lunch and dinner. The lunch menu includes soups, creative salads with grilled tuna, hot fried chicken or shrimp, overstuffed sandwiches with grilled chicken and smoked cheese or fish, crab cakes and pasta. Dinner appetizers include hot crab dip, pepper-fried calamari and black-bean and goat-cheese quesadillas. Try the herb-encrusted tequila grilled shrimp, seared tuna and grilled beef

Photo: Scott Taylor

Shrimp trawlers fill a lot of orders for Crystal Coast restaurants.

with tomato chutney. Nightly chalkboard specials are also featured. The chocolate-raspberry truffle cheesecake and Key lime cheesecake are favorites for dessert. Front Street Grill has all ABC permits plus an extensive beer and wine selection. Espresso and cappuccino are also available. Reservations are suggested.

Harpoon Willie's Restaurant & Pub
$$ • 300 Front St. • 728-5247

Why not relax and dine overlooking Taylor's Creek and an island that is home to roaming ponies? That's what Harpoon Willie's offers. Dinner appetizers include crab cakes, steamed clams, seafood gumbo and stuffed shrimp. Entrees feature fresh local seafood, especially shrimp and shellfish, and certified Angus beef. Favorites include shrimp Alfredo, savory scallops, baby-back ribs, rib eyes and seafood combinations, fried or broiled. The restaurant has all ABC permits and offers wine and domestic and imported beers. Harpoon Willie's pub is next door. A ferry to Shackleford Banks and Carrot Island leaves the restaurant dock several times each day during the summer.

Loughry's Landing
$$$ • 502 Front St. • 728-7541

With a beautiful view of Taylor's Creek and the Beaufort waterfront, Loughry's Landing is the restaurant we have always known

as the Beaufort House. Newly redecorated, the restaurant reopened this spring under the new ownership and management of Donna and Joe Loughry, well-known locally for running Ottis' Seafood Restaurant on the Morehead City waterfront. The lunch and dinner menus feature fresh local seafood — including steamed shellfish — and beef, ribs, chicken and pasta selections are also offered. On summer nights, the upstairs Crab Deck overlooking the activity at the docks is a great spot to enjoy cracking into steamed crabs or peeling shrimp. It's very casual. You just can't be too polite eating steamed crabs.

Mario's Pizzeria & Ristorante
$$ • U.S. Hwy. 70 E., Beaufort Square Shopping Center • 728-6602

Mario's, in the town's only shopping center, offers brick-cooked pizza that is fantastic and has a faithful following. Fresh vegetable toppings include spinach, broccoli and tomatoes, and garlic lovers find complete satisfaction in the fresh garlic pizza. Subs, calzones and strombolis are also packed with fresh vegetables. Mario's keeps a steady stream of return diners with very reasonable prices and delicious selections such as cavetelli pasta with broccoli sautéed with garlic, fettuccine Alfredo and chicken Marsala.

Net House Steam Restaurant & Oyster Bar

$$-$$$ • 133 Turner St. • 728-2002

If you ask where to go for seafood, most Beaufort residents will send you to the Net House. Just across the street from the Beaufort Historic Site, the Net House specializes in steamed shellfish broiled and lightly battered fried seafood. It also has an oyster bar. Guests can enjoy an atmosphere of weathered pine and nautical antiques at this family-owned eatery. Try the creamy clam chowder, conch chowder, crab soup or seafood bisque for lunch or as a dinner appetizer. Sandwiches, salads and seafood are also offered for lunch, which is served during every season except summer. Dinner favorites include steamed crabs, clams, oysters and shrimp or the broiled platter that includes flounder stuffed with crabmeat, scallops, oysters and shrimp. The Net House is known for its famous Key lime pie, and it has all ABC permits. No reservations are taken.

FYI

Unless otherwise noted, the area code for all phone numbers in this guide is 919.

Beaufort Inlet and Taylor's Creek. Summer diners can dine at shaded tables on the outside dock. Lunch favorites are the Spouter's soups, salads and sandwiches named for legendary local characters or haunts. Our favorite is the Out Island, a delightful assembly of shrimp, mushrooms, onions, provolone, tomatoes and sprouts on rye. Also renowned is the Spouter's banana cream crepe dessert. The dinner menu changes seasonally and entrees are announced that take advantage of fresh seafood availability. From the menu, appetizers and entrees are spectacular. We suggest starting with Cajun oysters served with a bourbon-spiked remoulade. Fire-roasted beef entrees, such as tenderloin served with wild mushroom sauce, get a big thumbs up. Another delicious taste combination is pecan chicken with hot pear compote. Entrees are served with a choice of smoked Gouda mashed potatoes or wild rice and seasonal vegetables. The Spouter Inn has all ABC permits. Dinner reservations are recommended.

No Name Pizza and Subs

$ • 408 Live Oak St. • 728-4978, 728-4982

This is as good as it gets in Beaufort for pizza, according to our own personal survey. No Name is also a great place for subs (everything from meatball to vegetarian), burgers and spaghetti with meatballs. The Greek salad is loaded with feta cheese and served with a loaf of garlic bread. No Name also serves pasta dishes, Greek dishes, sandwiches and chicken. The baklava is wonderful. The menu is the same for lunch and dinner, but dinner specials are announced daily. You'll leave satisfied, feeling like you got your money's worth. No Name offers dine-in or drive-through service.

The Spouter Inn

$$$ • 218 Front St. • 728-5190

A maroon awning marks the Front Street entrance to this intimate restaurant, which is over the water and offers a wonderful view of

The Veranda

$$$ • Town Creek Marina, 241 W. Beaufort Rd. • 728-5352

The Veranda, overlooking Gallant's Channel at Town Creek Marina, has all the ingredients for a stellar dining experience. It's just finding your way to it that is a bit awkward, but once you've done it once, you'll return for the seasonal American cuisine of executive chef Tad Whitaker. Crossing the bridge into Beaufort, the Veranda is easy to see across the harbor on the north side. The restaurant is upstairs at Town Creek Marina. Dining on the porch is the way to go for lunch, dinner or the Sunday champagne brunch. Whitaker uses fresh ingredients grown or caught locally and treats them simply. We recommend anything grilled with one of his salsas or fruit chutneys.

INSIDERS' TIP

There is nothing like camping beside Cape Lookout Lighthouse, watching the light sweep the beach and listening to the rolling waves.

The Veranda's mixed grill combines shrimp, scallops and the day's catch. Served with either black-bean salsa or pineapple-apricot chutney, freshly baked breads and vegetable salad with chef-made dressings, there is simply no way to dine any better. The Veranda has all ABC permits. Reservations are recommended.

Morehead City

Anchor Inn Restaurant & Lounge
$$-$$$ • 2806 Arendell St. • 726-2156

The Anchor Inn Restaurant is well-known by locals and visitors for fine food and quality service. For 27 years, the restaurant has offered a lavish breakfast and creative dinner. A variety of omelets, waffles, fruits, pancakes, quiches, biscuits and muffins are served at the hearty breakfast. Dinners are served by candlelight and include Angus beef and prime rib, fresh local seafood, fresh pasta, chicken and Mediterranean dishes. Seafood is black-ened, grilled, broiled or fried. A special lower-calorie menu is offered, and there are daily breakfast and dinner specials. Desserts are unsurpassed and include the famous tollhouse pie and chess pie. Private banquet and meeting rooms are available, and the restaurant has all ABC permits. The adjoining lounge often features live piano music.

Bistro By The Sea
$$$ • 4033 Arendell St. • 247-2777

Bistro By The Sea, a favorite of locals for both food and hospitality, is newly opened in its brand new digs next to the Hampton Inn. The hospitality extends comforts including a piano and martini bar and a cigar patio. The Bistro celebrates its space, like moving into a dream house, after five cramped years in the restaurant's old 1,000-square-foot area. Chef-owner Tim Coyne, in his new kitchen, serves reliably wonderful dinner entrees using very fresh vegetables, seafoods and tasty cuts of beef. Seafood entrees vary nightly according to freshness and availability. Other than seafood specialties, we also recommend the chargrilled filet mignon or rib eye, liver in orange liqueur or stir-fried chicken with rice and wontons. We also like the pasta creations, such as seafood-and-cheese-filled pasta shells, eggplant Parmesan and capellini with pesto, vegetables and scallops. Sandwiches are available along with a tempting selection of desserts. Bistro By The Sea has all ABC permits.

Blue Peter's Cafe
$$$-$$$$ • 509 Evans St. • 808-2904

If you're still thinking about the name, it's working. The same folks who brought us The Sanitary Restaurant opened Blue Peter's this winter on the Morehead waterfront and gave it a name you won't forget. Other than that, it's a colloquial name for a mud hen, or coot. The opening of this restaurant helped punctuate the presence of really fine dining on the Morehead waterfront. Lunch chef is Martha Bourne, pied piper of culinary talent from the well-remembered Bogue's Pocket Cafe. The dinner menu belongs to executive chef James Koebbe, who can't help showing his good training. Taking the best of a worldly exposure to cuisines and fresh local ingredients, the dinner menu offers such entrees as sautéed lump crab cakes with a Lowcountry remoulade; peach-glazed breast of duck with kielbasa, spinach, onions and polenta cakes; shrimp and scallops with a Southwestern red chili pesto cream sauce and linguine. Don't get us started — the experience is delightful, lunch or dinner.

Calypso Cafe
$$$ • 506 Arendell St. • 240-3380

Calypso Cafe is like a restaurant in the tropics that you'll never forget: Its small size, happily colored cement walls and steel-drum music will make you feel a world away. But it's the tropical cuisine that makes memories that stick in your mind, like grits to your ribs, and has created a dedicated clientele that doesn't even care if there are other good restaurants in town. Owners Dave and Mary Lindsay make it too easy, mon, and too good. We like to follow Dave's whims, announced nightly. Start with an appetizer — black bean torta, baked stuffed jalapeños or curried potato bisque. Then choose the grilled triggerfish with what-

ever enhancement Dave is making, like black bean mango chutney. Entrees are centered around local seafood presented with island fruits and spices. Desserts, such as paradise pie (a brownie and ice cream covered with strawberry puree), are an exquisite temptation. Share one. Guests can dine at a table, at the bar or on the patio. The cafe serves mixed drinks, wine and beer and is well-known for creative cocktails.

Capt. Bill's Waterfront Restaurant
$$ • 701 Evans St. • 726-2166

This family-style restaurant has served lunch and dinner on the Morehead City waterfront for 52 years. Owners John and Diane Poag maintain the waterfront tradition of good seafood. Locals know the weekday lunch specials, especially that Wednesday and Saturday are conch stew days. Capt. Bill's offers seafood fried and broiled, cold plates, salads, seafood casseroles, seafood combination plates, Cajun-style catfish, steaks, chicken and sandwiches. Desserts are made from family recipes and include a Down East Lemon Pie that alone is worth the trip. Don't leave without sampling one of the 13 flavors of fudge made at the restaurant.

Charter Restaurant
$$ • 405 Evans St. • 726-9036

On the Morehead City waterfront, the Charter specializes in fresh local seafood for lunch and dinner with a great view over the water. Announced specials and the lunch menu offer seafood specialties and sandwiches as well as ribs, hamburger steak, soups and salads. Our favorite is Crabby Dan, hot crabmeat heaped on an English muffin and topped with a tomato slice and cheese. Dinner appetizers may include oyster supreme, clam chowder or seafood bisque. Entrees include homemade crab cakes, shrimp and flounder stuffed daily. Seafood is steamed, fried or broiled. Chicken, charbroiled steaks and barbecue ribs are also offered. The restaurant's salad bar includes vegetables, breads, pasta and cheese. Our recommendations for dessert: Granny's apple-caramel pie or homemade tollhouse pie. The Charter offers menus for senior citizens and children and has all ABC permits.

Pull up a chair under a beautiful old oak and enjoy the sunset.

El's Drive-In
$ • 3600 Arendell St. • 726-3002

El's has been a Carteret County tradition since 1959. This is an old-fashioned drive-in — that means you are waited on by a car-hop and sit in your vehicle and eat. El's has great burgers, hot dogs, fries and milk shakes. The superburger is a Carteret County favorite and is a special one, assembled with slaw and chili. Try a shrimp or oyster burger, a BLT, a fish or steak sandwich, a shrimp or oyster tray or fried chicken. This is a favorite lunch and dinner spot for locals, so go early to get a parking place. And don't forget to lob a french fry or two out the window to the waiting sea gulls.

El Zarape
$ • 4138 Arendell St. • 808-2233

When only Mexican will do, this is nirvana. You're immediately served tortilla chips and salsa, the beer menu is extensive and entrees served with refried beans and all your favorites are offered — chili rellenos, fajitas, burritos, enchiladas, quesadillas, tacos, tostadas and hundreds of combinations of these. Service is speedy and mostly in English, but it's a good place to try your Spanish out and the summer air conditioning is truly chili.

Magnolia Tree Cafe
$$$ • 105 S. 11th St. • 726-2225

Lunch or dinner at the Magnolia Tree Cafe is a Southern hospitality experience. The genuine warmth of proprietor Ruthie King is attractive enough, but her kitchen charms all appetites. The restaurant is in a restored 18th-century house with private dining rooms and comfortable porches that are cooled by Bogue Sound breezes. For lunch, the sandwiches, omelets and hot specials are tempting, but if you haven't tried her chicken salad, the decision's made. Whatever's fresh in seafood inspires the specials announced each evening. Try her shrimp and grits with black-eyed pea salsa or the filet mignon with Ruthie's famous bourbon sauce. Whatever she's made for dessert, especially if it's chocolate, order it. You'll

Made To Order

"Hi, darlin' . . . What can I get for you?" asks Louise, the waitress at Morehead City's legendary El's Drive-In.

The answer from people in about 400 cars a day is, most frequently, a burger — a shrimp burger, oyster burger or El's Superburger. And no one forgets to order the fries. Nouvelle cuisine be damned. There are too many times in Carteret County when only an El's burger will do.

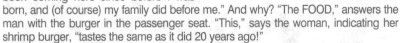

This is one of those times. Sitting in her truck with a sea gull waiting on the hood for any leftovers, one customer says, "I've been coming here since before I was born, and (of course) my family did before me." And why? "The FOOD," answers the man with the burger in the passenger seat. "This," says the woman, indicating her shrimp burger, "tastes the same as it did 20 years ago!"

And El's isn't just the locals' fancy.

"My uncle came from Germany with his wife who'd never been here," the woman behind the wheel continues, "and after all the seafood they caught and ate while they were here, their favorite thing was the burgers at El's."

"We just recently had some people from Seattle, Washington, order take-out shrimp burgers and ask us to wrap each ingredient separately so they could get them back home and put them together themselves," says Thursday's cook, Robin Paul, who has assembled burgers at El's for four years.

El's Drive-In is a Morehead City favorite for burgers, shrimp burgers and oyster sandwiches.

". . . California, Florida . . ." Louise adds. "We had a man land in a private plane in Beaufort and take a cab here for nine or 10 shrimp burgers to take to friends in Fort Lauderdale."

So, what is it that keeps them coming to El's from childhood and Fort Lauderdale?

"We start every day with 120 to 150 pounds of fresh ground beef, then press the burgers. The oysters and shrimp are from Beaufort. We make the slaw," says Robin. "We make everything. That's how they've always done it."

And they assemble it their way or yours. The El's way starts with the basic burger, fried shrimp or oysters. Add slaw, and you're holding the building block on which El's reputation is crafted. No special sauces here. Just flavors you can trust like real hamburger, ketchup, that sort of thing. Continuous customer satisfaction also comes from the custom features that distinguish each individual burger. If you want shrimp on your cheeseburger, so be it. Onions? Mustard? Oysters? It's your burger.

"This is the second grill in the history of the business," says Robin, indicating the

— continued on next page

shiny stainless centerpiece of the short-order kitchen. "From this 32-by-16-foot building, we serve about 800 burgers a day."

Some changes have taken place during the nearly 50 years of El's Drive-In history. The location has changed, small Coke bottles have been replaced by cans, and the soft-serve ice cream window was ditched because it became a hassle. When high school students began to collect the window trays, they had to be replaced with bags. No one minds the few modernizing changes — customers wait up to 45 minutes for an El's burger in summer. No one minds that either.

be encouraged to enjoy the ambiance for as long as you like. For food, price and atmosphere, the Magnolia Tree is a restaurant we always recommend.

Mer-Nan's
$$$$ • 3701Bridges St. • 247-9241

Beside Carteret General Hospital, Mer-Nan's is constantly being discovered. A combination of the initial syllables of the owners' first names, Mer-Nan's is simply delightful. Windows are filled with blooming orchids, tables are generously sized for the comfort of diners, service is professional, and Merlin in the kitchen is a magician. Lunch sandwiches (Monte Cristo is fabulous), salads, quiche, fresh fruits and seafood cold plates are faithfully demanded by local bridge clubs, book groups, mothers meeting daughters for lunch and New Bern societies. Dinner is equally satisfying. Entrees are served with a choice of salads including the best Caesar salad we've tasted in the area. The pecan-encrusted fresh filet with chili mango sauce says it all, but grilled salmon served on Dijon lime ginger sauce with spinach walnut ravioli and rice pilaf is irresistible as well. Desserts, too, are awesome. Flambé Cherries Jubilee and Bananas Foster are prepared tableside.

Mitzi's
$$$$ • 403 Arendell St. • 240-3601

This restaurant opened in 1997, adding to the upscale dining excitement on the Morehead City waterfront. Patrons who regularly enjoyed the Cajun and world-wise cuisine of Bourbon St. Cafe and the memorable hospitality and catering of Beverly Veasey of Jason's will find all of that expertise newly assembled at Mitzi's. Dinner is served in a stylishly casual setting that overlooks Bogue Sound. Seating on the second-floor deck is a perfect choice for sun-

sets and cool summer nights. Appetizers like escargot with herbed garlic butter or tempura shrimp with plum dipping sauce lead to entrees chosen from fresh seafood, Black Angus beef and executive specialties such as veal scallopini with shrimp in a Fontina cheese sauce. Be sure to check out the nightly seafood specialties and dessert board. You can expect a reliably wonderful evening at Mitzi's. Reservations are appreciated.

Nikola's
$$$ • Fourth and Bridges Sts. • 726-6060

Nikola's serves Northern Italian cuisine with a warm, Old World charm. This is the perfect place to take someone special or to gather with a group of close friends. The 1920s-era, two-story Victorian house provides eight separate dining rooms, and guests can enjoy three course meals as well as à la carte selections. Meals include a choice of homemade soups or pasta, tossed green salad, two vegetables and an entree. Exquisite dinner options include veal selections, fresh seafood, prime beef cuts, chicken and made-from-scratch pastas, all prepared in authentic style. Our favorites are the numerous veal preparations, especially the simple and rich flavors of veal Piccata sautéed with lemon and wine. Nikola's has all ABC permits and has opened a second restaurant in New Bern.

Ottis' Waterfront Restaurant
$$$ • 711 Shepard St. • 247-3474

Fresh seafood from the adjoining market is Ottis' specialty. Dinner is served nightly featuring fresh catch specialties prepared blackened, Cajun, pan-fried, sautéed, grilled, broiled or steamed. From the steamer, clams, shrimp and snow crab legs are always available, and oysters are offered in season. Appetizer selections include calamari served with sweet-

and-sour sauce, crab-stuffed mushrooms and shark bites grilled "on the barbie." Popular selections don't include only seafood. For a change, try choice rib eye and New York strip steaks, pasta primavera and chicken Marsala. Ottis' features an extensive selection of California wines, a good selection of beers and has all ABC permits.

The Plant
$$$ • 105 S. Seventh St. • 726-5502

Opened in 1996, The Plant was another sure sign that upscale dining had arrived on the Morehead City waterfront. From the architectural redesign of the building to the chocolate, truffles and champagne, The Plant is flawless. The executive chef makes gracious use of fresh seafood and herbs, successfully introduced sushi to a skeptical local population and sets the pace with seasonally changing menus that keep the tables occupied. Favorites from the dinner menu are blue corn-crusted tuna served with a ginger and carrot puree and red chile pasta or beef tenderloin with five-peppercorn sauce and roasted potatoes. For lunch, those who try the grilled portabello mushroom sandwich with goat cheese, basil and red onions seem to keep ordering it over and over. Sunday brunch, daily lunch and dinner are delightful at umbrella-canopied tables on the patio. Large parties are accommodated easily in The Plant's Warehouse, which is also a full-service bar.

Rapscallions
$$ • 715 Arendell St. • 240-1213

Raps is a favorite downtown spot for lunch, dinner or drinks in a casual 1890s family atmosphere. House specialties include steamed clams and crabs, Philly cheesesteaks, the original Raps Burger and seafood Alfredo. You'll also find ribs, crab legs, soups and steaks. Raps has a wonderful taco salad and dressed-up hamburgers, seafood gumbo and overstuffed sandwiches. Lunches feature a light and lively special that could be shrimp salad one day and a delicious fruit plate the next. The bar at Raps is a popular gathering place on weeknights and weekends. Bar patrons are served hot popcorn and can watch the big-screen television.

Sanitary Fish Market & Restaurant
$$ • 501 Evans St., Morehead City
Waterfront • 247-3111

Sanitary has been a landmark on the Morehead City waterfront for nearly 60 years. In 1938, Ted Garner and Tony Seamon, both now deceased, opened a waterfront seafood market in a building rented for $5.50 per week with the agreement that no beer or wine would be sold and that the premises would be kept clean and neat. The name Sanitary Fish Market was chosen by the partners to project their compliance. When 12 stools were set up at the counter, the first seafood restaurant on the city's waterfront was in business. Today, Ted Garner Jr. operates the family-oriented business. Customers find old favorite menu items along with many new additions, all ordered by number. Best-known for fresh seafood served broiled, steamed, grilled or fried, the Sanitary also offers steaks, poultry, pork and pasta entrees. Lunch always includes a good selection of vegetables and attracts lots of locals. The Sanitary Fish Market at the restaurant still sells fresh local seafood for those who prefer to cook it themselves. And, just before the new millennium, the Sanitary now offers beer and wine.

Summer Palace
Chinese Restaurant
$ • 3402 Arendell St. • 726-6000

Summer Palace offers Mandarin, Szechuan and Cantonese cuisine. Lunch and dinner buffets offer a huge variety, but menu selections are far more distinctive. Dinner appetizers including fantail shrimp and steamed or fried dumplings offer a nice variety. Entrees feature chicken, duck, beef, seafood and pork. Peking duck for two served with scallions and Chinese pancakes is, singularly, reason enough for dinner at the Summer Palace. It is spectacular. A children's menu, American menu and takeout service are available.

Texas Steakhouse & Saloon
$-$$ • U.S. Hwy. 70 at N.C. Hwy. 24
• 240-2633

Beefing up Morehead City with steaks hand-cut to your specifications, Texas Steakhouse & Saloon also offers a selection of 27 types of longneck beers to wash off the

Photo: NC Aquarium

A blue crab by any other name would taste as sweet.

road dust while you wait for that steak to be seared. Have some roasted peanuts and go ahead and toss the shells on the floor. It really is a lot of fun, and the aged beef is excellent. Seafood and pasta alternatives are also offered, but it's best to stick with the program. There's constant country music in the air just in case you think you're not in Texas.

Town House Restaurant
$ • 907 Arendell St. • 726-5101

The very local clientele of this small, downtown lunch staple is joined on Thursdays every week by the great numbers who faithfully show up for a traditionally complete Lebanese lunch plate. The choice is vegetarian or not, and the plates may include kibby, hummus, tabouli, salata, stuffed grape leaves, koosa — all straight from the old country. All Insiders know the schedule and are either there or have called ahead for take-out.

The Waterfront Seafood Deli & Cafe
$ • Jib of Shepard and Evans Sts.
• 247-3933

This small cafe is in the jib, or triangle, between Shepard and Evans streets and across from Ottis' Waterfront Restaurant. During lunch and dinner hours, walk up to the counter and order seafood plates and platters, crab-cake sandwiches, shrimp or oyster burgers, hamburgers, hot dogs, soups, chowders and salads. Take-out lunches are convenient for boaters, waterfront workers and, at any booth, it's an Insiders' favorite for a fast business lunch.

WestSide Cafe
$$$ • 4370-A Arendell St. • 240-0588

WestSide Cafe is a favorite among locals and regulars. This upscale cafe offers creative lunches and gourmet dinners. The lunch menu offers soups (try the almost-famous tomato soup), specialty sandwiches, burgers, hot dogs, subs and salads. Favorites include the pastrami, knockwurst and Swiss grilled on rye with Russian dressing; the stadium dog with slaw, kraut and chili; the grilled shrimp salad; and the smoked turkey sandwich.

While lunch is wonderful, dinner is when the WestSide Cafe shines. Favorite appetizers are glazed shrimp, seafood potstickers with Oriental dipping sauce and soups. Entrees include shrimp and sun-dried tomatoes in a cream sauce over linguine, grilled beef in a cognac cream sauce and sautéed breast of chicken in a raspberry glaze. Each week a "temptations" menu is prepared to accompany the regular dinner menu. WestSide Cafe has all ABC permits and serves beer, wine, select coffees and wonderful juices. There is take-out available, and live jazz is a house special twice a week.

Mrs. Willis' Restaurant
$-$$ • 3004 Bridges St. • 726-3741

Mrs. Willis and her family have been serving home-cooked meals since 1949. The restaurant actually began in the home of "Ma" Willis as a barbecue and chicken take-out place specializing in mini-lemon pies. Customers ate right in the kitchen, which is now Capt. Russell's lounge. In 1956, the restaurant moved into the garage, which is the front of today's restaurant, and additions were made through the years. The restaurant is a favorite of locals and visitors who want a meal made from family recipes without going to the trouble themselves. Specialties include fresh pork barbecue, local seafood, chargrilled steaks and fresh vegetables. We recommend the Down East conch chowder for starters and then the prime rib — it's one of the best around for the money. Other entree suggestions include the seafood combination plate, chicken livers, pork chops, stuffed crab, rib eye or roast beef. There is a special every day and night. Mrs. Willis' can accommodate groups of any size and has all ABC permits.

Windansea
$$$-$$$$ • 708 Evans St. • 247-3000

The well-known chefs of the Coral Bay Club opened Windansea on the Morehead City waterfront in February 1997 in a location known for upscale dining and downscale decor. A complete remodeling, however, fit the decor to the dining and created a delightful setting for the artistry from the kitchen. Among the wonderful aspects of the new atmosphere is a wood-fired brick oven that bakes specialty crusty sourdough breads and inventive individual pizzas. If you can't make up your mind among the dinner entrees, try the grilled triggerfish served with cheese-filled ravioli and fresh asparagus, Tandoori chicken or roasted lamb. Menus change seasonally, but the Creme Brulee dessert will likely be offered throughout the year, so try it. There are no disappointments, unless you didn't call for reservations. Seating is limited.

Swansboro

Capt. Charlie's Restaurant
$$$ • N.C. Hwy. 24 at Front St.
• (910) 326-4303

Capt. Charlie's Restaurant specializes in fresh seafood, prime rib and steaks. The traditional menu offers lots of fried seafood, although there are plenty of other choices. Try

the stuffed flounder or broiled shrimp and scallops. The steaks have an enormous following too. Well-prepared food served in ample amounts brings people back to Capt. Charlie's again and again. With all ABC permits, you can have a drink in the lounge while you wait for your table or with dinner if the mood strikes you.

The Flying Bridge
$$$ • N.C. Hwy. 24 E. • (910) 393-2416

The Flying Bridge has a location advantage overlooking the Intracoastal Waterway and a neighboring sandy island. The restaurant has three delightful components: a restaurant that serves lunch and dinner featuring fresh grilled seafood, pasta, chicken, veal and steaks; a steam and raw bar offering oysters, clams, crabs and shrimp; and a ship's store deli, bakery and seafood market that makes subs and bagels and sells fresh seafood. The restaurant and bar have all ABC permits. The restaurant offers daily specials and wonderful desserts.

White Oak River Bistro
$$$ • 206 Corbett St. • (910) 326-1696

Just past the bridge in the familiar white building with the inviting porches, White Oak River Bistro offers European cuisine for lunch and dinner. Service is in the brightly varnished dining room or on the lovely porch overlooking a lawn that spreads under willow trees to the river. The appetizing wafts from the kitchen bring on an expectation of the fresh herb sauces used. Among the lunch entrees, choose from a number of pastas and a selection of sauces or specialty Italian sandwiches including a delightful focaccia. Dinner entrees include pastas with veal, chicken and seafood. White Oak River has all ABC permits.

Yana's Ye Olde Drugstore Restaurant
$ • 109 Front St. • (910) 326-5501

Just about everybody in Swansboro eats at Yana's at some time during the day. Whether it's the food or the company that attracts you, once you've been in, you'll come back again and again. Breakfast specialties are all are cooked to order. Lunch can include a variety of sandwiches or soups, but the Bradburger, a beefy hamburger with egg, cheese, bacon, lettuce and tomato, is worth a sample. And the desserts? See for yourself! Try the milk shakes — made with real ice cream and milk.

Down East

Driftwood Restaurant
$$ • Cedar Island • 225-4861

On the banks of Core Sound, the Driftwood includes a motel, restaurant, campground, gift shop, convenience store and hunting guide service, but locals refer to all those things at the complex by simply saying "at the Driftwood." The restaurant is known far and wide for the Friday night prime rib special and Saturday seafood buffet. Other entrees feature all types of seafood, including fresh crabmeat, shrimp salads, five-seafood combination plates and softshell crabs. You'll also enjoy ham, pork chops, chicken, barbecue and a children's menu. The restaurant is beside the Cedar Island-Ocracoke ferry terminal. This is a very popular restaurant year round, and we suggest you call for the off-season schedule. For information about the motel, see our Accommodations chapter; for information about the campground, see our Camping chapter.

Island Restaurant
$-$$ • Harkers Island • 728-2214, 728-2247

Liston and Carolyn Lawrence have been serving island residents and guests for 15 years from the same location. Open for breakfast, lunch and dinner, Island Restaurant offers everything from pizza and sandwiches to seafood platters and prime rib. Shrimp and eggs, along with all the traditional dishes, are served for breakfast. The lunch menu includes hamburgers, subs, pizza and spaghetti. Sandwiches range from oyster and shrimp burgers to flounder and crab sandwiches, and there is take-out service. The restaurant's prime rib

special and weekend seafood buffet just can't be beat and are well worth the drive from wherever you are. There is a full menu that includes shrimp and fish dinners, roast pork and cold seafood platters. You can have your meal prepared as you like it — fried, broiled, steamed or charbroiled. The "little mates menu" offers selections for children.

Sea Level Inn Restaurant
$$ • Sea Level • 225-3651

Twelve miles from the Cedar Island ferry terminal, Sea Level Inn Restaurant offers casual waterfront dining on Nelson's Bay off Core Sound. The inn has been converted to condominiums, but the restaurant is open to the public. It serves lunch and dinner most weekdays, dinner on Friday and Saturday and breakfast and a lunch buffet on Sunday. The breakfast menu offers traditional Southern items. There is usually a hot lunch special along with salads, seafood plates and sandwiches. Fresh local seafood and beef are favorites on the dinner menu, and everything is cooked to order.

Western Carteret County

Newport Family Diner
$ • 41 Chatham St., Newport • 223-5336

This cafe has a reputation for serving ample portions of homestyle food every day, all day. Full breakfast specials for 99¢ are actually served and served a lot. For lunch or dinner, guests will enjoy steak, seafood, roast turkey, chicken and pastry and more. There are sandwiches, soups, salads and daily lunch and dinner specials. Newport Family Diner is in downtown Newport.

Granny's Diner
$ • U.S. Hwy. 70, Newport • 223-6106

Granny's Diner is country cooking in a family atmosphere. Open at 5:30 AM every day, Granny's serves a hearty breakfast that can't be beat. You'll find pork tenderloin, hamburger gravy on toast, eggs and all your favorites. For lunch and dinner, the menu features such entrees as barbecue ribs, steak, chicken and fish. Each Friday and Saturday night features prime rib and seafood. It draws quite a crowd, but it's the homemade banana pudding that keeps folks coming back. Granny's serves three meals a day Monday through Saturday. On Sunday, it's open for breakfast and lunch only.

Fairway Restaurant
$$ • N.C. Hwy. 58, Cape Carteret
• 393-6444

The Fairway Restaurant is a popular lunch spot for golfers, construction workers, business people, tourists and locals. Guests will find salads, quiche, specialty sandwiches, homemade soups and delicious burgers. Dinner turns to certified Angus beef and local seafood, and one of the specialties of the house is the prime rib. Done to perfection, exactly the way you request, it's moist and delicious. Italian selections, ribs and grilled chicken and chops are offered. Fairway is closed on Sunday.

McCall's Bar-B-Que & Seafood
$ • N.C. Hwy. 58, Cape Carteret • 393-2929

This eastern North Carolina favorite opened in Cape Carteret during the fall of 1995, offering the barbecue and chicken that eastern North Carolina was raised on plus all the country vegetables that Grandma fixed. Add fresh fried fish, beef ribs and steaks, and you've pretty much viewed the menu, but most folks go for the buffet. A seniors menu and take-out are offered.

Mazzella's Italian Restaurant
$$ • N.C. Hwy. 58, Cape Carteret
• 393-8787

About 2 miles north of Cape Carteret, Mazzella's is an authentic Italian restaurant with excellent dinners. The family-owned and operated business provides only the finest Italian cuisine and keeps diners coming back again and again. A number of Italian entrees are made with fresh pastas, homemade sauces and seafood. Sandwiches and pizzas are also offered during dinner hours.

T&W Oyster Bar and Restaurant
$$ • N.C. Hwy. 58, near Cape Carteret
• 393-8838

Since 1972, T&W has had customers coming from near and far for steamed oysters served in rustic surroundings — even a roaring fire when the weather is right. Try the combination of two or more seafood items, steak, chicken or a burger. Guests will also find sandwiches made with fried shrimp, oysters, scallops or fish. T&W serves beer and wine and has an ABC license for brown-bagging. Don't let the line fool you — the restaurant can accommodate parties of close to 400, and the bar can handle anyone who stops by to feast on steamed oysters.

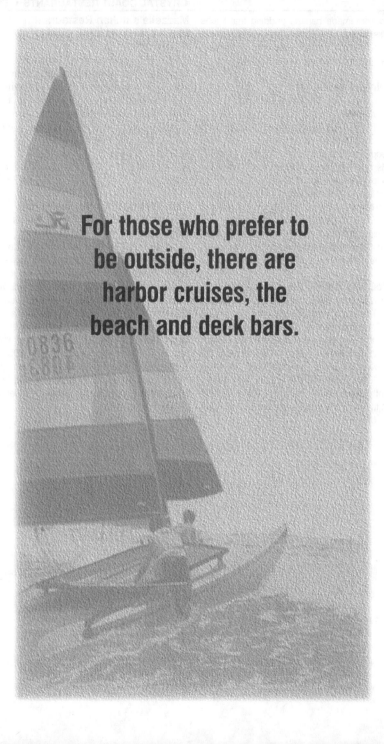

For those who prefer to be outside, there are harbor cruises, the beach and deck bars.

Nightlife

Most folks don't come to the Crystal Coast just for the nightlife. Many residents and visitors consider an after-dinner drink, a walk on the beach or a stroll along the boardwalk about all the nightlife they want after a full day of watersports or exploring the sites. Still, others want to dance and socialize in clubs.

The nightlife here can be divided into two categories: outside or inside. For those who prefer to be outside (the area's mild climate allows that most of the year), there are harbor cruises, the beach and deck bars. Some nightspots offer both, with lounges inside and out.

You won't find the number of rockin' and rollin' places other beach areas offer, but there are a few dance spots and watering holes for those who want to mingle.

Shagging to beach music is very popular here, and many clubs on the beach cater to shaggers. The shag is a type of dance that was probably a derivative of the beach bop, although it is smoother and done to rhythm and blues or North Carolina's own beach music. The dance is basically an eight-step, alternate-step that has a definite rhythm and distinct appearance. A few local beach clubs offer shagging lessons on certain weeknights.

Most coastal nightlife takes place on or around the water. In addition to the many waterfront bars, several local boats offer sunset trips or dinner cruises. Check our Fishing, Watersports and Beach Access chapter for more information about cruises.

We have listed the spots that cater primarily to nightlife seekers. Some of these nightspots close during the winter so calling ahead is a good idea in the off-season. If the business is on Bogue Banks, we have used the milepost (MP) number for easy location. Many restaurants are considered nightspots because they feature live entertainment or have a bar, so check our Restaurants chapter for more information too. The local newspaper or any one of the weekly vacation guides might also help you in selecting a nightspot. At the end of this chapter we have included information about movie theaters.

Bogue Banks

Atlantic Beach

Atlantic Beach is home to a number of reputable nightspots that have stood the test of time and continue to offer quality entertainment. There are others, but we'll only tell you about the ones we feel comfortable recommending. New spots often open each spring. If you see a nightspot that we haven't listed below, there may be several reasons for its omission — it may not be one we would recommend to a friend, it may have just opened in the spring or we may have unintentionally overlooked it. Check a place out with another Insider before you venture out if you have any doubts. Here are a few suggestions.

Channel Marker
Atlantic Beach Cswy. • 247-2344

The Channel Marker offers a fun bar and waterfront atrium lounge. An outside deck overlooks Bogue Sound, and dock space is available for those arriving by boat. The bar has all ABC permits and is a popular nightspot for all ages.

Capt. Stacy
Atlantic Beach Cswy. • 247-7501,
(800) 533-9417

The Capt. Stacy fleet is well-known for its deep-sea fishing charters, but it also offers moonlight cruises and harbor tours during the summer. Private party and dinner cruises can also be arranged. For more information about the Capt. Stacy fleet, see our Fishing, Boating, Watersports and Beach Access chapter.

Kelli's
Atlantic Beach Cswy. • 247-1094

The professional crowd frequents Kelli's on weeknights, but on the weekends, a more diverse crowd of all ages fills the bar. The lounge has all ABC permits. Patrons can sit at the bar, at inside tables or on the outside deck. Dock space is available for those arriving by boat. For information about meals see our Restaurants chapter.

Sha-Boom
Atlantic Beach Cswy. • 726-7000

Sha-Boom definitely caters to the younger, or those who consider themselves younger, crowd. The club DJ spins Top-40 tunes, and the dance floor is usually packed. If you're a fan of events such as bikini contests, lingerie shows and male burlesque shows, you'll find them here. Sha-Boom has all ABC permits.

Courtney's Beach and Shag Club
Crow's Nest Shopping Center, Atlantic Beach Cswy. • 247-7766

Courtney's caters to shaggers and beach music fans of all ages. The club is open to members and guests and has all ABC permits. Courtney's also offers weekly shag lessons, and they are sure to get you moving.

The Reef Restaurant and Lounge
Atlantic Beach Cswy. • 726-3500

The Reef's upstairs lounge is a very popular place after work and on weekends. At indoor tables, on the deck, or at the bar, creative appetizers and island-style drinks are served along with beers, wines and mixed drinks. Live entertainment is provided during the summer.

Skipper's Cove
Restaurant and Nightclub
MP 2, N.C. Hwy. 58 • 726-3023

Skipper's Cove is a popular nightspot for those seeking a dinner club or just some entertainment and dancing. The club's popular house band plays beach, country and Top 40. Live entertainment is included with your dinner, and the restaurant is well-known for its extensive all-you-can-eat buffet. For those who would like to stop by later for a drink, some music and dancing, there is a small cover charge.

Mary Lou's Beach Club
MP 2, N.C. Hwy. 58 • 240-7424

Mary Lou's is another nightspot for those interested in beach music and shagging. The DJ spins beach music with a little Top 40 and takes requests.

INSIDERS' TIP

Locals often travel to Kinston to watch the minor-league Kinston Indians play baseball.

Beach Tavern
MP 2½, N.C. Hwy. 58 • 247-4466

Beach Tavern has been around since 1972 and continues to attract a very diverse group of people who aren't looking for anything fancy. You can play pool and darts, listen to the jukebox and watch sports on a wide-screen TV. The grill serves burgers, hot dogs and good pizza. Beach Tavern is open year round, seven days a week.

Jolly Knave Restaurant and Lounge
Oceanfront, Atlantic Beach Circle • 726-8222

The Jolly Knave, also called Harpers, is right on the beach and offers a great view of the ocean and happenings on the beach. Kim's Upstairs Lounge provides a relaxed atmosphere for mingling. Downstairs, summertime guests will find a restaurant offering indoor or outdoor dining. The lounge and restaurant have all ABC permits and serve beer and wine.

No Name Grill and Lounge
Atlantic Station Shopping Center, MP 3, N.C. Hwy. 58 • 240-2224

The lounge and bar are separated from the dining room, and there is usually a crowd in the summer. Cold domestic and imported beer, wine and mixed drinks will quench the thirst you work up dancing. If you don't want to dance, you can play with the electronic games or watch the wide-screen TV.

Pine Knoll Shores

Molly's Bar & Grill
Sheraton Resort, MP 4¾, N.C. Hwy. 58 • 240-1155

Offering beach nightlife at its best, Molly's is an open-air bar and grill directly on the ocean. Enjoy drinks with grilled seafood or chicken while you relax by the pool and the ocean.

Woody's On The Beach
Sheraton Resort, MP 4¾, N.C. Hwy. 58 • 240-1155

Woody's is an oceanfront club featuring a DJ and Top-40 music. This is a comfortable place to go with a crowd or to slip away with a special friend. The nightclub opens around 8 PM.

Harry's Island Bar
Sheraton Resort, MP 4¾, N.C. Hwy. 58 • 240-1155

If you want some laughs on a weekend night, catch the Lafftrax comedy show. Comedians perform twice every Friday and Saturday night, at 8:30 and 10:30 PM. Harry's charges a $5 cover; reservations are recommended.

A waterman follows the cloud trail home.

Cutty Sark Lounge
Ramada Inn, MP 8¼, N.C. Hwy. 58
• 247-4155

This lounge in the Ramada Inn is very popular. The lounge is open every night, with a disc jockey entertaining some nights.

Indian Beach/Salter Path

**Frank and Clara's
Restaurant & Lounge**
MP 11, N.C. Hwy. 58 • 247-2788

The upstairs lounge offers a variety of music from beach and shag to country and rock. There is no cover charge and no membership required, so this is the perfect spot if you are visiting the area. The downstairs restaurant is excellent.

Emerald Isle

**RuckerJohn's
Restaurant and More**
Emerald Plantation Shopping Center, MP 19½, N.C. Hwy. 58 • 354-2413

This relaxing, upbeat nightspot is very popular with the younger and middle-age sets. You'll find a nice bar area separated from the dining area. Rucker John's has all ABC permits and is just the right place to meet friends.

Beaufort

Backstreet Pub
429 Front St. • 728-7108

This laid-back place is in an alley behind Clawson's Restaurant and is called

INSIDERS' TIP

The boardwalk in Beaufort is a great place to watch sunsets.

Back Bar by the regulars. In this small, out-of-the-way, popular spot, there is usually standing room only. An outdoor courtyard offers some respite from the crowds. Beer, wine and wine coolers are served at the huge wooden bar. Upstairs is a "sailors' library" where folks can bring a book to swap or to read. Live entertainment is often available.

Crystal Queen
708-B Cedar St. • 728-2527

This 82-foot coastal riverboat replica operates from the Beaufort waterfront and offers a variety of services. Guests can board for a sunset/moonlight cruise or a narrated daytime scenic tour. Private charters and catered events can also be accommodated. The vessel is licensed for 150 passengers.

Dock House
500 Front St., Beaufort • 728-4506

Dock House has long been the traditional gathering place for locals and for those traveling along the Intracoastal Waterway. In spring, summer and fall, patrons sit on the boardwalk or on the upstairs deck and watch the boardwalk and the Taylor's Creek boating activity. Live music is featured during the season. Dock House offers a great selection of beers, mixed drinks, wines and wine coolers, and it serves lunch and dinner.

Mystery Tour
Beaufort Waterfront, Beaufort • 728-7827

Docked in Beaufort's Taylor's Creek, the 65-foot double-decked *Mystery* tour boat cruises 18 miles of area waterways. See the writeup in our Attractions chapter for a complete description.

Royal James Cafe
117 Turner St. • 728-4573

Some consider the Royal James the best place in eastern North Carolina to shoot pool, and it is somewhat of a Beaufort tradition. You're likely to find players there whose fathers also frequented the place. The jukebox belts out country and rock. Ice-cold beer, wine, wine coolers, soft drinks and bar food are available.

Morehead City

Anchor Inn Restaurant & Lounge
2806 Arendell St. • 726-2156

The Anchor Inn is beside Best Western Buccaneer Motor Inn (see our Accommodations chapter). Patrons can sit at the bar or cozy up in comfortable chairs. This is a great place to wind down after work or to wind up for weekend nightlife.

Capt. Russell's Lounge
3002 Bridges St. • 726-3205

Beside Mrs. Willis' Restaurant (see our Restaurants chapter), Capt. Russell's serves munchies, sandwiches and your favorite beverages every day. The lounge opens at 5 PM and has all ABC permits. Inside, you can relax at the bar or at tables. A game area has darts and six pool tables.

Carolina Princess
711 Shepard St. • 726-5479,
(800) 682-3456

After unloading the anglers and their catches from a day of deep-sea fishing, the *Carolina Princess* is cleaned and prepared for a night of activity. The vessel offers cruises and is available for private charter.

INSIDERS' TIP

Mixed drinks, beer and wine are available in establishments in every incorporated town on the Crystal Coast except Newport. Mixed drinks are not allowed to be served in restaurants in the unincorporated areas of Carteret County, which includes the Down East area. Most of these area restaurants offer a good selection of domestic and imported beers and wines. According to North Carolina law, a restaurant serving mixed drinks cannot allow patrons to brown bag, or bring their own alcohol.

Continental Shelf
405 Evans St. • 726-7454, (800) 426-7966

The *Continental Shelf* offers spring and summer evening cruises and a chance to see the surrounding area and wildlife by night. This 100-foot vessel is also available for private charter year round.

Raps Grill & Bar
715 Arendell St. • 240-1213

Raps is a favorite gathering place among locals and is often packed during the summer. The downstairs bar area surrounds a huge oak bar and has tables and plenty of floor space. Upstairs are two levels of dining.

Movie Theaters

The area's movie theaters listed here offer discounts for seniors and children. They also run matinees at reduced prices, but check to make sure which days because off-season matinees are usually restricted to weekends. Movie listings are printed in the *Carteret News-Times*, published every Wednesday, Friday and Sunday.

Atlantic Station Cinema 4, MP 3, at the west end of the Atlantic Station shopping center in Atlantic Beach, 247-7016

Emerald Plantation Cinema 4, MP 20¼, in the Emerald Plantation Shopping Center, Emerald Isle, 354-5012

Plaza Cinema One, Two & Three, Morehead Plaza Shopping Center, Bridges Street in Morehead City, 726-2081

Morehead Theatre, 1309 Arendell Street in Morehead City, 726-4710

On the beach, as in all resort areas, rates vary according to the season and the lodgings' proximity to water.

Accommodations

The Crystal Coast is a diverse resort area with plentiful accommodations near natural and historic attractions. There are many attractive lodging choices, some rich with history and all full of our special Southern hospitality. Choose from luxurious oceanfront or soundside hotels and resorts, family-style motels and efficiency suites or cozy bed and breakfast inns.

On the beach, as in all resort areas, rates vary according to the season and the lodgings' proximity to water. If, for economy's sake, you are considering a location away from the water, you may want to ask about access either to the ocean or sound and if it is within easy walking distance.

The Crystal Coast is becoming a year-round resort. There is little off-season anymore when visitors aren't here in some abundance, so it is always wise to make reservations in advance no matter what time of year. However, during the early spring and late-fall shoulder seasons and in the winter, many establishments offer attractive weekend getaways, golf packages and special rates. The area is a popular site for meetings and conventions throughout the year, and many facilities offer meeting rooms and convention services. The Crystal Coast Civic Center (see our Attractions chapter) in Morehead City accommodates sizeable shows and gatherings with hotels and other lodgings conveniently nearby.

Each establishment has a different deposit and refund policy. While some require a deposit equal to one night's stay in advance, others will simply hold your reservation on your credit card. Often, a 24-hour notice is sufficient for a full refund, but some require as much as a three-day notice. Because of the area's popularity, extending your stay can be difficult but not impossible. Some places require up to 72-hours' notice for extensions past your originally scheduled departure date.

Many of the area's lodgings offer nonsmoking rooms by request. The older inns restrict smoking to certain areas and often do not offer facilities to accommodate small children. The pet policy in hotels, motels and bed and breakfast inns is the proprietor's option. Most do not allow pets in rooms, although some lodgings do make provisions for them. In our discussion of accommodations that follows, we have let you know when a facility makes allowances for pets. If there is no mention of a pet policy, assume that pets are not allowed.

This guide doesn't attempt to list all the accommodations available on the Crystal Coast. Rather, we've provided a sampling of some of our favorites. For more information about lodging, contact the Carteret County Tourism Development Bureau, P.O. Box 1406, Morehead City, NC 28557, (800) SUNNY NC or 726-8148. The bureau operates visitors centers at 3409 Arendell Street (U.S. Highway 70) in Morehead City and on N.C. Highway 58, just north of the Cameron Langston Bridge to Emerald Isle.

Price Code

For the purpose of comparing prices, we have placed each accommodation in a price category based on the rate for a double-occupancy room per night during the summer season. Winter rates can be substantially lower. Rates shown do not include state and local taxes. We've tried to be accurate, but amenities and rates are subject to change. It's best to verify information important to you, including credit cards accepted, when making your reservations.

$	$35 to $59
$$	$60 to $79
$$$	$80 to $124
$$$$	More than $125

Bogue Banks

Accommodations we'd recommend on the beach are just too numerous to list them all. Here, we offer a sample range of accommodations from full-service resorts to family and angler favorites with fewer frills. We also suggest you contact condominium developments on the beach (see the Crystal Coast Weekly and Longterm Cottage Rentals chapter) because most offer attractive vacation rates.

Atlantic Beach

Show Boat Motel
$-$$$ • Atlantic Beach Causeway
• 726-6163, (800) SHO-BOAT

With easy access to Bogue Sound, this familiar motel with a stern paddlewheel offers lodging as well as watersports at affordable rates. Guests can fish from the motel dock, complete with a fish-cleaning table, or take a dip in the pool. All rooms have refrigerators, and guests can enjoy picnic areas, grills and continental breakfasts. The motel offers family, corporate and AARP rates and is open all year. Also on site is Wreckreational Divers, 240-2244, a full-service dive shop for those who like to explore down under (see our Sports, Fitness and Parks chapter.)

Sundowner Motel
$-$$$ • Atlantic Beach Causeway
• 726-2191

This motel is a good choice for a fishing getaway. It offers quiet, clean waterfront accommodations that are hospitably comfortable for anglers and families. Kitchenettes are available, and patrons are offered free boat-launching access and a wet slip during their stays. Complete with a pool, the motel has picnic tables, barbecue grills, brewed coffee and storage spaces.

Oceanana Family Resort Motel and Pier
$$-$$$ • E. Fort Macon Rd. MP 1½
• 726-4111

This comfortable motel on the ocean provides guests with lots of extras. Long a favorite of families with children, the Oceanana offers a pool, children's play area, fishing pier, picnic tables and grills, free patio breakfasts in the warm season, free use of the adjoining fishing pier, beach chairs and a patrolled beach. Guests choose from standard rooms, oceanfront rooms or suites, all with refrigerators. The Oceanana closes for the season in mid-November and reopens the week before Easter.

Hollowell's Motel
$-$$$ • E. Fort Macon Rd. MP 1¾
• 726-5227

Hollowell's is a family-oriented motel operated by Don Hollowell. It is three blocks from the ocean, and an easy walk to restaurants and shopping. Guests are offered quiet rooms with kitchenettes or refrigerators, a bridal suite or private cottages. All rooms have telephones, cable TV and HBO. A swimming pool with a slide is popular with children.

Budget Inn
$-$$$ • 221 W. Fort Macon Rd. MP 2½
• 726-3780, (800) 636-3780

This clean, comfortable motel was recently remodeled and offers family and commercial rates by the day, week or month. All rooms have HBO, telephones and access to the pool. Kitchenette efficiencies are also available. The motel is an easy three-block walk from the ocean and is close to restaurants, shopping areas and the main beach amusement circle.

Days Inn Suites
$$-$$$$ • W. Fort Macon Rd. MP 2½
• 247-6400, (800) 247-2264

Days Inn Suites on the soundside offers 90 attractive units, all on the main floor. Each has a sunken sitting area and private porch with a

wonderful view of Bogue Sound. Suites offer either one king-size or two double beds, microwaves, refrigerators and coffee makers. Guests have use of the outdoor pool, the boat ramp and dock, and boat slips are available by reservation. Golf and dive packages are available. Days Inn Suites is within walking distance of the beach, shopping areas and restaurants.

Holiday Inn Oceanfront
$$$-$$$$ • Salter Path Rd. MP 4¾ • 726-2544, (800)465-4329

The completely redecorated Holiday Inn Oceanfront offers dependable Holiday Inn services and accommodations enhanced by its oceanfront location. The resort hotel offers 114 rooms with refrigerators. Guests enjoy the pool, High Tide pool bar and grill, weekend live entertainment, 800 feet of private beach, picnic area and special golf privileges. Mar Y Ceilo is the resort's full-service restaurant (see our Restaurants chapter) and lounge. Holiday Inn Oceanfront has meeting facilities for small or large groups.

Sheraton Atlantic Beach Oceanfront Hotel
$$$$ • Salter Path Rd. MP 4½ • 240-1155, (800) 624-8875

Sheraton is a full-service beachfront resort. All rooms include a refrigerator, microwave, coffee maker, hair dryer, iron and ironing board, and a private balcony. Suites with one bedroom, living room and a whirlpool tub are available. The staff will arrange anything from sameday dry cleaning to golf and tennis. Fine dining is available in the resort's Paradise Restaurant

INSIDERS' TIP

The Carteret County Tourism Development Bureau's (800) SUNNY-NC phone line offers information to all Crystal Coast vacationers, including up-to-the-minute room availability.

(see our Restaurants chapter), and in season an oceanfront grill serves casual fare and beverages. Lafftrax offers live weekend comedy shows, and Woody's nightclub (see our Nightlife chapter) is a local's favorite for dance music and drinks. The resort has its own fishing pier for anglers. Catering and full banquet services are available for small or large meetings. Guests enjoy the indoor and outdoor pools, spa, fitness room, game room and the gift shop.

Pine Knoll Shores

Windjammer Inn
$$$ • Salter Path Rd. MP 4½
• 247-7123, (800) 233-6466

All of the rooms at the attractive Windjammer Inn are oversized and oceanfront with private balconies, refrigerators, cable TV and two telephones. The glass-enclosed elevator is an unexpected surprise and offers a great view of the ocean. Guests enjoy the oceanfront pool, private beach area with beach services and complimentary coffee each morning. There is a two-night minimum during summer weekends and a three-night minimum on holiday weekends. We recommend you get a room on the top floor and relax.

FYI

Unless otherwise noted, the area code for all phone numbers in this guide is 919.

Sea Hawk Motor Lodge
$$$ • Salter Path Rd. MP 4¾
• 726-4146, (800) 682-6898

This comfortable and newly remodeled lodge offers 36 oceanfront rooms with balconies or patios, phones, cable TV and refrigerators. Connecting double rooms, a cottage and villas are also available. The coffee shop is open in season, and a pool is situated in the middle of a large, grassy lawn facing the ocean. Guests are offered bicycles, grills and fishing rods, but they especially enjoy lazing in hammocks on the oceanfront lawn.

Atlantis Lodge
$$$ • Salter Path Rd. MP 5
• 726-5168, (800) 682-7057

Set among the beautiful live oaks on the oceanside, the Atlantis Lodge was among the first hotels built on Bogue Banks. Its patrons are faithful and never disappointed. Most units are arranged as suites, offering efficiency kitchens, dining, living and sleeping areas. All have patios or decks facing the surf, cable TV and other expected amenities. Recreation areas, equipment, golf packages and complimentary beach furniture and lifeguard services are extended to guests. The outdoor pool is a quiet place for sunning and swimming, and the third-floor lounge has an adjoining library. Unlike most hotels, the Atlantis makes provisions for pets. In August the lodge hosts a popular sand-sculpture contest (see our Annual Events chapter).

Royal Pavilion Resort
$$-$$$$ • Salter Path Rd. MP 5½
• 726-5188, (800) 533-3700

This is the newest oceanfront resort and conference center on Bogue Banks. Many remember it as the former John Yancey Motor Hotel; however, it has been extensively renovated, and the new resort offers 115 light, airy guest rooms. Many rooms are equipped with special amenities, including complete efficiency kitchens. An outdoor pool, 1,500 feet of private beach, cable TV service and local activities arrangements, including golf packages, provide guests with an abundance of leisure-time choices. The resort has four conference rooms for meetings or private events and the Tradewinds Restaurant (see our Restaurants chapter) and lounge.

Iron Steamer Resort
$$-$$$ • Salter Path Rd. MP 6¾
• 247-4221, (800) 332-4221

On its quiet stretch of the island, the Iron Steamer got its name because the remains of a sunken Civil War blockade runner are visible from the resort's pier at low tide. Favored by families and anglers, it has 49 oceanfront rooms and a lighted fishing pier complete with tackle shop, fishing gear rentals and a 24-hour snack bar. Rooms are available with refrigerators and private balconies. Guests have access to the beach, pool and pier. The Iron Steamer's operating season is from Easter to Thanksgiving.

Strolling along the beach is a favorite way to pass time, no matter what the season.

Photo: Scott Taylor

Ramada Inn Oceanfront
$$$ • Salter Path Rd. MP 8¼ • 247-4155, (800) 338-1533

On the oceanside in a quiet mid-island residential area, this seven-floor inn offers all oceanfront rooms with double or king-size beds. Each room has a small private balcony, and guests have access to the beach, the pool, golf and tennis courts, and the Cutty Sark Lounge and the Clamdigger Restaurant, a favorite of locals who know all about the weeknight dinner specials. Meeting and banquet facilities are available. The Ramada Inn offers attractive getaway weekend packages from November through March.

Salter Path

William and Garland Motel
$-$$ • Salter Path MP 10½ • 247-3733

This small family-owned motel has eight rooms and three mobile units. Nine are effi-ciencies, and two provide only simple sleeping accommodations. Don't expect anything fancy, but do expect a family atmosphere and clean, comfortable surroundings. Guests have access to the ocean via a nature trail walkway (about 200 yards) and access to the 20-acre Salter Path Dunes Natural Area, perfect for walking, sunning and picnicking. William and Garland Motel is beside the Big Oak Drive-In, home of the famous shrimpburger.

Oak Grove Motel
$-$$ • Salter Path MP 10½ • 247-3533

We're impressed by this motel because it's so tidy, and in the shade of live oaks it always looks cool, even on the hottest days. It has one- and two-story stone-sided units with standard rooms and efficiency apartments with porch rockers for enjoying the shade. The motel is a family facility and has lots of repeat business. Seniors are offered a free night during a week's stay. Two-night minimums are required on weekends.

INSIDERS' TIP

The local Marine Mammal Strandings Network telephone number is 728-8762. It is not in the local directory and could be important if you encounter an out-of-place dolphin or whale.

Parkerton Inn

The Crystal Coast's Newest Motel!

- American Owned
- Complimentary Breakfast
- Cable TV, HBO
- Senior Citizen's Discount
- Outdoor Swimming Pool

"An unbeatable combination: Parkerton Inn guaranteed quality with golfing, beach access and The Crystal Coast Amphitheater nearby!"

1184 Highway 58 North Cape Carteret, NC
NC 800-393-9909 / 919-393-9000

Emerald Isle/Cape Carteret

Islander Motor Inn
$$-$$$ • Islander Dr. • 354-3464, (800) 354-3464

Islander is on the ocean in Emerald Isle, and although the rooms do not directly face the water, most offer a wonderful east-west view of the sea and beach. The two-story brick motel offers guests easy beach access, a pool, a luxurious lawn area, a restaurant, room refrigerators and large meeting rooms for conferences or gatherings.

Parkerton Inn
$-$$ • N.C. Hwy. 58 N. • 393-9000, (800) 393-9909

Only three years old, the Parkerton Inn is on the mainland just north of the intersection of highways 58 and 24. It is especially convenient for guests overnighting for the summer outdoor drama, *Worthy Is The Lamb*. Guests may choose any of several room arrangements including kitchenette efficiencies and rooms equipped for the handicapped. Golf packages are offered, and a complimentary continental breakfast is included.

Emerald Isle Inn and Bed and Breakfast
$$$-$$$$ • 502 Ocean Dr. • 354-3222

A.K. and Marilyn Detwiller accommodate their island guests in two-bedroom suites with private baths and patios or in double rooms with a shared bath. Guests enjoy views of the ocean and sound from porches with comfortable swings, nearby beach access and the use of beach chairs and umbrellas. A full breakfast is served each morning in the dining room. The Detwillers also offer apartments that accommodate eight guests, but they do not provide linens or breakfast in these apartments.

Harborlight Guest House
$$$-$$$$ • 332 Live Oak Dr. • 393-6868, (800) 624-VIEW

Situated on a spectacular peninsula on

Bogue Sound off Highway 24, the Harborlight Guest House offers bed and breakfast accommodations in its seven suite or room arrangements. The rambling three-story inn, once a restaurant used by the ferry service, is particularly graced with views, 530 feet of shoreline and a quiet setting close to Emerald Isle beaches and attractions. The hospitality of owners Bobby and Anita Gill includes gourmet breakfasts served in the dining room, on the waterfront terrace or privately for guests in the luxury upstairs suites. Suites have fireplaces and whirlpools that take great advantage of surrounding waterviews. Open year round, the inn offers its 20-person capacity conference room for seminars, weddings and other group gatherings. It is a no-children facility with guests who come from everywhere. Harborlight Guest House has been featured by *Southern Living Magazine* as one of five outstanding North Carolina bed and breakfast inns.

Beaufort

The majority of accommodations in Beaufort are historic bed and breakfast inns that offer charming surroundings, memorable views and warm hospitality. All are in the historic district and within walking distance of the waterfront, boardwalk, shopping areas, restaurants, N.C. Maritime Museum and historic sites.

Room arrangements and breakfast specialties vary in each inn. Most do not have facilities for young children or pets, and many limit smoking to certain areas of the house. There are two large hotel-like inns, Beaufort Inn and Inlet Inn. Both were constructed in the old Beaufort style, as required by the Beaufort Historic Preservation Commission.

Beaufort Inn
$$$-$$$$ • 101 Ann St. • 728-2600, (800) 726-0321

On Gallant's Channel, Beaufort Inn offers 44 rooms, all with private porches and rock-

Blackbeard's *Revenge*

After nearly 300 years, piracy may thrive again on the North Carolina coast as controversy takes shape over possession of Blackbeard's sunken flagship, *Queen Anne's Revenge*, which is believed to be lying off the coast of Beaufort. And, no one would be more pleased about it than Blackbeard, himself. As a career man who thrived on purchasing the favor of government officials, especially of Colonial Governor Charles Eden, Blackbeard would be a valuable consultant for today's legislators who are staking claims on the ship's remains for their constituencies. He'd also be good at marketing the museum collection that the remains of *Queen Anne's Revenge* will surely, and soon, render.

On March 3, 1997, the announcement of the location of an 18th-century ship's remains was made jointly by Intersal, the Florida-based investment group responsible for the find, and the North Carolina Division of Archives and History. Historians and marine archeologists involved in examining items recovered from the wreck site just off the Beaufort Inlet are nearly 100 percent sure this is, finally and indeed, *Queen Anne's Revenge*.

The active search by Intersal for any sunken remains of the ship near Beaufort Inlet has been in progress for almost a decade. Area sweeps with magnetometers were made and metal finds were charted routinely. Local divers hired by Intersal would investigate underwater locations identified electronically on the surface. On November 21, 1996, the last day of scheduled operations for the year, Beaufort diver Will Kirkman dove on a sand bar in only 20 feet of water about 2 miles off Fort Macon. In murky water with visibility of less than a foot, he thought he could be among a mass of cannons. A ship's bell, a cannonball and the brass barrel of a blunderbuss — a wide-barrelled musket — were taken from the site.

The most valuable information from the recovered items in identifying the wreck was the bronze ship's bell. It bears the date 1709 and the inscription "IHS Maria" which state historians believe refers to Jesus and Mary.

Queen Anne's Revenge was launched in 1710 in England as a merchant ship commissioned the *Concord*. She carried 20 cannons and displaced around 300 tons. She had a short career in the service of England. In 1710, the French captured *Concord* and refit her as an armed transport ship renamed *Concorde*. She may have been involved in slave trade as she sailed routinely between Africa, South America and the Caribbean.

By 1717, Edward Teach of Bristol, England, had left the service of privateer-turned-pirate Captain Benjamin Horigold with whom he joined as crew in 1716. By this time, Caribbean and Colonial governments were souring on the common practice of privateering. It had been a lovely arrangement for quite a while in avoidance of duty payments to the Crown of England. Everyone profitted. Privateers bought the inattention of local government officials and sold to merchants who were able to make greater profits. But, when cargoes in which wealthy officials and merchants had invested were intercepted, privateers became criminals, or pirates. Edward Teach, who had shown great promise with Hornigold, took *Concorde* out of the service of France in 1717, doubled her cache of cannons to 40 and renamed her *Queen Anne's Revenge*.

From this point, Blackbeard's career was unbelievably short when you consider how legendary it is, how many marriages he managed while pirating and that it ended
— continued on next page

in 1718 when he was beheaded in a battle for his death in Ocracoke. Presumed literate, Blackbeard was a genius at marketing an image. History doesn't document a single death to his credit. His method was intimidation. A statuesque man, he wore a full black beard when beards weren't the style. His hair was long and he wore it thickly braided, probably like dreadlocks, at sea. For attacks, he braided his beard, which grew from just under his eyes. In his hair and beard, he laced fuse cords used to ignite cannons. They were treated in saltpeter and lime water to burn slowly. When he appeared on the deck of *Queen Anne's Revenge* to demand the surrender of a halted vessel, he had guns and knives strapped to him and was surrounded by smoke like a demon from Hell. So effective was the image that more than 45 ships are known to have surrendered to Blackbeard and one city — Charleston, South Carolina — from which he demanded medicine to cure his crew of venereal disease. In fact, there are no recorded battles with ships of Blackbeard's fleet except for the battle at Ocracoke. Ships just surrendered.

Not surrendering without a struggle, the North Carolina towns of Beaufort, Bath and Manteo are now claiming that the Blackbeard heritage is theirs and, consequently, they should house the artifacts. At this point, Beaufort has the advantage of possession as the wreck is near Beaufort Inlet, as well as North Carolina's only maritime museum to house the collection. Bettie Bell, one of Carteret County's most feisty commissioners, has taken the matter to the merchants in the form of petitions to the local legislators to battle strong and hard for the potentially valuable tourism attraction to the Crystal Coast. In the context of the history of Blackbeard the pirate, he'd probably comment on the whole thing: What goes around comes around.

ing chairs for viewing the activity in the waterway. Rooms are furnished in early American decor incorporating local arts and crafts.

Owned and operated by Bruce and Katie Ethridge, the inn opened in 1987 and has become well-known for its complimentary breakfasts. A typical breakfast, served in a cozy dining room with a fireplace, includes Katie's breakfast pie, croissants, cereal, Danish pastries, fresh-squeezed juice and coffee. The inn has one large meeting room and two smaller meeting rooms, which accommodate 18 to 20 people. An exercise room, spa and boat slips are available, and Katie can loan you a bike and help you with area information.

Captain's Quarters Bed & Biscuit
$$$ • 315 Ann St. • 728-7711, (800)659-7111

This two-story white home with its luxurious wraparound porch offers guests the quiet elegance of a Victorian summer at the shore. You'll find Ms. Ruby, Capt. Dick Collins and daughter, Polly, to be delightful hosts.

The three upstairs bedrooms feature private powder rooms and baths. House traditions include a fresh biscuit continental breakfast and a toast to the sunset each evening, which is celebrated with wines or fresh fruit juices. The Collins family assists guests with area information, reservations and services, including use of a PC, modem and fax machine. Payment by personal check is preferred.

The Cedars by the Sea
$$$-$$$$ • 305 Front St. • 728-7036

At the corner of Front and Orange streets, the two stately homes that comprise The Cedars are surrounded by gardens whose summer flowers color each lovely guest unit and the inn's dining rooms. Both houses, c. 1768 and 1851, are beautifully restored and furnished with period pieces. Owners Linda and Sam Dark extend their hospitality in every detail. There are 12 rooms and suites with private baths and second-floor porches with rocking chairs. Some rooms are designed with separate sitting rooms; one has a whirlpool tub and others have fireplaces. The inn is open all year, and a full breakfast served in the dining room is included in the price. The Cedars

offers executive retreats and weekend spa packages.

Cousins Bed and Breakfast
$$$ • 303 Turner St. • 504-3478

Hosts Martha and Elmo Barnes extend their hospitality in Beaufort at the Ward-Adair House, c. 1855, across the street from the county courthouse. Accommodations include four private rooms with baths, breakfast prepared by Elmo, who has authored his own cookbook, and use of the house and private garden for special occasions. The dining room will comfortably seat 20 for small meetings, parties or wedding receptions, which the Barnes are happy to cater. Cousins welcomes guests year round and offers winter weekend cooking packages featuring Elmo's guidance and instruction.

Delamar Inn Bed and Breakfast
$$$ • 217 Turner St. • 728-4300,
(800) 349-5823

Delamar Inn, c. 1866, is restored to its original charm and accommodates guests in four antique-furnished guest rooms with private baths. The Scottish charm and hospitality of hosts Mabel and Tom Steepy begins with a breakfast of homemade breads, muffins, jams, cereals and fruits and extends to helpful arrangement of their guests' plans to enjoy the beaches, explore the town by bicycle, golf, tennis or whatever suits the moment. Cookies and refreshments await at the day's end. The Steepys welcome guests year round.

Inlet Inn
$$$-$$$$ • 601 Front St. • 728-3600

The 37-room Inlet Inn opened in 1985 in the same block of Front Street occupied by the original Inlet Inn of the 19th century. Today's inn offers harborfront rooms with a sitting area, bar, and refrigerator with ice maker. Many rooms open onto private porches. Others offer cozy fireplaces or window seats for viewing the Cape Lookout Lighthouse, Beaufort Inlet and Beaufort waterfront from the best vantage available. Guests are served a continental breakfast of homemade pastries, fruits, coffee and tea in the lounge. Boat slips, a courtyard garden, the rooftop

INSIDERS' TIP

To catch the Cedar Island Ferry to Ocracoke with your vehicle, you must be in line half an hour before departure time or your reservation will be cancelled. No exceptions!

Photo: Scott Taylor

The Beaufort Oars bring home frequent competitive honors.

Widow's Walk Lounge and an on-site meeting room are also available for guests' use year round.

Langdon House
$$$, no credit cards • 135 Craven St. • 728-5499

Innkeeper and restorer of the Langdon House (c. 1733), Jimm Prest extends the hospitality of a good friend and provides all the extras that give his guests a personalized experience of Beaufort. He'll arrange for boating to the best getaway beaches and send you there with a beach basket of comforts. He can tell you where and how to catch sea trout, take care of an ache or pain, help with a restaurant selection or reservation and take care of needs you didn't know you had. Each of the four guest rooms has a queen-size bed, a private bath and is furnished with antiques in keeping with the old Colonial/Federal home. Go there to relax: Sleeping late is considered a compliment to the innkeeper. The hallmark of Jimm's hospitality is the full breakfast, served until 11 AM. A hearty helping of fresh fruits is followed by one of the house specialties such as stuffed French toast or Belgian waffles. With a word in advance, he's happy to cater to special diets and preferences. Just ask. There are no problems unless you plan to pay with a credit card, none of which are accepted, but personal checks are just fine as long as you promise there's money in your account. Bring a change of clothes and a good attitude, and Jimm will take care of the rest.

Pecan Tree Inn
$$$ • 116 Queen St. • 728-6733

This 1860s two-story Victorian home, complete with gingerbread trim and turrets, is a

INSIDERS' TIP

The deep roots of sea oats help anchor the sand dunes. The plant is protected by law, so don't even think of harvesting a few, even if they're dead.

Photo: Scott Taylor

Bodysurfing when the waves are just right can top off your trip to the beach.

charming seven-guestroom bed and breakfast remodeled by hosts Sue and Joe Johnson. Each spacious room has special character and a private bath, and two romantic suites have king-size canopied beds and Jacuzzis. A stay at the inn includes an expanded continental breakfast served in the formal dining room or on the inviting wraparound front porch. You will enjoy Susan's fresh-baked homemade muffins, cakes and breads, fruit, cereal and specially ground coffee. The Johnsons are glad to assist with daytrip plans or arrange for box lunches, beach chairs or bicycles. They encourage simple relaxation on the cool porches overlooking the inn's ever-expanding herb and flower gardens.

Morehead City

Best Western
Buccaneer Inn
$$-$$$ • 2806 Arendell St. • 726-3115, (800) 682-4982

The Buccaneer Inn has 91 attractive rooms with refrigerators, some with a king-size bed and Jacuzzi. Guests are offered complimentary full, hot breakfasts, newspapers, free local calls and cable TV. Meeting and banquet facilities are available. Special rates apply for corporate, commercial and military guests, and golf packages are available. The inn is beside Morehead Plaza and is a short driving distance from Atlantic Beach. The Anchor Inn Restaurant and Lounge (see our Restaurants chapter) is beside the motel.

Comfort Inn
$-$$$ • 3012 Arendell St. • 247-3434, (800) 422-5404

The Comfort Inn, like others in the national hotel chain, offers reliably comfortable rooms, a pool and complimentary continental breakfast each morning. Convenient to the Crystal Coast Civic Center and all beach and historic attractions, the Comfort Inn has 100 rooms and additional meeting facilities to accommodate any gathering. Local phone calls are free, fax service is available and each room has cable TV. Golf, diving and winter getaway packages are also available. The inn neighbors two restaurants and the Morehead Plaza. Corporate, AARP and AAA discounts are offered.

Econo Lodge Crystal Coast
$-$$$ • 3410 Bridges St. • 247-2940, (800) 533-7556

The Econo Lodge is two blocks from the Crystal Coast Civic Center and offers 56 rooms at very attractive rates. Amenities include cable TV, free local calls, a pool and complimentary continental breakfasts. Special value packages for golf and scuba diving are offered and meeting facilities are available. Restaurants are within a short driving distance.

Hampton Inn
$$$ • 4035 Arendell St. • 240-2300, (800) 538-6338

Hampton Inn, overlooking Bogue Sound, offers beautiful views of the Intracoastal Waterway and the island of Bogue Banks. The 120-room inn has a fresh nautical decor. Guests enjoy an outside pool and deck area, free continental breakfasts served in a sunroom, free accommodations for children and an exercise room. Meeting rooms, plenty of parking and golf, tennis and fishing packages are available. Restaurants and shopping areas are nearby.

Down East

There are a few motels in the Down East area and we've listed them here. Many people also enjoy the kind of island getaway that is a real back-to-basics experience, so we've also told you about accommodations available on Core Banks. For information about Down East campgrounds, see the Camping chapter.

Morris Marina Kabin Kamps
$ • 1000 Morris Marina Rd., Atlantic • 225-4261

Rustic cabins that vary in size to accommodate four to 12 people may be rented on North Core Banks by the day. The price indicated here is a per-person rate based on a full cabin. "Rustic" means mattresses or bunks, gas cooking stoves, a sink and a toilet. Most cabins have hot water and showers; some have lights. Although water is potable, most visitors bring their own. Pack as you would for a camping trip and you'll be most comfortable. Long a guarded secret of

Photo: Scott Taylor

Waterbirds like this heron are a common site in the area's marshes, lakes and waterways.

anglers, this cabin settlement is also the choice getaway for shellers in the spring and bird-watchers in the fall. Three ferries a day (until December) run from Atlantic to the cabins. Making reservations well in advance is recommended. Take your four-wheel drive vehicle and drive the 22 miles of beach to historic Portsmouth Village at Ocracoke Inlet. See our Getting Around chapter for more information.

Alger G. Willis Fishing Camps
$ • Hwy. 70E., Davis • 729-2791

Twenty-five rustic cabins are available on South Core Banks at Shingle Point. Cabins accommodate four to 12 people and are rented on a per-night basis for about $11 per person if full. All that is provided is mattresses, a gas stove, potable water (but don't forget to bring your own), sinks, toilets, a roof, a floor and walls. Bring everything else you'll need, but expect a beautiful getaway. A caretaker is available when you run out of kerosene, ice, bread or whatever. He'll get supplies you need on the next ferry from the mainland. Four ferries arrive daily between early April and late October. It's not just for anglers anymore, so plan ahead and reserve early. See our Getting Around chapter for more information.

Driftwood Motel
$ • Cedar Island • 225-4861

This remodeled motel at the Cedar Island-Ocracoke Ferry Terminal consists of 37 rooms, each with two double beds and a television. There are no phones in the rooms, so this is a good place to get away from it all. The motel complex also has a restaurant known for fresh local seafood and prime rib, a campground (see our Camping chapter), a gift shop, a grocery store and a guide service for hunting and fishing. The motel closes from mid-January to mid-March.

Calico Jack's Inn and Marina
$ • Harkers Island • 728-3575

During summer and fishing seasons, this 24-room motel offers comfortable accommodations with two double beds and a restaurant. The marina accommodates boats up to 50 feet and offers gas and diesel fuel, supplies, refreshments and a complete tackle shop. Charter boats and ferry and water-taxi service to Cape Lookout are also available at the marina.

Fisherman's Inn
$-$$ • Harkers Island • 728-5780

This six-room motel faces the water and is owned and operated by Don and Linda Flood. The Floods also have a cottage with a full kitchen and bath available. The inn offers a marina, campground, boat slips, tackle and bait shop and charters.

Harkers Island Fishing Center
$ • Harkers Island • 728-3907

Harkers Island Fishing Center has a 20-room motel that sits back off the road and offers standard, no-frills accommodations. Ten efficiencies containing two double beds, a refrigerator and a stove are available. Guests have easy access to the marina, boat ramp, charter boats and ferry service to Cape Lookout.

Sea Level
Extended Care Facility
Cost determined by amount of care required • Sea Level • 225-4611

Sea Level Extended Care Facility provides long-term care as well as day-to-day care for those who need nursing care. The facility has a guest program that allows vacationers to bring a family member requiring special care along. The program is used by many people who want a vacation but find it difficult to leave someone behind. Contact the facility for more information about this program.

Weekly & Long-term Cottage Rentals

The Crystal Coast is the perfect place to vacation. If this is your first visit, you are about to discover why so many people come back year after year. The climate is moderate year round, the scenery is spectacular and the people are friendly and welcoming.

Now, let's make your stay on the coast as easy as possible. There are about 10,000 beds for rent on the Crystal Coast. That's the figure the Tourism Development Bureau, 726-8148 or (800) SUNNY NC, uses, and those options range from small fishing units near the pier — perfect if you spend all your time surf casting or pier fishing — to plush condominiums and seaside cottages. All you need to do is make a few simple decisions, starting with when to visit the coast.

The Rate Season

Rental rates change according to the season and that's sometimes confusing. To add to the confusion, not all rental agencies on the Crystal Coast use the same season schedule. It's always best to check with each company for specific season/rate changes.

Generally, most rental agencies on the east end of Bogue Banks use two seasons: in-season (Memorial Day through Labor Day) and off-season (any other time). On the west end of Bogue Banks, many rental agencies use these descriptions: prime season (mid-June through mid-August), mid-season (May through mid-June and mid-August through September), off-season (September through November and March

through April) and winter (December through February).

Vacation rentals can vary from $275 a week to more than $2,000. Costs can be as much as 25 to 30 percent less in off-season than in-season. For that reason, and because the weather is relatively warm year round, many people decide to vacation here in the "shoulder seasons" of spring, fall and winter. Decide what you need, and call rental agencies listed in the following pages or others listed in the phone directory to see what is offered.

Most visitors to the Crystal Coast come in the months of June, July and August. Tourism plays a big part in the county's economy. The average visitor stays 4 nights, and all totalled, visitors have an estimated $2.4 million annual impact on the Crystal Coast.

Locations and Types of Accommodations

Rental agencies can help you find the perfect place, whether that's the angler's cottage close by the pier, the family cottage within walking distance of the beach or the oceanfront condo with all the amenities of home. Rental costs vary with the type of accommodation and the location. Always check rental brochures or with an agent about the location. This is very important if you are planning to walk to the beach. Carrying chairs, coolers and an umbrella while watching out for your children can make a short trip seem a lot longer if you are several rows back from the water. Of course, generally speaking, the farther away from the water, the less expensive the rental rate.

Here's the general idea of what location descriptions mean. Oceanfront means facing the ocean with no physical barrier, road or property lines between you and the beach. Oceanside means you can walk to the beach without crossing a major road, but there might be other rows of houses between your cottage and the ocean. Soundfront means the cottage fronts the sound and you have easy access to the water. Soundside means you are on the

sound side of the road and in walking distance of the sound. Often, soundside cottages and developments offer guests access to the ocean and beach by means of a walking path.

Pets

If you plan to bring a pet, tell the agent. Some places allow them but charge an additional fee, and others don't allow them at all. Vacationers who choose to violate this rule are subject to eviction and the loss of their deposit. Boarding kennels are available in the area. Check the Yellow Pages for options.

Furnishings and Equipment Rentals

If you are renting an apartment or condo, it will likely be fully furnished. Most rental brochures list the furnishings (small appliances,

FYI

Unless otherwise noted, the area code for all phone numbers in this guide is 919.

TVs, VCRs, stereos, toasters, microwaves) and other items that are provided, such as beach chairs and umbrellas, hammocks and grills. You might only need to bring your sheets and towels, or you can rent those from the rental company. If not, there are a few independent agencies that rent linens along with other extras, such as baby furniture and extra folding beds. In many of the units, a telephone is available for local calls and for credit card or collect long-distance calls. Some do not have phones, so if that's important check ahead.

Occupancy

Most vacation rentals are offered on a weekly basis, particularly in the summer. If you would like just a few days at the beach, check with an agency and see what can be arranged. Everything is more flexible in the off-season. Each rental unit is governed by rules and regulations spelled out in rental brochures and contracts.

INSIDERS' TIP

Spring and fall are exquisite at the Crystal Coast. The weather is temperate, the beaches sparsely populated, the restaurants less hurried and the roads uncrowded. Visitors will enjoy the relaxed pace and the breathtaking beauty of sea and sky.

Other Tips

Renting vacation accommodations is a business on the coast, so approach it that way. Be sure to read the rental agreement carefully and ask questions if there is anything you don't understand. By getting all your questions answered, you can often reduce the number of items you bring and make it an enjoyable vacation for everyone. If you are a smoker, check to see if smoking is permitted. If you are planning a house party, let the agent know in advance. If large parties are prohibited and you ignore this rule, you could be evicted and lose your money.

Most visitors who arrange rentals on the Crystal Coast are family-oriented people who prefer a quiet, relaxed beach vacation.

Rental Companies

The Crystal Coast offers numerous cottages and condos to choose from, but you need to shop early. Many places are booked early in the year. Below is a listing of just a few of the many Crystal Coast companies that handle rentals. If you spot a particular place

you would like to rent, just jot down the location and contact one of these rental companies. Or, simply tell the company representative what you want in the way of size and location and let them guide you. Most can send a picture-illustrated brochure featuring the available cottages and condos to help you make your choice. We have alphabetically arranged these companies and given their telephone numbers and addresses for your convenience.

Bogue Banks

Atlantic Beach Realty Inc.
Causeway Shopping Ctr., 407 Morehead Ave. • 240-7368, (800) 786-7368

Atlantic offers condo and cottage rentals in Atlantic Beach and Pine Knoll Shores, as well as some rentals in the Morehead City area.

Bluewater Associates Better Homes and Gardens
**200 Mangrove Dr., Emerald Isle
• 354-2323, (800) 326-3826,**

Bluewater handles 118 cottages and condominiums in the Emerald Isle area. Let Carol or Faye handle your special rental needs.

Century 21 Coastal Properties
**610 Morehead Ave., Atlantic Beach
• 726-2718, (800) 849-1995**

This agency can suit your every vacation desire. Whether you are seeking a cottage,

INSIDERS' TIP

Recycling is easy and popular along the Crystal Coast. Most towns offer curb-side pickup of recyclable items. Residents outside town limits can call the county office, 728-8450, for directions to the closest drop-off point.

an efficiency or a condo — oceanfront, soundfront or something in between — Coastal Properties can help.

Century 21- Coastland Realty Inc.
7603 Emerald Dr., Emerald Isle
• 354-2060, (800) 822-2121

Handling rentals of cottages and condos in a variety of styles and prices, this agency deals mainly in Emerald Isle.

Coldwell Banker Spectrum Properties
515 Morehead Ave., Atlantic Beach
• 247-1100, (800) 334-6390
7413 Emerald Dr., Emerald Isle
• 354-3040, (800) 367-3381

Both offices offer condo and cottage rentals along Bogue Banks from Atlantic Beach to Emerald Isle, in Cape Carteret and in Morehead City.

Colony By the Sea
885 Salter Path Rd. (MP 10), Indian Beach
• 247-7707

Colony By the Sea has oceanfront and ocean view one-and two-bedroom condo units.

Emerald Isle Realty Inc.
7501 Emerald Dr., Emerald Isle
• 354-3315, (800) 849-3315

This agency offers about 700 vacation properties in Emerald Isle, Atlantic Beach and Pine Knoll Shores.

ERA Carteret Properties Rental
7801 Emerald Dr., Emerald Isle
• 354-3005, (800) 448-2951

Continuing to offer a large selection of cottages and condos in Emerald Isle, this agency will provide extra attention to meet your every vacation need.

Gull Isle Realty
611 Morehead Ave., Atlantic Beach
• 726-7679, (800) 682-6863

Gull Isle handles vacation rentals of cottages and condos from Atlantic Beach west to Salter Path.

Ketterer Realty
N.C. Hwy. 58 at Mangrove Dr., Emerald Isle
• 354-2704, (800) 849-2704

Ketterer offers a wide variety of vacation rentals — everything from oceanfront homes to beach cottages and condos — in Emerald Isle.

Sound 'n Sea Real Estate
205 Morehead Ave., Atlantic Beach
• 247-7368, (800) 682-RENT

This agency specializes in the renting of vacation houses and condos in Atlantic Beach and Pine Knoll Shores.

Ocean Resorts Inc. Condo Rentals
2111 W. Fort Macon Rd., Atlantic Beach
• 247-3600, (800) 682-3702

This agency handles the vacation rentals for the condo subdivisions of Dunescape Villas, Island Beach & Racquet Club, Bogue Shores and Beachwalk Villas at Pine Knoll Shores.

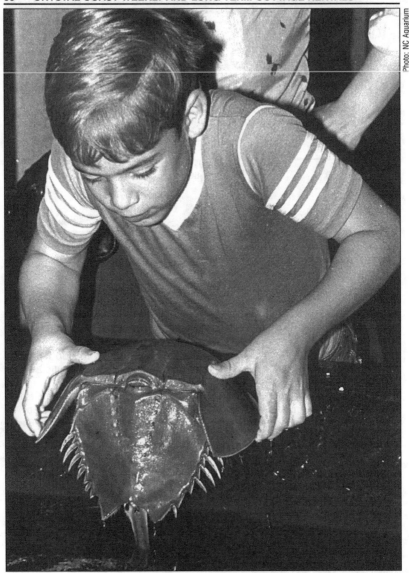

The touch tank at the North Carolina Aquarium offers
a great hands-on way to experience the sea.

Prudential Sun-Surf Realty
7701 Emerald Dr., Emerald Isle
• 354-2658, (800) 553-SURF

Handling the rental of more than 250 homes,
cottages and condos, this agency handles property from Emerald Isle to Pine Knoll Shores.

Realty World-Johnson Realty
Ste. 1, 407 Morehead Ave., Atlantic Beach
• 247-5150, (800) 972-8899

The features of this agency are seasonal
rentals of all types including oceanfront rentals and first- or second-row rentals.

Sands Oceanfront Resorts
**Fort Macon Rd., Atlantic Beach
• 247-2636, (800) 334-2667**

Vacation rentals for Sands Villa Resort, A Place At the Beach and Sea Spray, all in Atlantic Beach, are the specialties of this agency. For information about timeshare units at A Place at the Beach, see the Timeshare section below.

Sunny Shores
**Salter Path Rd., Pine Knoll Shores
• 247-2665, (800) 626-3113**

Sunny Shores handles many vacation rentals of condos and cottages in Atlantic Beach, Pine Knoll Shores and Emerald Isle.

Tetterton Management Group
**513 Morehead Ave., Atlantic Beach
• 247-3096, (800) 334-2727
Salter Path Rd., Indian Beach • 247-1000, (800) 334-6866**

Tetterton offers a variety of vacation cottages and condo rentals from Atlantic Beach to Emerald Isle south to Topsail Beach.

Whaler Inn Beach Club
**Salter Path Rd., Pine Knoll Shores
• 247-4169, (800) 525-1768**

Attractive oceanfront one- and two-bedroom condominiums are for rent for the two-night minimum or for a week.

Windward Dunes
Salter Path Rd., Indian Beach • 247-7545, (800) 659-7545

Windward Dunes is an eight-story condo development in Indian Beach that offers 50 direct oceanfront one- and two-bedroom units.

Beaufort

Beaufort offers no condos to vacationers, but there are a few rental apartments and houses available. Rates vary for one night, a week or longer.

While a few people advertise their own rentals with a sign out front, many list them with local agents. If you are looking for a rental in Beaufort, we recommend you contact a Beaufort real estate company, look in the *Carteret County News-Times* or ask another Insider.

Down East

A drive Down East, particularly to Harkers Island and Cedar Island, will turn up several nice rental cottages/houses. Many of these are not handled by a real estate agency; they simply have the owner's name and a phone number posted out front. Most rental places are booked year after year by the same people, so we suggest you find the one you are interested in and make arrangements early.

Timeshare, Interval Ownership

There are several developments on the Crystal Coast set up for interval ownership or timesharing. Billed as a way to have a lifetime of affordable vacations, the plan is set up so you actually purchase a block of time, one or more weeks in length, for a specific unit. Each year, the time you purchased is yours at that unit. Of course, your plans may change one year. With almost all of the companies you can exchange your week on the Crystal Coast for another location, some around the nation or world. Check on this before you purchase.

Before you arrange to buy into an interval ownership condo, there is a maintenance fee to consider. Once you pay off the note, you receive the deed to your week in your specific unit. Some organizations do put restrictions on resale, even after you own the time in that unit, so check on that before you put your name on the dotted line.

The unit will be completely furnished, down to the linens, dishes and pans, so you just stop by the supermarket to pick up food, bring in your suitcases, unload the sporting equipment, and you'll be set for the duration. Each of these interval-ownership facilities is loaded with amenities, and each one is different.

If you are seriously considering purchasing into a timeshare or interval ownership property, give the resort a call and arrange a tour. A few of the facilities on the Crystal Coast that offer interval or fractional ownership are listed here.

Coldwell Banker-Spectrum Resort Properties Inc.
7413 Emerald Dr., Emerald Isle • 354-3070

This company offers fractional ownership of resort properties. This concept involves 10 individuals owning a 10th of a deeded interest in resort property. For this, each individual gets five weeks occupancy of the condos; weeks and holidays rotate each year. Two weeks are left for maintenance.

Peppertree
Salter Path Rd., Atlantic Beach • 247-2092

Peppertree offers one-, two- and three-bedroom units, many with an ocean and sound view. Owners can use the facility property year round. The facility offers a daily club membership that you might want to use if you move to the area but live somewhere other than on the beach. You can park at the resort and use its private beach house for your visits to the shore. Peppertree has four pools, three outdoor and one indoor and a security guard. New units are under construction.

Sands Oceanfront Villas
Fort Macon Rd., Atlantic Beach • 247-2636

There are 98 units for timeshare purchase at A Place at the Beach. Designed as one-, two- and three-bedroom units, each provides all the luxuries of home and then some. Each unit is fully furnished, and linens, towels and a fully-equipped kitchen are provided. A laundry facility is on site. Additionally, the two- and three-bedroom units feature washers and dryers. A Place at the Beach has an indoor heated pool and outdoor pool with a waterslide. For information about rentals at A Place at the Beach, see the rental section above.

Whaler Inn Beach Club
Salter Path Rd., Pine Knoll Shores • 247-4169

Attractive oceanfront one- and two-bedroom condominiums are the feature here. Completely furnished, the units offer fully equipped kitchens complete with dishwashers and all the kitchenware and utensils vacationers need. Units also offer balconies for relaxing and washers/dryers for cleaning up. Owners have immediate and full access to the ocean and sandy beaches in front of the club as well as to the club's heated pool and Jacuzzi. Ownership also allows those living or visiting nearby to continue to use the facility for parking, beach access, showers, swimming and other amenities. Whaler Inn is part of Interval International, allowing owners access to more than 11,000 resorts worldwide. Whaler Inn's helpful staff can offer more information about the beach club.

Rental Services

Instead of hauling so many extras (baby cribs, beach chairs, blankets, towels, linens, etc.) to your rental house, consider renting items from one of the rental service companies listed

It does not take much for kids to have fun at the beach.

here. It saves packing, unpacking and cleanup time, giving you more time for fun.

General Rental
Hwy. 24 east of Cape Carteret • 393-2220

General Rental rents beds, baby furniture, car seats, all kinds of home repair tools (saws, drills, sanders), carpet cleaners, party tents, mowers, tillers and midsize construction equipment.

PR Rentals and Sales
4803 Arendell St. • 247-9411

PR offers furniture, appliances, vacuums and electronics rentals.

Walston's True Value Hardware
Cedar Point • 393-6111

Walston's rents carpet cleaners and all types of tools from a half-inch drill to a ditchwitch. It also has ladders, tillers and mowers.

Country Aire Rental
U.S. Hwy. 70, Morehead City • 247-4938
U.S. Hwy. 70, Beaufort • 728-2955

This company rents a little bit of everything — beds, baby furniture, tools, equipment (tillers, mowers, trailers, sanders, tractors, paint sprayers, etc.) tents of all sizes and wedding and catering supplies.

You will need longer tent stakes for the sandy soil to hold things down in the strong ocean breezes.

Camping

If camping is a pastime you enjoy, one of the best places to camp is on the Crystal Coast. Our area offers excellent camping opportunities, from rent-a-space RV camping with all the conveniences of home to tent camping with no conveniences at all. Primitive camping is available at Cape Lookout National Seashore, Bear Island and in the Croatan National Forest (see the Attractions chapter).

Camping along the coast is popular almost year round because of the mild winter climate. Summer campers may need to create shade with tarps or overhangs to protect themselves from the hot sun. Campers will find beach camping a little different from mainland camping. You will probably need longer tent stakes for the sandy soil to hold things down in the strong ocean breezes. Netting is almost a must, except in the dead of winter, to protect against the late-afternoon and early-morning mosquitoes and no-see-ums, those barely visible flying insects. A roaring fire and a good insect repellent help also. If you aren't fond of plastering yourself with pesticides, try mixing Avon's Skin So Soft with water and spraying it on. This mixture will fend off most insects and it smells good too. It also works on dogs.

To really get away from it all, try camping at Cape Lookout or Bear Island, both of which are only accessible by boat or ferry. There are no designated camping sites on Cape Lookout National Seashore, and camping is allowed everywhere except on a small amount of well-marked, privately owned land. Bear Island has quiet, secluded campsites. Croatan National Forest, which includes land in Carteret and Craven counties, offers two options: Stay in one of the two planned campgrounds or pitch a tent anywhere on National Forest land that isn't marked for private use.

Overnight fees vary from campground to campground and usually depend on the location (whether oceanfront or off the beaten path) and the facilities offered. Fees for commercial campgrounds generally range from $15 to $35 a night and reservations are suggested. There is no charge to camp at Cape Lookout National Seashore or at some sites in Croatan National Forest.

Most piers along Bogue Banks also rent RV and tent spaces (see our Fishing, Boating, Watersports and Beach Access chapter).

Bogue Banks

Arrowhead Campsite
N.C. Hwy. 5, MP 11½, Indian Beach
• 247-3838

Next to Bogue Sound in the heart of Bogue Banks, Arrowhead Campsite offers 12 acres with full hookup, tent sites and clean restroom/shower facilities. Most types of water activities, such as sailing, shelling, fishing and clamming, are enjoyed in the sound. The campsite has a boat ramp, a pier and a protected swimming area, and ocean access is just 600 feet away. Popular restaurants, shops and a grocery store are within walking distance. The campground has a lot of regulars who return every year, so reservations are a good idea. Arrowhead usually closes in late November and opens before Easter.

INSIDERS' TIP

If you're planning to take a vehicle to Cape Lookout, schedule your trip well in advance to ensure room on the ferry from Davis or Atlantic. (See our Getting Around chapter.)

Salter Path Family Campground
N.C. Hwy. 58, MP 11¾, Salter Path
• 247-3525

This campground offers sites on the ocean or the sound. It has been owned by the Lindsay family since 1967. All sites have electrical outlets, water taps and picnic tables, and most sites have sewer and cable hookups. Shower facilities, volleyball, basketball, fishing, wind surfing, a laundry room, a camp store, a boat ramp, a pond and a dump station are available. This campground is within easy walking distance of a grocery store, restaurants and shops. It is open mid-March through early November. Reservations are suggested, and it might save you a few bucks to check out the spring and fall weekly and monthly rates. Clam rakes are rented at the office for 15¢ per hour and users are asked to contribute one clam to the campground saltwater aquarium. They also provide instructions for preparing your catch.

Watersports Rentals and RV Campground
N.C. Hwy. 58, MP 12, Indian Beach
• 247-7303

This camp spot is on Bogue Sound right across the road from the Indian Beach Pier. The watersports equipment rental business offers spaces for RV full-hookup camping and tents. The business rents sailboats, motor boats and Jet Skis and gives lessons on how to use the equipment and how to water ski (see our Fishing, Boating, Watersports and Beach Access chapter).

Beachfront RV Park
N.C. Hwy. 58, MP 19¼, Emerald Isle
• 354-6400

On the oceanfront with about 158 full-hookup and tent camping sites, Beachfront RV Park is beside Bogue Inlet Fishing Pier. The park owners pride themselves in offering pleasant surroundings and clean bathhouses. A camp store with RV supplies, a dump sta-

tion, a pier, surf fishing and a game room are available. Campers can walk to the nearby seafood restaurants. The campground is closed from early December to early March. Good Sam members can get a 10 percent discount.

Holiday Trav-L-Park Resort
N.C. Hwy. 58, MP 21, Emerald Isle
• 354-2250

This oceanfront camping resort offers 365 grass sites with full-hookups along with a host of amenities, including paved streets, shower facilities, shaded tent sites, a complete grocery store with RV supplies and LP gas, a yogurt shop, a recreation hall, a dump station and an outdoor swimming pool. You can rent mopeds and bicycles and play on the basketball and tennis courts. Kids and parents alike enjoy the shuffleboard area and the go-cart track. A summer activities director lines up live entertainment, so there is always something going on for those who want to stay active. But there is also plenty of peace and quiet. In business since 1976, Holiday Trav-L-Park enjoys a large following of repeat customers. The park is the site of the huge Emerald Isle Beach Music Festival in mid-May. (See our Annual Events chapter.) Storage facilities are available for campers, boats and motor homes. The park is within walking distance of grocery stores, restaurants, movie theaters and shops. Trav-L-Park offers a 10 percent discount to Good Sam members, and it is open all year except two or three weeks in late December and early January.

Bridgeview Family Campground
N.C. Hwy. 58, MP 21, Emerald Isle
• 354-4242

Bridgeview is near the foot of the high-rise bridge connecting Bogue Banks with the mainland. The campground sits off the highway and fronts Bogue Sound. About 113 RV sites are available for lease for 9- to 12-month peri-

INSIDERS' TIP

Dune vegetation keeps dunes from washing out to sea. Sea oats are the tall, thin, grain-headed grasses that anchor and beautify our dunes. It's against the law to pick sea oats — alive or dead.

Photo: Scott Taylor

Wild horses of Shackleford Banks are now protected by legislation.

ods. Overnight camping is limited to five primitive tent sites, which do not include water. Bridgeview has a boat ramp, a swimming pool and a fishing pier. Several lots are wooded, and picnic tables and a playground are featured.

Western Carteret County

Whispering Pines Campground
N.C. Hwy. 24, 12 miles west of Morehead City • 726-4902

Situated on Bogue Sound, Whispering Pines has 140 full-hookup sites, a swimming pool, paddleboats, a miniature golf course, a freshwater pond and fishing. The camp store and the park are open all year. The park has mail and phone message services. Whispering Pines offers special off-season monthly rates. On-site and off-site storage is available for boats and campers.

Waterway RV Park
N.C. Hwy. 24, Cedar Point • 393-8715

This park is situated on 28 acres on the Intracoastal Waterway between Cape Carteret and Swansboro. Tim Stanley and Patricia Wilkinson, who also own the Beachfront RV Park at Emerald Isle, purchased this camp two years ago and have been working to make it a great place to vacation. Waterway offers 300 RV sites with full hookups (water, sewer and electric), 167 of which have cable TV. For larger RVs, 30-amp, 50-amp or 100-amp service is available. A favorite among anglers and their families, the campground provides two boat ramps and 29 boat slips, fish-cleaning stations and a storage area for campers and boats. Kids have a lot to do here; there's a big swimming pool, game room, a playground with stuff to play on and a volleyball court. Grown-ups will be pleased with the full supply store, laundry room, paved streets and card-entry security gate. A 10 percent discount applies for Good Sam members. Waterway is open year round.

Swansboro

Bear Island
Hammock's Beach Rd., west of Swansboro Ranger Station • 326-4881

Access to Bear Island is provided from Hammock's Beach State Park (see the Attractions and the Getting Around chapters) or by private boat. The 3.5-mile island offers primitive, private camping at designated spots for a small fee. Campers must register with the park office on the mainland before going over to Bear Island. Be aware that the bathhouse in the center of the island is a good distance from the camping areas. Campsites for boaters are also offered, but some sites are tricky to get to because of shallow water. Campers traveling by ferry are advised to travel light because it is close to a mile walk from the ferry landing to some sites. To minimize human disturbance of nesting loggerhead sea turtles, Bear Island is closed to camping during the full-moon phases of the months of June, July and August.

Goose Creek Resort
N.C. Hwy. 24, 7 miles east of Swansboro • 393-2628

Goose Creek Resort offers 300 RV sites, with full hookups, for family camping on Bogue Sound. Campers will find two boat ramps, a pool, a waterslide, a game room, a heated/air conditioned bathhouse, a camp store, tent sites, a 250-foot fishing pier, basketball, skiing, clamming and crabbing and a dump station. Goose Creek has an amphitheater for dancing and offers church services Easter through Labor Day. In addition to the regular RV sites, the resort has 12 extra-wide units that accommodate Park Models. Open year round, Goose Creek offers special long-term rates and on-site boat and RV storage.

Down East

Coastal Riverside Campground
216 Clark Ln., Otway • 728-5155

Otway is a small Down East community just east of Beaufort. This campground has all the extras you would expect, plus a security gate to ensure privacy, 55 sites with hookups and additional tent sites. This shady campground is on North River and has a pier, a pool, a boat ramp, a bathhouse, a store, a game room, cable hookups and a dump station. They also offer RV and boat storage and seasonal rates. The campground is open all year.

Cedar Creek Campground and Marina
U.S. Hwy. 70, Sea Level • 225-9571

Cedar Creek caters to family camping with shady sites and easy access to Core Sound and Drum Inlet. Guests will find a swimming pool, flush toilets, hot-water showers, a dump station, boating, fishing, horseshoes and basketball, along with 20 sites with full hookups and 35 additional sites for RVs and tents. Parts of the campground and marina are open all year, although the facilities are only fully operational between April 1 and November 30. About 12 miles from the Cedar Island-Ocracoke ferry terminal, the campground also offers an RV storage area. Cedar Creek gives a 10 percent discount to Good Sam and AAA members.

Driftwood Campground
N.C. Hwy. 12, Cedar Island • 225-4861

This waterfront campground is beside the Cedar Island-Ocracoke ferry terminal. Its 65 sites consist of tent, water and electric and full hookup. Swimming, fishing, volleyball, horseshoes and video games are offered along with a bathhouse, a store and a dump station. AARP members receive a 10 percent discount. The campground is open March 1 through December 15. It is part of the Driftwood complex, which includes a restaurant and a convenience store and grill. Driftwood is well-known for its hunting and fishing guide service and its great food. (See our Restaurants and Accommodations chapters for more information.)

Cape Lookout National Seashore
Ranger Station, Harkers Island • 728-2250

Cape Lookout National Seashore (see the Attractions chapter) offers waterfront camping at its best. This is the place to go if you want privacy. You might see a ranger and a few anglers around the cabins or folks around the lighthouse keeper's quarters; otherwise, you are on your own. Imagine sitting around the fire at dusk, listening to the sound of waves and watching the sweeping light of the Cape Lookout Lighthouse. Water as far as you can see, with the Atlantic Ocean on one side and Core Sound on the other. This camping area has no developed campsites, no bathhouses (the lighthouse has a toilet), no fees and no access without a boat. There are two primitive cabin complexes with flush toilets and showers. So how do you get to this wonderland? By boat or by ferry. Ferry service is provided by several concessionaires permitted by the National Park Service (see our Getting Around chapter) and numerous charter boats. Like all National Parks, some restrictions apply, so talk to a ranger before scheduling your trip.

Croatan National Forest
Ranger Office: 141 E. Fisher Ave., approx. 25 miles north of Morehead City off Hwy. 70 • 638-5628

Croatan National Forest is made up of 157,000 acres spread between Morehead City and New Bern. Recreational areas are available for a day's outing or for overnight camping. The forest has two planned campsites, Cedar Point and Neuse River, where you will find drinking water, bathhouse facilities and trailer space. Primitive camping is permitted all year and campfires are allowed. Much of the park is closed November through March, except the Cedar Point and primitive camping sites that are open year round. For more information on the Croatan National Forest, see our Attractions chapter and our New Bern chapter.

Cedar Point Campground
Croatan National Forest, Cape Carteret • 638-5628

On the White Oak River a mile north of Cape Carteret (follow signs from Highway 58), this campground is a good stopover if you want to experience coastal marsh and maritime forest in their truest forms. At Cedar Point lovers of the outdoors can enjoy many activities: camping, picnicking, fishing, boating and hiking. The site offers 40 camping units with electrical hookups, a bathhouse with flush toilets and warm showers, drinking water and an unimproved boat ramp. Formerly open year round, Cedar Point is now open April through October.

Cedar Point Tideland Trail
Ranger Station, 1 mile north of Cape Carteret • 638-5628

This is one of the two planned camping sites in Croatan National Forest. On the banks of the White Oak River, the area offers 50 camping spaces, drinking water, toilets and an unpaved boat ramp. Cedar Point can be reached by following the signs from N.C. 58 about a mile north of Cape Carteret. Reservations are not required. The Cedar Point Tideland Trail, an interpretive nature trail, is here and offers a short loop, a one-hour walk and a two-hour walk.

Morehead's Waterfront shopping area continues to benefit from revitalization. Sidewalks, trees and benches invite visitors to take a stroll.

Shopping

Shopping is a favorite recreation for many vacationers, and the Crystal Coast accommodates that activity with plenty of unique stores and boutiques.

Initially, a newcomer or visitor may find it difficult to locate what he or she needs because there are no single, all-inclusive large shopping centers or malls. However, lots of shops and stores do exist. There are mini-malls, strips of shops and several good-size shopping centers. This combination affords you plenty of places to find what you need and want.

Because the Crystal Coast is considered a resort area, you'll find dozens of shops that cater to the beachgoer or surfer. Whether you're looking for a beach souvenir, a gift for someone back home, the perfect-fitting swimsuit, a special T-shirt or a beach wrap, you'll find it here. If you need clothing or equipment for your favorite summer sport, you will find many brands of goods including everything from surf boards to tennis togs. Since there aren't as many tourists here in the win-

ter, some shops, particularly those on Bogue Banks, close in the winter.

We have designed this section to offer you a brief look at a few of the shops in each Crystal Coast community. Antiques shops, decoy shops and flea markets are listed separately at the end of this chapter. We can't mention every shop that warrants your attention, so explore on your own and ask around. Other Insiders will be delighted to share information with you.

Bogue Banks

Most Bogue Banks' shopping is focused on the active lifestyle of beachgoers — both residents and visitors. Shops offer swimwear, watersport accessories, casual wear, seashells and souvenirs. Here is a sampling of some of the shops you'll find on Bogue Banks, beginning in Atlantic Beach and wandering west to Emerald Isle. We have given the milepost (MP) number for the shops on N.C. 58 (the main road on the island).

Photo: NC Travel and Tourism

Walking on the beach is one of our favorite activities in this area.

Atlantic Beach

Bert's Surf Shop, MP 2, stocks swimwear, activewear, beach T-shirts, a large variety of sports equipment and sunglasses. Bert's also has a shop in Emerald Isle. **Marsh's Surf Shop** on the Atlantic Beach Causeway offers everything from dresses and shorts to T-shirts and jackets for men, women and children. There are plenty of beach items too — sunglasses, surfboards, swimsuits, beach bikes and all the accessories. Marsh's also carries a wonderful selection of leather clogs and active footwear.

Sandi's Beachwear, MP 2, offers a variety of swimwear and activewear. You are sure to find the perfect suit and accessories at this store. **Atlantic Beach Surf Shop**, MP 2, offers quality beachwear, casual clothes and officewear. Footwear, jewelry, sunglasses, surfboards, beach bikes and all the accessories are for sale. **Davis Beachwear Shop**, on the Circle, has been in business for years and carries a complete line of sportswear and swimwear for adults and children.

Presents, Atlantic Beach Causeway, is the place to shop for unique gifts, gourmet foods, toys, decorator and garden items, stationery and gift baskets. **Catco**, also on the Atlantic Beach Causeway, offers distinctive handcrafted nautical jewelry. **Wings**, MP 2, has two beach-oriented retail stores within the same block and carries lots of T-shirts, bathing suits and casual apparel along with shells and jewelry.

Hi-Lites, MP 2, specializes in discounted clothing in juniors, misses and plus sizes with an emphasis on sporty separates with nothing over $15. You'll also find swimsuits, belts, earrings, bags and hats. **Tony's Beach Shop**, MP 4, is across from the Sheraton. The store offers everything from ice cream and yogurt to swimwear and boogie boards. Tony's also offers gifts, souvenirs, hermit crabs and the largest selection of seashells in the area.

Christmas By The Sea, MP 5, is a shop filled with holiday decorations, ornaments and more. There are plenty of wonderful gift ideas for Christmas, or for any occasion.

The Atlantic Station Shopping Center, MP 3, offers a variety of shops. The center is anchored by **Atlantic Station Cinemas** and **Pak-A-Sak Food Store**. **Outer Banks Outfitters** is just the store for anglers. This is a marine electronics store that, along with radios, stereos and spotlights, carries fishing tackle, clothing, jewelry and much more. **Beach Book Mart** offers a great selection of paper and hardback books at reduced prices. Beach Book Mart also offers a good selection of local books along with bestsellers, cookbooks and much more. **Kites Unlimited** has hundreds of wind-borne treasures in designs and sizes for all ability levels. Inside you will find quality kites, windsocks, flags, unique games and puzzles. Other shops include **Atlantic Photo**, providing film processing services; and **Video City**, offering a wide selection of movies for rent. **Coastal Crafts Plus** features the work of more than 30 crafters — pottery, jewelry, paintings, and woodcrafts. The **Bake Shoppe Bakery** tempts shoppers with donuts, bagels, fresh breads, pies and some health food items. **Great Mistakes** features savings on brand-name clothing for women and men. They also have stores in Beaufort and Emerald Isle. **Special Moments** arranges anything for any occasion — gift baskets, balloons, cards, stationery, gourmet candy, coffee, mugs, stuffed animals, T-shirts, souvenirs and more. Let them create a fabulous gift arrangement for that special moment. **Budding Artists Ltd.** is the in-

FYI

Unless otherwise noted, the area code for all phone numbers in this guide is 919.

INSIDERS' TIP

No discussion of shopping Down East would be complete without mention of Phil's Barbecue Sauce. The sauce is a home creation of Philip Willis of Davis and is a spicy vinegar-based sauce that is great on grilled fish, pork and chicken. Phil's Barbecue Sauce is sold in many local grocery stores.

spiration of Leigh Humphries, who takes pride in showcasing local and regional artists. Her new gallery offers prints, water colors, sculpture, pottery, photographs and other original art pieces. Leigh also has a full-service frame shop and will gift wrap upon request.

Across N.C. 58 from Atlantic Station Shopping Center is Coral Bay Shopping Center, MP 3. This small center includes **Eckerd Drug Store** and **Food Lion** supermarket.

Pine Knoll Shores

There are no outright shopping areas in Pine Knoll Shores. This residential town does offer a convenience store and several hotels and piers with gift shops or tackle shops.

Salter Path and Indian Beach

Vacationers will find a few places to shop in Salter Path and Indian Beach. **Village Gift Shop & Beach Wear**, MP 11, offers beachwear, T-shirts, shell items, gifts, jewelry, hats, suncatchers and lots more. **Fishin' Fever**, MP 11, is a seafood market and tackle shop. Someone around the store can always tell you where to go to wet a line, what bait to use that day and how to prepare your catch. For unlucky anglers, the fresh seafood market will save the day.

Old Island Store, MP 11, offers nautical beachwear, gifts, shells, beach supplies, art, lamps, flags and windsocks. **Dog Island Outfitters**, MP 10, is on the sound a block off the highway. Here you will find outdoor apparel and watersport rentals.

Island Rigs, MP 12, is a watersport rental business (see our Fishing, Watersports and Beach Access chapter) that also offers watersport accessories, sportswear and beachwear. **Food Dock**, MP 11, is the local grocery store.

Emerald Isle

Shops line Emerald Drive (N.C. 58) and are in Emerald Plantation (see below). Here, we have included a sampling of the shops you'll find in town.

Fran's Beachwear, MP 19, carries an excellent selection of swimwear for everyone from the daring to the shy, along with sporty and dressy separates and a wide range of shoes, accessories and souvenirs. **Fran's Gifts** (same location) offers such collectibles as Tom Clark Gnomes, Dept. 56 Snow Village and Precious Moments. You'll also find gifts, jewelry and accessories.

Especially for You, MP 19, offers clothing and accessories for the fuller-figured woman. This shop is very popular and enjoys much repeat business. **BeachMart**, MP 20, is filled with T-shirts, souvenirs, bathing suits, beachwear, sunglasses and more. BeachMart also has a location in Atlantic Beach at MP 2.

Bert's Surf Shop, MP 19, was the town's first surf shop. The shop stocks beach clothing for all ages, skateboards, windsurfing equipment and surfboards. Bert's always has activewear, sunglasses, hats and beach T-shirts. **Wing's**, MP 19, offers T-shirts, bathing suits, casual apparel, shells and jewelry. **Great Mistakes**, MP 20, features discount brand-name clothing for women and men. There are sister stores in Beaufort and Atlantic Beach.

The Emerald Plantation Shopping Center, MP 20, offers stores in a courtyard-type setting. The center is anchored by **Food Lion**, **Revco Drug Store**, **Sound Ace Hardware** and **Emerald Plantation Cinema 4**. **Tom Togs Factory Outlet** sells a large selection of well-known clothing brands at drastically reduced prices. Inside you will find items for women, men and children along with accessories. Be sure to check Tom Togs, with locations also in Beaufort and Morehead City, before you pay full price elsewhere. **J.R. Dunn Jewelers** features distinctive jewelry for women, men and children, along with many nautical creations. J.R. Dunn also has a shop in Cypress Bay Plaza in Morehead City. **Elly's Personal Touch** is packed with children's clothes, games, books and all kinds of gifts including stained glass, pottery, decoys and wreaths. **Emerald Isle Books & Toys** has books and magazines for all ages. **Country Store** offers baskets, windsocks, flags, cards, wreaths, brass, clocks, frames and Christmas items. At **Carolina Video** you

may choose from a large selection of movies and video games. VCR rental is also available.

Beaufort

The specialty shops in Beaufort are sure to suit anyone's taste. Although there are others, most shops are along the downtown waterfront area. Only a few of Beaufort's shops close in the winter.

Beaufort's many attractions — the waterfront, the museum, historic sites and pubs — provide respite for those who find themselves in Beaufort with a born shopper. We couldn't

possibly list all the shops, so we hope you will do some exploring on your own. The shops we have listed are all located on Front Street.

Fabricate Apparel specializes in clothes of natural fibers. The shop offers trendy, expressive clothes as well as conservative outfits for women, men and children. You'll find jewelry, belts, bags, a small selection of shoes, T-shirts and sweatshirts that feature Beaufort scenes, environmental messages and drawings by M.C. Escher.

Next door owner Barbara Pearl has opened a new shop, **Ibis.** It features upscale women's clothing such as Eileen Fisher and Kaminiski hats.

INSIDERS' TIP

Want some free reads for the beach? Collect your old paperback books and visit the Bogue Banks Public Library, 320 Salter Path Road, MP7, Pine Knoll Shores, 247-4660. There, you may choose up to 10 paperbacks from the library's Trading Post. All that's required is for you to trade in as many books as you take.

Scuttlebutt specializes in "nautical books and bounty." An outstanding selection of nautical books and charts, clocks, music, games, toys, models and galleyware are available.

Mary Elizabeth's caters to women seeking the career look in traditional clothing, shoes and all types of accessories. Mary Elizabeth's also offers sportswear.

Stamper's Gift Shop sells fine china, all kinds of gifts and novelty items as well as an extensive line of collectibles by Gorman, Lee Middleton, Susan Wakeen, M.I. Hummels and Tom Clark Gnomes. Stamper's also offers a variety of throw rugs and blankets, including those featuring scenes from Beaufort. Next door, **Stamper's Jewelers** offers a full line of jewelry items as well as engraving and excellent repair services.

For great ice cream or a few more souvenirs, stop by **The General Store**, where you'll find all kinds of memorabilia to take home — hats, T-shirts, shells, saltwater taffy and jewelry. **Top Deck** is one of the best places in town for name brand clothing, shoes, T-shirts,

casual wear, Ray Bans and things labeled "Beaufort." The **Harbor Shop** offers all kinds of things — baskets, rugs, stained glass, art, jewelry and so much more. Owner Rob Davis carries some cards, drawings and jewelry created by local artists. **La Vaughn's Pottery** has plenty of gourmet coffees and wines, some from North Carolina vineyards. As the name reflects, the store has pottery items along with furniture, collectibles and jewelry.

Local artist Alan Cheek displays his work at **Down East Gallery**. Alan's artwork will serve as a lovely reminder of time spent in the Beaufort seaport. Down East Gallery does custom framing. On the Beaufort Historic Site, the **Mattie King Davis Art Gallery** features paintings, sketches, note cards, carvings, photographs, weavings and gifts created by local artists. At **Chachkas** (that's Yiddish for little things around the house that you have to pick up and dust) gift shop, the staff will show you beautiful and unusual jewelry at very attractive prices. These Insiders find it hard to resist the charming slide bracelets made to resemble

Carving A Niche

Well-known for its excellent hunting grounds, the Carteret County area has been hunted by locals and sportsmen from near and far for hundreds of years. Catering to the many hunting visitors, locals took to the task of chopping the forms of ducks and geese from blocks of wood to lure waterfowl to within firing range. Today the carving of wooden decoys has developed into a local form of art. Old working decoys and new handcarved ones are plentiful in the area, and collecting these art forms is becoming very popular.

Core Sound Decoy Carvers Guild was formed about nine years ago to bring back the art of carving and to support those locals who had never quit chopping at blocks of wood. Of course, the ducks, geese and other waterfowl these men and women now craft are not all used in the water. Instead, many are collected, bought, sold and displayed. The Guild's membership is made up of handcarvers of working, decorative and realistic waterfowl, collectors, painters, taxidermists, photographers and breeders.

Each year since 1987 the Guild has hosted a large and impressive festival at Harkers Island Elementary School. Scheduled for the first weekend each December, the Core Sound Decoy Festival attracts local and nationally known carvers, goose callers and other artists. Many men, and a few women, gather to exhibit and sell their work. Decoys are judged, sold, displayed, made and auctioned. There are booths set up to display artifacts, promote conservation and preservation efforts and focus on wildlife clubs. But most of all, there are decoys, lots and lots of decoys. This is one educational festival not to be missed — even if you're not a collector.

The 10th Annual Core Sound Decoy Festival is scheduled for early December on Harkers Island. For more information about Core Sound Decoy Carvers Guild, Core Sound Waterfowl Museum or area carvers and shops, contact the museum at P.O. Box 556, Harkers Island, North Carolina 28531, or call 728-1500.

Though it might seem otherwise, the ability to carve decoys is not something one is born with. All it takes is interest and patience.

Just ask Keith Gaskill of Sea Level, who didn't pick up a carving knife until 1992. Since then, Keith, now 42, has won prizes in competition and is hooked on the traditional art form of Down East residents. After an auto wreck at age 18 left him paralyzed below the waist, Keith engaged in a number of activities but didn't focus on carving until a few years ago.

"It's good therapy and occupies my time. I get a great deal of enjoyment from taking a block of wood and turning it into a bird," says Keith.

Keith says his success should inspire others and recommends that those interested in learning the art should attend any of the numerous decoy shows along the East Coast, visit a hobby shop or look for the advertisements of carving suppliers often found in the back pages of outdoor sporting magazines.

Many shops along the Crystal Coast offer a few decoys, but the majority available, old or new, are sold by the collectors or from the crafter's home.

If you are looking for a decoy, keep your eyes open for yard signs and stop by the Core Sound Waterfowl Museum on Harkers Island for a flyer listing area decoy shops. The museum also sells decoys and has hundreds on display.

Most of the area's decoy shops are east of Beaufort and in the Down East area. Not

— continued on next page

Photo: Claire Doyle

A teal made from wood makes a stunning decorative decoy. This one was carved in 1995 by local artist Cliff Bain and shown at the Ninth Annual Core Sound Decoy Festival.

all the "shops" are really shops. You might be browsing in someone's living room or garage and discover a real treasure. They advertise using signs along the road. But don't let that fool you. These guys aren't just messing around with some wood — they are creating works of art. One stop will prove that to you. Whether you are looking for carved ducks, geese or shorebirds, you are sure to find them here.

shells and sea animals. For a really special piece, select an Italian silver and gold bracelet, pendant or earrings — sophisticated, lightweight and feminine. Chachkas is Carteret County's exclusive retailer for jewelry made of Italian silver. But that's not all. Owner Sandra Santafede does decorative hand painting of furniture, walls and almost any wooden object you'd care to have transformed into something uniquely your own. Sandra will devise her own design or use yours. Ask to see her portfolio of completed work.

Chadwick House is a retail interior design store offering lamps, prints, paintings, furniture, upholstery, wallpaper and window treatments. The shop's lovely accessories include glass vases, picture frames, baskets, garden ornaments and kitchen accents. **For Nature's Sake** offers art, clothing, gifts and products, all aimed at passing on the messages of conservation, preservation and peace. For Nature's Sake also has a store on Evans Street in Morehead City. **Great Mistakes** offers

brand-name clothing for women and men at discount prices. The store features first-quality overruns, closeouts, samples and imperfects.

Bell's Drug Store has been serving the people of Beaufort and visitors since 1918 and continues that same friendly, professional service today. Along with drugstore items, Bell's has fountain drinks, film, personal care items, gifts and cards. Across the street from the Maritime Museum are several shops. Among them are **Cabin Fever**, which sells handmade wood crafts and specializes in Christmas ornaments, two gift shops, the **Bag Lady** and the **Peddler**, and **Tom Togs**, a clothing outlet that sells discounted brand-name sportswear for the whole family. Atlantic Boat Works, near the end of Front Street, houses the new **Montana Wine and Coffee Store**, which carries wine and gourmet coffee and plans to add a wine bar and a baked goods section.

Somerset Square houses a number of

shops. This two-story building is on Front Street at the south end of Turner Street. **Handscapes Gallery** specializes in works by North Carolina artists and craftspeople and is the perfect place to find special gifts and treasures. Owner Alison Brooks fills the shop with pottery, jewelry, paintings, glass and wood items. The **Rocking Chair Book Store** is celebrating its 17th year of offering books for adults and children. Be sure to check the selection of regional books, sailing books and helpful book lights. Owners Neva Bridges and Josephine Davis are full of information, and they will order any book for you. The **Fudge Factory** makes creamy, sinful fudge from natural ingredients on marble-top tables right before your eyes. **Containing Ideas** carries an extensive line of Patagonia apparel (jackets, pants, hats and accessories) and lots of T-shirts, bags and hats with environmental messages.

Just outside the downtown area is **Gaskill's True Value Farm & Garden Center** on U.S. 70. One step inside will take you back in time. Bo Sullivan and his helpful crew stock this country seed store with everything you need to get the garden going, the lawn tamed, the house and boat fixed or the animals fed.

Holland's Shoes in Beaufort Square Shopping Center on U.S. 70 carries an excellent selection of shoes for the entire family with great prices to match. You'll find brand-name shoes, including Reebok, Nike, Rockport and Sperry, along with handbags, socks, laces and shoe-cleaning items.

A number of grocery stores, drug stores and variety shops are on U.S. 70 east of downtown Beaufort.

Morehead City

Morehead City offers the largest selection of shops on the Crystal Coast. Shopping opportunities are spread from one end of the city to the other and range from clothing boutiques and craft shops to book stores and marine hardware suppliers. Here we have described a few of the shops in the city and have arranged them by area.

Waterfront

Morehead's Waterfront shopping area continues to benefit from revitalization. Sidewalks, trees and benches invite visitors to take a stroll. The shops, however, are hard to pass by. Facing Bogue Sound, most shopping runs along Evans and Shepard streets. The businesses we describe here are all located within the confines of these waterfront streets.

Dee Gee's Gifts and Books is a tradition on the waterfront and continues to offer a huge selection of books, cards and novelties. Dee Gee's features special sections of local and regional books, children's educational books, games and nautical charts. Let owners Doug and Jane Wolfe help you with your special book request.

Waterfront Junction is the place to stop for craft supplies, needlework, prints, crewel embroidery and nautical gifts. The shop is well-known for its custom framing and its stock of ready-made frames. **Windward Gallery** offers oils, watercolors and pastels by acclaimed local artist Alexander Kaszas and many others. Inside you will also find jewelry, pottery, scrimshaw and glass pieces. For women's clothing, **Lee's "Of Course"** has it — and specializes in one-of-a-kind fashions in all sizes. Don't leave the Morehead waterfront without stopping by **The Sea Pony**. This shop abounds with attractive gifts for that special person — or even for yourself. Among many enticing items, you'll find pottery, clothing, pictures, cards, English antiques and fine jewelry.

The owners of **The Purple Marlin** travel far and wide to find intriguing gifts featuring fish and fish-related themes. The Purple Marlin carries fine American and imported handmade collectibles and decorations for the home. Shoppers will be delighted with the

---

INSIDERS' TIP

As you drive around on Bogue Banks, be careful to observe the towns' posted speed limit. Pedestrians constantly cross Highway 58, the main drag on the island.

Murano and Blenko glass pieces and the washable silk pillows and lamp shades. For entertaining, pick from porcelain and stoneware dishes depicting fish of all types, styles and colors. Nifty kitchen items are made of pottery, carved aluminum and lead-free pewter. Most of The Purple Marlin's home accessories are as practical as they are beautiful. The shop will gift wrap and ship your purchases.

Downtown

As you travel east (toward Beaufort) on Arendell Street, several shops between 12th and 5th Streets are well-worth a visit. **Ginny Gordon's Gifts And Gadgets** carries a great collection of cookware, cookbooks from near and far, and every cooking utensil imaginable. Ginny's also offers occasional cooking classes.

Kennedy's Office Supply has a complete line of office supplies and paper products along with calendars, art supplies, pens and furniture for the office. **Carolina City Smoked Seafood** has delicious varieties of smoked seafood, spreads and delicacies. Our favorites are the smoked salmon and bluefish in lemon pepper. It offers party trays and has a mail-order service. At **Sew It Seams** you will find sewing patterns and notions, fabrics, books, craft and quilting supplies. Owner Lillian Lawrence offers sewing and quilting classes as well as many different kinds of craft workshops.

At **Morehead City Floral Expressions**, shoppers can select from potted plants and very special floral arrangements. **Parson's General Store** has an extensive collection of gifts, local crafts, books, home accessories, seasonal decorations and sweets.

At **City News Stand**, those who wish to keep up with world happenings can choose from among an endless number of magazines and many major newspapers. Greeting cards are available and so are bestsellers and books about local lore.

At **Branch's** you will find a traditional office supply shop with lots of enticing extras. Besides cards and supplies for drafting, art

Photo: Scott Taylor

Wild horses and boaters gather at the Beaufort waterfront.

and school, you'll find gifts, interesting home accessories and cute stuffed animals.

When you visit **Sullivan's** photography studio, owner Hardy Sullivan will show you marvelous examples of restored, repaired and airbrushed photographs. He takes family, group, passport and publicity photos and will custom-frame anything you wish. Hardy and his wife, Joyce, enjoy photographing animals; lots of Crystal Coasters go to Sullivan's for pictures of their birds, cats and dogs. (Don't leave without meeting Chole, the talking Cockatoo who hangs around the studio.)

Across Arendell Street from Sullivan's, Don and Ellie Zurek, proprietors of **Crystal Coast Crafters**, recently relocated from the 900 block, will teach you how to make any of the craft items displayed in their store: stained glass, shell craft, lamps and shades, holiday decorations and more. Don and Ellie specialize in stained-glass repair and restoration; they are the artisans who restored and remounted

the stained-glass panels in Rucker John's bar in Emerald Isle (see our Restaurants chapter). The Zureks also carry a large selection of art and craft supplies. Next door, **Fannie's Attic** showcases antiques, collectibles, pottery, afghans, holiday items, art-to-wear, dolls, pottery, dried flowers and wind chimes.

Through the Looking Glass, with a sister store in Swansboro, creates and delivers distinctive floral arrangements for every occasion. This attractive store makes it hard to pass up the glass and crystal selections, exclusive gifts for that very special person, irresistible nautical items and the delightful stuff in the Christmas shop.

Around Morehead City

When you turn around and leave the downtown and waterfront sections of Morehead City, you will be traveling west on Arendell Street (toward Newport and Havelock). Going in this

direction you will encounter a number of small shopping centers. We have listed a few of them here, enterprises that are in or just outside the city's limits, but not clustered in any single area. The street addresses should make them easy to find.

Recreation enthusiasts should check out **EJW Outdoors**, 2204 Arendell Street, for new fishing gear and outdoor clothing or to have a bike tuned up. **Teacher's Pet** and **A Sea of Learning**, 2408 Arendell Street, are two of the most wonderful shops in the area. Whether you are a teacher, a parent or learning yourself, you are sure to enjoy these two stores. Teacher's Pet focuses on all types of learning aides, everything from charts and artwork to books and equipment. A Sea of Learning features educational games and toys for children of all ages.

Morehead Plaza is between Arendell and Bridges streets and is anchored by **Belk**, a full-line department store; **Roses**, a discount retail store; **Byrd's Food Store**, a grocery store with a good deli section; and **Eckerd Drugs**, a drugstore and pharmacy. **The Light Within**, with items that will help you focus on your overall health and healing, is a wonderful store to explore. Natural herbs, essential oils, mineral salts, books and tapes are sold. The Light Within also offers a complete yoga school with day and evening classes for all levels. **Maurice's** carries trendy clothing for women

and men. **Crystal Sports** offers sporting goods equipment, clothing, training shoes and plaques and trophies ready to be personalized.

Dubbed a '60s shop, **Yesterdaze Closet** offers vintage clothing, music and jewelry along with incense, books and memorabilia.

At the back of Morehead Plaza, facing Bridges Street, is **Williams Hardware**, one of the best-supplied hardware stores in the area. It has a helpful staff that won't keep you waiting. **Anderson Audio** is the perfect place to look for that home or car stereo system or other electronic sound machine. **Crystal Coast Brass** cleans brass, silver and copper and sells items ranging from vases and cups to decorative pieces.

Morehead Plaza West is a strip of shops behind Morehead Plaza that can be reached from Bridges Street. The largest store in the plaza is **Western Auto** where you can find everything you need for do-it-yourself auto repairs or have one of their mechanics do it for you. It has tires, batteries, accessories, cleanup kits and bicycles. **Jewelers' Workbench** is our favorite place to go for custom-made jewelry — everything from wedding rings to earrings. They will place special pieces in just the right setting. Owner Laurie Stinson professionally handles any jewelry creation, repair or cleaning and offers her own designs for sale. Laurie can bring new life to your old jewelry pieces.

Twin Book Stores, 3805 Arendell Street, is the place to find thousands of new and used hardbacks, paperbacks, comic books, cookbooks and North Carolina books.

Diamond Shoal Jewelers, 4637 Arendell Street, offers a wonderful selection of jewelry and watches for men and women. Diamond Shoal's specialists also make repairs. The **Painted Pelican**, 4645 Arendell Street, features the work of local artists and craftspeople in the form of prints, pottery, shorebirds, jewelry, scrimshaw and much more. Here you'll also find a frame shop offering custom work and readymades. **Wind Creations**, 4109 Arendell Street, offers all kinds of special flags and banners. A number of their own creations are on hand, and the shop will design special orders.

Howard's Furniture Showrooms, 4024 Arendell Street, offers a full line of home furnishings, bedding, accessories and window treatments. Howard's staff also offers a complete home design service. Sharing the same building is **Superior Carpet and Appliance**, which offers top-of-the-line carpets and vinyl and wood floorings, GE appliances and all types of outdoor furniture. Superior installs and services carpet and appliances. Next door, **Creative Lighting** is filled with fixtures for kitchens and baths along with cabinets and countertops of all types. You'll love the many unique chandeliers.

The **Gourmet Galley**, 4050 Arendell Street, offers gourmet cheeses, pastas, domestic and imported wines, some gourmet candies, spices, plenty of coffees and an espresso bar. The shop is where Carolina Swamp Sauces were created and are offered for sale. **Consider the Lilies Florist** has relocated to 4130 Arendell Street and has expanded its offerings to include home interiors. Patrons can now find Cal-Tone paints, wallpaper and custom-designed window treatments. The shop continues to deliver and wire flowers and create wedding floral arrangements.

Auto Brite, 4303 Arendell Street, is the best place in town to pamper your car with a professional cleaning job and to get a car-related gift. While your car is being cleaned, you can browse among car coffee mugs, tapes and CDs, shirts, cards or any number of small items for the maintenance and upkeep of your car.

Pelletier Harbor Shops, 4428 Arendell Street, includes a number of specialty shops. For women's clothes, visit **The Golden Gull**, featuring the latest fashions and accessories for ladies. The **Jewelry Nest** offers custom designed nautical jewelry created with 14K gold and sterling silver. **Lynette's** carries distinctive fashions for women. The shop offers lovely jewelry, handbags and all the right accessories. **Knowledge of Christ Books & Gifts** is a wonderful store filled with books, gifts, stained glass, collectibles, dolls, prints and paintings. The store also offers Bibles for adults and children. **Over The Rainbow** is a great place to shop for distinctive clothing, footwear and accessories for that favorite little person and maternity wear for a special mom. **Cameo Boutique** offers all types of lingerie for women plus a few items for men. There are also accessories, adult games, lotions, stockings and gifts. **ETC... Ladies Apparel** sells everything from denim to sequins. **Crystal Palate** features gourmet food items such as coffees and teas, cheeses and crackers, domestic and imported beers and wines and scads of those one-of-a-kind kitchen gadgets that are perfect as gifts — or better yet, for your own kitchen. **McQueen's Furniture and Interiors** has lovely home and office decorations, furniture, lamps, prints and accessories. If you are shopping for clothes and accessories for that favorite gentleman or lady, stop by **Graff's Fashions**. **Shoe Splash** can provide just the right shoes to go with any ensemble, and **Sun Photo** offers a reliable one-hour color photo service. **J. Alden Limited for Women** and **J. Alden Limited for Men** offer dress and adventure wear.

The Marketplace is a strip mall at 4900 Arendell Street at the junction of U.S. 70 and Country Club Road. **Rack Room Shoes** carries a wide selection of women's, men's and children's name-brand shoes — everything from casual to dressy to athletic, plus lots of handbags. The **Dress Barn** sells women's clothes at discount prices. **Paper Plus** offers a variety of paper products for the office or the home. This is the place to go when planning your next party. If you want to stay home and watch a movie, pick from a wide selection at **Blockbuster Video**.

The **Parkway Plaza Shopping Center**,

4917 Arendell Street, is anchored by **Kmart** and a **Winn-Dixie** supermarket. Shoppers will also find the **Book Shop**, whose knowledgeable staff will help you choose from a wide selection of paper, hardbound and children's books at discounted prices; **Sherwin Williams** for an extensive choice of paint and wallpaper; and **Mail Boxes, Etc.**, which packs and ships all manner of items and offers fax and copying services. **Tal-Y-Bont Interiors, Ltd.**, 5113 C Highway 70 W., sells all styles of furniture and accessories but emphasizes items appropriate for beach living. This store also offers custom window treatments and a free interior design service.

Cypress Bay Plaza is between highways 70 and 24, and **Wal-Mart** is the plaza's largest store. **Sears Roebuck And Co.** features appliances, hardware, clothing, shoes and an auto shop. **J.R. Dunn Jewelers** features distinctive jewelry for men, women and children, along with many nautical creations. **Carolina Linen** has a large inventory of bed and bath accessories. Other stores in the center include **Food Lion** supermarket, **Revco Drug Store**, and **Gloria's Hallmark**. Shoppers will also find a **Baskin-Robbins Ice Cream & Yogurt Shop**, the **Sub-Sational Deli & Sub Shop**, a video rental store, clothing stores and more.

Truckers Toy Store, U.S. 70 W., handles a full line of truck, sport utility and van accessories, and has a full installation department. The staff's goal here is to help people personalize their vehicles, whether that means truck caps, hitches, step bumpers, running boards or toolboxes. They stock hundreds of accessories and can order hard-to-find items. You'll even find things for your car such as sun roofs and window tinting.

William's Floor Covering and Interiors, U.S. 70 W., offers a full line of floor coverings — everything from carpet to ceramic to hardwood to vinyl. Customers will also find a large selection of wallpapers, blinds, fabric, drapes and more. Let the consultants at William's work with you on your new construction or remodeling project for a home or an office.

At **Munden Garden Center Inc.**, 5178 U.S. 70 W., across the highway from Wal-Mart, Dennis Munden and his staff will help you pick out the right plants for our windy, salty coastal environment. To fill your gardening needs, the center sells shrubs, trees, flowers, vegetables, seeds, feed, fertilizer and lawn and garden supplies. There is also an attractive selection of indoor plants and decorative garden objects. At Christmas time, Munden's locally grown poinsettias are breathtaking. The second location, where much of the plant stock is propagated and made ready for sale, is Down East, on U.S. 70 in Williston.

Inside **Colonial Carolina Pottery**, off U.S. 70 W., you'll find china, crystal, glassware, brass, gifts, bird feeders, rugs, baskets, cookware, furniture, linens, candles, housewares and silk flowers. A separate department offers a huge selection of bath and bed linens and lamps. **Sunshine Garden Center** is next door and offers potted plants, silk flowers and arrangements, baskets, home decorations and every lawn and garden item imaginable.

Swansboro

Shops in Swansboro are basically in two areas — along the waterfront and its adjoining side streets, and along the highway. We suggest you take some time to walk along the White Oak River, shop a bit, enjoy lunch at one of the restaurants and relax in Bicentennial Park.

The waterfront shops are clustered along Front Street. Inside **Russell's Olde Tyme Shoppe** you'll find country crafts, jewelry, handcrafted clothing, pottery, furniture, baskets, silk and dried flowers and kitchen and cooking items. Each purchase in Maxine Russell's store is placed in a handpainted shopping bag, a gift in itself. **Noah's Ark** offers novel gifts for adults or children. The shop carries women's and children's clothing, plenty of accessories, some toys, books and cassette tapes.

Keepsake Originals is on the second floor of the 1839 William Farrand Store. The shop features cards, rubber stamps, handmade alpine lace, beautifully crafted gift boxes and soothing music on tape and CD.

Through the Looking Glass offers memorable floral arrangements for any occasion along with candles, greeting cards, wines and porcelain and crystal sculptures. The **Christmas House** is packed with all the seasonal items you can imagine. **Sunshine and Silks** features baskets, silk flowers, wreaths, ribbons, knickknacks, gifts and wood art.

Down East

There are only a few Down East shops, but each is uncommon and special and well-worth the trip. Because hours vary, we suggest you call ahead.

Lucky Duck's, 728-1331, in Bettie is a wonderful shop filled with antique decoys, waterfowl carvings by local artists, wildlife art, gifts and accessories. Artists Gail and Bernie Corwin also carry a complete line of supplies at the store.

The **Core Sound Waterfowl Museum Gift Shop**, 728-1500, on Harkers Island is filled with unique Down East gifts, most of which have waterfowl and environmental themes. There are decoys, wildlife art, books, cards, house flags, windsocks, clothing, bird houses, bird feeders and much more. The shop also features decoy and local history exhibits.

Somethin' Special Craft and Gift Shop, 729-1176, in Smyrna sells handmade baskets, decoys, stained-glass items, furniture, pillows, afghans, lamp shades, craft supplies, cross-stitch patterns, thread, a good selection of fabric and antiques too.

Newport

Newport offers a number of shops in the downtown area and a few along U.S. 70, just outside the town.

In the downtown area you'll find **C.M. Hill Hardware**. This traditional hardware store carries everything from guns and fan belts to mowers and Westinghouse appliances. **Newport Garden Center** offers everything for the lawn and garden and also sells and services equipment. The center's greenhouse provides fresh, locally grown plants.

Cape Carteret

The town's shopping center features **Piggly Wiggly**, a chain food store; **Kerr Drug Store**, a drug store and pharmacy; **Max-Way**, a discount clothing and supply store; and **Village Cleaners & Laundry**, a dry cleaners offering alterations and shoe repair. **West Carteret Medical Center**, operated by Carteret General Hospital, is in the town's shopping center.

Western Carteret County

A number of good stores are scattered throughout the western part of the county. Most communities have a convenience/gas store, a beauty salon and tanning booth, or maybe a craft and flower shop. We have listed a few of the stores you will find there.

Carolina Home and Garden (formerly Russell's Hardware), N.C. 24 in Bogue, offers a variety of hardware, gardening and lawn-care supplies at reasonable prices. The shop is also home to **Yardworks**, a quality landscaping and lawn-care company. **Walston True Value Home Center**, Cedar Point, is an extremely well-equipped store with hardware and building products along with plants and gardening supplies. **Redfearn's Nursery** in Cedar Point has landscaping and potted plants, planters, garden seeds, fertilizers, herbicides or pesticides.

Wild Birds Unlimited, Cedar Point, is a fascinating shop offering special blends of bird seeds, unique feeders for a variety of animals and books and videos on bird types and how to attract birds to your feeder. Wild Birds also has educational items for children, clothing and gifts.

Winberry Farm Produce, N.C. 24, Cedar Point, and **Smith's Produce**, N.C. 24, Ocean, are two well-known roadside stands that offer seasonal local vegetables, Bogue Sound watermelons and cantaloupes.

Antiques

Antiques shops are plentiful along the Crystal Coast. Beaufort offers several antiques shops, and we will highlight just a few. **The Flea Market**, 131 Turner Street, has old furniture, toys, jewelry, kitchen items and hardware. A good number of old nautical items are usually around.

Also in Beaufort is **Waterfront Antiques & Collectibles**, 121 Turner Street, a cozy shop with several rooms displaying a large selection of brass and lots of plates, kitchen gadgets, old furniture, trunks, jewelry, toys, advertising collectibles and children's clothing. **Craven Street Antiques & Collectibles**, 121 Craven Street, buys items and sells antiques, collectibles and furniture. Often you'll find some wonderful items from old Beaufort homes.

Morehead City is also home to a number of antiques shops. **Cheek's Antiques**, 727 Arendell Street, is a good place to start your search. Long established, this shop has a variety of antiques certain to keep you busy browsing. The shop's specialty is matching old sterling. **What Not Shop**, 1015 Arendell Street, is an antiques and collectibles shop that features lots of old Pepsi and Coke memorabilia. **Seaport Antique Market**, 509 Arendell Street, offers more than a dozen vendors' booths set up in an attractive manner to give you an opportunity to see more than one collector's wares at a time. You'll find furniture, books, glassware, knickknacks, jewelry and even some clothing and accessories. On U.S. 70 W., across from the Truckers Toy Store, you'll find **Trash & Treasures**. This is a good place to browse. Take the time to walk through the large collection of old and new stuff — books, porcelain and ceramic statuary, dolls, phonograph records, furniture, lamps and lots of nifty miscellany.

Swansboro's Front Street and the associated side streets are home to several antiques stores. A sampling of those shops is given here. **Lighthouse Antiques**, Front Street, fills a two-story historic house with antiques of almost every sort — miniatures, furniture, clocks, dishes, old decoys and jewelry. One room features pottery, another Chinese antiques and another children's furniture and toys. Shoppers will also find a few decoys, some rugs and jewelry. The **Barber Shop Antiques and Collectibles**, Front Street, features quilts, collectibles, dishes and furniture. **Lazy Lyon's Antiques**, also on Front Street, is an interesting shop to visit. Shoppers may browse among vintage post cards and photographs, old crockery, clothing, antique furniture and much, much more.

Cedar Point is dotted with antiques shops. The town's 5-mile stretch of N.C. 24 between Cape Carteret and Swansboro is a great place to stop and browse. **Swansboro Antique Center** shows the wares of many dealers in a 12,500-square-foot building. You'll find kitchen collections, decoys, hunting and fishing equipment, furniture, quilts, paintings, toys, books, old radios and cameras, political memorabilia, clothing, tobacco and medical products and original stained glass. **Calico Village Antiques and Carpentry Shop** offers oak furniture, bric-a-brac, toys and collectibles. Next door is **The Grapevine**, a rustic old house with antiques, baskets and furniture.

Flea Markets

There are two large flea markets in the area — one between Newport and Morehead City and the other outside Cape Carteret. Both are very active in the summer and have varying winter hours.

Newport-Morehead Flea Mall, U.S. 70, is actually several large open-air buildings joined together. Dozens and dozens of vendors gather here to sell all kinds of items — crafts, appliances, clothing, food, books, antiques, artwork, vegetables, plants and hardware. **Cedar Point Open Air Flea Market**, junction of N.C. highways 24 and 58, offers a tremendous variety with booths rented to dealers who sell everything from baseball cards to original paintings. You'll also find handmade wooden items, plants, uniforms, clothing, cosmetics, produce and jewelry.

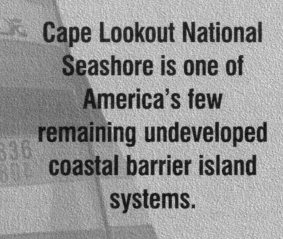

Cape Lookout National Seashore is one of America's few remaining undeveloped coastal barrier island systems.

Attractions

Ocean-related activities and coastal parks are much of what make the Crystal Coast so attractive to tourists and so protected by residents. Natural attractions such as Cape Lookout National Seashore, Fort Macon State Park, Hammocks Beach State Park, Theodore Roosevelt Natural Area, Rachel Carson Estuarine Research Reserve, Croatan National Forest and Cedar Island National Wildlife Refuge offer a wide variety of pristine beaches, maritime forests and waterways to enjoy and explore.

In this chapter we highlight the Crystal Coast's many attractions — the unique cultural and natural histories of the area, natural attractions, the aquarium and museums — that enhance the visit of every tourist and the daily lives of every resident. Among the attractions we've included in this chapter are tours and an outdoor drama that, for some visitors, are the sole reason to be here. Some folks come particularly for annual events that are discussed in detail in our Annual Events chapter. Other things that we Insiders think are particularly attractive about living here, such as county and local parks, we've described in the Sports, Fitness and Parks chapter. For more attractions the whole family will enjoy, especially the kids, see our Kidstuff chapter.

General Attractions

Bogue Banks

North Carolina Aquarium at Pine Knoll Shores
MP 7, Salter Path Rd. (N.C. 58), Pine Knoll Shores • 247-4003

The North Carolina Aquarium at Pine Knoll Shores is one of the most popular attractions on the Crystal Coast and one visit will tell you why. Visitors enjoy exhibits indoors and out, films, talks, programs and workshops on coastal topics, outdoor field trips and other fun and educational activities.

Tucked away in the maritime forest of the Theodore Roosevelt Natural Area, the North Carolina Aquarium is open year round and bustles with activity from spring through fall. The Pine Knoll Shores facility is one of the state's three aquariums. Another is on Roanoke Island near Manteo and one is at Fort Fisher near Wilmington.

Each aquarium conducts a variety of activities and displays numerous exhibits. Showtanks are home to colorful fish and other marine life native to North Carolina waters. The aquariums educate the public about our state's fragile aquatic and marine resources. In fact, the aquariums were first called Marine Resources Centers. They were renamed in 1986 as part of their 10-year anniversary.

While all the programs and exhibits are designed to educate, much fun is involved too. The popular hands-on touch tanks allow everyone to get a feel for and a close-up look at common marine animals. At the Pine Knoll Shores Aquarium, visitors find a collection of freshwater and saltwater plants and animals. The Precious Waters exhibit features a 2,000-gallon salt-marsh tank and a riverbank display with live alligators. Its accompanying video presentation explains conservation issues such as loss of habitat and coastal water quality.

A popular exhibit is the loggerhead nursery, where turtle hatchlings that have been injured, abandoned or for some reason were unable to reach the sea are monitored until they can be safely released into the ocean. Each year, usually in May, the aquarium stages a Turtle Release trip, the aquarium's most popular annual event. This is when these sea turtles are returned to the open sea.

Other popular programs include onboard collecting cruises, canoe trips, snorkeling instruction, interpretive beach walks and excur-

Photo: Scott Taylor

Fishing is fun for everyone!

sions to remote barrier islands. The aquarium's surf-fishing weekend workshop held each fall is a favorite for anglers of all ages.

The aquarium publishes a calendar of events four times a year that lists all programs and activities. Some field trips, classes and workshops require a nominal fee and all require advance registration. To register or to find out about programs call 247-4003.

The aquarium's outdoor Salt Marsh Safari exhibit along Bogue Sound features overlooks, bird scopes and informational signs that discuss the importance of the salt marsh and the plants and animals living there. The exhibit's winding boardwalk leads to the Alice G. Hoffman Nature Trail, a short half-mile loop through an ancient maritime forest. An interpretive trail brochure is available at the visitor service desk. The aquarium's newest exhibit is an outdoor Fossil Dig. Visitors can sign up for a program that allows them to sift through fossil-bearing soil in search of sharks' teeth, animal bones, fish vertebrae, plant imprints and other age-old relics.

Back inside, the aquarium gift shop offers an inviting selection of educational and environmentally aware items ranging from pens, pencils and puzzles to T-shirts, CDs and pottery. For gift shop information call 247-3599.

Admission fees are: adults, $3; senior citi-

zens and active military, $2; children (6 to 17 years old), $1; registered school groups, Aquarium Society members and children younger than age 6, free of charge. Admission fees have created a special fund to be used for expansion, renovations and improvements of the three state aquarium facilities. Plans have been designed for each facility and the funding phase is in progress. Membership in the Aquarium Society entitles participants to newsletters, calendars, special functions and discounts on programs and gift-shop purchases. Aquarium society members are also entitled to free admission to each of the state's three aquariums and to more than 120 other zoos and aquariums across the country.

Aquarium hours are 9 AM to 7 PM daily Memorial Day through Labor Day and 9 AM to 5 PM daily the remainder of the year.

Beaufort

Beaufort Historic Site
100 Block of Turner St., Beaufort
• 728-5225, (800) 575-SITE

The Beaufort Historic Site is a large area in the center of town that is the home of 13 restored houses and buildings. Cared for by the Beaufort Historical Association, the site is avail-

able for tours as well as classes, workshops and events throughout the year.

Most of the restored buildings were moved to the site from other locations in town. These moves were necessitated in many cases by property owners who were ready to tear down an old structure to build a new one. Among the restored buildings on the site are those described below.

Josiah Bell House, c. 1825, is the large yellow house used as the welcome center for the Beaufort Historic Site. Its Victorian furnishings reflect the typical customs of its original era. **Samuel Leffers Cottage**, c. 1778, was once the schoolmaster's house. It is furnished in a primitive style and features a Beaufort-type roof line.

Carteret County Courthouse of 1796 was the county's third courthouse and is the oldest public building remaining in Beaufort. It has been restored with authentic furnishings. **Old County Jail**, c. 1829, is in excellent condition. Its three cells and jailkeeper's quarters were in use until 1954. There is a museum room in one of the cells. The **Apothecary Shop and Doctor's Office**, c. 1859, features a wonderful collection of medical instruments and memorabilia from the first county doctors and dentists. **R. Rustell House**, c. 1732, is home to the Mattie King Davis Art Gallery. In its time, it was a typical Beaufort cottage and was owned by prominent early citizen Richard Rustell Jr.

Guided tours of the Beaufort Historic Site depart the Safrit Historical Center (at the south end of the historic site) Monday through Saturday year round.

After a tour of the historic site, hop on the old English double-decker bus for a terrific narrated tour of Beaufort's historic district complete with stories of town residents who colorfully peopled local history. Bus tours depart the historic site on Monday, Wednesday and Saturday. Architectural walking tours of Beaufort's historic district are guided on Monday and Thursday, and guided tours of the **Old Burying Grounds** are offered anytime with a minimum of five people. In addition, the Beaufort Historical Association conducts its annual Beaufort Old Homes Tour during the last weekend in June (see our Annual Events chapter). Activities include tours of private and association-owned homes, musical performances, an antique show and sale, military re-enactments and more.

The Robert W. and Elva Faison Safrit Historical Center, in the first block of Turner Street on the south end of the site, welcomes and orients visitors to the historical site with exhibits, video presentations and demonstrations before they begin touring the buildings. The gift shop is located here. For information about the Beaufort Historic Site or any of its activities, stop by the Safrit Historical Center. We guarantee you'll wish you had a few more days in town.

N.C. Maritime Museum
315 Front St., Beaufort • 728-7317

The N.C. Maritime Museum interprets North Carolina's historical alliances with the sea. The museum's theme, "Down to the Sea," celebrates the state's coastal heritage, maritime and natural history and natural resources.

The 18,000-square-foot building is constructed of wood and resembles facilities used in the 19th century by the U.S. Lifesaving Service, the forerunner of the U.S. Coast Guard. The museum's interior is designed to impart the feeling of being in the hold of a large ship. On the ground floor are exhibit areas, offices, an auditorium, a classroom, library and gift shop.

The museum houses an impressive collection of ship models, ranging from sailing skiffs to full-rigged ships, including a model of

---

INSIDERS' TIP

Phillips Island is in the Newport River just north of the N.C. State Port in Morehead City. From the high-rise bridge passing by the port, it is the most visible of several local islands leased by the National Audubon Society for the protection of nesting colonial waterbirds. A brick chimney on the island is all that remains of a defunct fish processing facility.

the *Snapdragon*, once captained by the privateer Otway Burns of Swansboro. Burns sailed the North Carolina coast during the War of 1812. Other museum exhibits include native coastal birds, fish and mammal specimens, marine fossils and artifacts, decoys, small watercraft and salt water aquariums. The museum also houses a huge collection of sea shells, the Brantley and Maxine Watson collection, from international and local waters. The museum's library offers the best references and periodicals collection you'll find in maritime topics, and you're welcome to use it while you're there.

Museum programming reflects maritime and natural history of North Carolina. Films, talks, lectures, concerts, field trips and instruction are conducted for the public year round and are announced in the museum's quarterly calendar. Preregistration is required for some activities. The museum's gift shop is the best place to find a special book on natural or maritime history or a navigational or topographical map.

The Cape Lookout Studies Program is a special educational program that began operating through the museum in 1989. It has been a smashing success. The program is actually an intense short course of study designed to meet the needs of any particular group. Groups of eight to 15 people stay at the old Coast Guard Station on Cape Lookout to learn about and experience coastal ecology. Courses of study have included dolphin behavior, tern and turtle nesting, barrier island ecology and other marine-related subjects.

Each year, the museum hosts its Traditional Wooden Boat Show, which features beautiful handcrafted boats, music, boat races, talks, entertainment and displays (see our Annual Events chapter).

The N.C. Maritime Museum is open year round and designs its programs and activities for the interests of all ages. Its Junior Sailing Program offers sailing skills instruction in classes scheduled from June through August, and Summer Science School for youngsters addresses such subjects as sea shells, ma-

Keep Your Eyes on the Sea for Dolphins

If you're walking along the beach and see fins gliding in and out of the water just offshore, don't be alarmed. Chances are you're being treated to a passing display of bottle-nosed dolphins. If you're really lucky, you'll see one catapult from the watery depths to leap above the horizon simply for the fun of it.

Close-up

These friendly, sleek, streamlined marine mammals are permanent residents in waters along the Crystal Coast. People often call them porpoises, but on the Eastern Seaboard, porpoises range only as far as New Jersey. What we have here are bottle-nosed dolphins.

Worldwide, there are about 80 species of whales and dolphins. Several species live and pass through offshore waters along our coast, including spotted, striped and common dolphins. Technically, dolphins are small-toothed whales, and because they give live birth and nurse their young, they are marine mammals. During summer, when calves are born, dolphins tend to concentrate in tidal rivers and estuaries along our coast. These areas provide plenty of food and shelter from large sharks. Still, many dolphins swim in and out of the inlets and can be seen traveling in groups just beyond the breakers along shore.

Dolphins don't eat anything that can't be swallowed whole. In local waters, their main diet consists of crabs, mullet, menhaden, flounder and other small fish. Studies have shown that some dolphins are local residents, while others are seasonal or migratory. Along the Crystal Coast, dolphins are commonly seen during the summer months in Back Sound, Core Sound, Bogue Sound, North River, Newport River, Nelson Bay and the community of Straits. Here they feed, mate and raise their young. Feeding activity can frequently be seen late on summer afternoons around the rock jetties off Radio Island and Fort Macon. In late fall, they leave the estuaries and head for open water, where they live and feed through April.

Photo: Scott Taylor

Bottle-nosed dolphins are a delight to see in coastal waters.

— continued on next page

Dolphins are air breathers. They have lungs, not gills, and must come to the surface to breathe. Rather than breathing through a nose like humans, dolphins breathe through a blowhole in the top of their heads. Boaters anchored in creeks, coves and bays often hear dolphins blow nearby. Exhibiting an unusual friendliness and perpetual smile, dolphins may follow alongside boats, sometimes swimming ahead or body surfing on the boat's wake.

The intelligence of dolphins is hard to determine, although there seems little question that their brains are highly developed. Marine parks have trained them to perform amazing stunts, and the military has been able to teach them to carry out complicated maneuvers. In the wild, however, they don't always display dolphin-perfect judgment. They sometimes wind up in places they're not supposed to be — like stuck in water that's too shallow. Similar to a sailboat that's run aground, they have to wait until the tide rises before they can float to freedom. Such a predicament poses a threat to these animals because they can become overheated in the sun and die. If you see a stranded dolphin, call the local Marine Mammal Strandings Network at 728-8762.

Dolphins' eating habits are perplexing. Stomach contents of dead dolphins have turned up cigarette lighters, fishing lures, rocks, camera lens caps and other foreign materials. Whether the dolphin ate them, or whether the dolphin ate a fish that ate them, is not known.

People often confuse the dolphin mammal with the dolphin fish. Believe us, when you see dolphin on a restaurant menu, you are not eating Flipper. The dolphin fish is now commonly listed on restaurant menus as mahi-mahi, dorado or other names to avoid confusion.

When you are out on the beach, scan the waters just past the breakers and you might see these graceful marine mammals surfacing and descending in a smooth flowing line as they feed, play and enjoy their water world.

rine archaeology, pirates, fishing and salt marsh habitats (see our Kidstuff chapter). Field trips and programs for both adults and children range from how to harvest, clean and cook clams to hands-on trawl and dredge trips aboard a research vessel. A trained naturalist might take adventurers on a hike through the marshes, on a trek to look for waterfowl or on a boat ride to explore one of the area's many surrounding undeveloped islands. Whatever the topic, a unique coastal experience is sure to follow.

No admission fee is charged; museum hours are from 9 AM to 5 PM Monday through Friday, 10 AM to 5 PM Saturday and 2 to 5 PM Sunday.

Late in 1996, North Carolina budgeted $1 million for expansion plans of the N.C. Maritime Museum. Plans include a waterside expansion of the existing facilities on Front Street and the acquisition of property north of the Grayden Paul drawbridge on Town Creek. The new property could involve the restoration of a closed menhaden processing plant now on the site, the necessary facilities to move the junior sailing program to the site, natural history areas, underwater archeology and boat-restoration labs. Projected plans for the N.C. Maritime Museum would render it the largest maritime museum on the East Coast.

Harvey W. Smith Watercraft Center
Front St., Beaufort • 728-7317

This beautiful watercraft center is an extension of the N.C. Maritime Museum and is just across the street on the waterfront. The watercraft center is a busy, bustling arena of activity, where the sounds of hammers, saws and drills and the smells of wood chips and salt air bring images of traditional boatbuilding and early seafarers. The center's viewing platform above the boatshop floor allows visitors to observe the process of making boats. In addition to boatbuilding and restoration projects, the center offers classes in boatbuilding carpentry, oar making, lofting, tool making and halfmodeling. It also houses the John S. MacCormack Model Shop, where model builders construct scale models of a variety of vessels, including the colonial merchantmen, small craft and other historical ships. No admission is charged. Hours are 9 AM to 5 PM Tuesday through Friday; 10 AM to 5 PM, Saturday; 1 to 5 PM, Sunday.

Morehead City

Carteret County
Museum of History and Art
100 Wallace Dr., Morehead City • 247-7533

In 1985, the Carteret County Historical Society was given the old Camp Glenn School building, c. 1907, which had served the community first as a school and later as a church, a flea market and a print shop. The society moved the building from its earlier location to Wallace Drive, facing the parking lots of Carteret Community College and the Crystal Coast Civic Center, just off Arendell Street in Morehead City. The members renovated the building and created a museum to show visitors and residents how life used to be in Carteret County. There are rotating exhibits with emphasis on the area's Native American heritage, schools, businesses and homes. The museum houses the society's research library, including an impressive Civil War collection, that is available to those interested in genealogy and history. The museum conducts occasional genealogy workshops. Monthly exhibits feature area artists, and there is a gift shop. The museum is open Tuesday through Saturday from l until 4 PM. There is no admission charge.

Crystal Coast Civic Center
3505 Arendell St., Morehead City
• 247-3883

On the campus of Carteret Community College overlooking Bogue Sound, the Crystal Coast Civic Center is the largest facility of its kind on the North Carolina coast. A multiple-use facility with a 12,000-square-foot exhibition hall, the civic center can accommodate meetings of 1,000 people or dinners for 800, or its space can be divided into smaller areas. Each year the Crystal Coast Civic Center hosts events that are major attractions to the resort area, from the North Carolina Commercial Fishing Show to the Festival of Trees. Exhibitions and trade shows are frequent throughout the year, as are peripheral events such as awards dinners for the Big Rock and the Hardee's Atlantic Beach King Mackerel fishing tournaments and the Opening Ceremonies Luncheon and the Blessing of the Fleet during the North Carolina Seafood Festival weekend. Many private businesses and families schedule use of the Crystal Coast Civic Center for events involving a large number of people. Accommodations include a snack bar, full-service catering kitchen, public address system, portable stage and a 5,600-square-foot outdoor plaza overlooking beautiful Bogue Sound.

Down East

Core Sound Waterfowl Museum
S.R. 1335, Harkers Island • 728-1500

Established in 1988 as an outgrowth of efforts by the Decoy Carvers Guild, the Core Sound Waterfowl Museum is funded entirely by its own membership, which numbers more than 2000. Each December, the museum hosts the Core Sound Decoy Festival (see the Annual Events chapter), a weekend-long gathering of waterfowl artists and decoy carvers held at the Harkers Island Elementary School.

Truly a grassroots effort, the museum, located just east of the school, houses decoys from the collections of such renowned local carvers as the late Homer Fulcher, Eldon Willis and Julian Hamilton. It has pieces by Jack

---

INSIDERS' TIP

Both the N.C. Aquarium and the N.C. Maritime Museum schedule guided tours focused on specific ecological environments of the Crystal Coast. Quarterly calendars are available at each facility for making trip plans, and all trips require reservations.

Dudley, author of *Core Sound Waterfowl Heritage*, and a Dixon reproduction decoy. Also exhibited are the blue-ribbon pieces from all past Core Sound Decoy Festival competitions in the decoy painting, gunning shore birds and best-in-show categories. Carving demonstrations are continuous living history exhibits. The museum gift shop carries books, stationery, shirts, canvas geese and decorative decoys.

Plans are progressing to build a permanent museum building at the end of the road in Harkers Island next to the Cape Lookout National Seashore Park Service headquarters. Fund-raising efforts for the planned $2 million museum facility, which will be completely financed by membership contributions, began at the 1994 Core Sound Decoy Festival. Willow Pond, the 4-acre freshwater centerpiece of the museum's environmental education program, was restored in 1996 with financial efforts of Ducks Unlimited and volunteer labors.

There is no admission charge to enjoy the Core Sound Waterfowl Museum. Hours from Easter to Christmas are Monday through Saturday, 10 AM to 5 PM; Sunday, 2 PM to 5 PM. Winters, museum hours are Wednesday through Saturday, 10 AM to 5 PM. Membership categories range from $25 for individuals to various statuses of contribution support.

Outdoor Drama

Crystal Coast Amphitheater/ Worthy Is The Lamb
N.C. 58, Peletier • 393-8373, (800) 662-5960

This 2,100-seat amphitheater overlooks the White Oak River in the little community of Pelletier, just north of Cape Carteret. The amphitheater is home to *Worthy is the Lamb*, the only fully orchestrated musical passion play in production in the country. The spectacular presentation is a sensitive, moving composition of art, spoken word and music with insightful, spiritual reflections that reveal a com-

Built in 1859, The Cape Lookout lighthouse is still an active aid to navigation.

pelling portrait of the life and times of Christ. The amphitheater was awarded the Nisbet Award in 1995 by the Travel Council of North Carolina based on its positive impact on state tourism.

The production features costumes, ships, horses and chariots that reflect the pageantry of the period when Christ was alive. Sets have been carefully constructed to create a replica of the city of Jerusalem. State-of-the-art technology in computer-coordinated sound, lighting and special effects provide consistently outstanding performance quality. The

soundtrack was recorded in London at the same historic English cathedral where the soundtracks for such movies as *Greystoke: The Legend of Tarzan* and *Yentl* were produced.

Worthy is the Lamb performances are staged at 8:30 PM Thursday through Saturday from mid-June through August. In September, performances begin at 7:30 PM on Friday and Saturday only. Adult tickets are $11; senior citizens, $9; children ages 6 through 12, $6. Discounts are offered to groups of 15 or more and active military.

Tours

Crystal Queen
600 Front St., Beaufort • 728-2527

Docked in Taylor's Creek on the Beaufort waterfront, the red, white and blue 82-foot paddle wheeler *Crystal Queen* is available for a variety of scenic tours. Licensed for 150 passengers, the *Crystal Queen* includes a snack bar with soft drinks, beer and wine on its enclosed, heated and air-conditioned lower deck. It also has a canopy and sundeck (complete with foul weather curtains) on its upper deck.

The tour boat offers several daily 1½-hour narrated sightseeing cruises in season. Two-hour evening dinner cruises are scheduled by reservation and usually have live musical entertainment aboard. Departure times for tours and dinner cruises are generally fixed during the summer months and change according to demand; call for departure times.

Tours take sightseers along the Morehead and Beaufort waterfronts, Shackleford Banks and surrounding waterways. The *Crystal Queen* also accepts private charters so you can choose your own route. Help is available with food planning, and the boat has all ABC permits.

Group rates, active military and senior discounts are available; children ages 6 to 12 ride at a reduced rate; children 5 and younger ride free. Call for rates, departure times and reservations or fax to 728-1644.

Mystery Tours
Front St., Beaufort • 728-7827

Docked in Taylor's Creek in front of the Beaufort House Restaurant, the 65-foot double-decked *Mystery* tour boat takes cruises along 18 miles of area waterways. Complete with a covered cabin, snack bar and resident pirate who delights all the passengers, especially kids, the boat provides visitors with a water view of Beaufort's historic homes, island ponies, salt marshes, bird rookeries, Morehead City State Port, Fort Macon, Shackleford Banks and other islands along the Intracoastal Waterway. Tours last 1½ hours and are conducted daily at 2, 4:30 and 7 PM, April through October. Costs are $8 for adults, $5 for children ages 6 through 12, and free for children younger than 6. The *Mystery* also charters half-day fishing trips from 8 AM to noon and can make arrangements for dinner cruises. The boat is available for special-occasion charters such as birthdays, weddings and anniversaries. Special-interest trips can be arranged for birders, shell collectors and other groups.

White Sand Trail Rides
N.C. 12., Cedar Island • 729-0911

There are beach trails to explore on horseback about as far Down East as you can go before getting wet. Lots of packages are available, but owner Wayland Cato also offers a half-hour ride just for kids. The 45-minute drive from Beaufort through Down East is a great exploration trip too. Stop along the way at Harkers Island to visit the Core Sound Waterfowl Museum or at the Cedar Island Wildlife Refuge. In fact, this trip could pretty much devour a whole day.

Ecology Tours

Coastal Adventures
N.C. Coastal Federation
3609 N.C. 24, Ocean • 393-8185

The North Carolina Coastal Federation is an active organization focused on protection of the coastal environment and culture through its activities in education, information and legislative accountability. It conducts fascinating tours from May through October as part of its education effort.

On Mondays, a Croatan National Forest Safari takes explorers into the land of carnivorous plants. Venus's-flytraps, sundews, butterworts and four varieties of pitcher plants proliferate in the Croatan. A one- or two-hour trail exploration of longleaf pines and the Patsy Pond natural area departs by appointment and is free of charge.

On Tuesdays an Open Beach and Inlet Investigation is offered to observe the changes effected on Bogue Inlet and nearby beaches by modern and historic development. The small boat trip explores a salt-marsh habitat and allows for shell-collecting at Hammocks Beach State Park.

Each Wednesday, a Barrier Island and Sound Adventure is a boating trip to sample marine life from sound waters and islands. The importance of the sound as a food source and critical habitat is discussed as are the conflicting demands within this ecosystem.

Thursday's boating venture is into the estuaries of Bogue Sound on a Trawl and Seine Expedition. Samples of marine life are collected in shallow waters for a look at their dependence on water quality.

All trips are scheduled through the Coastal Federation office, and all but the trail tour require a small but well-spent fee.

State and National Parks

The Crystal Coast is fortunate to have national, state and local parks scattered from one border to the other. Here, we offer a look at national and state parks. Local parks are described in our Sports, Fitness and Parks chapter. Our coastal area parks are dazzling with historic interest and natural beauty, so get out there and enjoy them.

Fort Macon State Park
MP 0, E. Fort Macon Rd. (N.C. 58), Atlantic Beach • 726-3775

Fort Macon State Park, at the east end of Bogue Banks, is North Carolina's most visited state park, and with around 1.4 million visitors each year, it is the Crystal Coast's most visited attraction. Initially the fort served to protect the channel and Beaufort harbor against attacks from the sea. Today the danger of naval attack is remote, but during the 18th and 19th centuries this region was very vulnerable. The need for defense was clearly illustrated in 1747 when Spanish raiders captured Beaufort and again in 1782 when the British took over the port town.

Construction of Fort Dobbs, named for Governor Arthur Dobbs, began here in 1756 but was never completed. In 1808-09 Fort Hampton, a small masonry fort, was built to guard the inlet. The fort was abandoned shortly after the War of 1812 and by 1825 had been swept into the inlet.

Designed by Brig. Gen. Simon Bernard and built by the U.S. Army Corps of Engineers, Fort Macon was completed in 1834 at a cost of

---

INSIDERS' TIP

Expansion plans for both the N.C. Aquarium and the N.C. Maritime Museum promise big changes. These tourist attractions of the late-20th century promise to be tourist destinations in the 21st century.

$463,790. The fort was named for Nathaniel Macon who was speaker of the House of Representatives and a U.S. Senator from North Carolina. The five-sided structure was built of brick and stone with outer walls 4.5 feet thick. The fort was deactivated after 1877 and then regarrisoned by state troops in 1898 for the Spanish-American War. It was abandoned again in 1903, was not used in World War I and was offered for sale in 1923. An Act of Congress in 1924 gave the fort and the surrounding land to the state of North Carolina to be used as a public park. The park, which is more than 400 acres, opened in 1936 and was North Carolina's first functioning state park.

At the outbreak of World War II, the Army leased the park from the state and, once again, manned the fort to protect a number of important nearby facilities. In 1944, the fort was returned to the state, and the park reopened the following year.

Today, Fort Macon State Park offers the best of two worlds — beautiful, easily accessible beaches for recreation and a historic fort for exploration. Visitors enjoy the sandy beaches, a seaside bathhouse and restrooms, a refreshment stand, designated fishing and swimming areas and picnic facilities with outdoor grills. A short nature trail winds through dense shrubs and over low sand dunes. The park is abundant with wildlife, including herons, egrets, warblers, sparrows and other animals.

The fort itself is a wonderful place to explore with a self-guided tour map or with a tour guide. A museum and bookstore offer exhibits to acquaint you with the fort and its history. The fort and museum are open daily year round. Fort tours are guided through late fall. Re-enactments of fort activities are scheduled periodically from spring to fall. Talks on the Civil War, natural history and a variety of nature walks are conducted year round. The fort is open daily from 9 AM to 5:30 PM. The fort office is open Monday through Friday from 8 AM to 5 PM.

Beside the park is Fort Macon Coast Guard Base, home port of four large cutters and several smaller vessels. The base is charged with patrolling the area from Drum Inlet on Core Banks south to the North Carolina-South Carolina border (see our Military chapter).

Theodore Roosevelt Natural Area
MP 7, Roosevelt Dr., Pine Knoll Shores
• 726-3775

This little gem of a nature trail is alongside the N.C. Aquarium on Roosevelt Drive in Pine Knoll Shores. Maintained and operated by Fort Macon State Park, the 265 acres have extensive maritime forests and freshwater ponds. The land was donated to the state by the family of Theodore Roosevelt, the country's 26th president. The forest attracts naturalists, birdwatchers and photographers. The nearby aquarium offers a nature trail guide that is available in the aquarium gift shop.

This soundside trail is a good place to see land birds. The marshes along this section of Bogue Banks are not extensive, so there are few marsh or water birds. The best birding along the trail is from mid-April through May or in late fall and winter. Mosquitoes take over the trail from late spring through early fall, so arrive prepared.

Rachel Carson Component of the North Carolina National Estuarine Research Reserve
430-B W. Beaufort Rd., Beaufort
• 728-2170

Just across Taylor's Creek from the Beaufort waterfront is a series of islands that make up the Rachel Carson Component of the North Carolina National Estuarine Research Reserve. Most locals refer to the entire chain of islands as Bird Shoal or Carrot Island, the names the islands were known by before the state acquired the land.

These islands are roughly 3.5 miles long and have an interesting recent history. Through the years, the land was privately owned by individuals or groups. In 1977, when the owner of 178.5 acres announced plans to divide the land and sell it in tracts, locals formed The Beaufort Land Conservancy Council and began collecting money and support for preserving the island chain. They sought the aid of the Nature Conservancy, a national nonprofit organization dedicated to the protection of natural areas, and together the groups raised $250,000 from individuals and businesses for the purchase of the islands. Now the state of North Carolina manages the island reserve.

In the late l960s Congress recognized the need to protect coastal resources from pollution and the pressures of development. In particular danger were the nation's estuaries, those valuable, fragile areas where rivers meet the sea. So the National Estuarine Research Reserve was established. Now administered by the North Carolina Division of Coastal Management, the reserves are sites for walking, exploring, researching and educating about the natural and human processes that affect the coast.

Estuary waters make up the bays, sounds, inlets and sloughs along the coast and are among the most biologically productive systems on earth. More than two-thirds of the fish and shellfish commercially harvested in coastal waters spend part or all of their lives in estuaries. The economy of many coastal areas depends heavily on the health of these environments. North Carolina is fortunate to have four protected sites: Zeke's Island, Currituck Banks, Masonboro Island and Rachel Carson.

This site was named in honor of the late scientist and author, Rachel Carson, who did research on the islands in the 1940s and, through her research and writing, made people aware of the importance of coastal ecosystems. The Rachel Carson site is made up of salt marshes, tidal flats, ellgrass beds, sand flats and artificially created dredge spoil islands. It is a favorite spot for beachcombing, swimming, sunbathing and clamming but camping is not allowed. Visitors are encouraged to leave everything — the animals, plants and research equipment — undisturbed. You'll need a boat to get there, and there are a few that can be hired to take you (see our Getting Around chapter).

The Rachel Carson site is home to a number of feral ponies descended from domesticated ponies that were taken to the islands to graze. They now roam the sandy expanse, living in small bands called harems, each consisting of one stallion, several mares and the year's foals. Bachelor males roam the island alone or in pairs. These are either older stallions who have lost their harem to a younger, stronger male or young stallions who have not yet challenged the dominant males. The ponies paw watering holes in the sand and often fight over the limited supply of water. As a result of the damage to the marsh caused by grazing and the seasonal food shortages that affect the ponies, the Division of Coastal Management began to control the size of the herd with birth control medication in 1996. Optimal herd size for the available food and water supply is around 30. The research reserve is also home to about 160 species of birds.

Site education coordinators conduct free tours of the reserve twice a month from May through August, but boat transportation arrangements must be made to get there (see Getting Around). A self-guided trail brochure is available at the N.C. Maritime Museum, the reserve office or at ferry service offices. An information sign about the reserve is displayed on Front Street in Beaufort across from the Inlet Inn.

Hammocks Beach State Park
1572 Hammocks Beach Rd., Swansboro • (910) 326-4881

Venture to Hammocks Beach State Park on Bear Island and be rewarded with one of the most beautiful and unspoiled beaches in the area. The park consists of a barrier island off the southernmost point of Bogue Banks and a small area off N.C. 24 just south of the residential area of Swansboro where the park office and ferry landing are located. Watch for state directional signs. There is a small fee for the ferry to Bear Island, which operates on a schedule year round. Weekend ranger programs are conducted for visitors.

On Bear Island loggerhead turtles come ashore at night during nesting season to nest above the tide line. Explorers can discover marine life in tidal creeks and mudflats. The island is accessible only by ferry (see our Getting Around chapter), and camping is allowed (see our Camping chapter).

A bathhouse with snack bar used to provide the only shade and comfort facilities on the island, but they were destroyed by Hurricane Fran in the fall of 1996. Go prepared to shade yourself and with the refreshments you'll need. It's a half-mile walk from the ferry landing to the ocean beach. With picnic baskets, umbrellas and beach supplies, the arriving passengers huffing over dunes are reminiscent of beachgoers in the 1920s. The trip is always worth any trouble along the way.

Cape Lookout National Seashore
131 Charles St., Harkers Island • 728-2250

Cape Lookout National Seashore is one of America's few remaining undeveloped coastal barrier island systems. It includes about 28,500 acres of barrier island environment bounded on the north by Ocracoke Inlet and on the south by Beaufort Inlet. Three islands make up the 56-mile seashore: North Core Banks, also known as Portsmouth Island; South Core Banks, or Cape Lookout; and Shackleford Banks. Each island is distinctive in history and characteristics.

Cape Lookout National Seashore was authorized by the United States Congress to be included in the National Park System in 1966. The National Park Service (NPS) maintains authority over the seashore.

The seashore's pristine ocean beaches offer surfcasters, sunbathers, surfers, snorklers and shell collectors a wonderful escape. Other recreational pursuits in the park include picnicking, primitive camping, migratory waterfowl watching and hunting. The area is noted for its natural resources. Birds and animals are the only permanent residents. The endangered loggerhead sea turtle nests on the beaches each summer and seldom nests any farther north. The park is an inviting habitat for the plentiful resident and migrant birds. Raccoons, rabbits, nutria, a variety of insects, snakes and lizards are also among the park's permanent residents. Ghost crabs, mole crabs and coquina clams populate the beaches.

Cape Lookout National Seashore is surrounded by water and can only be reached by private or commercial boat. For some sites, limited ground transportation can be arranged with the ferry operator prior to departure, as can accommodations (see the Ferries section of our Getting Around chapter). Camping is permitted anywhere in the park (see our Camping chapter) except in posted areas.

One objective of the National Park System in preserving the banks was to return them to their natural state, and the acquisition of privately owned cabins, which are visible from the Cape Lookout light, caused some ruffles. Some owners proved their points and were granted lifetime or 25-year leases on property that have mostly, by now, reverted to the National Park Service. No further development on the islands is allowed.

The horses on Shackleford Banks are also considered by the National Park Service to be unnatural, or exotic, to the island environment. The removal of horses from the island is a heated controversy with few paths for an easy compromise. The NPS proposes removal of 75 percent of the herd, all but around 50 horses, and use of birth control medications on the remaining horses. Defending the horses' presence as natural to the island, groups have presented historical documentation of their presence more than 400 years ago. From the beginning of the relationship between residents with personal history on these islands and the NPS, controversy has been the most natural state.

The Cape Lookout Lighthouse is still an active aid to navigation. The first lighthouse was built on Core Banks in 1811-12 and was painted with red and white stripes. The current lighthouse was completed in 1859 as the prototype for other North Carolina lighthouses and wears a distinctive black and white diamond pattern.

Visitors are welcomed in the restored lighthouse keeper's quarters that houses a small natural history collection. Other associated structures (coal shed, etc.) are also preserved near the lighthouse where there is shelter for picnicking, a nice swimming beach and a boardwalk that leads from the lighthouse area, over the dunes, to the ocean beach.

At the northernmost end of Core Banks at Ocracoke Inlet is **Portsmouth Village**. The village was established in 1753 to serve as the main port of entry to several coastal communities. Named for Portsmouth, England, the port village was busy with lightering incoming vessels, an unloading and reloading process that allowed vessels to pass through the shallow Ocracoke Inlet. During its heyday in the 1860s, the village had a population of about 600. After Hatteras Inlet opened, the village became less important in its port services.

From 1894 to 1934, the population of Portsmouth was mainly concerned with its lifesaving station. After a severe hurricane in 1935, the village population declined, and by the early 1970s, no year-round residents remained.

Today, the village looks much like it did in the early 1900s. The remaining homes, cemeteries, church and pathways are still used by former residents and their descendants. A reunion occurs each year in Portsmouth Village. Structures that are not privately owned are maintained by the Park Service. Portsmouth Village was placed on the National Register of Historic Places in 1979 and is guided by policies of the National Historic Preservation Act.

Looking east from Fort Macon, **Shackleford Banks** is the island across the Beaufort Inlet. It stretches 9 miles east to Cape Lookout, bordered by the Atlantic Ocean on the south and Back Sound on the north. The island's sound side has long been a favorite weekend destination for residents escaping the peopled mainland beaches. The rock jetty is a favorite spot for anglers.

Shackleford Banks officially became part of Cape Lookout National Seashore on the first day of 1986. Until then, the island was dotted with cabins, or camps, that former banks residents and their descendants continued to use as getaway shelters. The acquisition of Shackleford Banks meant removing the structures and livestock that had been left to roam the island. Before 1986, the island was home to hearty herds of wild cattle, sheep, goats, pigs and horses. Today, only the horses have been allowed to remain, and management plans for them are currently in question.

The island was named for Francis Shackleford, who was granted the land in 1705. Permanent residents once populated communities on Shackleford. The largest community was Diamond City at the east end. By 1897, about 500 people populated Diamond City in a community complete with church buildings, stores, a post office and a school. According to information provided in *Island Born and Bred*, a history/cookbook compiled by Harkers Island Methodist Women, the most growth occurred in the 1850s because of a boom in the local whaling industry.

New England whaling vessels visited the area as early as 1726. By 1880 six crews of 18 men from Diamond City were whaling off the banks' shores. The whalers were a hearty people and included families of Davises, Moores, Guthries, Royals and Roses — names still common in Carteret County. When a lookout spotted a whale, crews would launch their

THE NORTH CAROLINA
SEAFOOD  FESTIVAL

always the

First Weekend in October

Morehead City Waterfront

 Live Entertainment

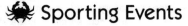 Sporting Events

 Activities

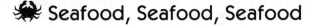 Seafood, Seafood, Seafood

---

P.O. Box 1812 • Morehead City, NC 28557
(919) 726-6273 (NCSF)

small rowing boats to harpoon the creature. If successful, a crewman would signal villagers on shore by holding an oar in the air. When the boats came ashore, pots of boiling water would be ready to process the blubber into valuable oil. Merchants in Beaufort and Morehead City sold the oil as lamp oil and lubricating oil or used it to make soap. Whale bone was valuable in making corset stays, ribs for umbrellas and other items. They sold the rest of the whale as fertilizer.

East of Diamond City, across what is now Barden's Inlet, was the community of Cape Lookout. West of Diamond City was Bell's Island, a settlement known for bountiful persimmon trees. The western part of Shackleford Banks was known as Wade's Shore. Two hurricanes that followed each other closely in 1896 and 1899 convinced most island inhabitants to move to the mainland. Many moved their homes by boat to Harkers Island or Morehead City. Others resettled in Salter Path on Bogue Banks.

Cedar Island National Wildlife Refuge
Lola Rd., Cedar Island • 225-2511

This 12,500-acre wildlife refuge on the southern end of Cedar Island is maintained by the U.S. Fish and Wildlife Service, which provides areas for hiking, bird-watching, launching boats, picnicking and hunting. No ranger services are available.

Waterfowl abundant during the year include mallards, black ducks, redheads, pintails and green-winged teals. Other wildlife at home in the refuge are raccoons, deer, bears, woodpeckers and river otters. In the spring and fall, this is a delightful picnicking and birdwatching destination.

The Cedar Island Wildlife Refuge was formed in 1964 to build waterfowl impoundments, primarily to help the black duck. All the planned impoundments were not created due to government funding interruptions. There are some restrictions for hunting on the impoundment.

The access is well-marked on Cedar Island. Turn on Lola Road and follow it to the refuge office. One boat ramp is across from the office, and another is at the base of the Monroe Gaskill Memorial high-rise bridge.

Croatan National Forest
141 E. Fisher Ave., New Bern • 638-5628

Croatan National Forest is made up of 157,000 acres spread in a triangle between Morehead City, Cape Carteret and New Bern. Forest headquarters are on Fisher Avenue, approximately 9 miles east of New Bern off Highway 70. Well-placed road signs make the office easy to find.

Because the Croatan is so expansive and undeveloped, it is best to pick up a forest map from the headquarters if you plan to explore extensively. For short daytrips or hiking excursions, site brochures are sufficient.

The name Croatan comes from the Algonquian Indians' name for "Council Town," which was once located in the area. Because of the forest's coastal location, you'll find many unusual features here. Some of the components of the ecosystem are pocosins, longleaf and loblolly pine, bottomland and upland hardwoods.

Sprinkled throughout the Croatan are 40 miles of streams and 4,300 acres of wild lakes, some fairly large such as Great Lake, Catfish Lake and Long Lake. Miles of unpaved roads lace through the woodland providing easy, if sometimes roundabout, access to its wilderness.

The forest offers excellent hiking, swimming, boating, camping, picnicking, hunting and fresh and saltwater fishing. Boat access is provided at several locations. Rangers advise that lake fishing is generally poor because of the acidity of the water. All fishing, hunting and trapping activities are regulated by the N.C. Wildlife Resources Commission. The forest has several camping sites (see our Camping chapter) that are open most of the year. Primitive camping is permitted all year and sites are plentiful. Some areas of the forest close seasonally, and fees can vary, so call headquarters for current rates and availability.

As with all national forests, the Croatan's natural resources are actively managed to provide goods and services for the public. Pine timber is harvested and replanted each year, and wildlife habitat for a wide range of animals is maintained on thousands of acres. Endangered and sensitive animal and plant species are protected. The red-cockaded woodpecker is among the endangered animals that find safety here. More common animals that abound include the southern bald eagle, alligators, squirrels, otters, white-tail deer, black bears, snakes and wild turkeys.

The area is known for its beautiful wildflowers, including five genera of insectivorous plants, a combination rarely seen elsewhere. Among the insectivorous plants are pitcher plants, round-leaved sundew, butterworts, Venus's-flytraps and bladderworts, all of which die if removed from their natural habitat; it is against the law to disturb them. Pamphlets about the wildflowers and insect-eating plants are available at the park headquarters.

Summer fires, whether spontaneous in nature or controlled for forest nurturance, are common. The insect-eating plants that proliferate in pocosin habitat are actually fire dependent, another reason not to try to take one home. After a good burning, they're well-nurtured and hungry for bugs. Nature is stranger than fiction.

For kids ages 8 through 15, the N.C. Maritime Museum's Junior Sailing Program teaches basic through advanced sailing skills during the summer's eight two-week courses.

Kidstuff

I went to find the pot of gold
That's waiting where the rainbow ends.
I searched and searched and searched
and searched
And searched and searched and then —
There it was, deep in the grass,
Under an old and twisty bough.
It's mine, it's mine, it's mine at last . . .
What do I search for now?
— Shel Silverstein

If the pleasure is in the search, not the treasure, there's a lot of kid in you. For that kid, and any other kids you have on board, great explorations are ahead on the Crystal Coast. Of course the beaches are the main attraction, and the adventures and challenges they offer are as endless as imagination. But, when you reach the what-do-I-search-for-now point, the choices present you with another bountiful quest.

Set out for fun in the jungle, on a pirates' island or on a water-boggan slide. School up with other minnows at the North Carolina Aquarium and explore things that live in the ocean. Make wonderful creations from stuff you find on the beach or go on a snorkeling adventure in the sound. Ride a Ferris wheel and see forever. Take the helm of a bumper boat, try your skills in a round of mini-golf or take a spin in a go-cart. We've got horseback rides on the beach and some of the best summer camps on earth. And if you're interested in how the seashore environment works or want to learn how to sail a boat, the thing for you is North Carolina Maritime Museum's Summer Science School or Jr. Sailing Program. The courses are short and are out in the wild

for only a few hours each day, so they won't take up your whole vacation.

When you've exhausted the suggestions we've listed and you're told, "Go fly a kite!," you actually can! Flying anything is best on a North Carolina beach, you know. The Wright Brothers knew.

Many of the sites for adventures that follow are also described in other chapters and, for further details, we have referred you to them. We just thought you might appreciate having a concentration here in case you have the misfortune of finding a pot of gold.

Amusements

Ballastic Adventures
The Circle, MP 2¼, Atlantic Beach
• 726-7759

It's zero to 80 in two seconds on the Slingshot, the newest way to terrorize yourself on The Circle. And, of course, every kid wants to do it. For $25, or two for $40, you can be projected 150 feet into the air, then free fall for 130 feet before the bungee whips you back up again, turning you end over end until, when you quit rolling, you're lowered to the ground. Best of all, there's a "no hurl guarantee" because it's simply impossible while pulling four to five G's. For an extra $10, you can buy the video tape of your face during the experience. And, no kidding, there's always a line, noon until midnight. The Slingshot propels all kids tall enough to be strapped in (at least four feet) from Memorial Day until the N.C. Seafood Festival weekend at the beginning of October.

Carteret Lanes
U.S. Hwy. 70 W., Morehead City • 247-4481

Everyone in the family can enjoy knocking down a few pins at Carteret Lanes. It's bowling in a family atmosphere with an arcade and snack bar available. Of course leagues and competitions bring out the matching shirts, but the unpolished amateurs also have lots of fun. Carteret Lanes is open year round.

Fun 'n' Wheels
The Circle, MP 2¼, Atlantic Beach • 240-0050

Depending on your age, you may well think of The Circle when you consider Atlantic Beach. This was the site of the beach arcade, it's where you'd go for the best bands and where the younger kids were jostled all day and night on the rides that were the centerpiece. Well, it still is. The Circle's center is home of Fun 'n' Wheels amusements that, in the summer months, features the largest Ferris wheel on the island, a go-cart track, bumper boats, kiddie cars and the Amazing Gyro for kids who like to see things from many angles. Between Memorial Day and Labor Day and weekends April through October, the Fun 'n' Wheels rides are open from noon until midnight.

Golfin' Dolphin
Manatee St., Cape Carteret • 393-8131

This expansive family entertainment complex, off N.C. 24 in Cape Carteret behind Hardee's, is where athletes of all ages and stages can hone their competitive edges. The complex includes a 50-tee driving range, baseball and softball batting cages and an 18-hole miniature golf course. While the bigger kids are sharpening their skills, the little ones enjoy the arcade games, bumper boats and go-karts. The Golphin' Dolphin also has a snack bar and a pro shop that sells high-quality golf accessories. A party room is available for private birthday parties and celebrations. The complex is open daily, "9 AM until," from March through December. Winter hours vary.

Jungleland
Salter Path Rd., (N.C. Hwy. 58), MP 4½, Atlantic Beach • 247-2148

This large amusement park has something for the whole family. Here you will find bumper boats, miniature golf, an arcade, a snack bar and rides for the kids. Admission to the park grounds is free, and tickets (or day passes) are available for individual rides. The park opens daily at 11 AM from April through October. Jungleland is one of the best places to keep kids amused for hours.

Playland
204 Islander Dr., MP 20½, Emerald Isle • 354-6616

Playland in Emerald Isle has eight superfast water slides and all sorts of rides for toddlers and youngsters, including bumper cars, bumper boats and slick and grand prix tracks. Home of "the original" Water Boggan, 354-2609, and Lighthouse Golf, 354-2811, an 18-hole miniature golf course, Playland also has a snack bar and a picnic area to keep the kids completely happy and give moms and dads a break. Playland is open daily during the summer months.

FYI

Unless otherwise noted, the area code for all phone numbers in this guide is 919.

Pirate Island Park
Salter Path Rd. (N.C. Hwy. 58), MP 10½, Salter Path • 247-3024

The family will enjoy an active day at this Salter Path park with two giant twister water slides, kiddie slides, a pool and bumper boats. A lounge area, showers and lockers are available for use before a round of miniature golf or a turn through the video arcade. Hot dogs and snacks are available. Group rates and a picnic area with volleyball are available for parties.

Sportsworld
U.S. Hwy. 70 W., Morehead City • 247-4444

The sport at Sportsworld is skating, and for the local crowd it's the meet-and-compete spot for the younger-than-driving-age set. Sportsworld is well-maintained and supervised with all the right music and activity changes

Photo: Bill Russ

It takes two to reel in the big ones.

on the skating floor. A snack bar with arcade games is a comfortable vantage for viewing the skating without actually having to relearn the sport. Sportsworld is open year round. Call for hours and activities.

Go Fish

Take-A-Kid Fishing
Carteret County Sportfishing Assoc.
• 726-5550

Take-A-Kid Fishing is a project organized annually by the Carteret County Sportfishing Association for underprivileged children from all over North Carolina. The August day of fishing involves every head boat on the Crystal Coast, at least 100 volunteers, loads of donated burgers and more than 300 young anglers. The event has grown since it began in 1989, and sponsorships are generous.

The Triple S Marina Kids Tournament
Triple S Marina, Atlantic Beach • 247-4833

This kids' tournament is held each summer in late July for anglers ages 2 to 14. There is a 50¢ registration fee and awards are presented for the largest and smallest fish. A fam-ily cookout for residents and guests at Triple S Village follows the awards ceremony.

North Carolina Seafood Festival Kids' Fishing Tournament
Sportsman's Pier, Atlantic Beach
• 726-NCSF

During the first weekend in October, this tournament brings close to 50 young anglers to Sportsman's Pier in Atlantic Beach. Prizes are awarded for the largest of any kind of fish caught, and each angler goes home with a tackle box.

Hot To Shop

A Sea Of Learning
2410 Arendell St., Morehead City
• 240-2732

This is the greatest place for games, videos, things to build, cuddle, paint, put together, discover and, OK, learn. It's a delightful place to take a kid or to shop for a birthday present surprise. The shop also houses educational materials for teachers and conducts workshops in the use of materials. That's because it's the enterprise of a couple of former teachers.

Kids' Events

Easter Egg Hunt
Beaufort Historic Site , 100 Block Turner St., Beaufort • 728-5225, (800) 575-SITE

Every spring on the Saturday before Easter, bring your basket and a grown-up for the annual Easter Egg Hunt at the Beaufort Historic Site. There are wonderful hiding places on the grounds, eggs are not too hard to find and there are lots of them. Prizes are awarded, some good cookies are served, and it's free.

Harvest Time
Beaufort Historic Site, 100 Block Turner St., Beaufort • 728-5225, (800) 575-SITE

All 4th-grade North Carolina history students know that preparing for the winter in Colonial times on the coast was a big deal. There were fish to salt, bears to skin, preserves to make, logs to split, wool to weave, cider to press. To say the least, it was a busy time. During three weeks in October at the Leffers House on the Beaufort Historic Site, students can talk to the Leffers family while they're doing all these things getting ready for the cold days to come. All Carteret County students get to participate, and many others come from all over the state to get this firsthand, real experience in history.

Hot Diggity Dog Show
Carteret County Parks and Recreation Dept. • 728-8401

Usually on a Saturday in November, the kids of Carteret County are invited to show off their dogs. They can dress them up and demonstrate their best tricks at the event held at Swinson Park off Country Club Road in Morehead City. The show is for kids from five to 12 years old and, of course, their dogs.

N. C. Kidfest
Morehead City Parks and Recreation Dept. • 726-5058

Celebrated the first Saturday in June at The Circle in Atlantic Beach, Kidfest is a full-day early summer festival staged for and by children. It involves entertainment on multiple stages, educational tents, puppet shows, storytelling, a petting zoo, a tractor-pulled train and other fun rides and booths where kids can sell products to benefit civic and charitable organizations focused on kids. It's a spectacular day that ends, spectacularly, with fireworks. Parking is limited in Atlantic Beach for Kidfest. The best parking is at Carteret Community College in Morehead City, which offers a shuttle service throughout the day.

Lots To Learn

Jr. Sailing Program
N.C. Maritime Museum, 315 Front St., Beaufort • 728-7317

For kids ages 8 through 15, the Junior Sailing Program teaches basic through advanced sailing skills during the summer's eight two-week courses. Sailing courses also include seamanship, navigation skills and maritime traditions, but kids also learn safety, adapting to forces of nature, self-reliance, sportsmanship and respect for others, boats and the sea. Each student uses an Optimist Dinghy, and class size is limited to 14 students with two instructors per class. This is a first-class program and classes fill quickly. Call for a schedule and an application.

Programs Just For Kids
N.C. Aquarium at Pine Knoll Shores, N.C. Hwy. 58, Pine Knoll Shores • 247-4004

Everything at the N.C. Aquarium Pine Knoll Shores (see our Attractions chapter) will keep a kid fascinated, but each summer the aquarium plans programs and activities with a kid's point of view in focus. Activities are scheduled each week through the summer months for kids from 4 to 11 years old. The 1½-hour programs introduce preschoolers to marine life with live animals, craft projects, stories and films. Early grade students enjoy art projects, games and sea life videos; older children learn about coastal environments and marine life via field trips, crafts and live animal activities. Beginning snorkelers of any age are offered instruction on a regular basis at the aquarium during the summer months. Preregistration is required for all these activities, and we suggest you make reservations early.

Summer Science School for Children
N.C. Maritime Museum, 315 Front St., Beaufort • 728-7317

This popular summer program of the North Carolina Maritime Museum (see our Attractions chapter) is for students entering 1st through 9th grades. The various hands-on study activities include explorations of delicate marine ecosystems with guidance of researchers and instructors at area marine laboratories. Maritime heritage projects are assisted by the museum staff. Most classes are offered in one-week sessions for about three hours a day. Five-day classes at Cape Lookout explore the wonders of the barrier island. Class sizes are small and activities are often wet. Call the museum for schedules and applications.

Other Good Stuff

Charisma Kids
Glad Tidings Pentecostal Holiness Church, Morehead City • 726-0160

The children's ministry at Glad Tidings on Country Club Road in Morehead City involves about 100 kids between the ages of 4 and 12

Photo: Scott Taylor

It's a seadog-eat-sea robin world out here.

in a very active program that is met with a very positive response from kids. Charisma Kids meet for their own church on Sundays, 10:30 AM to noon in Glad Tiding's Family Life Center. For the kids it's an exciting celebration that positively reinforces lifetime Christian habits. Their activities include music, mission trips, games, interesting community guests and involvement in the church through projects. This youth program is so highly motivating, we've heard of kids asking to be dropped off if their parents aren't planning to attend Sunday services. Anyone is welcome, and parents are encouraged to participate.

Sandy's Kids Club
Sands Oceanfront Resort, Atlantic Beach • 247-2636, (800) 334-2667

Kids ages 5 to 12 years old who vacation at A Place At The Beach, SeaSpray or Sands Villa Resort in Atlantic Beach and rent through Sands Rental Management register at a special kids' desk while their parents check in at the regular desk. Kids get an identification wristband so they won't get lost, a free gift and access to many fun activities of the kids' club. Daily, between mid-June and mid-August, club activities are scheduled at the resort pool and waterslide, on the beach or on field trips to exciting places such as the North Carolina Aquarium, the North Carolina Maritime Museum, Jungleland or Fort Macon State Park. Everyday resort activities include fun stuff like pool games, T-shirt tie dyeing, kite flying, treasure hunts and lots of things parents don't want to do. Sandy, the kids' club mascot, sends each member a birthday and Christmas card each year to remember the summer fun.

Outside Fun

Kites Unlimited
Atlantic Station, Atlantic Beach • 247-7011
Kites Unlimited sponsors Sunday morning kite-flying exhibitions at Fort Macon State Park, and everyone is invited to join. Bring a kite because you'll want to try the things you see after the demonstrations. For the truly competitive kite fliers, the Carolina Kite Fest at Sands Villa Resorts in October (see our Annual Events chapter) is also sponsored by Kites Unlimited.

White Sand Trail Rides
N.C. Hwy 12., Cedar Island • 729-0911
Mount up, cowpokes. There are beach trails to explore on horseback about as far Down East as you can go before getting wet. Wayland Cato offers lots of packages including a half-hour ride just for kids. Young cowpokes can also ride double for half price. The 45-minute drive from Beaufort through Down East is a great exploration trip too. Stop along the way at Harkers Island to visit the Core Sound Waterfowl Museum or at the Cedar Island Wildlife Refuge (see our Attractions chapter). In fact, this trip could pretty much devour a whole day.

Summer Camps

The Crystal Coast has camping opportunities that offer summer programs and are available for group use year round. And nearby at the mouth of the Neuse River are some of the most prestigious summer camps in the eastern United States for campers 6 to 17 years old.

Camp Albemarle
1145 Hibbs Rd., Newport • 726-4848
This Presbyterian camp in a beautiful setting on Bogue Sound operates year round and is open to the public. Summer camp sessions are divided into age groups, with weeks dedicated to campers from 3rd through 12th grades. Activities include swimming in the pool and sound, tennis, basketball, sailing and canoeing, along with other traditional camp activities. A sailing camp is also operated each summer. The camp is on N.C. 24 south of Morehead City.

Camp Sea Gull
Camp Seafarer
Rt. 65, Arapahoe • 249-1111 Sea Gull, 249-1212 Seafarer
Camp Sea Gull for boys and Camp Seafarer for girls are on the Neuse River in Arapahoe about 27 miles north of Morehead City and 21 miles east of New Bern. The camps share an outpost and docks on the Morehead City waterfront. Camp Seafarer for girls opened in 1961, and Camp Sea Gull for boys has been in operation since 1948. Both are owned and operated by the capital area YMCA in Raleigh, 832-4744. Sea Gull and Seafarer feature a nationally recognized seamanship program including sailing, watersports and ocean excursions from the Morehead City waterfront outpost. In addition, both camps offer horsemanship, archery, golf, tennis, soccer, riflery and

---

INSIDERS' TIP

Those opaque gray jellyfish, locally called "jelly bombs," that bob along on the water's surface in the tide are not the stinging kind. Their short tentacles transport other small seagoing creatures wherever the jellyfish go.

group camping. The camps conduct environmental education programs that serve schools throughout the state and offer facilities for corporate training and conferences.

Summer Day Camps

Arts and Enrichment Camps
Morehead City Parks and Recreation
1600 Fisher St., Morehead City • 726-5083

The Morehead City Parks and Recreation Department sponsors Arts and Enrichment Camps at Morehead Elementary School at Camp Glenn throughout the summer for school-age children. Week-long camps, full- or half-day, are designed for fun in art, dance, drama, computers and math. A small fee is charged.

Morehead City Parks and Recreation Day Camp
1600 Fisher St., Morehead City • 726-5083

An eight-week summer day camp for preschool and school-age kids offers field trips, arts and crafts, swimming, skating, music, drama, sports, games and T-shirts. It's a lot of supervised entertainment for an incredibly reasonable price for both city residents and non-residents.

Sound To Sea Day Camp
Trinity Center, Pine Knoll Shores
• 247-5600

If you're planning to spend a week or two with Nana and Gramps in Pine Knoll Shores this summer, ask them to arrange for you to spend some time each day at the Trinity Conference Center's environmental education day camp. The kids who do get a great hands-on exposure to five coastal habitats: the sound, marsh, pond, maritime forest and ocean dunes. They learn about the creatures living in each environment, play interesting games, swim, make crafts and learn about coastal cultures starting with Native Americans. From 9 AM to 4 PM, you'll be with other kids your age, from 6 to 12 years old, who are fun to play and learn with. You'll have lots to tell Nana and Gramps about the stuff you did, and your teachers will think you're very smart when you get back to school.

Many artists find the pace of coastal living conducive to developing their talents and move here for that purpose.

The Arts

Art often imitates life on the coast, and the arts reflect the relationship of coastal people with the sea. Here on the Crystal Coast, art enjoys a special place in many of our museums and public buildings. Our most treasured annual events reflect the value of the arts to our communities with the omnipresence of performing and visual arts. On the Crystal Coast, the state of the arts is active, varied, visible and valued.

Many artists find the pace of coastal living conducive to developing their talents and move here for that purpose. It's not unusual to meet professionals from other locations earning a living here painting, writing or making pottery. Our active community of coastal artists is involved in an eclectic array of artistic production — music, drama, dance and the visual arts. Arts organizations actively support artists' endeavors and welcome new members and volunteers.

In this chapter we list arts organizations, arts groups in the visual arts, theater, music and dance, and galleries. If there is no address for a group, we have listed the name and phone number of a person to contact.

Arts Organizations

Carteret Arts Council
801 Arendell St., Ste. 3, Morehead City • 726-9156

This nonprofit organization, partially funded by the North Carolina Arts Council, is a distributing agent that funds arts events and education, promotes arts organizations, assists artists seeking grants in support of their professional development and sponsors workshops and lectures. Every February it sponsors the Art From The Heart exhibition, which involves artists from three surrounding counties. The council also sponsors the Carteret Arts Festival, a June weekend of music and exhibits by selected artists. Both events take place in Morehead City (see our Annual Events chapter).

The addition of programs conducted or assisted by the Carteret Arts Council since 1976 has resulted in an ever-expanding community arts concept that embraces drama, literature, dance, music, traditional crafts and the visual arts. Its new offices allow for a display gallery staffed by volunteers. Long-range plans envision an art center for the county with expanded services for the community. Volunteer assistance and membership support keep the program active and growing.

Carteret County Arts and Crafts Coalition
Donna Graff • 726-3354

What began in the late 1970s as a small group of professionally oriented artists seeking an outlet for their work has grown into a juried, professional art group of almost 70 members. The coalition conducts four major shows each year — on Memorial Day weekend, on the Fourth of July holiday, on Labor Day weekend and a three-week Christmas gallery show before the Thanksgiving holidays. New members are welcome, and jurying of new work takes place twice each year.

INSIDERS' TIP

The Sunday Afternoon Concert Series at the First Presbyterian Church in Morehead City often features classical music on the church's remarkable pipe organ and by the Morehead Brass Consortium.

Core Sound Decoy Carver's Guild
Wayne Davis • 728-7316

Born from an idea of seven decoy carvers at a birthday party in 1987, the Decoy Carvers Guild now has a membership of more than 300 active decoy carvers, collectors, breeders, taxidermists and waterfowl artists in more than 25 states. The Core Sound Decoy Festival (see our Annual Events chapter) in December and Core Sound Waterfowl Museum (see our Attractions chapter) in Harkers Island are outgrowths of the efforts of the Decoy Carvers Guild. The guild welcomes new members and meets each month on the third Wednesday at Harkers Island Elementary School.

Dance

The Carteret Arts Council brings professional talent in dance, drama and music each year through a variety of grants and its own budget. Visiting artists hold concerts as well as instructional programs in the public schools in conjunction with these public performances. Such concert and instructional programs have featured African, jazz and contra dancing.

Private dance studios on the Crystal Coast offer classes for toddlers through adults in ballet and modern dance. Students perform recitals and often participate in area festivals, group functions and parades. Dance organizations are also active in community events.

Carolina Strut Performing Arts Centre
303 N. 35th St., Morehead City • 726-0431

Classes for adults and children in tap, ballet, point or jazz are offered by instructor Melanie Galizia.

Dance Arts Studio
123 Bonner Ave., Morehead City • 726-1720

Myrna Eure offers tap, ballet and jazz instruction in classes for ages 3 through adult.

Gulls and Buoys Square Dance Club of Carteret County
Dottie Gorman • 223-4641

This group stages an annual Square and Round Dance for adults that gathers dancers from nearby states and across North Carolina

at the Crystal Coast Civic Center. The club meets each Friday at the First Presbyterian Church in Morehead City. New members are welcome.

Hi-Tiders Square Dance Club
Ruby Wilson • 362-5789

This group meets every Wednesday night for dancing at Swansboro Primary School. New members are welcome.

Music

The Crystal Coast is home to several choral groups that perform frequently and occasionally audition new prospects. We are fortunate to host some extraordinary concert series, a wonderful music festival weekend in the spring and active jazz and folk arts music societies that promote, in concerts and education, America's most innovative music styles.

American Music Festival
Julie Naegelen • 808-ARTS

An exquisite chamber music series, the American Music Festival Series is composed of five extraordinary concerts performed in the acoustically complementary North Carolina Maritime Museum auditorium in Beaufort. Now in its seventh season, the concert series is supported by membership, sponsorship and a volunteer staff. From late fall 1996 through spring 1997, the series brought world-class performances of East Carolina Winds, Duke University's Ciompi Quartet, the Scampati Piano Quartet and musicians of the North Carolina Symphony, Vienna Symphonic Orchestra and London Philharmonic. Series memberships are $50 or, if you take chances, concert tickets may be available at the door.

Beaufort By-The-Sea Music Festival
Ann Carter • 728-5501

This beautifully organized annual spring weekend event is jam-packed with a complete range of music, performed in downtown Beaufort. The Beaufort Business and Professional Association sponsors and schedules the festival. See our Annual Events chapter for more about this event.

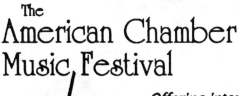
Carteret Chorale
Laurence Stith • 726-6193

This group of 40 talented vocalists from Morehead City, Newport and Beaufort has performed together for 18 years, creating a chorale known widely for its top-notch performances. The chorale performs benefit concerts regularly in Carteret County and has taken its talent as far as Carnegie Hall, the National Cathedral and Russia. Annually, the group performs at Bruton Parish Church in Williamsburg, Virginia. Director Laurence Stith, retired professional pianist, vocalist and educator, is also a composer, and the group often performs his original music. "Have tux, will travel," say the members, who pay their own travel expenses and provide their stage wardrobes for performances.

Carteret County Chapter of the North Carolina Symphony
Cynthia M. Cummins • 354-9376

The Carteret County chapter of the North Carolina Symphony brings our superb state symphony to the area to perform three annual concerts. A well-supported annual fund drive, A Day for the Symphony in September, provides for three additional free concerts for elementary and middle school students. Volunteers are always needed.

Coastal Jazz Society
Marjorie Hoachlander • 247-7778

The society's primary mission is jazz education for all ages. The organization also aims to increase awareness and enjoyment of jazz within coastal areas of the state. The Coastal Jazz Society presents well-known musical groups in concert at its annual Jazz Fest By The Sea in October and hosts other popular jazz-interest events including speakers on jazz history and development. The society welcomes the membership of anyone who enjoys listening to, learning about or playing jazz.

Crystal Coast Choral Society
Finley Woolston • (910) 347-6317

Originally formed in the mid-1980s in Swansboro to perform at the town's bicentennial celebration, this group has continued to appear in concert every year since and includes nearly 70 vocalists from Onslow and Carteret counties. Several members are retired professional musicians, and others are talented amateurs. The society rehearses each Tuesday in the band room at Swansboro High School. The group welcomes new members.

Crystal Strings Dulcimer Club
Donnell Meadows • 726-7699

This group meets each month, except December, from September until May to make music with mountain and hammer dulcimers and other acoustic instruments. Interest in traditional music is the only prerequisite; beginners, professionals and appreciators are welcome.

The Freshest Fish In Town

You won't find his sculptures in any art gallery — he's just not that kind of artist. And although they're not edible, you will find Craig Gurganus' ping-pong-eyed flounder, triggerfish, crabs, clown fish and barracuda at some of the best restaurants in the Crystal Coast and Outer Banks areas, Wilmington and Chapel Hill. Craig's puffy works of art are called Fish Bouffant.

Art took this surfer by surprise, and the startled looks that characterize his personable fish and sea creatures are very much an exclamation point of *artiste remarque*. Craig, a handy and personable Rocky Mount boy compelled by the surf, spent one winter painting houses — when the surf was contrary — but knew he had undeniable art genes. His family has produced a best-selling novelist and screenwriter, a psychologist, a landscape designer and primitive artist, and Craig. It was inevitable.

He found the perfect fodder for his art while watching a friend's surf shop that winter in Rodanthe on Hatteras Island. In the forms of broken surfboards Craig saw Fish Bouffant. ("They're in there. I don't make them," said Craig.) He carves the fish out of the broken polyurethane foam of the boards, applies spray paint and resin then trims them out with fins of structured wooden skewers, fiberglass cloth and resin. The finished product, with an appropriately protruding eye, is a Fish Bouffant.

After a show at the North Carolina Aquarium in Manteo a little more than 10 years ago, then more shows in specialty coffee shops and at Crook's Corner in Chapel Hill, Craig finally learned the value of making himself known. "Someone wanted to buy all of them, but nobody knew how to find me," he said. "A close friend advised, 'Craig, it's got to be either house-painting or art.'"

He chose art. After all, an artist whose work sells without being in a gallery and for whom the main factor navigating any day is the surf conditions, is one who will take a chance.

Craig's designs are named things such as Yikes (his signature surprised flounder), Rickles (the clown fish), Elvis (the star-quality seahorse) and Buster (a blue crab, of course). The home of Fish Bouffant is in Beaufort in a perfect house for their creation. A former neighborhood grocery surrounded by collards and tropical plants bordered with bowling balls, Craig Gurganus' studio is in the garage.

Photo: Coaster Magazine

Craig Gurganus creates a Shark Bouffant in his studio.

Inside, in the Board Room — where the director is Craig's own surfboard — broken boards quietly wait to be relieved of the Fish Bouffant inside.

Down East FolkArts Society
Judy Orbach • 726-2399

If you think folk music sounds like the mountains, you need to hear more folk music by the sea. Between September and June, each month brings a concert to the Crystal Coast for the Folk Concert and Dance Series. Organized and sponsored by the Down East FolkArts Society, concerts and dances occur at Clawson's 1905 on Front Street in Beaufort, the Duke University Marine Lab auditorium on Pivers Island and Beaufort Elementary School. Instruction in New England contra dancing, which requires no partner and has no age requirements, precedes the dances. Call for series membership information and concert schedules, or watch the newspaper for announcements.

La Musique Club of Carteret County
Rachel Mundine • 223-4538

This music fellowship is open to performers and music lovers. Members meet at 11 AM on the first Monday of each month at Webb Civic Center, 812 Evans Street in Morehead City. The group performs a number of concerts, including benefit concerts, each year.

Saturday in the Park Concert Series
Jaycee Park, Morehead City • 726-5083

On Saturday evenings between Memorial Day and Labor Day, this popular concert series brings an interesting range of music to the Jaycee Park on the Morehead City waterfront. Gospel, flamenco guitar, acoustic rock, reggae — it's all there for the listening on those beautiful summer evenings. Just bring a chair or blanket. The rest is absolutely free. It's sponsored by the Morehead City Parks and Recreation Department.

Theater

Carteret Community Theater
Richard Evans • 726-6340

This group of amateur actors puts on a series of plays each year that are greatly appreciated by the community, including children's productions in summer and at Christmas, dinner theater and other staged performances. Always receptive to talented newcomers, the community theater welcomes everyone at widely advertised cast calls. The group meets monthly at Carteret Community College.

Writers' Organization

Carteret Writers
Les Ewen • 354-4339

This active group of professional writers and aspirants gathers on the second Thursday of each month for lunch and a scheduled speaker at Mrs. Willis' Restaurant in Morehead City. Carteret Writers sponsors workshops, seminars and competitions throughout the year as well as an ongoing outreach program in the public schools.

Regular Art Exhibits

In this area, art can be seen in a number of public places. The North Carolina Maritime Museum, 315 Front Street, Beaufort, 728-7317, exhibits the finest work of state and local artists. These works complement the museum's maritime focus. Monthly exhibits are sponsored by the Arts for the Hospital committee, and are shown at Carteret General Hospital, 3500 Arendell Street, Morehead City, 726-1616. The Carteret County Museum of History and Art, 100 Wallace Drive, Morehead City, 247-7533, features at least one local artist a month. The county's three public libraries sponsor artists in revolving displays that change monthly.

Carteret Community College, 3505 Arendell Street, Morehead City, 247-6000, displays work by students in the school's arts and crafts courses in the college library. The Upstairs Gallery at the college also features student work and work by other local and re-

A great white heron takes off to hunt his next meal.

gional artists. And on Harkers Island, the Core Sound Waterfowl Museum, 728-1500, exhibits the best of hand-carved decoys and wildlife art.

Art Lessons

Continuing Education Department
Carteret Community College • 247-6000

The Continuing Education Department offers courses in specific visual arts techniques each semester. For county residents age 65 or older there is no tuition charge, only the cost of materials. Call for further information.

Commercial Art Galleries

To our great advantage, some coastal artists have also become involved in the business of art galleries that showcase and sell their works. Some galleries represent local and regional artists; others bring art works from much farther afield. Discover many of our treasured local artists at the following galleries.

Budding Artists Ltd.
Atlantic Station Shopping Center, Atlantic Beach • 247-5111

Budding Artists represents an interesting variety of visual arts by students and "becoming" artists. At various times, you may find new collections of paintings in varied media and pottery. Prints, poster art and complete framing services are also offered.

Carteret Contemporary Art
1106 Arendell St., Morehead City • 726-4071

This gallery shows an extraordinary selection of paintings and sculpture by regional, national and local artists in frequently changing exhibits.

Down East Gallery
519 Front St., Beaufort • 728-4410

This gallery exclusively represents the paintings of local artist Alan Cheek. There are published prints of his work and also framing services.

Handscapes Gallery
400 Front St., Beaufort • 728-6805

Handscapes represents local and regional artists in jewelry, pottery and varied media. Occasionally the proprietor finds something that isn't always North Carolinian, but it's always irresistible. This is the best destination for accent jewelry in the area.

Laughing Gull Gallery
Salter Path Rd., Atlantic Beach • 726-2362

A nice collection of local and regional artists is represented at this gallery that also offers framing services.

Mattie King Davis Gallery
Beaufort Historic Site • 728-5225

This summer-only gallery exhibits and sells the varied works of more than 100 local and regional artists from Memorial Day through Labor Day.

Painted Pelican Art Gallery
4645 Arendell St., Morehead City • 247-5051

Local artist/owner Beth Munden is represented at this gallery. Prints, poster art and framing services are also offered.

Turner Street Gallery
126 Turner St., Beaufort • 728-1447

The nautical watercolors of Beaufort artist Dee Knott are represented at this small, delightful gallery.

Windward Gallery
508 Evans St., Morehead City • 726-6393

This waterfront gallery represents the paintings of local artist Alexander Kaszas as well as other artists in varied media.

The Traditional Wooden Boat Show of the North Carolina Maritime Museum in Beaufort was the first, and is the largest, gathering of wooden watercraft in the Southeast.

Annual Events

Traditions are very important on the Crystal Coast. One strong indicator of this is that festive events are usually announced with the number of years that event has occurred. From the seventh season of the American Music Festival concert series in January through the 10th annual Core Sound Decoy Festival in December, we Insiders anticipate and enjoy each event with zest and, frequently, guests. The area's traditional festivals often have a very salty flavor that seasons them like a family reunion. In the midst of what may appear to be a public festival gathering of endless random strangers, hugs and greetings are likely to break out anywhere.

Fold in with the crowd and feel right at home. The simple pleasures of just being on the Crystal Coast provide a full plate, but including any of the following events in your plans expands a sample taste of the area into a real feast.

January

American Music Festival
N.C. Maritime Museum, Beaufort
• 808-ARTS

This chamber music series has brought extraordinary concerts to our coast for seven years. Five concert performances are scheduled yearly from October through May in the auditorium of the North Carolina Maritime Museum in Beaufort (see our Arts chapter). Series tickets are $50, and, incredibly, tickets are usually available at the door for $10 to $12.

February

Art From the Heart
Morehead Plaza, Morehead City
• 726-9156

This two-week exhibition of original, innovative and traditional works by selected area artists occurs each year in mid-February. Carteret Arts Council organizes and funds the event. Proceeds benefit the local arts council and provide scholarships to Children's Art Camp. Admission is free.

Mardi Gras Ball
Crystal Coast Civic Center, Morehead City
• 728-5216

Habitat For Humanity is very visible and active through the year, but this is the organization's most fun fund raiser. It involves dinner, dancing, a nicely profitable cash bar and an art auction. The crowd is masked, tuxed and ready to get out of the house. Tickets go fast so call the Habitat office to get your name on the invitation list, or purchase a ticket from any Habitat volunteer.

March

Coastal Home Show
Crystal Coast Civic Center, Morehead City
• 247-3883

This annual trade show in early March assembles the services, wares and expertise of local businesses that focus on aspects of building, landscaping and decorating. Gather ideas, good advice and the right products for do-it-yourself projects, or shop for professional services during the weekend show. An admission fee is charged to get into the show.

St. Patrick's Day Festival
Emerald Plantation Shopping Center, Emerald Isle • 354-6350

Winter hibernations are halted by this mid-March weekend of fun and games, corned beef and cabbage, traditional beverages, music and wearing of the green in Emerald Isle. Sponsored by the Emerald Isle Parks and Recreation Department, the festival supports local craftspeople and civic organizations. It's free.

The Core Sound Decoy Festival, held each December at Harkers Island Elementary School, is fun for the whole family.

North Carolina Commercial Fishing Show

Crystal Coast Civic Center, Morehead City
• 633-2288

This annual trade show features boats and fishing equipment displays and demonstrations and information forums about the commercial fishing industry in North Carolina. An admission fee is charged.

Swansboro Oyster Roast

Cape Carteret Fire and Rescue Building, Cedar Point • 326-5066

This annual fund-raiser of the Swansboro Rotary funds the scholarships awarded each year by the civic organization. From Swansboro through Emerald Isle and beyond, the population turns out for all-you-can-eat oysters, clams or a pig-pickin' with traditional slaw and hushpuppy trimmings. The mid-March event usually happens on St. Patrick's Day. Tickets are $20 or $25 depending on the choice of menus.

FYI

Unless otherwise noted, the area code for all phone numbers in this guide is 919.

April

Newport Pig Cooking Contest

Newport Park, Howard Blvd., Newport
• 223-PIGS

This huge barbecue competition draws folks from all over eastern North Carolina for the best barbecue on earth, accompanied by homemade baked goods, live entertainment and children's activities. Delicious "Down East" barbecue goes on sale after the contest is judged. The event benefits numerous civic organizations and occurs in early April. Admission is free but food costs extra.

Publick Day

Beaufort Historic Site, Beaufort
• 728-5225

On a Saturday in mid-April, this annual event features the outdoor sale of flea-market merchandise and crafts in the colonial tradition, entertainment, mock trials and exhibits. Proceeds benefit

preservation of historic structures through the Beaufort Historical Association. Admission is free.

Easter Egg Hunt
Beaufort Historic Site • 728-5225

On Easter weekend, the Beaufort Historic Site is the perfect setting for a traditional Easter egg hunt for kids. It's a bring-your-own-basket event heaped with small-town warmth. Admission is free.

Easter Sunrise Services
Various locations

The dawning of Easter morning is celebrated in services at several locations across the county, many on the waterfront or beach. The *Carteret County News-Times* lists service locations and times the week before Easter.

Beaufort By-the-Sea Music Festival
Various downtown locations, Beaufort • 728-5501

This full weekend celebrates all that's right about Beaufort. Everyone is out enjoying the late-spring weather and a panoply of music that must be a great surprise greeting for the northbound boats arriving in town during the weekend. Fun for all ages and appealing to all musical tastes, the Beaufort Music Festival is always the last weekend of April. Free concerts of classical, country, traditional, jazz, rock and reggae music are presented on various stages within a three-block area of downtown Beaufort. The Beaufort Business and Professional Association

sponsors and schedules the weekend events. Bring a chair or blanket and a picnic to enjoy on the lawn or have lunch or dinner at any of the downtown restaurants. Parking is available at any of the downtown parking areas.

Lookout Spring Road Race
Sports Center, Morehead City • 726-7070

This annual road race in Morehead City adds 5K and 1-mile race competitions to the Beaufort Music Festival weekend. The event is sponsored by the Lookout Rotary Club to benefit local charities and civic organizations. There is an entry fee for race participants.

May

Nelson Bay Challenge
Sprint Triathlon
Sea Level • 247-6902

This annual event includes a 750-meter swim, a 20K bike ride and a 5K run the first Saturday of May. Proceeds from the race, raised by entry fees, benefit the Sea Level Rescue Squad and various county youth programs.

Traditional Wooden Boat Show
N.C. Maritime Museum, Beaufort • 728-7317

The Traditional Wooden Boat Show of the North Carolina Maritime Museum in Beaufort was the first, and is the largest, gathering of wooden watercraft in the Southeast. Not a commercial show, it's an early May weekend of scheduled demonstrations, talks and races that annually assembles people who share a well-honed interest in the art, craftsmanship and history particular to wooden boats. Admission is free.

Salter Path
Clam and Scallop Festival
Salter Path ballpark, Salter Path
• **247-7994**

The first Saturday in May brings an island community celebration with good local seafood and music to the heart of Salter Path. Organized by and benefiting the Salter Path Fire and Rescue Department and the Crystal Coast Pentecostal Holiness Church, the festival begins with a clam chowder cookoff at the fire department on Friday night. Saturday's food and music is all local, but the people come from great distances for food and local color like this. Admission is free but food costs extra.

Mile of Hope
Beach strand at Atlantis Lodge, Pine Knoll Shores
• **354-5400**

In early May each year, the Mile of Hope Foundation organizes a beach getaway for pediatric cancer patients and their families. Local businesses and sponsors donate lodging, food, entertainment and gifts to make it a very special weekend. A mile of beach beginning at Atlantis Lodge is the site of a Saturday sandcastle building contest. Wonderfully imaginative structures evolve throughout the day. Music, food and entertainment add to the relaxed beach fun. It's a nice destination for the day, especially with a kid.

Emerald Isle Beach Music Festival
Holiday Trav-L-Park, Emerald Isle
• **354-2250**

If you don't know beach music, this Saturday in mid-May is a crash course. Concerts feature top beach music groups (some who invented it), dancing in the sand, a beauty pageant and other entertainment. Peripheral events benefit the Children's Hospital of Eastern North Carolina and civic organizations. Tickets may be purchased in advance or at the gate for a full day of music, dancing and sun. Food and beverages are available, but coolers are prohibited.

Storytelling Festival
Various locations, downtown Swansboro
• **(910) 455-7354**

The Swansboro waterfront is the setting for this delightful, entertaining two-day event in mid-May. Stages and workshops are scheduled and organized by the Onslow Public Library for children, adults and both. The adult storytelling events are usually the scary ones. Admission is free.

Turtle Release
N.C. Aquarium, Pine Knoll Shores
• **247-4004**

Every year in late May, the North Carolina Aquarium returns rehabilitated sea turtles to their natural environment. Loggerhead and other types of turtles are taken offshore and released into the sea by aquarium staff, volunteers and the interested public. Anyone who has preregistered may go along, but register early. (See our Attractions chapter.) A lot of people love turtles. A participation fee is charged.

Memorial Day King Mackerel & Blue Water Tournament
Casper's Marina, Swansboro
• **(910) 326-1500**

This annual holiday weekend fishing competition with a variety of categories is sponsored by the Swansboro Rotary Club. Tradi-

Chrome Domes Gather in Morehead

MOREhead, less hair — get it? Well, the Bald Headed Men of America got it and have been gathering for their annual September convention on the shores of the Crystal Coast for the last 24 years. In 1997 this wacky, good-natured group of "chrome domes" will convene on Sept. 12, 13 and 14 for another of their whimsical conventions.

So unique are these gatherings that national and international news media focus attention on the small coastal town of Morehead City each fall. Otherwise Morehead City draws little outside media attention except when a big hurricane threatens the Crystal Coast.

Close-up

Founder and local resident John Capps, whose head is as slick as a peeled onion, has more one-liners than you can shake a stick at: "If you haven't got it, flaunt it"; "No drugs, plugs or rugs"; "God gave some men hair and others brains"; or "The convention is a hair-raising experience." And that's just for starters.

John and his wife, Jane, own and operate Capps Printing, located — where else — on Bald Drive in Morehead City. John formed the Bald Headed Men of America organization after being rejected for a job. He was in his mid-20s, and the employer who turned him down told him his baldness made him look too old for the position and that he didn't project the image the company wanted. Since then John has changed the minds of thousands of people and has led a campaign focusing on baldness as both a humorous and painful issue.

Since the formation of the group, which now has a membership of more than 30,000 around the globe, John and many of the members have appeared on numerous

Photo: Jimmy Sparkman

The second weekend in September brings bare heads from around the country, and around the world, to Morehead City for the Bald Headed Men of America's annual convention.

— continued on next page

entertainment news magazine shows on TV. They have been featured in hundreds of magazines and newspapers, both in the United States and in foreign countries. At the 1996 convention media guests included the BBC, the Australian TV Network, Fox Television, CNN, *The London Times* and even a television crew from India. Members periodically receive *The Chrome Dome Newsletter*, and the organization has its own site on the Internet — http://www.ipass.net\@bald.

Attendance at the group's annual September convention varies but is never less than several hundred. Polished-pate pals travel across the country to join the fun, and members from such far-flung locations as Australia, London and Ireland often travel to the United States to attend the convention. The annual gathering includes family members, too, and many couples load up the kids and make the jaunt a fall vacation.

The three-day affair includes activities such as cookouts, golf, boat cruises, picnics, a social and the official bald banquet, where contest winners of such challenging competitions as "the sexiest bald head," "the smallest bald spot," "most kissable" and "smoothest" carry away prizes.

The annual get-together does have a serious side, though, and offers self-help sessions for wives of bald men, workshops for those having trouble coming to terms with their baldness and a variety of open forums. The organization contributes annually to the Aleopecia Areata Research Foundation, which conducts research in baldness, especially in children.

Collectively, the group is jovial about the bare facts of being bald. Their sense of humor is both infectious and inspirational. At the 1990 convention, Great Britain's Tim Hibbert showed up to write a feature story for the *Daily Mail*, a newspaper with a circulation of 4 million. Hibbert commented, "In England, people are too insular, too private, to ever get into a group like the Bald Headed Men of America. All these domes together, having a good time, would be unthinkable. At home, the thought of growing bald is traumatic, and the man suffers in private. But it's a silly thing to worry about. Here, believe it or not, they celebrate being bald. It's incredible. It would help if the English could be more like this."

Bald John eschews all the remedies on the market that are supposed to cure baldness. He labels them gimmicks and believes they instill false hopes among users and compound the stigma that bald is bad. Bald is just bald. Why is bald bad? Why isn't bald beautiful? To the Bald Headed Men of America, it is.

John's wife is as active in the group as her husband. In the office one day she fielded a call from an anxious and despondent Jim in Poughkeepsie, N.Y. After listening and chatting for a few minutes she said with a wide smile, "Jim darlin', you need some humor in your life. Come on down to the convention and you'll see a whole new side of things." Jim came . . . and he left smiling.

---

tionally, some big surprises have been brought in including billfish in the huge range. Proceeds from the tournament benefit local charities and civic organizations. Participants pay a fee to compete in the tournament.

NCYRA Championship Regatta
Racing boats arrive and depart Beaufort Docks • 728-3155

Memorial Day weekend begins with the excitement of arriving sailboats racing offshore for the Wachovia Cup. Throughout the week-end triangular course races are scheduled as well as social events in downtown Beaufort.

Carteret County Arts and Crafts Coalition Spring Show
Beaufort Historic Site, Beaufort
• 726-3354

This outdoor exhibition and sale of arts and crafts by juried coalition members is the first show of the year during Memorial Day weekend. Demonstrations, food and music enhance the festive atmosphere, and quality is tops. Admission is free.

June

N.C. Kidfest
Atlantic Beach Circle, Atlantic Beach
• 726-5083

Kids from miles and miles around are out for the fun and, did someone say learning opportunities? Most kids hope not at this time of year, but it's amazing how much fun learning can be. With sponsorship of area businesses, churches, arts and civic organizations, the day is full of events "for kids, by kids" but is great fun for adults too. See our Kidstuff chapter for details. Admission is free.

Big Rock Blue Marlin Tournament
Events at various locations • 247-3575

One of the oldest and largest sportfishing tournaments in the country, the Big Rock involves fish-fry festivities, parties and daily public weigh-ins during the week on the Morehead City waterfront. The early June event benefits charities and nonprofit organizations, not to mention the winners. Participants pay an entry fee.

Arts By the Sea
Waterfront, Swansboro • (910) 326-7222

This annual arts and crafts festival in early June, brings lots of music, food and people to the downtown Swansboro waterfront for a Saturday of enjoyable strolling among numerous artists booths. Proceeds from the festival go to local civic organizations. Admission is free.

Carteret Arts Festival
City Park, downtown Morehead City
• 726-9156

Sponsored by Carteret Arts Council and the Downtown Morehead City Business Association in mid-June, this two-day arts event brings artists, craftspeople, dramatic artists and musicians for scheduled events. Lots of art-related activities for youngsters and art creations are part of the fun. Most activities are free. Funds raised support area art programs.

Worthy Is The Lamb
Crystal Coast Amphitheater, Peletier
• 393-8373, (800) 662-5960

One of the Crystal Coast's major attractions, this outdoor passion play begins its sum-

The traditional Wooden Boat Show is held each May in Beaufort.

mer performance season in mid-June. Plays are presented each Thursday, Friday and Saturday through Labor Day, weekends through September, at Crystal Coast Amphitheater off Highway 58 in Peletier. See our Attractions chapter for more information.

Beaufort Old Homes Tour
Beaufort Historic Site, Beaufort
• 728-5225, (800) 575-SITE

Always the last weekend in June, the Old Homes Tour of Beaufort opens some of this country's oldest private homes and buildings for narrated tours. New restorations and those in progress keep the tour fresh and interesting each year. Crafts, music, demonstrations and re-enactments occur throughout the weekend at the Beaufort Historic Site, where the tour begins. A fee is charged.

Antiques Show and Sale
Crystal Coast Civic Center, Morehead City
• 728-5225, (800) 575-SITE

Held in conjunction with the Beaufort Old Homes Tour in late June, this large show features about 40 dealers and repair and restoration specialists. Come and bring a broken family treasure for repair or advice on restoration. An admission fee is charged.

July

Independence Day Celebrations
Various locations

Fourth of July fireworks and festivities, including a street dance, are held on the Morehead City waterfront to celebrate Independence Day. Consult the *Carteret County News-Times* for times and other festive locations before the weekend or call the town office at 726-6848. Fireworks also light up the Swansboro waterfront every Fourth of July.

Down East Fish Fry
Sea Level • 225-7721

Never miss a volunteer fire and/or rescue department feed Down East. This one features fish, shrimp and other seafood, plus live entertainment on the Fourth of July in Sea Level. Proceeds help to operate the Sea Level Rescue Squad. A fee is charged per plate.

Coastal Invitational Showcase
Crystal Coast Civic Center, Morehead City • 729-7001

This semiannual show spotlights artists and craftspeople from all over the southeastern United States who demonstrate and sell work during the weekend show in mid-July. The Showcase returns during the Thanksgiving holiday weekend. An admission fee is charged.

Historic Beaufort Road Race
Front St., downtown Beaufort • 726-7070

This year's 18th annual mid-July road race includes a certified 10K, 5K and 1-mile walk and run and a wheelchair event with starts in downtown Beaufort. The popular race is organized by Beaufort Old Towne Rotary and St. Egbert's Track Club and brings out lots of participants. Participants pay an entry fee.

Bogue Sound Watermelon Festival
Open Aire Flea Market, Cedar Point • 393-2281

The harvest begins in late July, and the Crystal Coast celebrates one of our most valuable summer resources: watermelon. The festival, like Bogue Sound melons, is growing in Cedar Point. The day of fun and entertainment benefits the Carteret County Domestic Violence Program. Admission is free.

Ladies King Mackerel Tournament
Town Creek Marina, Beaufort • 726-8452

Annually in late July, this popular tournament involves only women anglers. The women manage to land the big ones — mackerel, that is — and the weigh-ins are late afternoon celebrations. Participants pay an entry fee.

August

N.C. Ducks Unlimited Band the Billfish Tournament
Various marinas • 787-0522

This early August tag-and-release billfish tournament funds preservation projects for state wetlands. Participants pay an entry fee.

Atlantic Coast Soccer-on-the-Sand Jam
Main beach, Atlantic Beach • 859-2997, (800) 375-GOAL

This annual sporting event gathers statewide soccer and volleyball team competitors to Atlantic Beach for an early August weekend of sandy competition. The well-organized weekend is a great spectator sport too. Admission is free.

Atlantis Lodge Sand Sculpture Contest
On the beach at Atlantis Lodge, Pine Knoll Shores • 726-5168

What began as one energetic family's pastime at a reunion now draws some serious competition in early August for adults and children. Seeing is believing every year, and it's well-worth the trip. The competition entry fees benefit the Outer Banks Wildlife Shelter.

September

Carteret County Arts and Crafts Coalition Fall Show
Beaufort Historic Site, Beaufort • 726-3354

The organization of fine artists and craftspeople gather for an outdoor show and sale of excellent quality and original arts and crafts on Labor Day weekend. Food and music add to the festive atmosphere. Admission is free.

Hardee's Atlantic Beach King Mackerel Tournament

Sea Water Marina, Atlantic Beach
• 247-2334, (800) 545-3940

This year's is the 19th annual tournament and the nation's largest all-cash king mackerel fishing competition event. The mid-September tournament benefits local nonprofit organizations and includes a memorable fish fry. Participants pay an entry fee.

N.C. Big Sweep

Locations on Crystal Coast waterways
• 728-8430

Big Sweep is an annual statewide cleanup of waterways, beaches and roadsides by volunteers in mid-September. Locally, volunteers are organized by several interests including the Rachel Carson Reserve, 728-2170, and centrally, by Carteret County's office of the North Carolina Cooperative Extension Service.

Bald Headed Men of America's Convention

Bald Headquarters, 102 Bald Dr., Morehead City • 726-1855

The 1997 gathering is the 24th annual convention of this international hairfree group. The weekend includes self-help workshops, testimonials, golf games, picnics, contests for the most kissable head and other activities in mid-September. Proceeds benefit the Aleopecia Areata Research Foundation, which conducts research in baldness, especially in children. The organization was founded by Morehead City's John Capps. See the close-up in this chapter for more about the event.

October

North Carolina Seafood Festival

Waterfront, Morehead City • 726-6273

The first weekend of October brings nearly 100,000 people to the Morehead City waterfront for this two-day outdoor major annual festival. Highlights are an endless variety of seafood prepared in a multitude of ways, street dances and concerts both days. Crafts, educational exhibits and programs, games and contests are also part of the many festivities that spread between the North Carolina State Port and Ninth Street. Admission is free.

Harvest Time

Beaufort Historic Site, Beaufort
• 728-5225

This is an educational program of the Beaufort Historical Association for 4th grade students of North Carolina history that occurs during three weeks of October. Living history re-enactments of winter preparation activities in the daily lives of a coastal village family of the 1700s occur around the Leffers Cottage at the Beaufort Historic Site. School groups and visitors are treated to interesting preparation activities and demonstrations that make history seem more real. All Carteret County Schools participate as well as many schools all over the state. It's free for the participating students, visitors must pay a fee.

Mullet Festival

Downtown Swansboro • (910) 326-5754

This is the area's oldest festival that started 43 years ago to celebrate the completion of the new bridge over the White Oak River in Swansboro and the crew that built it. It was so fun, it's been celebrated ever since with a parade, a street carnival, arts and crafts and, oh yeah, bountiful mullet and seafood. The festive

INSIDERS' TIP

February promotes creativity in Down East gatherings and annual celebrations. In Cedar Island on February 15, the Boom Truck Festival celebrates the commercial fisherman's next-best friend, his rigged truck; at the Gloucester Community Center, Mardi Gras season prompts the annual gumbo, dance and music of the local Cajun/zydeco musicians, Unknown Tongues.

Spring on the Crystal Coast
makes all Insiders frisky.

early October event, held on a Saturday, benefits local civic organizations. Admission is free.

Carolina Kite Fest
Sands Villa Resort, Atlantic Beach
• 247-7011

On this late-October Saturday, the sky fills with kite demonstrations, competitions and night kite flying on the beach. Participants arrive from as far away as California, Japan and all over North Carolina. Kites Unlimited in Atlantic Station sponsors the annual event. Admission is free.

Havelock Chili Festival
Havelock City Park • 447-1101

Here's a spicy competition that puts any lost heat back into late October. The sparks fly and chili is sold all day Saturday. Lately, salsa has entered the competition. Take your heartburn remedy. Admission is free, and food costs extra.

November

Mill Creek Oyster Festival
Mill Creek Volunteer Fire Dept., Mill Creek
• 726-0542

Here's another all-day feed and family event not to miss. The annual oyster roast in early November is all you can eat for one reasonable price.

The Saturday festival co-stars other seafoods for the less adventurous seafood tastes and also includes music and crafts. The event benefits the Mill Creek Volunteer Fire Department.

Photo: Scott Taylor

Saltwater Light Tackle Fishing Tournament
Crow's Nest Marina, Atlantic Beach
• 240-2744

In early November, this annual weekend tournament offers anglers their choice of surf, pier or boat fishing for king mackerel, puppy drum or flounder. The largest fish takes the cash and the competition challenges more than 200 anglers each year. Participants pay an entry fee.

Ducks Unlimited Banquet
Crystal Coast Civic Center, Morehead City
• 240-1794

The annual fund-raising benefit for the preservation of waterfowl habitat is eagerly anticipated on the first Thursday of November each year. Ticket price includes membership, a wonderful dinner and an evening at the Crystal Coast Civic Center with about 400 people committed to waterfowl habitat preservation.

Swansboro By Candlelight
Downtown Swansboro • (910) 326-7222

In mid-November, Swansboro's downtown merchants host this evening event with open shops decorated for the Christmas season. Admission is free.

Community Thanksgiving Feast
Beaufort Historic Site, Beaufort
• 728-5225, (800) 575-SITE

On the Sunday before Thanksgiving a traditional Thanksgiving feast is served at the Beaufort Historic Site. Beaufort restaurants contribute the feast fixings, and the community gathers together in thanks. Proceeds from this ticketed event benefit preservation efforts of the Beaufort Historical Association. Tickets are sold at the Beaufort Historic Site.

Carteret County Arts and Crafts Coalition Holiday Show
Morehead Plaza, Morehead City
• 726-3354

At the Thanksgiving holidays, this three-week show and sale of original juried artwork by members of the Carteret County Arts and Crafts Coalition opens in Morehead Plaza. More than 40 local artists combine their work to create the gallery show for Christmas gifting opportunities. Admission is free.

Coastal Invitational Showcase
Crystal Coast Civic Center, Morehead City
• **729-7001**

This annual Thanksgiving holiday show brings numerous crafters and their wares to Morehead City. Admission is free. A small admission fee is reduced by 50¢ with a can of food contributed to Martha's Mission.

Christmas Flotillas
Waterfronts, Morehead City and Beaufort
• **728-4646; Swansboro waterfront**
• **(910) 393-6997**

On the Crystal Coast, Santa arrives by yacht. At sunset on late-November and early December Saturdays, evening parades of decorated and lighted boats bring him in to open the Christmas season celebration on the coast. In late November, the Swansboro Christmas flotilla lands Santa at a downtown dock where spectators greet Santa and the participating captains. In early December on the Crystal Coast, the celebration starts in the afternoon with open house at the Beaufort Historic Site and town bed and breakfast inns. The Coast Guard greets visitors aboard their vessel at the town docks. The town lights luminaries that greet the Crystal Coast Christmas Flotilla as it parades by the Morehead City waterfront to the Beaufort waterfront. The boats dock, and Santa and the crews gather for a festive awards ceremony hosted by the North Carolina Maritime Museum.

December

Core Sound Decoy Festival
Harkers Island Elementary School and various locations, Harkers Island
• **728-1500**

Held the first weekend in December on Harkers Island, the two-day festival includes competitions in carving and painting decoys, exhibits and sales of old and new decoys, a loon-calling contest, special competitions and activities for children, educational exhibits and an auction. The event benefits the Core Sound Waterfowl Museum and is the area's largest off-season event. An admission fee is charged.

Festival of Trees
Crystal Coast Civic Center, Morehead City
• **247-2808**

Sponsored in early December by Hospice of Carteret County for the benefit of those receiving hospice services, the annual Festival of Trees features a display of more than 60 decorated trees, breakfast with Santa, luncheon and a festive party. An admission fee is charged.

Coastal Carolina Christmas Celebration
Beaufort Historic Site, Beaufort
• **728-5225**

Historic homes and buildings at the Beaufort Historic Site are decorated for Christmas in traditional styles in mid-December. The opening event offers tours with entertainment and refreshments and benefits preservation of historic structures through the Beaufort Historical Association. An admission fee is charged.

Fishing, Boating, Watersports and Beach Access

The Crystal Coast is well-known as a perfect place for water-related activities. Surfers looking for ocean waves, windsurfers and water-skiers looking for calm sound waters and anglers looking for something in between will find what they want here. And a wonderful bonus for everyone is our generally mild climate, which allows folks to participate in their favorite watersports year round.

In this chapter we offer a look at fishing, including lessons, gear, piers; boating, including charters and rentals; watersport equipment rentals; swimming; and beach access areas. For businesses on Bogue Banks, we have given the milepost (MP) number to help you locate them.

Fishing

The Crystal Coast hosts numerous fishing tournaments. One of the nation's largest king mackerel tournaments, Hardee's Annual Atlantic Beach King Mackerel Tournament, is held in September, and one of the largest and oldest blue marlin tournaments, the Big Rock Blue Marlin Tournament, takes place in June. For details and dates, see our Annual Events chapter.

Federal government studies have shown that your chances of catching fish in North Carolina waters are unsurpassed along the entire East Coast. Of the 21 recorded catches of Atlantic blue marlin in excess of 1,000 pounds, five have been caught off the North Carolina coast. In fact, a 1,002-pounder is on display in the parking lot behind the Crystal Coast Visitors Center in Morehead City.

The Crystal Coast has many opportunities for anglers. Whether you surf fish from the barrier island beaches, dangle your line from one of the piers dotting the coastline or catch one aboard a private charter or head boat, you're sure to have the time of your life. Sport fishers are not required to obtain a fishing license. However, to make sure your fishing experience is fun, contact the N.C. Division of Marine Fisheries before you fish for a list of size and catch limits and harvest restrictions.

Fishing Schools

Most anglers come to the Crystal Coast equipped with fishing skills and knowledge, but a growing number of people want to know more about fishing in area waters or want to improve their chances of hooking the big one. Lucky for them, some good fishing lessons are available.

The **N.C. Aquarium at Pine Knoll Shores**, 247-4004, conducts several fishing classes. Special Activities Coordinator Jeff McBane plans classes and workshops for beginners, folks who have some fishing experience and 4th- and 5th-grade kids vacationing on the Crystal Coast.

During spring, summer and fall, beginners can sign up for the 8-hour Surf Fishing Course (last year's format spread the 8 hours over two days). Participants first receive classroom training: knot tying, lures and bait for catching fish in the surf, hooks and sinkers, rods and reels and where to catch fish. Armed with this knowledge, participants then go fishing at the Salter Path Public Beach Access early in the morning. Walking up and down the beach, Jeff demonstrates how to cast a line and encourages each beginner. This is an enjoyable and fun experience even for those who are not nuts about fishing. Bait, tackle and accessories are provided.

For a real treat (also mostly for beginners), go with Jeff on his annual fall 2½-day Surf Fishing Workshop. For this session, you must bring your own tackle, but you get to ferry across Core Sound and fish all day on Cape Lookout. Experienced teachers and fishermen Joe Malat and Mac Currin demonstrate techniques, explain how to "read the beach" for the best fishing and even show you how to clean and fillet your catch! (This last bit of information is very comforting to the family members of fishing folk. Woe to the fisher who can't clean his own fish!)

People who already know how to fish can register for Surf Fishing at Cape Lookout, an all-day fishing excursion. Jeff offers these expeditions several times throughout the spring, summer and fall. The Aquarium provides the bait and tackle and makes the transportation arrangements.

Nine and 10-year-olds who hanker to learn about fishing will enjoy the half-day beginners' sessions designed just for them. Throughout the season, Jeff starts these classes with a little orientation, which includes a tour of the aquarium and a quick lesson on the kinds of fish that can be caught in the surf. Then everybody piles into a van and goes over to Sportsman's Pier in Atlantic Beach and fishes until noon. All equipment and a snack are provided. Kids will love this!

If you want a short but informative read on surf fishing, buy Joe Malat's booklet, *Surf Fishing: Catching Fish from the Beach —When,* *Where, How.* It's full of illustrations and available at the N.C. Aquarium Gift Shop, 247-4003.

Last, but not least, to learn how to cook all kinds of fish, ask at the Aquarium about the Succulent Seafood Cooking Class. Jeff McBane teaches this one too.

Capt. Joe Shute's Bait & Tackle, 601-H Morehead Avenue, Atlantic Beach Causeway, 240-2744, gives free instruction on the last Saturday of the month from April through November. Capt. Joe teaches folks how to cast a net, make a rig, tie a knot, bait a hook and the basics of inshore and offshore fishing.

Fishing Reports

What's biting when and where is as important to avid fisherpeople as the world news is to the rest of us. Information about catches is available at most bait and tackle shops, marinas, piers or charter boat rental offices. Television station WCTI TV 12 offers a fish and game report during the sports segment of its news shows.

You can also call News Talk 24, 247-6396 ext. 1212 for an up-to-date, daily saltwater fishing report. To get the inside track on where to fish, read the *Carteret News-Times*. Every Friday it publishes "On the Line," a column by Bill Hitchcock, a coastal fishing writer. Bill also gives a daily radio update at 8:20 AM and a half-hour show on Thursdays at 6:30 PM on WTKF 107.3. Every Friday on Fox 8 and Fox 14 at 1 PM, watch his TV program, "North Carolina Saltwater."

Fishing Gear

Now that you have boned-up on how to fish, it's time to get your gear. Local tackle shops not only have the fishing stuff you'll need, but they also offer a bit of advice about what fish are biting and where. We've listed just a few of the many good shops in the area.

Freeman's Bait & Tackle
Atlantic Beach Cswy., Atlantic Beach
• 726-2607

This is a complete saltwater tackle shop selling rods and reels, along with a repair and cleaning service. Freeman's also has bait, clothing and other supplies.

Photo: Scott Taylor

A bad day surfing is better than a good day doing anything else.

EJW Outdoors
2204 Arendell St., Morehead City
• 247-4725

EJW's has been in business for more than 50 years and continues to offer gear for a variety of sports including hunting, biking and archery. But, the main focus is on fishing. EJW sells rods and reels and all kinds of bait and clothing and also services rods and reels. The shop is owned by David Willis.

Pete's Tackle Shop
1704 Arendell St., Morehead City
• 726-8644

Pete's is a N.C. Official Weigh Station for the citation program. Pete Allred sells rods and reels and is well-known for the repair and cleaning service his store provides. Pete offers everything an angler needs for offshore and inshore fishing, including specialized clothing and bait. He has been in business since 1977.

K&V Variety
K&V Plaza, 307 Mangrove Dr., Emerald Isle
• 354-7100

K&V Variety is a convenience store as well as a bait and tackle shop. At this year round shop, anglers will find all kinds of bait, crabbing supplies and tackle boxes. Also for sale

are rods and reels and rain gear for those dedicated to fishing no matter what the weather.

Fishing Piers

Fishing and crabbing (or simply walking out to see other people's catches) from local piers is a favorite pastime. Most of the fishing piers along the Crystal Coast are on Bogue Banks with access to the Atlantic Ocean. They are popular spots during the spring, summer and fall. Most piers close during the winter and those that don't only open during the day. The majority are privately owned and a fee, usually between $3 and $5, is charged for a day/night of fishing. Take your kids with you, or your mother-in-law who has never fished; it's fun.

Triple S Fishing Pier
MP½ • 726-4170

This pier is at the east end of Bogue Banks. Patrons are offered a lighted pier, tackle/snack shop and plenty of parking.

Sportsman's Pier
MP 1¼ • 726-3176

Sportsman's carries the slogan, "You should have been here yesterday." The pier has a tackle shop and a cafe that serves sandwiches, seafood and steaks, and has all ABC permits.

Oceanana Fishing Pier
MP 1½ • 726-0863

This pier is right beside the Oceanana Resort Motel. It is lighted with a tackle/snack shop and plenty of parking.

Iron Steamer Resort and Pier
MP 7½ • 247-4213

This 800-foot pier is beside the Iron Steam Motor Inn. It offers a tackle shop and fishing equipment rentals.

Indian Beach Fishing Pier
MP 12 • 247-3411

This fishing pier is about 825 feet long and offers a grill and tackle shop, efficiency apartments, a camping area and plenty of parking.

Emerald Isle Fishing Pier
MP 15 • 354-3274

This pier has a snack/tackle shop. It extends 742 feet and is lighted.

Bogue Inlet Fishing Pier
MP 19½ • 354-2919

This 950-foot pier is lighted and offers a snack bar and tackle shop.

Causeway Pier
Beaufort Cswy. • 726-7851

Causeway Pier is at the east foot of the high-rise bridge. This lighted pier offers a snack and tackle shop.

Straits Fishing Pier
Harkers Island • No phone

This pier is on Harkers Island Road and is maintained by the Carteret County Parks and Recreation Department, 728-8401. The pier extends over Back Sound, and there is no fee.

Head, Charter and Tour Boats

Fortunate fishers can fish from their own boats, but lacking your own (or a friend's) you can chose from the dozens of commercial rentals and charters. One good way to enjoy a day of fishing is on a head boat. These large vessels take as many as 50 people out into the Gulf Stream for a day's worth of deep-sea fishing. The name came about because you pay by the head, or per person, for the trip. You don't hire the entire boat, just a spot on the deck. The crew provides the rods, reels and bait; you just take your personal belongings (maybe a cooler of drinks and snacks, some extra clothing, weather gear and sun protection).

Charter boats are smaller vessels generally hired by a private party of four to six individuals for a half day or a full day of fishing in the Gulf Stream. If you don't have a full party, a charter captain may be able to hook you up with another half-party willing to share the expenses of chartering the boat.

Most head and charter boats operate year round, with less frequent trips in the dead of winter. For more information about head and charter boats, we recommend you walk along the Morehead City waterfront, check out the marinas on the Atlantic Beach Causeway, talk with other anglers and contact the Crystal Coast Charter Boat Association, Morehead City, 729-1661.

Regardless of how you get to the Gulf Stream, once there you will have a chance at red and silver snapper, king or Spanish mackerel, cobia, tuna, wahoo, blue fish, sailfish, dolphin, bass grouper or other fish abundant to Crystal Coast waters.

Seventy-three licensed charter boats and three head boats operate year-round on the Crystal Coast, so we can't list them all here. Our descriptions are representative samples of the vessels available for hire. We have also included a vessel that offers a chance to trawl for shrimp and a sailing tour that takes you on an ecology exploration of local waters.

Capt. Stacy Fishing Center
Atlantic Beach Cswy., Atlantic Beach • 247-7501, (800) 533-9417

Capt. Stacy's fleet consists of more than 14 vessels, including everything from sportfishing boats to an 83-foot head boat and a 65-foot head boat. The head boats offer half- and full-day trips along with a 22-

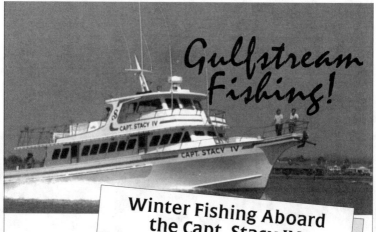

A speckled trout is a fine catch from local piers.

hour trip and a 36-hour trip. The fleet's charter boats can be hired for half- and full-day trips. The Capt. Stacy Center also offers moonlight cruises and harbor tours and can handle private parties.

Carolina Princess
Eighth St., Morehead City • 726-5479, (800) 682-3456

Owner Captain WooWoo Harker is one of the area's best-known captains. Since 1952,

the 95-foot *Carolina Princess* has offered a variety of ways to enjoy the area and the Gulf Stream. Full-day, 18-hour and 22-hour fishing trips are available year round, and half-day trips are offered each Wednesday. The *Carolina Princess* can accommodate 100 people. Group fishing trips, parties, receptions and weddings can also be arranged. The *Carolina Princess* also offers dinner cruises.

Continental Shelf
400 Evans St., Morehead City • 726-7454, (800) 775-7450

The *Continental Shelf* is a 100-foot head boat that goes out on full-day, 18-hour and 22-hour excursions. Half-day trips are offered on Tuesdays. The boat docks on the Morehead City waterfront beside the Charter Restaurant. Summer evening cruises aboard the boat offer guests a chance to see the area's islands and wildlife and enjoy a quiet, relaxing night. The *Continental Shelf* is available for private charter groups, fishing, evening cruising or daytime sightseeing.

Mary Catherine
Beaufort • 726-8464, 726-6519

Here is a chance to have a new experience and fill your freezer with shrimp. The *Mary Catherine* is a 55-foot commercial trawler equipped with the latest fishing gear. Shrimp trawling charters are available from May through mid-October. After a trip, you take home the catch. The boat is licensed for up to six passengers and operates every day during the season.

Good Fortune
Beaufort • 247-3860

If you are fascinated by coastal ecology — or want to know more about the subject — arrange to sail with Capt. Ron White, a marine biologist and owner of the 42-foot sailboat *Good Fortune*. This custom-built craft is available for half-day, full-day and 2-hour sojourns, educational trips, group and corporate charters and evening sails. Capt. Ron will also take you snorkling and will provide the gear. Sunset excursions conclude with complimentary wine.

A Sportfishing Guide for North Carolina's Coast

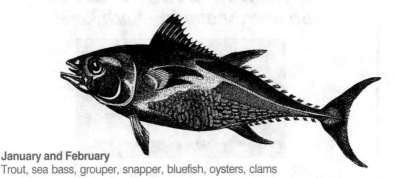

January and February
Trout, sea bass, grouper, snapper, bluefish, oysters, clams

March
Grouper, sea trout, sea bass, bluefish, croaker, snapper, oysters, clams, king mackerel, some yellowfin tuna

April
Bluefish, channel bass, grouper, snapper, croaker, sea trout, sea mullet, some king mackerel, some oysters, clams, tuna

May
King mackerel, bluefish, grouper, flounder, cobia, tuna, shark, sea mullet, crabs, soft crabs, blue marlin, sea bass, wahoo, dolphin, Spanish mackerel

June
Blue marlin, white marlin, sailfish, dolphin, wahoo, cobia, king mackerel, bluefish, tuna, summer flounder, snapper, grouper, Spanish mackerel, shark, crabs, soft crabs

July
Dolphin, wahoo, tuna, blue marlin, white marlin, sailfish, snapper, grouper, summer flounder, bluefish, Spanish mackerel, sea mullet, shark, crabs, soft crabs

August
Dolphin, wahoo, tuna, grouper, snapper, Spanish mackerel, bluefish, speckled trout, spot, sea mullet, shark, crabs, blue marlin, white marlin, sailfish, king mackerel

September
Grouper, snapper, Spanish mackerel, king mackerel, spot, shark, bluefish, speckled trout, sea mullet, channel bass, flounder, sea bass, dolphin, blue marlin, white marlin, tuna

October
King mackerel, bluefish, snapper, grouper, channel bass, spot, speckled trout, flounder, shark, oysters, sea bass, tuna

— continued on next page

November

King mackerel, bluefish, speckled trout, flounder, snapper, grouper, shark, sea mullet, clams, sea bass, tuna

December

Bluefish, flounder, speckled trout, sea trout, snapper, sea bass, grouper, oysters, clams, some king mackerel

(Provided by N.C. Marine Fisheries)

Boating

Motor and Sail Boat Rentals

Water Sports Rental
MP 12, Indian Beach • 247-7303

Here you can rent a variety of sailboats as well as pontoons and power boats. You can sign up for sailing lessons too.

The Sailing Place
Atlantic Beach Cswy. • 726-5664

The Sailing Place rents many kinds of boats — power boats, catamarans, Sunfish, sailboards, daysailers and canoes. The company provides navigational information and charts with each boat, and you will receive instruction for the type of boat you rent. In addition, you may arrange for captained charters of yachts from 19 to 45 feet. Sailing lessons and sails of new and used sailboats are also available.

Causeway Marina
Atlantic Beach Cswy. • 726-6977

Causeway does not charter, but it does rent do-it-yourself, outboard-driven Carolina skiffs and pontoons.

Barrier Island Adventures
Beaufort • 728-4129

This business rents and charters boats for trips to Carrot Island, Shackleford Banks or Cape Lookout, and offers guided tours and fishing guide service.

Rose's Marina
Harkers Island • 728-2868

Rose's rents motor boats from 16 to 30 feet in length.

Kayaking

The kayaking enjoyed on the Crystal Coast is really sea kayaking and very much unlike the wild, crashing rides through North Carolina's roiling mountain waters. Here, kayaking is a peaceful, safe way to explore the naturally shallow waters of our abundant inlets, creeks and estuaries, which are home to an incredibly rich diversity of wildlife. Kayaking is growing ever more popular because it's such an interesting way to have fun and commune with nature. And as interest grows, so do the number of businesses offering rentals and tours.

Island Rigs
MP 12, N.C. Hwy. 58 across from the Indian Beach pier • 247-7787

Island Rigs rents kayaks and conducts tours and lessons.

Waterway Marina and Store
1023 Cedar Point Blvd., Swansboro • (910) 393-8008.

Kayaks, canoes and skiffs are avail-

INSIDERS' TIP

One of the best ways to really get to know the Crystal Coast is to escape to Shackleford Banks and explore on your own. Take your own boat or catch one of the passenger ferries described in our Getting Around chapter.

able for rent at this Swansboro establishment.

Coastal Kayak Outfitters
Front St., Beaufort, 728-7070, (800) 636-0373

John Maloney is in his third year of business and is an enthusiastic proponent of taking people on a kayak trip in beautiful Crystal Coast waters. John conducts tours to Portsmouth Village, Bear Island, Cape Lookout and Shackleford or sets up custom trips. Coastal Kayak Outfitters is the exclusive North Carolina dealer for Necky Kayaks, which are available for rent or purchase. The business offers instruction and sells all manner of accessories and safety equipment.

Rowing

The Beaufort Oars is a rowing club headquartered at the N.C. Maritime Museum's Harvey Smith Watercraft Center on Front Street in Beaufort. The group meets for fun and exercise, and new members are encouraged to join. For more information call the museum, 728-7317.

Boat Ramps

Whether you've rented a boat or have your own, you'll need to know where you can launch it. The Crystal Coast has many boat ramps, large and small, public and private. Below is a short list of just a few of the state-maintained public ramps. Because most ramps don't have names, we've listed them alphabetically according to location. Private ramps are in every part of the Crystal Coast, and most marinas and campgrounds have boat ramps. Remember, our list contains only the free, state-maintained ramps, so call the marina closest to you and, chances are, you won't have to drive far to put your boat in the water.

Beaufort

Curtis A. Perry Park is at the east end of Front Street near the tennis courts. It has four launching areas. Two ramps and a dock are offered off West Beaufort Road beside Town Creek Marina. These are maintained by Carteret County Parks and Recreation Department.

Cedar Island

A ramp is beyond the Cedar Island National Wildlife Refuge office on Lola Road at the south end of the island. The refuge also maintains a ramp on the west side of (and almost below) the new high-rise bridge, N.C. Highway 12, just west of the island.

Cedar Point

A ramp maintained by the N.C. Wildlife Commission is on the south side of N.C. High-

Photo: Scott Taylor

Dunes that can sustain grasses are less likely to wash away.

way 24 between Cape Carteret and Swansboro.

Morehead City

Municipal Park behind the Crystal Coast Visitors Center on Arendell Street, U.S. Highway 70, has several launching areas and a large parking area. The park is just east of Carteret Community College.

Sea Level

A ramp is maintained on the east side of the high-rise bridge on Highway 70 just before you get to the Down East community of Sea Level.

Watersports

Personal Watercraft Rental

The popularity of one-person (or sometimes two-person) watercraft is growing quickly, and shops renting Jet Skis, sailboards, skim and boogie boards, Waverunners, windsurfers and Sunfish are keeping up with that popularity. Most of the rental places also give lessons.

The Sailing Place
Atlantic Beach Cswy. • 726-5664

The Sailing Place offers rentals, charters and lessons in sailboards, sailboats, motorboats, skiffs and waterskis. You can rent by the hour, half-day, day or week. Skilled instructors, guides and captains will accompany you on your trip.

Island Rigs
MP 12, Indian Beach • 247-7787

Island Rigs offers sailboard rentals and lessons as well as rentals of kayaks, boogie boards, Sunfish and skim boards. The shop at Island Rigs carries a complete line of accessories, beachwear, sportswear, car and bike racks,

You've Caught the Fish. Now What?

Next to having a fish, the most important thing is cleaning it. Do it wrong and waste a good chunk of meat; prepare it the right way and savor every bite. Bought at a fish market, your finny meal probably already has been cleaned. But if you're given a fish or have caught your own, do this simple test to see whether it's really fresh: Lift the gill covering behind the fish's head to see if the gills are still red. You may want to pass on this one if the gills are only a light pink, and you'd definitely discard a fish with gray-colored gills.

Decide now whether to scale the fish. If barbecuing fish with soft flesh, such as blue fish or jumping mullet, you may leave the scales intact and place the fish on the grill with the scale side down to prevent the flesh from searing. A sharp knife edge rubbed counter to the scales, from the tail forward, will scrape them off. A store-bought fish scaler will make the job a little easier. Make the fish easier to hold in place for scaling and cleaning by rinsing it in cold water to remove the slippery covering. It's also a good idea to place a sheet or two of newspaper under the fish, atop a wooden or plastic carving board. When you're done, just wrap the remains in the newspaper and save on cleanup time.

Now comes the surgery. Key to success here is a sharp knife, preferably a filleting knife. Sharpen the blade after every few cuts and you'll glide right through the work. If you want the head removed, cut with a sawing motion behind the gills. Next, lay the fish on its side and cut from the top down the midline of the fish until you reach the small orifice toward the tail. Remove the entrails and discard them. Small specimens, such as hog fish or spot, don't need to be filleted. Just make several crosswise cuts on each side and they're ready for the frying pan.

It's not difficult to fillet fish. With the fish on one side, lift the other side and place the knife edge at the top of the fish's spine. Slowly start cutting close to the bone in the direction of the tail, while gently pressing the outside of the fish with your free hand to hold the knife in line as the blade separates flesh from bone. When completed, flip the fish onto its other side and repeat the process. The result should be two nice fillets. If you want to see how the pros clean fish, visit the Morehead City

Photo: P. Harrison

In a few quick steps you'll have these in the frying pan.

docks in season and watch as party boat crew members clean the day's catch. They make it look easy, and with a little practice there's no good reason why it shouldn't be as easy for you.

footwear and sunglasses. The outside deck overlooking Bogue Sound is a good place to have a cold drink and watch the action.

AB Jet Ski Rentals
Atlantic Beach Cswy. • 726-0047
This business is next to Marsh's Surfshop; it rents Jet Skis and other personal watercraft.

Water Sports Rental
MP 12, Indian Beach • 247-7303
Water Sports rents Jet Skis and other watersports equipment and offers lessons as well as half-day scenic guided Jet Ski tours.

Island Harbor Marina
Old Ferry Rd., Emerald Isle • 354-3106
This marina rents Jet Skis and motor boats.

Morehead Marine Inc.
4971 Arendell St., Morehead • 247-6667
If your Waverunner breaks down, Morehead Marine will get you back into the waves. This company also sells and services Yamaha Waverunners.

Scuba Diving and Snorkeling

The Crystal Coast is fast becoming a popular diving and snorkeling spot, and local businesses meet the demands of the sport. Diving is an all-year activity thanks to the Gulf Stream's warm waters, which lie about 35 miles off our shoreline. In summer, water temperatures range in the 80s, with visibility of 75 feet to as much as 150 feet. Ideally the best dive months are June through September when most tropical fish are present.

A national scuba diving magazine selected a local wreck site — a German submarine sunk off Cape Lookout in 1942 — as the fifth-favorite wreck dive. It was the only dive site on the list that is an actual wreck, not a man-made reef. Readers of *Rodale's Scuba Diving* magazine also voted Olympus Dive Center of

Morehead City third in the United States in both the "favorite resort/operator" and the "day boat operator" categories.

Olympus Dive Center
713 Shepard St., Morehead City • 726-9432

Olympus is operated by the Purifoy family. With five custom diver boats, Olympus is a full-service shop offering full- and half-day dive charters, equipment rental and instruction. The shop is also a Nitrox facility.

Discovery Diving Company
414 Orange St., Beaufort • 728-2265

Discovery can teach you to scuba dive or snorkel. On the water on Orange Street, the company offers Professional Association of Diving Instructors (PADI) Open Water Diver training, rentals, repairs, service and dive trips.

Wreckreational Divers
702 Morehead Ave., Atlantic Beach • 240-2244

Wreckreational provides instruction (PADI approved), all types of training and rentals. These folks can also arrange for large or small group dive trips.

Skiing

We are talking water-skiing here! Is there any other kind? Most surf stores carry water skis and related information. Both **Water Sports Rental**, MP 12, 247-7303, and **The Sailing Place**, Atlantic Beach Causeway, 726-5664, can give you water-skiing lessons and then set you up in a boat for an hour or a day of practicing.

Favorite skiing spots are the Bogue Sound west of the Atlantic Beach high-rise bridge, the sound between Beaufort and Shackleford and Core Creek north of Beaufort. These ar-eas all have places that are free from no-wake zones and are wide enough to allow for skier safety.

Surfing

Surfing is very popular along the North Carolina coast and always has been. There are plenty of places to catch the swell on the Crystal Coast. Any of our surf shops can provide information about wave conditions and surf contests. Most local outfits also rent surfboards and boogie boards. Listed below are some of the surf shops that can handle your needs.

Bert's Surf Shop, MP 2½, Atlantic Beach, 726-1730

Surf Zone Boards & Bikes, MP 4¾, Atlantic Beach, 247-1103

Marsh's Surf Shop, Atlantic Beach Causeway, 726-9046

Hot Wax Surf Shop, MP 20¼, Emerald Isle, 354-6466

Bert's Surf Shop, MP 19½, Emerald Isle, 354-2441

Sweet Willy's Surf Shop, MP 19½, Emerald Isle, 354-4611

77 Degree Surf Shop, Belk of Morehead City, 726-5121

Swimming

You can swim just about anywhere along the Crystal Coast, with the exception of a few posted areas. But even the most skilled pool swimmer may have difficulty dealing with ocean waves and undertows, so be careful and never swim alone. Riptides and undertows are very common along the North Carolina shoreline. If you find yourself being pulled by frightening currents, the most important thing to do is to stay calm. If you are caught in a riptide, relax and let it carry you toward the sea. Eventually it will dissipate. You should

INSIDERS' TIP

In Crystal Coast waters, the best fish to catch in the surf are striped bass, bluefish, summer flounder (also known as fluke), weakfish, speckled trout, red drum, kingfish, croaker, spot, pompano and Spanish mackerel. (Source: *Surf Fishing—Catching Fish from the Beach*, by Joe Malat, 1993.)

swim parallel to the shore to get out of the riptide, and then swim toward the shore. Be aware that not many lifeguards are around. Some places along Bogue Banks, such as the Atlantic Beach circle area and Fort Macon State Park, post lifeguards during the summer season. Swimming is not allowed around Fort Macon's rock jetties or on the inlet side. There are no public pools on the Crystal Coast, only those at hotels, condominiums, private communities and fitness centers. (Read our chapter on Sports, Fitness and Parks to learn more about fitness center swimming pools.)

Beach Access

If you want to swim, walk or run, collect shells or sun bathe, how do you get onto our marvelous Crystal Coast beaches? As is true in many coastal areas, getting onto the beach can be confusing. You aren't sure what is private property and what is public or where to park. But Insiders know where to go, and we list here the spots that take you directly to the ocean or sound. We also tell you which places have parking and bathroom facilities and are handicapped accessible. At some areas, vehicle access is available for permitted vehicles only. Public Beach Access areas are marked with signs that feature blue letters and a sea gull flying in an orange circle. We give the milepost (MP) number for those on Bogue Banks. Some beach access areas have gates that open at first light and close at dusk.

Atlantic Beach

Atlantic Beach offers pedestrian access at the **east end of the Sheraton Resort parking lot**. Vehicular access is provided at the south end of **Raleigh Avenue**.

A good place for beach access is **The Circle**, at the south end of Atlantic Beach Causeway. The character of The Circle changes from day to night, and it might not be the place where Insiders would recommend you let your kids roam free at night. But its atmosphere is improving and provides good access to the beach in the daytime. A go-cart track and Ferris wheel have been added in the center of The Circle, giving it more of a family atmosphere. The beach has been renourished, so beachgoers will now find a larger stretch of

beautiful beach, volleyball nets and plenty of parking.

On the **west side of The Circle**, there is a facility that offers limited paved parking, a bathhouse with outdoor showers, a ramp over the dunes and gazebo/picnic areas. It is equipped for handicapped beachgoers.

Les and Sally Moore Public Beach Access at MP 1½ offers toilet facilities, outdoor showers, a covered gazebo and a boardwalk over the dunes to the beach. It is equipped for the handicapped. Parking meters operate during the summer. Once on the beach, the young and not-so-young will find swings, a climbing area and an old boat to hide in.

Fort Macon State Park at the east end of Bogue Banks offers visitors miles and miles of sandy beaches on which to roam. The park has two popular access areas. The one at the west end of the park features a large bathhouse, outdoor showers, a seasonal refreshment stand, picnic shelters and outdoor grills. The other is near the fort and has a good deal of parking. The only restroom is at the entrance to the fort. For more information about Fort Macon State Park, see the Crystal Coast Attractions chapter.

Pine Knoll Shores

Town residents have access to the water at a few places, but there are no public access areas.

Indian Beach/Salter Path

The **Salter Path Regional Public Beach Access**, MP 10¼ off Salter Path Road, offers paved parking, a boardwalk over the dunes to the ocean, a picnic area and a comfort station with dressing area and outdoor showers. It is equipped for handicapped beachgoers as well.

A **Public Beach Access** at MP 11 off Salter Path Road on the west side of Squatter's Restaurant, offers parking for cars and racks for bikes. The south end of the parking lot opens directly onto the beach to allow beach access for vehicles with permits during the off-season.

Emerald Isle

Third Street Park, MP 12¼ at Second Street, is a good public access. Visitors to this park actually turn on Second Street just west

Photo: Scott Taylor

"I'd rather be sailing."

of the Indian Beach town line. A small gravel lot offers parking for a few cars and a bike rack. A ramp over the dunes takes oceangoers to the beach.

Beside **Emerald Isle Pier**, MP 15 off Salter Path Road, is a large access that has parking for more than 100 cars on a gravel lot. Visitors will have a short walk to the ocean beach.

Another access is at **Ocean Drive**, MP 15¼ off Salter Path Road. No parking spaces are offered here, only access to the beach for walkers or cyclists and vehicles with permits.

At **Whitewater Drive**, MP 17½ off Salter Path Road, beachgoers will find a wooden walkway to the beach and two vehicle parking places for handicapped visitors.

The access on **Black Skimmer Road**, MP 19 off Salter Path Road, offers visitors a place to walk to the beach and beach access for vehicles. No parking is offered.

The sound access on **Cedar Street**, MP 19¼ off Salter Path Road, has a small gravel parking lot and a short pier over the water.

Beaufort

On the east side of Beaufort-Morehead City high-rise bridge, **Newport River Park** off the causeway on U.S. 70 has a pier, sandy beach, picnic area, bathhouse and a launching ramp sufficient for small sailboats. The park entrance is directly across from Radio Island.

Radio Island, off the Causeway on U.S. 70, is the largest island between the Beaufort-Morehead City high-rise bridge and the draw-bridge into Beaufort. It is home to a variety of businesses — marinas, boat builders and a fuel terminal complete with large tanks. This beach access is a favorite spot for locals because it fronts Beaufort Channel, offers few to no waves and affords an impressive view of Beaufort and the surrounding islands. Portable toilets are provided and there's plenty of parking.

Curtis A. Perry Park, at the east end of Front Street, is not a swimming spot, but it does provide picnic tables, grills and a dock overlooking Taylor's Creek. Bathroom facilities and a boat ramp are also provided.

Because many boaters enjoy the shallow, protected waters along the Crystal Coast, numerous marinas are available to serve the fleet of water traffic.

Marinas

North Carolina has the largest area of inland waters on the East Coast. The Outer Banks enclose several large inland sounds: Currituck, Albemarle, Pamlico, Core and Bogue, which are laced together north to south by 265 miles of the Intracoastal Waterway (ICW). This liquid highway of inland waters makes the numerous coastal resorts and historical points of interest easily accessible by boat.

Of Carteret County's total 1,063 square miles, 531 miles are water. The bountiful brine giving definition to the Crystal Coast challenges the greater portion of the populace and most annual visitors to see the area by water. The weather lures pleasure boaters and sailors almost year round. Even in the coldest months, you'll find a few days each week that are too pretty to stay ashore.

Because many boaters enjoy the shallow, protected waters along the Crystal Coast, numerous marinas are available to serve the fleet of water traffic. There are more than 35 marinas, most on or just off the ICW. And, via the ICW, boaters can sojourn to nearby Oriental and New Bern, where a number of marinas serve power and sailing vessels. See the Marinas section of the New Bern chapter for those listings.

Crystal Coast marinas have varying water depths, services, amenities, transient accommodations and proximity to sights and services. Many condominium developments provide owners the use of private docks. Here we have provided a listing of Crystal Coast area marinas. Please call ahead or write to inquire whether a marina offers the specific services you'll need.

For you boaters who don't leave home without your craft trailing behind, we've also given you the locations of public launch ramps at the end of this chapter. There is no launch fee at these locations. At most of the marinas we've listed, launch ramps are available and a small fee is charged for use and to leave your vehicle and trailer while your boat is in the water.

Marinas

Bogue Banks

Triple S Marina Village, E. Fort Macon Road, MP ½, Atlantic Beach, 247-4833

Anchorage Marina, 517 E. Fort Macon Road, MP 1½, Atlantic Beach, 726-4423

Fort Macon Marina, E. Fort Macon Road, MP 1¾, Atlantic Beach, 726-2055

Bailey's Marina, Atlantic Beach Causeway, Atlantic Beach, 247-4148

Angler Inn and Marina, Atlantic Beach Causeway, Atlantic Beach, 726-0097

Captain Stacy Fishing Center, Atlantic Beach Causeway, Atlantic Beach, 247-7501

Crow's Nest Marina, Atlantic Beach Causeway, Atlantic Beach, 726-4048

Sea Water Marina, Atlantic Beach Causeway, Atlantic Beach, 726-1637

Causeway Marina, Atlantic Beach Causeway, Atlantic Beach, 726-6977

Island Harbor Marina, Old Ferry Road at the end of Mangrove Drive, Emerald Isle, 354-3106

Beaufort

Boaters who arrive in Beaufort via Taylor's Creek may drop anchor in the designated anchorage and out of the main channel. A number of moorings are privately owned, and boaters are asked to respect waterway courtesies of space and anchorage. There is no charge for anchoring and no limit for length of stay. A public dinghy dock and restrooms are available. The dock master at the Dock House is available to answer questions. Town Creek on the north side of Beaufort is also a designated anchorage with dinghy landing.

Beaufort Town Docks, Taylor's Creek, 728-2503

Beaufort Gulf Dock, Taylor's Creek (fuel only), 728-6000

Airport Marina, W. Beaufort Road on South Creek, 728-2010

Sea Gate Association, N.C. Highway 101, 1 mile north of Core Creek Bridge on the ICW, 728-4126

Town Creek Marina, W. Beaufort Road, north of the Beaufort drawbridge, 728-6111

Radio Island Marina, Morehead City-Beaufort Causeway, 726-3773

Morehead City

Dockside Marina and Ship's Store, 301 Arendell Street, 247-4890

Portside Marina, 209 Arendell Street, 726-7678

Morehead City Yacht Basin, Calico Creek, north of the Morehead City high-rise bridge, 726-6862

Island Marina, Morehead City-Beaufort Causeway on Radio Island, 726-5706

Morehead Sports Marina, Morehead City-Beaufort Causeway, 202 Radio Island Road, 726-5676

Coral Bay Marina, Pelletier Creek, U.S. Highway 70 W., 247-4231

70 West Marina, Pelletier Creek, 4401 Arendell Street, 726-5171

Harbor Master, Pelletier Creek, 4408 Central Drive, 726-2541

Spooner's Creek Yacht Harbor, N.C. Highway 24, 726-2060

Western Carteret/ Swansboro

Almost every home or business on the White Oak River or Bogue Sound has a dock, boat ramp or both. But the commercial docks, particularly the ones big enough and with channels dredged deep enough to accommodate a very large motor or sailing yacht, are few.

Casper's Marine Service, on the ICW south of town at 102 Broad Street, Swansboro, 326-4462

The Flying Bridge, off the ICW north of town on N.C. Highway 24, Swansboro, 393-2416

Dudley's Marina, off the ICW north of town on N.C. Highway 24, Swansboro, 393-2204

Down East

Barbour's Harbor, Harkers Island, 728-6181

Calico Jack's Inn & Marina, Harkers Island, 728-3575

Fisherman's Inn, Harkers Island, 728-5780

Harkers Island Fishing Center, Harkers Island, 728-3907, (800) 423-8739

Morris Marina, 1000 Morris Marina Road, Atlantic, 225-4261

Boat Sales and Service

We hope it doesn't happen to you, but boat motors have been known to fail. If you have a breakdown while boating along the Crystal Coast, one of these businesses should be able to help. For your convenience, we've organized the businesses according to the type of motor-repair services they specialize in. If you're in the market for a new boat or motor, call around or visit the businesses to find out who sells what.

INSIDERS' TIP

The Sanitary Restaurant on the Morehead City waterfront offers its dock to transient boats for $5 a night without water or electricity.

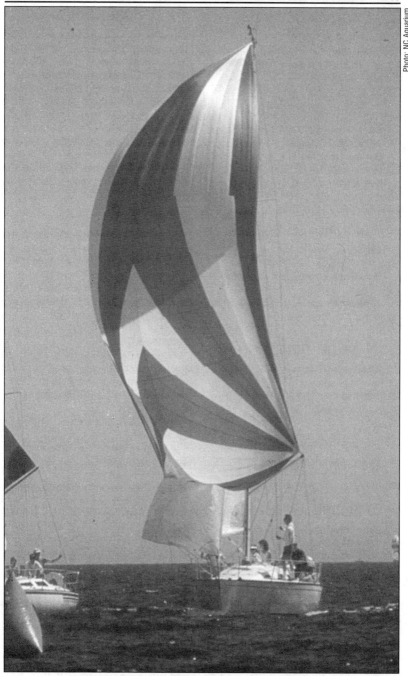

Photo: NC Aquarium

Spinnakers pop on the downwind leg of the race.

Evinrude Outboards

Morehead Marine Inc., 4971 Arendell Street, Morehead City, 247-6667

Lane's Marina Inc., Morehead-Beaufort Causeway, 728-4473

Johnson Outboards

Boats Inc., 4838 Arendell Street, Morehead City, 726-2196

Crow's Nest Marina, Atlantic Beach Causeway, 726-6161

Fort Macon Marina, 417 E. Fort Macon Road, Atlantic Beach, 726-5676

Mercury Outboards

Morehead Sports Marina, Morehead-Beaufort Causeway, 726-5676

Precision Marine, 1058 N.C. Highway 24, Cedar Point, 393-3036

70 West Marina, U.S. Highway 70 W., Morehead City, 726-9993

Suzuki Outboards

Atlantic Beach Causeway Marina, Atlantic Beach Causeway, 726-6977

Walsh Marine, 213 U.S. Highway 70 W., Havelock, 447-BASS

Volvo Penta

Town Creek Marina, 232 W. Beaufort Road, Beaufort, 728-6111

Yamaha Outboards

Jones Brothers Marine, 5136 U.S. Highway 70 W., Morehead City, 726-8404

Boat Ramps

The Crystal Coast area has a great deal of boat ramps, large and small, public and private. Below is a short list of just a few of the state-maintained public ramps. Because most ramps don't have names, we've listed them alphabetically according to location. There are private ramps in every part of the Crystal Coast area, and most marinas and campgrounds have boat ramps. Remember, this is only a list of the free state-maintained ramps, so call the marina closest to you and, chances are, you won't have to drive far to put your boat in the water.

Beaufort

Curtis A. Perry Park is a public ramp with four launching areas. The park is at the east end of Front Street near the tennis courts.

Two ramps and a dock are offered off W. Beaufort Road beside Town Creek Marina. These are maintained by Carteret County Parks and Recreation Department.

Morehead City

Municipal Park behind the Crystal Coast Visitors Center on Arendell Street has several launching areas and a large parking area. The park is just east of Carteret Community College.

Cedar Island

A ramp is beyond the Cedar Island National Wildlife Refuge office on Lola Road at the south end of the island.

The refuge also maintains a ramp on the west side of (and almost below) the new highrise bridge, N.C. Highway 12, just west of the island.

INSIDERS' TIP

The U.S. Coast Guard will refer all emergency calls that are not life-threatening to commercial towing operations, so you might as well call them first. A handful of towing businesses in the Beaufort, Morehead City and Emerald Isle areas monitor VHF channel 16 all day and night.

Cedar Point

A ramp maintained by the N.C. Wildlife Commission is on the south side of N.C. Highway 24 between Cape Carteret and Swansboro.

Sea Level

A ramp is maintained on the east side of the high-rise bridge on U.S. 70 just before you get to the Down East community of Sea Level.

Emergency Numbers

Coast Guard Information, 247-4598

Search and Rescue Emergencies, 247-4545

Swansboro Lifeboat Station in Emerald Isle, 354-2719

The Historic Beaufort
Road Race is the area's
most popular race.

Sports, Fitness and Parks

North Carolina's Crystal Coast has plenty to offer in the way of sports. Whether it's running, basketball, beach volleyball or bicycling, the year-round mild climate and wonderful coastal scenery make any activity more fun to do. And if the weather just won't cooperate or you need some equipment, you can visit our fitness centers, stretch and bend in a yoga class or work off stress in a karate session.

This section introduces you to a few of the area's most popular sports and, in most cases, gives you a contact. Watersports are described in our Fishing, Boating, Watersports and Beach Access chapter. At this chapter's end, we list some of the county and city parks on the Crystal Coast. Information about state and national parks is given in our Attractions chapter.

Sports

Like most areas, the Crystal Coast has its share of sports enthusiasts who participate in their favorite events casually or as part of an organized team. Here we have listed popular sports and how to contact someone in the know.

Baseball and Little League

Teams for children and adults are sponsored by the **Carteret County Parks and Recreation Department**, 728-8401.

If you'd rather watch, the **Kinston Indians**, a minor league professional baseball team based in nearby Kinston, provide great family entertainment. Games are played on week nights and weekends during the season in a newly renovated park with all the extras.

Kinston is a two-hour drive from Morehead City. For ticket information and a game schedule, call 527-9111 or (800) 334-5467.

Basketball

Most of the Crystal Coast parks have basketball courts, as do a few of the area fitness centers. The **Carteret County Parks and Recreation Department**, 728-8401, sponsors a basketball league.

Bicycling

As far as this Insider is concerned, the beach is absolutely the best place to ride your off-road bike (as long as it's low tide). Consult our chapter on Fishing, Boating, Watersports, and Beach Access to find out where and how you can access the beaches. For road or fat-tire bikes, **Salter Path Road** (N.C. Highway 58) is fun cycling, as is Emerald Isle's **Coast Guard Road**, which now has a bike path. The **Beaufort Bicycle Route** is a 6-mile loop of this beautiful, old town. Pick up your route map at the Safrit Historical Center at the Beaufort Historic Site on Turner Street.

The **Swansboro Bicentennial Bicycle Trail** is 25 miles of exhilarating biking that begins in historic Swansboro. The looped trail crosses the White Oak River to Cape Carteret, winds through the Croatan National Forest, crosses the river again and returns to Swansboro.

North Carolina's **Bicycle Program** has an excellent color map that shows bicycle enthusiasts where to cycle on the Outer Banks. Three loop and two linear bicycle routes are highlighted and include portions of the mainland as well as the barrier islands. Contact the Bicycle Program, N.C. Department of Transportation, P.O. Box 25201, Raleigh, N.C. 27611, 733-2804.

Bowling

We have only one local bowling alley, but it's a great place to have fun.

Carteret Lanes
U.S. 70, 1 mile west of Morehead City (across from Wal-Mart) • 247-4481

Carteret Lanes is equipped with 24 lanes, pool tables, electronic darts, video games and a snack bar. You'll also find a pro shop where you can buy bowling balls and shoes as well as get any of your bowling gear serviced.

Manager Mike Eskew reports that Carteret Lanes always has special summer programs. Last summer, twice every week, teenagers were encouraged to come in and bowl and socialize and just generally hang out. Also twice weekly, the lanes sponsors a senior citizen social, which does pretty much the same thing as the teenagers' get-togethers. Call to find out what's doing this summer. Carteret Lanes rents bowling shoes, and you may bring your own ball or use one of theirs.

Fitness Centers

Emerald Isle Municipal Complex
Emerald Dr. MP 19, Emerald Isle
• 354-6350

This center is open to residents and non-residents for a nominal fee. The facility offers a full-size gym for indoor tennis, basketball, volleyball, soccer and shuffleboard. Classes vary and often include aerobics, gymnastics and karate. There is also a weight room, a game room with pool and Ping-Pong tables,

an exchange library and a fully equipped kitchen. Space for meetings and parties is also available. Outside you will find tennis courts, a basketball court and a children's play area.

Body Quest
1 Medical Park Ct., Morehead City
• 247-2763, 726-0764

Body Quest offers one-on-one personal fitness under the guidance of owner Brian McArtan, a Certified Personal Trainer. For 10 years, he has helped folks of all ages (and both genders) lose weight, reshape their bodies and strengthen their muscles. Training can be scheduled at your convenience, in your home or at the Body Quest facility. Fees are by the session, which are typically 35 minutes to an hour, three times a week for eight weeks. Brian's approach to a healthy body emphasizes prevention. He has practiced on the Crystal Coast for three years.

Total Fitness Gym
U.S. Hwy. 70 W., Morehead City
• 247-6747

Total Fitness Gym is next to the Wal-Mart shopping center. Gay and Ross LaPointe own and operate this new facility and have a schedule convenient for vacationers and year-rounders alike. There are single and family memberships, senior citizen discounts and student memberships as well as nonmember passes. Rates are charged by the visit, month or year. Total Fitness Gym users have a lot to choose from: nautilus resistance machines, muscle dynamic Maxicam, unlimited aerobics, racquetball and a complete cardiovascular complex. If you want to relax after working up a sweat, try the steamroom, sauna and whirlpool. To keep your tan during the winter, use the tanning facilities. Personal training programs are also available, as is on-site childcare. The gym operates Monday through Friday from 6 AM to 9 PM; Saturday hours are 9 AM to 5 PM.

INSIDERS' TIP

Beaufort's waterfront is a popular early morning walking and running spot, with many folks arriving by 5:30 AM to enjoy the peace and quiet while exercising.

Photo: Wayland Cato

You can ride horses on the beach in Cedar Island.

Morehead City Recreation Department
1600 Fisher St., Morehead City • 726-5083

This is the area's most affordable fitness center with modest yearly rates for both city and non-city residents. Members may use the fully equipped weight room with free weights and equipment, a gym with a full-size basketball court and a game room with pool and Ping-Pong tables. The department offers aerobics, dance and karate classes, dog obedience classes and various youth sports programs such as basketball, T-ball and softball.

The Sports Center
701 N. 35th St., Morehead City • 726-7070

The Sports Center is a complete fitness center, offering a fully equipped weight room, Nautilus equipment and fitness equipment, an indoor swimming pool, racquetball courts, an indoor walking/running track and classes of all kinds including karate, water and floor aerobics and swimming. Sports Center also has a basketball/volleyball court, tanning salon, stair climbers, treadmills and NordicTrack. An Olympic-size outdoor pool with a waterslide and surrounding picnic tables have been added to the facility. For relaxing, you'll find saunas, a whirlpool and a steam room. The center has a vitamin and equipment store, a snack bar and child-care services. Daily and weekly rates are available, as is a short-term three-month membership.

Flying

Michael J. Smith Airport
102 Airport Rd., Beaufort • 728-1777

This airfield offers services for private planes and private lessons. This airfield was named in memory of the pilot of space shuttle *Challenger*, which exploded January 28, 1986. A Beaufort native, Navy Capt. Michael Smith learned to fly at this airfield.

Horseback Riding

Acha's Stable
1341 Nine Mile Rd., Newport • 223-4478

Acha's provides lessons and trail rides and offers boarding and stall rentals by the month for horse owners. The stable is just west of Morehead City.

Eterna Riverview Stables
Lake Shore Dr. • 726-8313

Eterna offers trail rides, lessons and boarding. The stables are off Country Club Road in Morehead City.

WhiteSand Trail Rides
Cedar Island • 729-0911

WhiteSand provides the horses, and you have the fun. Ride along the beach during the day, at sunset and in the moonlight. With stables on Cedar Island, WhiteSand also offers camping trips. Horse owners can bring their own horses to join the fun any time of year.

Zeigler Stables
Off Howard Blvd. (across from the ballpark), Newport • 223-5110

The stable offers riding lessons, boarding, summer riding camps and a tack shop.

Hunting

Guide services have long been a popular means for duck and goose hunters to experience a new locale. Using a guide cuts down the chances of spending time in the wrong spot.

Driftwood Motel and Restaurant
Cedar Island • 225-4861

The folks here operate a hunting and fishing guide service. Hunting dates depend on those set for the season but are usually mid-December through late January. The Driftwood's hunting package includes guide service by a local and use of a boat, decoys and blinds, accommodations in the motel and hearty meals. Blinds are scattered along 1,100 acres of marsh from Cedar Island to Portsmouth, in Core Sound and on Core Banks. Hunters can rent waders, have their kill cleaned, buy hunting accessories or get a hunting license at the Driftwood. Folks come to the Driftwood from all parts of the country each year to have a crack at the abundant redheads, pintails and other ducks and geese.

Adams Creek GunSports
6240 Adams Creek Rd., Havelock
• **447-7688, 447-6808**

June and Rusty Bryan provide guides for hunting quail, pheasant, duck and dove. They offer accommodations in an 1870 country farmhouse lodge overlooking Adams Creek, a part of the Intracoastal Waterway. Their daughter, Julie Brown, and her husband, Jim, keep the lodge and Julie prepares the meals. Her good Southern cooking emphasizes seafood, beef and game (guests are particularly fond of Julie's venison), and she sends the hunters off with breakfast in the morning and welcomes them with dinner on their return.

Adams Creek GunSports maintains impoundments, natural woodland ponds, and marsh and floating blinds. They also have a Sporting Clays course consisting of targets in the woods and fields. An on-site pro shop and shooting instructors are also available. The Bryans welcome hunting parties, and the lodge is also open for business meetings, parties and weddings. Be aware, however, that reservations are a must and that the Bryans book months in advance.

Karate

Karate lessons are often offered by the **Morehead Recreation Department**, 726-5083, and several of the local fitness centers (see Fitness Centers section in this chapter).

Kite Flying

There's something joyous about flying a kite. The Crystal Coast's beautiful seashore brings out the kite-flying urge in adults and children alike. For folks who want to fly with others, visit Fort Macon State Park on Sunday mornings. From 9 AM to noon, **Kites Unlimited**, 247-7011, Atlantic Station Shopping Center, sponsors friendly kite-flying competitions. (See our Annual Events chapter for information about the annual Carolina Kite Fest in October.)

Running/Walking

Running and walking are favorite forms of exercise along the Crystal Coast. This area's mild temperatures mean that one seldom has to miss a day of exercise and outdoor enjoyment. The Beaufort and Morehead City waterfronts and the beaches continue to be the most favored running and walking spots, and they are heavily traveled by early morning and evening exercisers.

Those runners who like to test their skills, or just run with a group, can avail themselves of the races described below. Most of them include walks too.

Lookout Rotary Spring Road Race
Morehead City • 726-7070

This race kicks off the local race season on the last weekend in April with a flat 5K and 1-mile run/walk beginning and ending at the Sports Center, N. 35th Street in Morehead City. The race is sponsored by the Lookout Rotary Club of Morehead City. For more information, call the Sports Center at the number above.

Beach Run Series
Atlantic Beach • 728-8401

This series of runs sponsored by the Carteret County Parks and Recreation Department usually begins in late May. This low-key weekday series attracts lots of local runners and walkers. The 1-mile run/walk, 5K and 10K are on the beach and begin and end at the beach access area at The Circle in Atlantic Beach. Dates vary depending on the tides.

Historic Beaufort Road Race
Beaufort • 726-7070

This is the area's most popular race. Hundreds turn out in mid-July to tackle the 1-mile run/walk, 5K run/walk and 10K courses. The courses are flat and fast, and runners can be assured of plenty of heat and humidity. For more information, call the Sports Center at the number above.

INSIDERS' TIP

Beach volleyball is increasing in popularity and the Atlantic Beach waterfront is the place to watch, or take part in, the action.

Photo: Burnie Batchelor

Campers from Camp Sea Gull explore the waters of the Neuse River.

Twin Bridges Race
Beaufort to Atlantic Beach • 726-6273

You'll have few choices with the Twin Bridges Race. You either run the 8K or stay on the porch. And because there aren't any hills on the coast, the race directors throw in two high-rise bridges. The race kicks off Saturday's events at the N.C. Seafood Festival the first full weekend in October on the Morehead City waterfront. It begins at the drawbridge in Beaufort and ends on the Atlantic Beach Causeway.

Soccer

There's lots of action on the soccer fields across the area for children and adults. **Carteret County Parks and Recreation Department**, 728-8401, sponsors leagues for younger players and for women and men. Soccer Dome of America organizes the annual **Soccer-on-the-Sand Jam**, North Carolina's only sand soccer tournament. See our Annual Festivals and Events chapter for more information.

Softball

The **Careret County Parks and Recreation Department** sponsors a men's and women's softball league each year. The teams are usually sponsored by local businesses and are very competitive. Call 728-8401 for information.

Tennis

The Crystal Coast is host to a number of tournaments each year. For more information, contact **Spooner's Creek Racquet Club**, 726-8560, or call **Island Beach and Racquet Club**, 726-2240. Public tennis courts are scattered throughout the area (see the Parks listings at the end of this chapter).

Three of the area's open-to-the-public golf clubs offer tennis courts: **Bogue Banks Country Club**, **Silver Creek Country Club** and **Star Hill Golf and Country Club**. See our Golf chapter for more information about these clubs. In addition, the **Emerald Isle Municipal Complex** (see Fitness Centers in this chapter) has tennis courts.

Triathlons

Nelson Bay Challenge
Sea Level • 247-6902

This popular sprint triathlon takes place in Sea Level in early May. The race includes a 750-meter swim in Nelson Bay, a 20K bike ride and a 5K run. For many, the race is a warm-up for the triathlon season ahead. This well-organized race offers spectators easy viewing of the transition area and a great post-race clambake. The funding sponsor is J.M. Davis Industries of Morehead City, 247-6902. Money raised benefits local youth programs.

Volleyball

Beach volleyball is catching on. Tournament nets are on the main beach at **The Circle** in Atlantic Beach, and there is usually plenty of action there. For information about beach volleyball tournaments, call the **Atlantic Beach Recreation Director**, 726-2121. An indoor volleyball league is sponsored by the **Carteret County Parks and Recreation Department**, 728-8401.

Yoga

Want to stretch and bend after all that sun and surf and good seafood? Try yoga to loosen strained muscles and gain flexibility. Visitors and vacationers can join the open, walk-in classes held at **The Light Within Natural Herbs, Healing and Yoga Center**, 726-6500, Morehead Plaza. Beginner and intermediate classes take place every day in the mornings and early evenings. Classes are also held on Saturdays. The instructor is Elizabeth Holliday, a yoga master and a teacher of teachers. Twelve-week yoga sessions are also available.

Sherry Wells, Suite 5, 704 Arendell Street, Morehead, 247-2137, has been a Phoenix Rising yoga therapist for two years. She conducts one-on-one sessions, by appointment, and helps people release emotional energy.

Parks

County Parks

The seven parks listed here are managed by the Carteret County Parks and Recreation Department, 728-8401, and all offer a picnic area and comfort station. Additional amenities are listed along with the location. Other area parks are included at the bottom of the list.

The **Salter Path Ball Field**, N.C. 58 in Salter Path, is behind the community fire department and is used for sports as well as community events.

Freedom Park, off Lennoxville Road in Beaufort, is surrounded by woods and has lighted regulation and youth fields, basketball courts and a picnic and play area.

Newport River Park, on the east side of the high-rise bridge between Beaufort and Morehead, has a short fishing pier, a boat ramp sufficient for launching small sailboats, a picnic area and restroom facilities. The park entrance is directly across from the entrance to Radio Island.

Swinson Park, Country Club Road in Morehead City, is a popular spot for athletics. Beside the new Morehead City Primary School, Swinson Park offers lighted regulation and youth athletic fields, tennis and basketball courts and a picnic area.

Western Park, off N.C. 58 in Cedar Point, offers a lighted youth softball/baseball field and a multipurpose field.

Eastern Park, U.S. 70 in Smyrna, is a lighted park that features regulation and youth fields, basketball courts, tennis courts and a picnic area.

Mariner's Park, off U.S. 70 in Sea Level, is across from the Sea Level Extended Care Facility and has lighted youth athletic fields and tennis courts.

City and Community Parks

Bogue Banks

The island doesn't have many parks, so most residents and visitors go to the beach to picnic and play. For a listing of the access areas, see our Fishing, Boating, Watersports and Beach Access chapter.

INSIDERS' TIP

Use a fishing reel to hold your kite string. Some say that's cheating but a reel sure makes it a breeze to bring a high-flying kite back to you.

Photo: Scott Taylor

Nothing like a lazy fall afternoon for some intense fishing.

Emerald Isle Parks and Recreation Department, 354-6350, maintains two small public parks. The park, behind the town hall on Emerald Drive at MP 19, has a children's play area and picnic tables. Merchant's Park is on the south side of Emerald Drive at MP 19½ and offers parking, picnic tables, shelter and restroom facilities.

Beaufort

The town's most popular park, **Freedom Park**, is maintained by the county (see County Parks above). It is about three blocks from Front Street on Leonda Drive. The town also maintains two others, described below.

Grayden Paul Jaycee Park is on Front Street at the south end of Pollock Street. The small area offers a dock, a swimming area, a gazebo and a grassed picnic spot, although there is no beach. The park was named for the late Beaufort raconteur Grayden Paul.

Curtis A. Perry Park is at the east end of Front Street across from the boat ramp. You'll find a basketball court, two lighted tennis courts, bathroom facilities, a dock and waterfront picnic areas complete with grills. The park was named in memory of the town's public works director.

Morehead City

Morehead City Recreation Department, 726-5083, oversees several city parks. Each park offers different amenities. At 1600 Fisher Street, behind the recreation department, are two multipurpose fields used primarily for softball and baseball. Inside this facility, members may use the weight room, loaded with free weights and machines; a gym with a full-size basketball court and a game room with pool and Ping-Pong tables. Membership fees are very reasonable. The department also offers aerobics, dance and karate classes, dog obedience classes and youth sports programs (basketball, T-ball, softball, etc.) and more.

City Park, 1000 Block, Arendell Street, is a shady park with playground equipment and a few picnic tables.

Jaycee Park, on the water at the south end of 9th Street, is the site of the city's Summer in the Park concert series hosted by the Parks and Recreation Department on Saturday evenings in summer. You'll find parking, picnic tables and a short pier at this park.

Municipal Park, behind the Crystal Coast Visitors' Center, Arendell Street, offers plenty of parking, picnic areas and a boat ramp. The park borders Bogue Sound, just west of the Atlantic Beach high-rise bridge.

Piney Park, 2900 Block, Bridges Street, just east of Morehead Plaza, is tucked away in some trees and serves as a quiet picnic spot.

Shevans Park, 1600 Block, Evans Street, has four tennis courts (two are lit), four basketball goals, a practice field and a fence.

Swansboro

Bicentennial Park is at the base of the bridge into Swansboro on N.C. Highway 24. The park was dedicated in 1985 and contains a life-size statue of Otway Burns, Swansboro's favorite privateer from the War of 1812, and a memorial to Theophilus Weeks, founder of the town. The park is the perfect place to fish from the sea wall, play or simply sit and enjoy the beauty of the White Oak River.

Golf

The Crystal Coast's championship courses await the golf enthusiast, and most of the area's exceptional club courses are open to the public. Courses are busy year round, and many Insiders consider fall the most favorable time to play. It is best to call ahead, especially on weekends, to reserve tee times. Several area hotels offer golf packages that include accommodations, meals, guaranteed starting times, greens fees and a few extras.

Below you will find the area courses that are open to the public. Two local driving ranges are listed at the end.

Courses

Brandywine Bay
Golf and Country Club
N.C. Hwy. 24, Morehead City • 247-2541

Located west of Morehead City, this 18-hole, par 71 championship course was recently ranked in *Golf Digest* as the best course in the area. A very popular course, it is set in dense woods and laced with streams and ponds. Originally designed by Bruce Devlin and redesigned by Ellis and Dan Maples, this coastal course plays 6609 yards from the championship tees, 6150 from the regular tees, 5389 yards from the gold, 6138 for the regular's men's and 5191 yards for women's. Golfers will find a well-stocked pro shop, snack bar, lessons by appointment and putting greens. Coy Brown is Brandywine's PGA professional and is well-known in the area.

Bogue Banks
Golf and Country Club
N.C. Hwy. 58, MP 5, Pine Knoll Shores • 726-1034

This par 72 course is 6100 yards with four holes overlooking Bogue Sound. Numerous lagoons and lakes meander throughout the narrow bermudagrass fairways leading to lush greens. Beautiful water oaks and lofty pine trees enhance the overall beauty of the course. From the blue tees it measures 6100 yards, from the white tees, 5757 yards and from the red, 5043 yards. A pro shop, snack area, tennis courts and daily and weekly rates are available. Golf and tennis lessons can be arranged. Jeff Austin is the course PGA professional.

Silver Creek Golf Club
N.C. Hwy. 58, Cape Carteret • 393-8058

On Highway 58 just north of Cape Carteret, this par 72 championship course, with bentgrass greens and beautiful bermudagrass fairways and tees, was designed by Gene Hamm. The course plays 7005 yards from silver tees, 6526 yards from blue tees, 6030 yards from white tees and 4962 yards from women's tees. A Southern-style clubhouse has a wide porch overlooking the course. Also on the grounds are a snack bar, locker rooms, a driving range, a putting green, a pro shop, tennis courts and a swimming pool.

Star Hill Golf and Country Club
Club House Dr., Cape Carteret • 393-8111

This is one of the area's finest 27-hole championship courses, measuring more than

---

INSIDERS' TIP

Call the course you intend to play a few days early so you can find out how far in advance you can reserve a tee time.

Brandywine Bay

*Brandywine Bay Championship Golf Course
invites you to discover 18 holes of the finest
golfing experience on the North Carolina
Coast! This course, designed by Bruce Devlin,
boasts over 6600 yards of rolling fairways
and bentgrass greens, the challenge of 40
acres of water, fast putting greens and the
well known 555 yard par 5 hole #10. This is
truly a golfer's paradise for the novice
or seasoned veteran,*

-PUBLIC & GROUPS WELCOME-

LESSONS AVAILABLE
BENTGRASS GREENS
FULLY STOCKED PRO SHOP

Tee Time Reservations:
(919) 247-2541

Brandywine Bay Championship Golf Course
Hwy. 70 West
Morehead City, NC 28557

Golf is a way of life for some, and the Crystal Coast offers some of the area's best courses.

9000 yards. Comprised of the Sands, the Pines and the Lakes, Star Hill is at the junction of highways 24 and 58 and is nestled between the Intracoastal Waterway and Croatan National Forest. Patrons will find a driving range, rental clubs, tennis courts, a swimming pool and a grill and snack area. You'll also find PGA Professional Instructors Phill Hunt and Mick Brown on hand.

Driving Ranges

Bob's Golf Driving Range
N.C. Hwy. 24, Morehead City • 240-4653

Just outside Morehead City on Highway 24, Bob's Golf Range offers a 250-yard driving range. Patrons can hit from T-mats or grass areas. The range is open throughout the year, although the winter hours vary.

Golphin' Dolphin
N.C. Hwy. 58, Cape Carteret • 393-8131

This business offers a 300-yard driving range, an 18-hole miniature golf course with elevations up to 22 feet, a batting cage, a pro shop, a go-cart track, bumper boats and more. The batting cage is for softball and baseball, and golf equipment is offered in the pro shop. The go-cart track is loads of fun. A separate room is available for parties or meetings. Golphin' Dolphin is behind Hardee's in Cape Carteret and is open every day during the summer. Winter hours vary.

Homes on the Central Coast vary tremendously in price, and location is everything. Here, good locations are determined by proximity to water, historic districts or golf courses and upscale subdivisions.

Neighborhoods and Real Estate

If you are seriously considering purchasing property or relocating to North Carolina's Crystal Coast, this is the section for you. We, as Insiders, think you are making a wonderful decision. Welcome!

In this chapter we introduce you, first, to the neighborhoods that make up the expansive Crystal Coast and then to some of the area's real estate companies. Our list is by no means complete but will familiarize you with the area and help you locate neighborhoods, businesses and services. The realty firms recommended here are listed alphabetically. These are not the only companies of their type in the area; there are many other fine and reputable firms, but we simply couldn't list them all. We revise this book annually, and we welcome your comments concerning additions or omissions in the next edition.

Before we start with neighborhoods, we should point out that an invaluable source of free information for anyone seriously interested in purchasing property is *New Homes Magazine of the Crystal Coast*. This monthly guide, published in cooperation with the Multiple Listing Service of the Carteret County Association of Realtors, contains in-depth descriptions of all the residential and commercial property in Carteret County. You can pick up a free copy at supermarkets, drug stores, restaurants and hundreds of local commercial establishments.

We begin by looking at beach neighbor-

hoods. When we talk about the beach we are referring to the island of Bogue Banks, which encompasses the townships of Atlantic Beach, Pine Knoll Shores, Indian Beach, Salter Path and Emerald Isle. From there we move to delightfully different historic Beaufort, then to the central town of Morehead City, westward to Swansboro and finally to the Down East reaches of Carteret County.

Like everywhere else, homes on the Crystal Coast vary tremendously in price, and location is everything. Here, good locations are determined by proximity to water, historic districts or golf courses and upscale subdivisions. While you may find very comfortable living quarters in the $60,000 to $70,000 range, you can also spend hundreds of thousands for a large, plush home in an exclusive waterfront neighborhood with a slip for your boat. Significant development has taken place away from the water recently, and a wide range of housing is available.

There is no specific relocation service on the Crystal Coast; however, rest assured that most agents will move heaven and earth to ensure that your move is smooth. After all, they are in the business of sharing with newcomers what we Insiders have already learned — this is a great place to be!

A note on zoning: If the property you are considering is not in an incorporated city or subdivision, ask your real estate agent or the

county planning office what uses are permitted in that area. Large portions of Carteret County are unzoned and may permit certain uses you have not bargained for. Then again, some folks are looking for that kind of freedom. Ask questions so you'll know before you commit.

Neighborhoods

Bogue Banks — The Beaches

Like most beach resorts, the Crystal Coast has a number of condominium developments. We mention a few here; however, for a more complete list of what is available, check with a real estate agent. Also, for information on time-share and fractional ownership possibilities, check our Crystal Coast Weekly and Long-term Cottage Rentals chapter.

Many newcomers move to the Crystal Coast for one reason: to live at the beach. Atlantic Beach, Pine Knoll Shores, Indian Beach and Salter Path often have older homes on the market. Newer homes, condominiums and townhouses have been built in recent years.

Emerald Isle and Pine Knoll Shores are the more recently established towns. Both have many new structures and homesites in a variety of price ranges; so, whatever you want, you can probably find it on the beach.

Atlantic Beach

Atlantic Beach has a nostalgic air about it — a throwback to the 1950s when beach houses were functional and rambling, when small cottages nudged right up next to ponderous two-story clapboards on narrow streets running parallel to the ocean. Today, some see Atlantic Beach as a bit ramshackle and hodgepodge while others are inspired to reminisce about red convertibles, Sandra Dee and beach blankets. But changes are afoot. The

Circle, where most beach entertainment businesses used to be centered, has been renovated and new businesses are moving in.

Today, private homes and vacation rentals are mixed throughout this small oceanfront town and, over the years, building has extended several blocks back from the water to N.C. Highway 58, or Salter Path Road. Most all dwellings in Atlantic Beach are within walking distance of the ocean, and the majority of new homes are concentrated on the eastern end of the island, along Fort Macon Road. Here, too, are a number of condominium and townhouse developments, such as **Seaspray**, **A Place At the Beach**, **Southwinds**, **Sands Villa Resort**, **Island Quay** and others. **Angler's Cove** is one of Atlantic Beach's newest waterfront condo developments. On the causeway, this development offers five three-story buildings with 18 units starting at $160,000.

The residential area known as **Hoop Hole Creek** on Bogue Sound, a few miles from the downtown center, is beautifully forested with a few remaining lots. Condos and townhouses such as **Dunescape Villas**, **Island Beach and Racquet Club**, **Coral Bay East and West** and others are also in this section. **Ocean Ridge II** is a new small oceanfront community with 18 lots. The lots offer great views of the ocean and Bogue Sound, are covered by restrictive covenants and begin at $39,000.

Pine Knoll Shores

The developers of Pine Knoll Shores deserve credit for their farsightedness. Built in a maritime forest, the town has done an admirable job of minimally impacting the environment. Drive through and you will see what we mean — trees are everywhere. Restrictive covenants require a complete survey of all trees larger than 3 inches on each lot. Before you can get a permit to build, you have to prove you will save as many trees as possible and disturb the land as little as possible. The process can be tedious, but the result is worth it, as most all residents will agree.

The beauty of Crystal Coast wildlife is endlessly fascinating.

The area is nearly 75 percent developed, and both large and small homes come on the market fairly regularly. Lots not on the ocean or sound start at $35,000, and homes range from the low $100,000s to more than $400,000, depending on proximity to the ocean, the sound, canals or the town's 18-hole golf course. Within the central portion of the town, a good many homes are built on canals, with the option of private docks.

Bermuda Greens, located off U.S. 58, along Pine Knoll Shores Golf and County Club, is a patio-home community. This planned residential area has 17 two-bedroom, two-bath homes with private garages and views of the golf course and the sound. Prices start at about $105,000.

Pine Knoll Townes, **Bogue Shores Club** **and Beachwalk at Pine Knoll Shores** are townhouse and condominium developments between MP 6 and 7 on U.S. 58. All are on the ocean and in a lovely maritime forest setting. Design features include courtyards, sun porches, gourmet kitchens, private balconies and other upscale luxuries. Prices range from $119,000 to as much as $300,000 for plush living accommodations.

Beacon's Reach, MP 8½ through 9¼, is a large development in a maritime forest on land once owned by the Roosevelt family. It includes both multifamily and single-family dwellings. Each village is carefully planned, and residents have access to lighted tennis courts, swimming pools, a marina, and parks on the ocean and the sound. Villages include Ocean Grove, with three- and four-bedroom units; Westport, with one-two- and three-bedroom units and both soundfront and freshwater lagoon-front units; the Breakers, with oceanfront condominiums; Fiddlers' Walk with soundside condominium units; and Maritime West, with oceanfront units.

Condominiums and single-family homes in Beacon's Reach range from $99,000 to $600,000 or more on the ocean. Soundside and oceanside lots range from $50,000 to just more than $200,000.

Salter Path/Indian Beach

Many of the longtime residents in these two small communities are descended from fishermen, and some still make their living from the sea. Some homes are low, rambling structures on the soundside, nestled under windswept live oaks bent from prevailing winds. If you are lucky enough to find one of these cottages on the market, you will have a piece of paradise.

In the last few months, the town of Indian Beach has seen the development of a very swanky residential community. **Sea Isle Plan-**

tation is probably one of the priciest areas on the island, but it is extremely beautiful. Located at MP 10 Sea Isle offers homesites and custom-built residences on both sides of Salter Path Road, Bogue Sound and the ocean. Bogue Sound lots, each with a private boatslip, begin at $89,000; custom homes start at $295,000. On the ocean side, ¾-acre, single-family lots begin at $165,000. Luxurious, already built new homes that front the ocean are in the range of $800,000.

The **Summerwinds** condominium complex is a large, oceanfront complex offering spacious living quarters with prices starting at just more than $100,000. Recreational facilities include an indoor, heated swimming pool, a whirlpool, saunas, exercise rooms, a spa and racquetball courts. Outside are three oceanfront pools with sundecks and a boardwalk. Units at the oceanfront **Windward Dunes** in Indian Beach range between $90,000 and $149,500 with pools, saunas and tennis courts.

Emerald Isle

The western end of Emerald Isle is family-oriented, and not until a few years ago did a substantial number of residents become "year rounders." Originally, the only access to the island was by boat and, later, ferry. It wasn't until the 1970s that the B. Cameron Langston high-rise bridge opened the area to tourists and newcomers. Emerald Isle is now one of the fastest growing areas of the county. Sections along Coast Guard Road, off N.C. 58, have seen an astounding amount of development in recent years. Some of the nicer subdivisions are here.

You'll find many of the town's recently built residences quite impressive. Homes and cottages come in all styles, but most are multi-storied, with wide porches and decks, so residents can take advantage of the beach view and sea breezes. Although some developers have bulldozed dunes and cleared much of the natural vegetation, others have left stands of maritime forest. There are a number of condominium and townhouse developments as well, such as **Pebble Beach**, **Queens Court**, **Sound of the Sea** and others in the price range between $59,900 and $139,000.

Lands End is an exclusive planned residential community on Coast Guard Road off N.C. 58 near the Point in Emerald Isle. Ownership includes use of a spacious clubhouse, a pool, four lighted tennis courts, stocked freshwater lakes and a lighted boardwalk to the beach. All roads are private, and utilities are underground. Homes range from $149,000 to $2.1 million. Interior lots start around $47,000; waterfront and ocean-view lots are priced in the mid-to-high $60,000s.

Emerald Plantation is a relatively new soundside subdivision that extends from N.C. 58 to Bogue Sound. A mixed-use development with single-family homes, townhouses and patio homes, amenities include a clubhouse, a pool, a boat ramp, tennis courts and a security gate. Lot prices range from $18,000 to $135,000, and homes range from $110,000 to $300,000. The **Wyndtree** subdivision is a large tract near Emerald Isle Point that has restrictive covenants as to sizes of houses but offers a wide diversity of sites from oceanfront to ocean view. Lot prices range from $35,000 to about $49,000, and single-family homes from $110,000 to $400,000.

The Point on Coast Guard Road off N.C. 58 at the westward tip of the island is one of the most established areas and has a wonderfully wide beach. Homes range from $162,500 for new constructions to $400,000.

Deerhorn Dunes, **Sea Dunes** and **Ocean Oaks** are three well-planned subdivisions that are almost indistinguishable from one another. On Coast Guard Road off N.C. 58, all are relatively new and were built around the same time. They are made up primarily of single-family homes, nicely landscaped on spacious lots. Lot prices begin at $35,000, with ocean-view lots less than $70,000. Single-family homes range between $110,000 and $200,000, with oceanfront homes climbing to as much as $400,000.

Windfall is one of the newer subdivisions in Emerald Isle off N.C. 58. It is a small development made up of about 24 lots that offer second, third and fourth row locations away

from the ocean. Lot prices range from $70,000 to $96,000, with homes from $175,000 to $250,000.

Cape Emerald off N.C. 58 on the soundside of Coast Guard Road is a subdivision of primarily permanent residents. Amenities include a clubhouse, a heated pool and spa and two tennis courts. It also has a security entrance and a community sewage system. Lots range from $20,000 to $95,000, and homes from $100,000 to $350,000. **Emerald Landing**, **Royall Oaks**, **Dolphin Ridge** and **Pointe Bogue** are four new, beautifully landscaped developments that offer peace and privacy in a verdant, spacious wooded setting. Off Coast Guard Road, lots vary from 75-feet wide to 30-feet wide on ocean and road fronts. Interior lots also vary in size due to efforts to preserve the area's wetlands. Interior lot prices begin at $50,000. **Emerald Landing**, **Pointe Bogue** and **Royall Oaks** have soundfront sites, and **Dolphin Ridge** has oceanfront building sites. Houses in these developments start in the low $200,000s.

Also off Coast Guard Road is **Spinnaker's Reach**, a new area described as a "sound to sea community." This development is tucked into the maritime forest and features a community pool, guarded entrance and a soundside pier and nature trail. Single-family

dwellings and oceanfront duplexes are being constructed. Depending on location, prices range from about $198,000 to $250,000 for an oceanside home.

Beaufort

Beaufort's geographic design lends itself to small residential areas built around roads and water. Most new development is east of Beaufort along U.S. Highway 70 or north along N.C. Highway 101. This small port town is a haven for boaters and is a hub of activity during the summer months. Many of its historic homes have been restored as residences or bed and breakfast inns. Its lovely waterfront is a natural setting for music and socializing at outdoor cafes. The town's many shops, restaurants and tourist attractions give Front Street a festive air. Runners, strollers, walkers and bike riders flow constantly along the main Front Street thoroughfare, and the Historic District can easily be covered on foot.

Beaufort's Historic District is the oldest residential area in town, covering about 15 square blocks. Homes here date back to the 1700s, and exterior characteristics are governed by guidelines of the Beaufort Historic Preservation Commission. Charged with assuring the integrity of the area, the commission reviews all proposals for exterior changes such as paint color, siding, window treatments, redesign and other building changes.

Businesses and signage in the historic district are also regulated. The historic commission was not formed until the 1980s, so you will see a few things that do not meet their standards. Property prices vary greatly in the historic district, depending on distance from the water, size and age of the house or building and its condition. You could be looking at a $425,000 waterfront home, a $90,000 residence a couple of blocks away from the water or a home at the far end of Ann Street for somewhere in the $70,000s.

Beaufort homes outside the historic district also carry a variety of price tags, again depending on the distance from the water as well as size, age and condition. **Deerfield Shores**, **Gibb's Landing**, **Howland Rock**, **Jones Village**, **Tiffany Woods** and **Sea Gate** are examples of subdivisions north of the downtown area. **Taylor's Creek** is one of the newer developments on the east end of the Beaufort waterfront, and **Graystone Landing** is a new build-to-suit development along N.C. 101.

Deerfield Shores, off N.C. 101, is an attractive area on the Newport River and Intracoastal Waterway. Central to the development is the Carolina Marlin Club, a private boating (sail and motor) club complete with a 73-slip marina, a clubhouse and a swimming pool. Slip owners own the marina and clubhouse, which is also used by the Morehead-Beaufort Yacht Club. Interior lots in Deerfield range from $12,000 to $35,000; marina-front lots begin at about $40,000 and riverfront lots sell for about $75,000 to $100,000.

Gibb's Landing is a small subdivision on North River, reached by following U.S. 70 east and turning right on Steep Point Road. Subdivision amenities include a community dock, pool and gazebo. Large lots range from $70,000 on the waterfront to $25,000 for lots across the street from the waterfront.

Howland Rock might be considered one of Beaufort's most prestigious neighborhoods. The entrance road is on U.S. 70, just across from the Food Lion grocery store. This older subdivision offers residents such amenities as a boat ramp, a recreational area and a homeowners association. Most of the homes were custom built with attention to detail. Price tags start at about $135,000 and go up to $350,000. Some lots are still available, including a few on the waterfront that can go for as much as $175,000.

Jones Village is in the Beaufort town limits and is one of the area's oldest subdivisions. There are several entrances from Live Oak Street (U.S. 70) to the subdivision, which wraps around behind Jones Village Shopping Center. The development is a quiet, well-settled area that seems to attract a pleasant mix of people. You'll find retirees living alongside young couples. Homes sell for $70,000 to $125,000.

Tiffany Woods is a new development about 4 miles east of Beaufort on U.S. 70. Developers are offering large wooded lots for about $16,000 and up. Several cul-de-sacs extend from the lighted main road, giving the neighborhood a feeling of privacy. This is one of the nicer new neighborhoods in the area.

Sea Gate is a waterside resort community 7 miles from Beaufort on N.C. 101 at Core Creek. The development is on the Intracoastal Waterway with a deep-water marina, a ships' store, gas and diesel fuel, a clubhouse, a playground, a swimming pool, tennis courts, a boat ramp and a security entrance. Homes range from $60,000 to $250,000. Waterfront lots range from $27,000 to $45,000.

At the east end of Lennoxville Road is the pricey new development of **Taylor's Creek**. This community consists of only 10 very large waterfront homes; some are now on the mar-

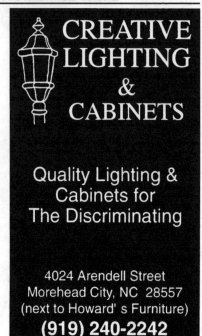
ket for more than $600,000. Residents also have use of a pool and boat docks.

Graystone Landing is about 3 miles up N.C. 101 from Beaufort. This neighborhood offers about 60 building lots. A few waterfront lots are available, although the majority are wooded interior lots in quiet surroundings. Lots range from about $20,000 to $120,000.

Morehead City

Morehead City is the area's largest city, and it has the most neighborhoods. Most early communities began at the water's edge because that's where the work was. Today, people continue to live by the water, but not so much for the work as for the beauty of the views and the breeze.

The city's earliest inhabitants lived near what is now the N.C. State Port, bounded by Bogue Sound, the Newport River and Calico Creek. As the area filled up, homes were built farther west.

Although Morehead City's downtown has

not seen as much restoration activity as Beaufort's, it is happening. Between Arendell Street and Bogue Sound, from about Ninth to 14th streets, is a neighborhood of small, wood-sided homes of active fishermen known as the **Promise Land**. Some of these houses were moved to the mainland by sailing skiffs at the turn of the century when severe storms almost destroyed the once-flourishing fishing village of Diamond City on Shackleford Banks. Homes were dragged out of the water and rolled on logs to their new foundation. As the story goes, one spectator commented on the sight, "It looks like the Children of Israel coming to the Promise Land." The name stuck.

Morehead City has expanded as its population has grown. Now, with improved access and all-weather bridges, more and more developments are popping up along the outskirts of town, many in the direction of Crab Point via N. 20th Street, Country Club Road and Barbour Road. Once an isolated farm community, **Crab Point** is one of Morehead City's oldest subdivisions and also the site of some

of the newest developments, so prices vary greatly. Clustered within each development are houses of a broad range of prices, mainly because of the high prices demanded by houses on the water.

Joslyn Trace is a relatively new subdivision on N. 20th Street at the junction of Country Club Road. Homes here are both one and two story, and lots range from $14,500 to $16,500. Creek Pointe and Mandy Farms are two neighborhoods just off Country Club Road, with homes ranging from $75,500 to $115,000.

South Shores is a new, private waterfront community on the Newport River. It offers members of its homeowners association lighted streets, curbs and gutters, a swimming pool and tennis courts. Lots begin at about $20,000 and go up to $45,000.

Country Club Road is a main thoroughfare along the backside of Morehead City. West Carteret High School is at the western end, and the Morehead City Country Club is toward the eastern end. In between lies mostly long-settled neighborhoods, although a few new developments have gone up in recent years. In most areas the lovely old trees have been left in place, and some homes are suitable for retirees or as first homes. An equal number are huge and obviously expensive. Generally speaking, the closer you get to the Morehead City Country Club, the more expensive the real estate becomes. In the more exclusive areas, there are very few lots left, but homes are being resold here as in all areas of the Crystal Coast.

Country Club East is a newer development across from and fronting the golf course. Here, two- and three-storied homes are the norm. Prices vary, depending on the size and features. Established homes with amenities such as a fireplace and two-car garage can sell for $134,500. A four-bedroom, two-story home with a partially finished attic can sell for up to $250,000.

River Heights lies to the east of the country club and is one of the older suburbs. Homes here are rarely on the market, and when they are, they are sold at premium prices.

Hedrick Estates on the west side of Country Club Road features nice one-and two-story homes, with well-landscaped yards. Lots are available, and established homes range from about $73,000 to $100,000. Adjacent to Hedrick Estates is Westhaven Village, made up of one- and two-story homes on large wooded lots. Homes here range from around $90,000 to $130,000.

West-Car Meadows off Country Club Boulevard is a well-established development, backed by Swinson Park and close to the new primary school, the high school and shopping areas. This is a good location for young families with children. **Northwoods** is a fairly new development off Country Club Road, with single-family dwellings on large tree-covered lots. A three-bedroom, two-bath home with a formal dining room and living room, screened-in porch, deck and garage can sell for between $100,000 and $160,000.

Greengate is a new residential neighborhood in Morehead contiguous to Mayberry Loop Road. It is a good place for the first-time buyer or anyone looking for low- to middle-priced new housing. Construction of single-family dwellings began in 1996 with prices starting at $78,000 for one- and two-story houses. Greengate offers nine floor plans and two-, three-and four-bedroom, energy-efficient homes.

Bonham Heights, **Mansfield Park** and **Mitchell Village** are older, spacious, well-established neighborhoods along the sound off U.S. 70. Homes vary from modest bungalows to two-and three-story residences. Most residents have lived in these areas for a number of years; however, homes do occasionally go on the market. Prices can vary from $85,000 several blocks away from the water to $350,000 for soundfront. Many waterfront homes have deep-water access at their back doors. It's worth a drive through these areas to see what is available.

The Bluffs is a condominium development at the end of Mansfield Parkway, overlooking Bogue Sound. Units are individually owned townhouses or condominiums, with a sound view from most units. A three-bedroom, two-bath condominium can sell for around $110,000; a four-bedroom, four-bath unit will sell for around $189,000.

Western Carteret County

As the county's population increases and annexation takes place, development in the western part of Carteret County continues, especially in response to the incoming personnel needs at Cherry Point. This area has some long-established neighborhoods, but many new ones are springing up along N.C. Highway 24 between Morehead City and Cape Carteret and along U.S. 70 between Morehead City and Havelock.

Spooner's Creek and **Spooner's Creek East** are long-standing neighborhoods, built around the marina at the mouth of Spooner's Creek and along Bogue Sound. The area features large homes, many with their own private docks. Homes are within walking distance of Spooner's Creek Marina, which has rental dockage and enough deep water for large yachts. Spooner's Creek Racquet Club has lighted tennis courts. Homes here are affordable to those in the upper income brackets. **Spooner's Creek North** is a new development in the area and offers many lots with boat slips. Building lot prices range from $44,000 to $200,000, depending on water access.

Brandywine Bay is an exclusive planned subdivision, stretching from Bogue Sound to U.S. 70. Begun in 1972, the project was built around the Earle Webb estate. The Webb Mansion, an impressive brick structure surrounded by majestic live oaks high on a bluff overlooking Bogue Sound, is now a private home. The waterfront portion of Brandywine Bay consists of a noncommercial marina with a community boat launch ramp surrounded by residential building lots. Marina slips are

INSIDERS' TIP

What's that shingle-covered dome on the north side of the Morehead City-Beaufort high-rise bridge? The dome keeps phosphates from the Texasgulf mining industry in Aurora out of the air as the chemical is processed for export from the N.C. State Port.

Photo: Scott Taylor

Build your own castle on the Crystal Coast.

individually owned. Three separate townhouse projects surround the harbor with space available for future construction. There are single-family residences and lots available on either side of the townhouses and harbor. Across N.C. 24 is the main residential section of Brandywine, which surrounds a beautiful 18-hole championship golf course. While some homes here were built in the 1970s, there is usually a nice selection of resales of both houses and lots. A new section, The Honors, recently opened.

Gull Harbor, **Soundview**, **Ho-Ho Village** and **Barnesfield** are all established developments along Bogue Sound on N.C. 24. While some homes are quite large and elaborate, others are moderate in size and style. Many have deep-water docks, and a few lots may still be available. Homes range from around $150,000 and up.

Somerset Plantation is one of the newest developments off N.C. 24 and features a swimming pool, tennis courts, a boat ramp, a residential day dock, boat slips and a secured entrance. Lot prices range from $33,000 to $145,900, depending on proximity to the water. Houses can range from $100,000 to $229,000, depending on size and water proximity.

In the Broad and Gales Creek areas are **Bluewater Banks**, **Fox Lair** and **Rollingwood Acres**. These are new subdivisions close to Broad Creek Middle School. Bluewater Banks is a soundfront development, and Rollingwood Acres is on Broad Creek. Home prices vary greatly, depending on location and water access. In Fox Lair, a nonwaterfront development, homes range from $90,000 to $140,000, whereas in Bluewater Banks prices range from $124,000 up.

Farther up N.C. 24 are **Pearson** subdivision, **Bogue Sound Yacht Club**, **Blue Heron Bay** and **Hickory Shores**. Again, some of these developments are longer settled than others. Homes vary from spacious and elaborate to small and practical. A few select lots remain for sale at Bogue Sound Yacht Club, beginning at about $40,000 and going up to $150,000. Blue Heron Bay is one of the newest developments, with lots ranging from $21,000 to $115,000 and homes from $149,000 to $350,000. Hickory Shores has interior lots,

beginning at $17,500 and going up to $75,000 for waterfront.

In Cedar Point, at the intersection of N.C. 58 and N.C. 24, the new community of **Magen's Bay** is under development. This is a residential soundfront community with a minimum lot size of 20,000 square feet. Magen's Bay features a private-gate entry, pool and bathhouse, tennis court, deeded water access and a 100-foot pier to Bogue Sound. Building lots range from $29,000 for interior sites to about $189,000 for waterfront. Brand-new homes range from the high $100,000s to the mid $200,000s.

Swansboro

Swansboro offers a variety of housing opportunities, including historic houses near the business district, mobile homes on the outskirts of town and charming new homes on unbelievably beautiful lots overlooking the water.

The **Swansboro Heights Extension** area is a 34-lot, fully built development with homes reselling in the $70,000 range. In the town itself, there are basically three types of homes. In the oldest part of town are the historic homes, some rehabilitated and restored and others in need of attention. Renovated and reproduction homes in Swanboro's historic district are on the market for $200,000 plus.

Around the fringes of the business district and extending several blocks in all directions are houses that were built about 50 years ago. They, like the older homes, are a mix of beautifully restored and maintained residences, with some that would be on the market as fixer-uppers. Closer to the city limits are homes built within the past 25 or 30 years. Most are still in good condition but not particularly distinctive in design.

In recent years, new developments have been opening, bringing a totally new look to Swansboro's housing picture. The **River Reach** development is perhaps the most dramatic change in Swansboro's real estate market and is almost fully settled. However, a few lots remain on the White Oak River and Stevens Creek, selling for around $60,000. Homes sell in the $175,000 to $200,000 range.

Plantation Estates is a waterfront subdivision on the White Oak River, with homes ranging from $125,000 to $150,000. **Hurst Harbour** is an exclusive new subdivision near the ferry landing at Hammocks Beach State Park. Prices for waterfront lots start at about $230,000; interior lots are in the $70,000 range. **Oyster Bay** offers moderately priced homes and lots and is being settled by the area's young professionals. Prices average from $100,000 up to $150,000. **Walnut Landing** was designed for more economical residences, with costs between $70,000 and $80,000.

Port West Townhouses are beside Swansboro Primary School and are made up of 13 buildings with four units each. Most units are rentals; however, some are owner occupied. The townhouses feature one, two or three bedrooms and range from the mid $40,000s to mid $50,000s.

Down East

Traditionally, the Down East communities themselves have made up the majority of neighborhoods. They string along U.S. 70 and

the waterfronts and revolve around the church, or the volunteer fire/rescue department. You should keep in mind that Down East living isn't for everyone. Newcomers must be ready to forfeit the conveniences of town living and be able to entertain themselves with the simple pleasures of day-to-day life. If you are ready to make those trade-offs, then you may have found your little piece of paradise.

Many of the county's traditional fishermen and boat builders live Down East, an area along U.S. 70 that merges into N.C. 12 and extends from Bettie to Cedar Island. As you cross the area's many bridges, it is not unusual to see clammers hip-deep in water with an inner tube in tow, harvesting salty-tasting mollusks from the sound bottom. Boat sheds are more common than garages, and the whir of saws and smell of wood chips are sure signs of happy boat builders. Fishing and shrimp boats ply the waters year round, and egrets, herons, ospreys and other shorebirds live in the marshes and wetlands along the highway.

Like many people who hold on to land settled by their ancestors and look to Mother Nature for their livelihoods, the indigenous people who make up these communities are

INSIDERS' TIP

When visiting any of the area's islands or hiking in the woods during the summer months, don't leave home without your insect repellent.

reserved and self-sufficient. They are fiercely independent and expect others to be the same. But in times of trouble or crisis, you will find none more kind or gracious than those living in the little fishing villages that make up Down East.

As more people move to Carteret County, its eastern sector has seen the development of a few subdivisions outside the fishing communities. Homes and acreage are becoming increasingly available and, although prices vary widely, they are going up — especially properties situated on the many creeks, inlets, bays, marshes and rivers that are the beauty of Down East. But if you want to get away from it all, this is the place to do it.

None of the Down East area is zoned and therefore the area falls under Carteret County jurisdiction.

Harbor Point in Straits has two sections and was established several years ago. Homesites are on a secluded peninsula, and the development offers a park area and boat ramp. Interior lots sell for around $20,000, with waterfront lots at about $46,000.

A new development on Harkers Island is **Harkers Point**. Twenty-seven waterfront lots (some fronting the Straits and some fronting Brooks Creek) are available as homesites. Each lot is priced at $125,000. All are ready for single-family home construction with water and sewer connections, power lines and paved roads. Harkers Point has an existing marina basin for residents, and the developers have set aside a large common area that will not be subdivided.

Osprey Isle in Smyrna has homes and lots on the water and paved streets. **Nassau Heights** is a new development in Williston, with lots ranging from $18,900 to $24,900. **Ward's Creek Plantation** and **Tranquility Estates** in Otway are both new developments. **Ward's Creek** offers waterfront, water view and water access lots, with prices starting at $12,500. **Tranquility Estates** is a waterfront and interior lot subdivision on Ward's Creek, with lots ranging from $13,500 to $62,000. Owner financing is available. **Whitehurst Landing** offers residential creekfront homesites in the Down East community of Straits. These large wooded lots are in peaceful surroundings and begin at $44,000.

Real Estate
Atlantic Beach

Al Williams Properties
407 Morehead Ave., Atlantic Beach Cswy.
• 726-8800, (800) 849-1888

Offices for this real estate sales and development business are in the Causeway Shopping Center. Listings often include exclusive condominium properties and waterfront homes on the beach and in Morehead City as well as building lots and acreage. Al Williams' Realtors are available to show you any of them.

Alan Shelor Realty
Crow's Nest Shopping Ctr., Atlantic Beach Cswy. • 247-7700, (800) 849-2767

This company offers properties all over the Crystal Coast. Listings often include exclusive condominiums and waterfront homes on the beach and in Morehead City as well as building lots and acreage. Five Realtors are on staff to help clients find just the right residential, resort or commercial property. Alan Shelor Realty has been in business for more than 20 years.

Cannon & Gruber, Realtors
509 Morehead Ave., Atlantic Beach Cswy. • 726-6600, (800) 317-2866

Formed in 1995 and combining more than 20 years of experience in local real estate, Cannon & Gruber offers many enviable listings not often on the market. Beach and soundfront condominiums are a specialty. Contact them for a listing of properties that are currently available.

Century 21 Coastal Properties
610 Morehead Ave., Atlantic Beach Cswy. • 726-4700, (800) 637-1162

This full-service agency handles both sales and rentals with nine agents on staff. It deals in properties throughout the county, including the western sector and Down East. Properties include condominiums, single-family homes, acreage, exclusive building lots and commercial sites. Other services include a building department that offers home design and construction services, and Auction Marketing Inc., which handles property auctions.

Coldwell Banker
Spectrum Properties
515 Morehead Ave., Atlantic Beach Cswy.
• 247-5848, (800) 237-7380

This Coldwell Banker firm is a full-service agency in Atlantic Beach. It also has offices in Emerald Isle, 354-3070, (see Emerald Isle section) and Greenville, (800) 355-6330. The two local offices each offer about 24 agents who specialize in properties throughout the county. It handles condominiums, homes, homesites and commercial property as well as long-term and seasonal rentals, 247-1100, and professional property management services.

Gull Isle Realty
611 Morehead Ave., Atlantic Beach Cswy.
• 726-0427, (800) 682-6863

In business for more than 20 years, Gull Isle Realty has earned a reputation of providing professional and individual attention to each client. The agency handles the sales of condominiums, homes, building lots and investment properties on Bogue Banks and the mainland. Gull Isle Realty also offers a number of resort rentals, 726-7679. The firm has a state-licensed appraiser. Call owner-broker David Waller for any real estate need.

Omni Real Estate/The Selling Team
513 Morehead Ave., Atlantic Beach Cswy.
• 247-3101, (800) 334-2727

Omni, a Tetterton Management Group Company, specializes in condominiums and homes for sale on the beach and in Morehead City, including the new nine-unit condominium development on the Atlantic Beach Causeway, Marlin Harbor. The full-service company also offers property listings county-wide and manages rentals for investment buyers. A vacation guide is published by Omni each year showing vacation rental properties. Its onsite rental office can lead you to the vacation location that fits your needs.

Realty World - Johnson Realty
407 Morehead Ave. Ste. 1, Atlantic Beach
Cswy. • 247-0077, (800) 849-4801

Realty World - Johnson Realty's team concept combines years of real estate experience in Carteret and surrounding counties. The group focuses on selling and marketing existing homes — those on the oceanfront or on the mainland. Realty World is noted for its professional property management group, which provides service-oriented care for properties. For information about seasonal rentals offered by Realty World - Johnson Realty, see the Weekly and Long-term Cottage Rentals chapter of this book.

Sound n' Sea Real Estate
205 Morehead Ave., Atlantic Beach Cswy.
• 247-7355, (800) 682-7368

Owned and managed by Demus and Ellen Thompson, Sound n' Sea specializes in the sale of homes, condos and commercial properties both on the island and mainland. The Thompson's firm is the oldest continuously owned and operated full-service real estate business in the Atlantic Beach-Pine Knoll Shores area. The Thompsons handle many ocean and soundfront properties. For more information about seasonal rentals from Sound 'n Sea, read our Weekly and Long-term Cottage Rentals chapter.

Pine Knoll Shores

Sunny Shores
N.C. Hwy. 58 (Salter Path Rd.) • 247-7347,
(800) 624-8978

Sunny Shores is a full-service company operated by a couple of veteran Pine Knoll Shores Realtors. The company offers sales, vacation rentals, property management and maintenance. Robert Lewis handles sales and partner Carol Piner handles rentals and property management. Sunny Shores' specialty is meeting unique rental requirements. For rental information, call 247-2665 or (800) 626-3113.

Emerald Isle

Bluewater Associates
Better Homes and Gardens
200 Mangrove Dr. • 354-2128,
(800) 326-3826

Across from the K&V Plaza, this full-service firm offers condominium and home sales on the beach and mainland with emphasis on sales of new constructions, building lots and resales in Emerald Isle and Cape Carteret. The company has its own construction arm that builds or finishes to client specifications. Its rental department, 354-2525, handles vacation and long-term rentals. Agents and other staff serve clients in Emerald Isle.

Century 21
Coastland Realty Inc.
7603 Emerald Dr. • 354-2131,
(800) 822-2121

The first realty franchise on the beach, this full-service company has been in business since 1980. It offers many completed homes, both new and previously owned, in some of Emerald Isle's most exclusive locations. It also sells building lots, constructions in progress and acreage on Bogue Banks and the mainland. Condominium resales and pre-construction sales are also their specialty. The staff includes 10 sales agents and a rental department handling vacation and long-term rentals.

Coldwell Banker
Spectrum Properties
7413 Emerald Dr. • 354-3070,
(800) 682-3423

This Coldwell Banker firm is a full-service agency in Emerald Isle with offices in Atlantic Beach, 247-5845, and Greenville, (800) 355-6330. The Emerald Isle office provides an extensive inventory of homes, condominiums and building lots in Emerald Isle and Cape Carteret. Knowledgeable agents match new homeowners with affordable property in the right locations. The Emerald Isle office also has a good reputation for its vacation and annual rental department, 354-3040, (800) 367-3381, and property management details.

Emerald Isle Realty
7501 Emerald Dr. • 354-4060,
(800) 304-4060

This agency has been a tradition on the coast for 35 years and hosts thousands of vacationing families each year. This family-owned property management, rental and sales firm is now in its new headquarters offering more than 700 vacation rental properties, a network rental reservations system and in-house maintenance and housekeeping departments. Rentals can be arranged by calling 354-3315 or (800) 849-3315. The company's sales team is equally strong, handling resales of homes and condominiums, commercial properties and building sites.

Emerald Properties
9100 Emerald Dr. • 354-4488,
(800) 398-8612

This agency is a small real estate firm that specializes in property sales in Cape Carteret and Emerald Isle. It offers residential and commercial properties, building lots and condominium resales. It also coordinates sales of remaining building lots in the Windfall and Wyndtree developments and the spectacular Tanglewood Ridge one-acre oceanfront lots.

ERA Carteret Properties
7801 Emerald Dr. • 354-3289,
(800) 448-2951

This full-service agency handles all types of properties both on the island and the mainland and has been in business since 1969. It is also very prominent in the property management field, with some 100 available rentals, 354-3005. Five agents conduct commercial and residential sales of new and established homes and offer business opportunities as well as lots and acreage. In addition, the firm offers other services that can be advantageous to clients, and it can help with custom construction and design.

Ketterer Realty
N.C. Hwy. 58 at Mangrove Dr. • 354-2704,
(800) 849-2704

This agency has a solid reputation earned through 22 years of service to home buyers

on the Crystal Coast. Company agents offer both new and resale homes in Emerald Isle and the western sector of the county as well as commercial sites, building lots and acreage. Ketterer Realty's services extend to guidance in developing house plans and construction details.

Prudential Sun-Surf Realty
7701 Emerald Dr. • 354-2958, (800) 849-2958

This full-service agency receives very high marks from other area Realtors. It has its own construction firm, Staebler Homes Inc. for custom-built homes, and offers a variety of vacation homes, building lots and condominiums on the island. It also has a very successful, professionally operated vacation rental program, 354-2658, (800) 553-7873. It represents sellers and is also a buyer's agency, meaning it negotiates price and terms in the best interest of the buyer. A free brochure explains the firm's buyer's agency policy.

Watson-Matthews Real Estate
9102 Coast Guard Rd. • 354-2872, (800) 654-6112

This business has been active since 1979 with sales of condominiums, single-family dwellings and duplexes as well as investment and commercial property. Watson-Matthews offers building sites in Lands End and other developments and pre-construction packages. The firm's agents will work with you in finding the perfect buy, whether it is a second home or a primary residence.

Beaufort

Beaufort Realty Company
325 Front St. • 728-5462, (800) 548-2961

This company specializes in residential and commercial property in the Beaufort historic district as well as throughout Carteret County. It handles some of the most handsome historic properties offered for sale. The company also offers sales of properties in Beaufort subdivisions, Down East, Morehead City and on the beach. The company does appraisals and offers annual and vacation rentals.

Century 21 Down East Realty
415 Front St. • 728-5274, (800) 849-5795

As the name states, Century 21 Down East Realty specializes in Beaufort and Down East property. It also handles property in Morehead City and is affiliated with the Morehead City Century 21 office. The firm handles residential and commercial sales as well as appraisals. It is Beaufort's oldest full-service real estate company, and its agents are knowledgeable and helpful.

Core Sound Realty
2622 U.S. Hwy. 70 E. • 728-1602, (800) 211-8202

Core Sound Realty handles all types of real estate — residential, commercial, acreage and lots — all over the county. It specializes in waterfront properties and acts as a buyer's broker. Owner Barbara Berrini's office is just outside Beaufort. You will drive right past it on your way to explore Down East.

Homeport Real Estate
400 Front St. • 728-7900, (800) 948-5859

Realtors and brokers Pat Kindell, Candy Rogers and Kerry Smith have lived in the area and operated businesses for more than 21 years. Upstairs in the Somerset Square building just off the Beaufort boardwalk, the company specializes in historic and resort properties as well as retirements and relocations along the Crystal Coast. Agents also work as buyers' brokers for clients. The company handles commercial and residential properties on the beach, mainland and Down East and also offers long-term rental services.

Morehead City

Ballou Enterprises Inc.
3332 Bridges St., Ste. 3 • 726-6811

This family owned and managed company has been in business since 1964. Ballou is a major developer of many of Morehead City's finest subdivisions and commercial enterprises. Ballou takes pride in the fact that it has

contributed to the growth and development of Morehead and its environs. For detailed information about the company's real estate holdings — both sales and rentals — call owner Sunnie Gail Ballou at the number listed above.

Brown and Swain Real Estate
4659 Arendell St. • 247-0055, (800) 366-5699

From Beaufort to Brandywine Bay, from points Down East to Cherry Point, owner-broker Betty Brown Swain always has interesting listings. She offers a range to interest any client from mobile home lots to Beaufort waterfront homes and always has a good buy in a fixer-upper. She handles sales of building lots in many area subdivisions as well as commercial property and acreage.

Century 21 Newsom-Ball Realty
4644 Arendell St. • 240-2100, (800) 849-5794

Ben Ball and Ken Newsom own both the Morehead City business and the Century 21 office in Beaufort. Both Realtor/brokers and the 14 sales associates working with them in the Morehead City office have well-rounded knowledge of the area. The company offers complete services, emphasizing the sale of homes, businesses and acreage. Century 21 also provides appraisals, property management services and rentals.

Chalk & Gibbs Realty
1006 Arendell St. • 726-3167, (800) 849-3167

This Better Homes and Gardens agency has been in operation since 1925. It handles sales of single-family dwellings, townhouses and condos as well as building lots and acreage. The company also offers property management and annual rental services for Morehead City and Beaufort as well as certified appraisals. In addition to real estate, Chalk & Gibbs has a complete insurance branch.

Choice Seacoast Properties
1512 Arendell St. • 247-6683, (800) 444-6454

This real estate firm is owned and operated by Trish and Tom Dale who, along with four other agents working with them, represent a variety of properties and innovative services. "Mailmost" increases exposure of homes listed through weekly mailings to qualified buyers, and "Netmost" enables buyers and sellers to save money through lower commissions. Choice lists residential and commercial properties, lots, acreage, condos and townhouses and offers property management services. For long-term rental information, call 808-2114.

Golf & Shore Properties
Brandywine Bay, U.S. Hwy. 70 • 240-5000, (800) 523-4612

Golf & Shore Properties specializes in properties in Brandywine Bay, which is on U.S. 70 in Morehead City. The company also represents properties throughout the county, and its experienced agents can help you select lots, single-family homes and townhomes. The firm's four agents can be relied upon to find you just the place you are looking for. The office is right inside the U.S.70 gate to Brandywine.

Home Finders
Robinson and Associates
304 N. 35th St. • 240-7653

Alan and Sharon Robinson own and operate this family business with the help of an additional agent. Alan Robinson has been in the real estate business since 1979, and his wife joined him in 1988. The company handles single-family homes from Morehead City to Newport plus lots and acreage. It also offers property management services and works with several builders in the area to offer building plans and construction. The firm is the exclusive agent for the new Greengate subdivision in Morehead City.

Putnam Real Estate Company
3800 Arendell St. • 726-2826

Putnam Realty is one of those companies that other real estate agencies recommend. It is a full-service agency that specializes in the sale of new and established homes and commercial properties throughout the county as well as building lots and constructions in progress in fast-growing Newport developments. Its agents also handle townhouses and mobile homes. The company offers full appraisal services, property management and long-term rentals.

RE/MAX Masters Realty
4459 Arendell St. • 247-3629, (800) 849-1144

In Colony Square on U.S. 70, this agency offers new homes and resales as well as townhouses, lots, acreage, condos and commercial property throughout the county. In addition, the firm assists clients in selecting and modifying house plans to meet their needs in Newport's recently developed Deer Park. The agency also offers commercial buildings and business opportunities as well as buyer's agent services.

Saunders Real Estate Company
100 N. 28th St. • 247-7444, (800) 587-2549

In the center of Morehead City, this company offers a great variety of properties from homes in some of the area's most exclusive residential districts to fixer-uppers with investment potential. The company offers lots and acreage and specializes in waterfront and residential properties. It also handles commercial business opportunities. The firm employs three agents and can provide appraisals, property management and relocation services.

Western Carteret and Swansboro

Ballard Realty
N.C. Hwy. 24 at Nine Foot Rd., Broad Creek • 240-2121, (800) COAST-NC

Brokers/owners Brenda Ballard and Joan Rife specialize in the western section of the county and especially in the subdivisions off N.C. 24 such as Fox Lair, Bluewater Banks, Soundview Park, Rollingwood Acres, Silver Creek and others. Ballard Realty also markets properties in Newport and Swansboro and manages long-term rental properties.

Shackleford Realty
415 W.B. McLean Dr., Cape Carteret • 393-2111, (800) 752-3543

With more than 20 years of experience, Shackleford Realty is well-known in the county for its market expertise in and around Cape Carteret, Swansboro, Cedar Point and Emerald

Isle as well as in subdivisions along N.C. 24. The agency handles many of the sales in the Star Hill, Hunting Bay, Quail Wood Acres and Fox Forest housing divisions and also offers town houses, lots and acreage. Ethel Shackleford operates the business, and the agency is recommended by other Realtors around the county.

Century 21 Waterway Realty
N.C. Hwy. 24, Swansboro • (910) 326-4152

This agency, one of the oldest in Swansboro, sells building lots, new homes and resales in the Swansboro/Cape Carteret/Emerald Isle area. Most of the company's agents are longtime residents of the area and can give you the real scoop about where the best buys are and about the best financing. The company also handles commercial properties, lots and acreage along the White Oak River and the Intracoastal Waterway and long-term rentals.

Down East

Most real estate agencies in Beaufort and Morehead City handle property east of Beaufort, and there are only a few real estate companies with offices actually in the Down East area. We suggest you contact your favorite Realtor if you are interested in property in the eastern sector of the county. Chances are he or she will be able to help you.

Eastern Gateway Realty
U.S. Hwy. 70, Bettie • 728-7790, (800) 205-5765

Owner Mary Hill and three agents handle properties all over the county and specialize in properties Down East. The company offers an enviable number of waterfront listings, lots and acreage. Mary's three agents are all experienced and knowledgeable about Down East property, and best of all, they're right there.

Builders

To find a builder in the Crystal Coast area, contact the **Carteret County Home Builders Association**, 223-5527. This organization is a membership group of builders and includes real estate companies, contractors and banks as associate members.

Utility Services

Carolina Power & Light
3504 Bridges St., Morehead City
• (800) 452-2777

CP&L offers electricity to the majority of residents and businesses. The amount of the deposit required depends on the size of your house or apartment, the service area and your credit. This deposit is refundable after one year if good credit is established. CP&L provides electricity to about 22,000 customers in Carteret County and in the Havelock area of Craven County.

Carteret-Craven Electric Cooperative
1300 Hwy. 24 W., Newport • 247-3107

Providing electrical service to much of western Carteret County, this member-owned corporation has about 28,000 members. It services all residents of Bogue Banks except those living in Atlantic Beach; all residents in Cape Carteret, Cedar Point and along Highway 58 to Maysville; residents along Highway 24 toward Morehead City and down Nine Foot Road and Lake Road to Havelock; residents along Highway 70 from Morehead City to the old residential district in Newport; and all Morehead City residents in the Country Club and Crab Point areas. A deposit is required when making an application.

Harkers Island Electric Membership
849 Island Rd. • 728-3769

Providing electricity to residents of Harkers Island, this is an electric distribution cooperative owned by the people it serves. The co-op was formed in 1939 and continues to provide electric utility service to residential property owners and commercial businesses on the island.

— continued on next page

Carteret-Craven Electric Cooperative

Locally owned and locally controlled by 27,000 member-owners

✦

Serving Morehead City Havelock Salter Path

A vital part of growth in Carteret and Craven Counties since 1940

Carolina Power & Light
1099 Gum Branch Rd., Jacksonville
• **455-1375**
　Call this CP&L office to arrange for electrical service in Swansboro.

Sprint Carolina Telephone
903 Arendell St., Morehead City
• **633-9011**
　Depending on your previous record, you may be asked to pay a deposit. That deposit usually is refunded after a year. Connection could take three or four working days, longer if there has not been telephone connection at that address before.

360° Communications
300 New Bridge St., Jacksonville
• **633-9011 (toll free)**
　Formerly Sprint Carolina Telephone, this company in Jacksonville can arrange for service in Swansboro.

With the variety of
sports, hobbies,
volunteer opportunities
and entertainment
available, most retirees
stay as busy
as they like.

Retirement

It doesn't snow all winter, it's not excessively hot all summer, golf and gardening are great nearly year round, fishing is fantastic, the people are charming, so retirees love this area. Our mild year-round climate, relatively low property taxes and property values on or near the water add to the attraction of retirees to the Crystal Coast. Because there is a lot of bang for the retirement buck here, the Crystal Coast enjoys a fast-growing population of highly educated, well-traveled and active retired senior citizens.

As our number of older residents increases, the county and its various towns develop more activities directed toward suiting the needs and interests of the senior set. With the variety of sports, hobbies, volunteer opportunities and entertainment available, most retirees stay as busy as they like.

Housing requirements can change quickly during the retirement years. Many townhouse and condominium developments are perfect for retirees who also decide to retire from house and lawn maintenance. All real estate companies can guide you toward more simplified living arrangements in beautiful locations.

Housing exclusively for older citizens on the Crystal Coast is available in a variety of settings, from federally subsidized accommodations for the elderly and handicapped to exclusive retirement complexes where you buy the unit and pay a monthly maintenance fee that includes taxes, meals, laundry and around-the-clock security service. In addition, there are nursing homes, rest homes and family care centers for those who need extra attention.

If you are shopping for one of these alternatives, it is very important to make several visits to the places you are considering. Information about all nearby facilities is available at the Department of Social Services at Craven and Broad streets in Beaufort, 728-3181 or, of course, at the facilities.

Services and Organizations

Leon Mann Jr. Enrichment Center for Senior Services
3820 Galantis Dr., Morehead City
• **247-2626**

The new Leon Mann Jr. Enrichment Center for Senior Services was opened in early 1997. The center replaced the Carteret County Senior Citizens Center at 1610 Fisher Street. The new center is fully accessible, bright, modern and well-designed with facilities that include space to expand for future tennis courts and a swimming pool. The new enrichment center, with large meeting rooms, classrooms, library, game room and health center, offers exciting opportunities, programs and services for Crystal Coast seniors older than 60.

Classes, exciting trips, workshops and entertainment events are planned for senior citizens, and facilities are also used for a variety of community activities including lively lessons in line dancing, exercise, billiards, table tennis, club meetings and the like. A hot lunch is available but arrangements need to be made at the center. The center also serves as headquarters for the SHARE food co-op. Each fall the center holds a Volunteer Opportunity Fair with representatives present from dozens of county institutions to share information on volunteer opportunities in the area. The center is open weekdays from 8 AM until 5 PM.

Senior Health Insurance Information Program
1610 Fisher St., Morehead City • 247-4366

The Senior Health Insurance Information Program (SHIIP) is a service of the Retired Seniors Volunteer Program (RSVP) that refers senior citizens' health insurance questions to trained volunteers. The volunteers help compare the benefits and disadvantages of various policies so seniors can make an educated buying decision. They also help file insurance and Medicare claims and find solutions to insurance problems.

Lifeline Program
Carteret General Hospital • 247-1616

The Lifeline Program operates out of the emergency room at Carteret General Hospital and was set up to help older or chronically ill persons live independently. The subscriber has a special machine attached to his or her home telephone and wears a small device at all times. In case of sudden illness, a fall or other emergency, the subscriber simply presses the button on the portable unit, which activates an alarm in the hospital emergency room where a staff member will respond. Newer devices include the capability of transmitting voice messages to and from the subscriber. A staff member calls the subscriber and if there is no answer or if the answer indicates an emergency, help is sent right away.

Meals-On-Wheels
Shirley Jackson, Coordinator • 726-9972, 247-5861

Area Meals-On-Wheels programs provide home delivery of hot meals, usually one a day, five to seven days a week. The program is designed to help the elderly, shut-ins, those recuperating from surgery and handicapped persons. Some systems require full payment for meals, some seek contributions and others operate entirely on donations. Volunteers and programs are coordinated by churches in areas throughout Carteret County.

Senior Games
Carteret County Parks and Recreation Dept. • 728-8401

Carteret County has its own Senior Games program for residents 55 and older. Local games are held each May, and a year-round program leads up to the annual games in July. Competitions include tennis, golf, swimming, biking, table tennis, horseshoes, croquet, walks, runs, jumps and shot-put. Get the picture? It's active. Games also include Silver Arts competition in painting, sculpture, writing, heritage crafts, instrumental and vocal music. Local winners compete in the state Senior Games during the summer and advance from there to the nationals. Nine Crystal Coast senior athletes were selected in 1996 to go to the national games. The Senior Games committee sponsors workshops to prepare the prospective athlete or artist to participate.

Week At Camp
Carteret County Parks and Recreation Dept. • 728-8401

Another special senior activity is Week At Camp, a week-long camping experience in August at a 4-H camp in the foothills outside Reidsville, North Carolina. Participants come from all over North Carolina and other states through both managing agencies, the Carteret County Parks and Recreation Department and the Dare County Cooperative Extension Service, 473-1101. For a fee of $230 per person, campers get transportation, insurance, room and board, nonstop entertainment, workshops and other extras. In addition, for those seeking a little more challenge, the High Adventure option takes participants white-water rafting and outdoor camping for two days out of the week. The camp has a swimming pool for exercise and a freshwater lake for paddleboating, canoeing and fishing. Classes and workshops are scheduled daily, and there's entertainment each evening. Meals are served family-style.

American Association of Retired Persons (AARP)
Morehead City Chapter • 726-4596, 726-8405
White Oak River Chapter • 354-2336, 354-3413

This nationwide organization has two active chapters on the Crystal Coast. The Morehead City chapter meets on the third Monday of each month for lunch at 11:30 AM at the Ramada Inn, MP 8¾, in Pine Knoll Shores. A speaker is scheduled for each meeting, and a newsletter is published to keep members apprised of goings-on of interest. To join the membership for lunch, reservations are taken in advance at one of the numbers above. Lunch is $6 per person. The White Oak River Chapter of the AARP meets at the Western Carteret Community Center in Cape Carteret on the second Monday of each month. Lunch reservations for this chapter meeting are taken at the numbers above.

Housing Options and Facilities

Americare of Eastern Carolina
3020 Market St., Newport • 223-2600, (800) 948-4333

Opened in November 1994, Americare offers 16 beautifully furnished two-bedroom apartments, each accommodating four residents who are able to live independently with some assistance. Assistance includes three nutritious meals a day (with special diet considerations) served in the dining room, laundry, housekeeping services, medication monitoring and administering, scheduled transportation and a variety of social, recreational and educational opportunities. The community-within-a-community complex is designed around an exterior courtyard with a gazebo-style bandstand for special performances and events or a village green for community gatherings. Each apartment has a courtyard patio. Monthly rental includes all services and an enthusiastic staff that is available at all times.

Ekklesia Apartments
Ekklesia Dr., Morehead City • 726-0076

Ekklesia Apartments is a HUD-subsidized retirement complex in a quiet part of town off Barbour Road. The complex was built by four area churches that retain much of the management authority. About two blocks from Morehead Plaza Shopping Center, Ekklesia includes 74 one-bedroom units and six two-bedroom units, all arranged in one-story clusters around the community center, which houses laundry facilities, a mail room and a large meeting room complete with a kitchen. The site manager and activities director offices are also in the community center. Regular activities include monthly birthday parties, special holiday parties, bingo, club meetings, a support group for the visually handicapped and such special events as an annual bake sale and the Watermelon Festival.

Harborview Towers
812 Shepard St., Morehead City • 726-0453

Harborview Towers is in a downtown residential neighborhood on the Morehead City waterfront overlooking Bogue Sound. The modern 10-story, 50-apartment complex is adjacent to Harborview Health Care Center, a skilled nursing and intermediate care facility for 125 patients and two family care facilities. Apartments are sold to residents, and a monthly fee includes maintenance, housekeeping, laundry, emergency and scheduled transportation, one meal a day in the dining room, all property expenses except telephone, property taxes and homeowner's policy on apartment contents. There are efficiency apartments and one- and two-bedroom units. All but the smallest units have balconies providing views of either Newport River or Bogue Sound. There is outdoor parking, with some covered parking on the building's ground floor. The newly renovated facility has an activities director, full-time security, and a live-in administrator, owner Doris Jernigan.

Sailors' Snug Harbor

U.S. Hwy. 70 E., Sea Level • 225-4411

Sailors' Snug Harbor is a retirement facility built specifically for retired Merchant Marines and operated by one of the oldest charitable trusts in this country. The facility is more than 160 years old although the building and location in Sea Level is around 20 years old. The trust was penned by Alexander Hamilton in the late 1700s for his friend Capt. Robert Richard Randall who wanted to build a "marine hospital for aged, decrepit, and worn out seamen" to be called "The Sailor's Snug Harbor." Properties of the trust included a small tract of land on Manhattan Island, now called Greenwich Village. The mariners, as Capt. Randall specified the resident retired Merchant Marines should be called, enjoy a lovely facility in a beautiful setting.

Nursing Homes

Nursing homes, by law, must provide registered nurses on duty at least 8 hours a day, seven days a week, with licensed nurses on duty around the clock under the supervision of the director of nursing. The following facilities provide both short- and long-term care. Generally, physical therapy and speech therapy are provided, according to doctors' orders. The homes provide planned activities, meals, regular classes and worship programs for the ambulatory.

Crystal Coast Rehabilitation Center

Penny Ln., Morehead City • 726-0031

Crystal Coast Rehabilitation Center is a facility that provides skilled nursing care for 92 patients who require intermediate or acute care. On-site staff members provide speech, physical and occupational therapy, and a full-time activities director keeps ambulatory patients active and alert. Center activities include current events, ceramics, painting, church ac-

tivities, parties and other social functions. The center accepts Hospice patients, and 11 Medicare beds are available.

Harborview Health Care Center

812 Shepard St., Morehead City • 726-6855

Harborview Health Care Center has an in-house therapy department and includes a nursing home for 125 patients who require skilled and intermediate nursing care. The center provides three nutritional meals daily, and both the second and third floors have two large glassed-in solariums that overlook Bogue Sound and Morehead City. It is certified for Medicare and Medicaid and is a member of the N.C. Health Care Facilities Association and the American Health Care Association. A staff activity director plans programs, and volunteers also conduct a variety of events for residents. Church services, Bible study, communion services, music therapy and other interactive functions are offered.

Sea Level Extended Care Facility

U.S. Hwy. 70 E., Sea Level • 225-4611

This extended care facility is owned by Carteret General Hospital. Housed in the former Sea Level Hospital building, acute and intermediate nursing home care are provided as well as custodial care for the aged. Sea Level Extended Care also offers a unique guest care service for those whose caregivers need a respite (see our Accommodations chapter).

Rest Homes

Rest homes provide custodial care, not nursing care, and have a doctor on call but only registered nurses on staff. There are nurses' aides on duty at all times under the direction of supervisors. While some residents use the facility for short-term care, most residents make use of the home on a long-term basis.

Carteret Care Rest Home
Professional Park, Morehead City
• **726-0401**

Carteret Care Rest Home is three blocks from Carteret General Hospital in Professional Park. The care facility is licensed for 60 patients, and residents are involved in programs aimed at keeping them active and interested. Twenty-four hour care is provided, and an in-house, facility-maintained physician's office is available to an assigned physician who visits once a month. Nurse's assistants and medication assistants are on staff, as is an activities director. The facility provides transportation for residents, and volunteers conduct church-related programs and activities. Local garden club members maintain gardens and bird feeders.

Family Care Centers

Family care centers provide a homelike atmosphere for those who need some care but can basically live independently. Residents must be ambulatory and perform some light housekeeping duties. They usually have kitchen privileges. Residents generally live in semiprivate bedrooms with a shared bath, have meals together and use the living room or other facilities jointly with other residents. There is a resident supervisor who does the heavy housework and cooking and, in general, looks after the residents. Transportation for medical attention, worship and shopping is provided. Medicine is under lock and key and is dispensed by the supervisor according to the doctors' directions.

Crystal Coast Family Care Center
238 Copeland Rd., Beaufort • 728-6065

In a quiet rural setting off N.C. Highway 101, Crystal Coast Family Care Center offers private rooms with shared baths and common-use living areas for 12 residents. Each of the two homes comprising the facility has a live-in supervisor to prepare meals, dispense medicines or any needed attention 24 hours a day.

Meals are served family-style. Planned activities are scheduled including cookouts, transportation, church and shopping. Owned and administered by Dean and Carolyn Graham, the Crystal Coast Family Care Center for ambulatory and semi-ambulatory residents has been operating since 1991.

Harris Family Care Center and Wadin' Creek Family Care Center
N.C. Hwy. 101, Beaufort • 728-7490

These are two separate care facilities in a country setting north of Beaufort. They are owned and operated by George and Millie Harris. Each house is licensed for six residents. The Harris house has only women residents, and the Wadin' Creek house can accommodate men or women. Each has three double bedrooms and two large bathrooms. Some outings and activities are planned. The live-in manager cooks, dispenses medicine and does heavy cleaning.

Veterans' Groups

Because of the proximity of several military bases and military hospitals, many people retiring to Carteret County are veterans. There are numerous veterans' organizations in the area, and all welcome new members. The Veterans' Service Office in Beaufort, 728-8440, offers problem-solving services to veterans.

American Legion Post 99, Jimmy Range, Beaufort, 728-3675

Disabled American Veterans Chapter 41, Wesley Jones, Newport, 223-5468

Military Order of the Purple Heart Chapter 639, Charles Woodward, Newport, 240-1583

Veterans of Foreign Wars Post 2401, Marvin Knox, Beaufort, 728-5112

Veterans of Foreign Wars Post 9960, Jim Broadus, Swansboro, 393-6278

Veterans of Foreign Wars Post 8986, Gary N. Bills, Newport, 247-2619

Vietnam Veterans of America, Jerry Birch, 728-5652; Charles Odell, 808-3766.

About 8,300 students attend prekindergarten through 12th grade in the county's 14 public schools.

Schools and Child Care

Educational opportunities in Carteret County include public and private schools. This section is designed to give you information about schools and child-care facilities on the Crystal Coast. Our Higher Education and Research chapter contains information about the local community colleges and research facilities.

Public Schools

Carteret County Schools

For information about the school system, contact the Carteret County Schools Central Office (Board of Education), P.O. Box 600, Beaufort 28516, 728-4583. Information booklets are available.

About 8,300 students attend prekindergarten through 12th grade in the county's 14 public schools. Each school is accredited by both the N.C. Department of Public Instruction and the Southern Association of Colleges and Schools. The local school system employs about 950 people. Carteret County public schools are governed by an elected five-member board of education. Members serve four-year terms and are chosen in countywide, nonpartisan elections. School board members meet in open session each month.

Technology is vital to instruction, and the amount of computer equipment each school has for its students to use continues to increase. In 1994 voters passed a $29 million school bond referendum that has funded more than $6.2 million for technology in the schools, allowing for an increase in computer equipment and software for student use and the networking of all county schools. The remaining bond funds were for construction and renovation projects.

Elementary school students follow a basic state-sponsored curriculum that features reading and language arts, math, science, social studies, health, physical education, music and art. The middle school concept is used in the three public middle schools and to varying degrees in grades 6 through 8 at other schools. This approach emphasizes teams of students and teachers working together to create consistency for each group.

The county's two high schools and three middle schools offer a comprehensive management program that emphasizes class attendance. Extended-day classes are part of this program. Students who need remediation are required to attend the after-school classes; other students voluntarily attend for enrichment opportunities.

The high schools have a handbook listing specific course offerings. Vocational education is offered in several areas: agriculture, home economics, distributive education, health occupations, business, occupational exploration and introduction to trade and industry.

Carteret County offers a voluntary year-round school for those living in the Newport district. The county's alternative high school, grades 9 through 12, offers innovative teaching methods for students having difficulty with traditional methods. Students attend this school year-round.

Student services include guidance counselors, psychologists, social workers and nurses. The school system provides bus transportation to and from school for students who live at least 1.5 miles from the school. Each school serves lunch, and many schools serve breakfast. Free or reduced-rate meals are available to those who qualify.

New students should register at the appropriate school before school opens in the fall, if possible. Students entering kindergarten and first grade must have immunization and physical examination records.

Each school has an advisory council that meets monthly to discuss issues. The councils report to the Board of Education. Most schools have a Parent-Teacher Organization (PTO) as well as booster organizations.

An elementary and a middle school are within the Town of Beaufort, and the high school, East Carteret High School, is on the outskirts. Students who complete 8th grade at Atlantic, Smyrna, Beaufort Middle or Harkers Island schools attend East Carteret High School.

In the Morehead City area, children in the public school system follow a path from primary to elementary to middle to high school. Which school children attend depends on where they live. Children living in the town limits of Morehead City and on Bogue Banks as far as Indian Beach attend a Morehead City school. Children living at the west end of the county and on Bogue Banks start school at White Oak Elementary School in Cape Carteret then advance to Broad Creek Middle School. From there students from the western end of the county go to West Carteret High School, along with students from Morehead City. Call the county School Board office, 728-4583, to find out which school district your home is in.

Several attendance zones in the western part of the county will change in 1998 and in 1999, when a new elementary school and a new high school are completed. Both will be off Highway 24, just west of the existing Broad Creek Middle School. The construction of both new schools was part of a $29 million school bond referendum county voters passed in 1994.

There are three schools in the Down East area of Carteret County. Each is named for its community, and each serves students through the 8th grade. When students complete 8th grade, they attend East Carteret High School.

Atlantic Elementary School has an enrollment of about 180 students in grades prekindergarten through 8th. Harkers Island Elementary School serves about 185 students from kindergarten through 8th grade, and it is the smallest school in the county system. Smyrna Elementary School, Marshallberg Road has about 380 students attending prekindergarten through 8th grade.

Three schools are in the western part of the county. White Oak Elementary School in Cape Carteret offers curriculum to about 580 students in kindergarten through 5th grade. Newport Elementary School has about 950 prekindergarten through 5th grade students. Broad Creek Middle School provides instruction to about 780 students in 6th, 7th and 8th grades. After completing 8th grade, students attend West Carteret High School.

Cape Lookout High School is the county's new alternative school, serving students in grades 9 through 12. Class sizes are small to ensure a lower student-teacher ratio. Students attend this school year-round.

Onslow County Schools

The four schools in Swansboro fall under the jurisdiction of the Onslow County Board of Education, Jacksonville, 455-2211.

Voters in Onslow County approved a $40 million school bond in 1994. The bond has

Photo: NC Aquarium at Pine Knoll Shores

The North Carolina Aquarium has lots of field trips to get kids out on water's edge.

provided for new construction and major renovations throughout the county, and the Swansboro area is included on the list. A new dining hall has been built at Swansboro Elementary and a new elementary school will be constructed just outside Swansboro.

Private Schools

Several private schools serve county students seeking an alternative to public education. Most offer instruction in four or five grade levels, with only two serving students from kindergarten through 12th grade. There is also a small group of home-school participants. For information about home schools, contact the Carteret County Schools Central Office, 728-4583.

Beaufort Christian Academy
U.S. Hwy. 70 E., Beaufort • 728-3165

Beaufort Christian is a ministry of Beaufort Free Will Baptist Church and enrolls students from kindergarten through 12th grade.

Grace Christian School
520 Roberts Rd., Newport • 223-6088

Grace Christian shares a facility with Grace Missionary Baptist Church and serves 5 year olds through 12th graders.

Gramercy Christian School
U.S. Hwy. 70, Newport • 223-4384

This school provides instruction for students in kindergarten through 11th grade.

Carteret Academy
1600 Fisher St., Morehead City • 808-2398

Carteret Academy is the county's newest private school. This private Christian school opened in August 1994 and serves students in grades 6 through 9.

The Tiller School
1950 U.S. Hwy. 70, Beaufort • 728-1995

The Tiller School serves students in kindergarten through 6th grade. The school is not church affiliated.

St. Egbert's Catholic School
1705 Evans St., Morehead City • 726-3418

This school is affiliated with St. Egbert's Roman Catholic Church and provides instruction to students in kindergarten through 5th grade.

White Oak Christian Academy
U.S. Hwy. 24, near Cape Carteret • 393-6165

Affiliated with the White Oak Church of God, this school serves students from 4 years old through 12th grade.

Newport Development Center
Church St., Newport • 223-4574

The Newport Development Center specializes in training for handicapped children and adults who need more specialized attention than regular classrooms can offer.

Child Care

A few day-care centers offer extended hours on weekends. Fees for day-care services vary and are often based on the age of the child, the number of hours the child spends at the facility and the number of children attending the facility. Many facilities provide transportation to and from school if needed, and most offer summer programs.

Cartert County and the State of North Carolina regulate day-care homes and day-care centers through the issuance of registrations and licenses. Regulations call for all such facilities to meet health and safety standards. In the case of nonsectarian child-care institutions, standards for children's learning and play programs must be met. For a list of regulated day-care homes and licensed day-care centers, call Michelle Rose at the Carteret County Department of Social Services, 728-2301.

Day Care

Beaufort

Ann Street
United Methodist Church
500 Ann St. • 728-5411

The church provides preschool care for 3, 4 and 5 year olds. Day care and an after-school care program are also offered.

Beaufort Christian Academy
Hwy. 70 E. • 728-3165

Beaufort Christian offers day-care services

during the week for children ages 2 through 5 and after-school care for older students.

Colony Day Care Center
103 Fairview Dr. • 728-2223

Colony offers care for children from 6 weeks to 12 years of age. Colony also offers day care, preschool and before- and after-school care.

Morehead City

My School
3415 Eaton Dr. • 247-2276

My School serves youngsters from 6 weeks through elementary-school age with preschool and before- and after-school programs.

Colony Day Care Center
700 N. 35th St. • 247-4831

Colony offers child care for kids from 1 to 5 years of age.

ABC Day Care
Mandy Plaza, 500 N. 35th St. • 240-2222

ABC serves children from 6 weeks to 12 years old and offers before- and after-school care.

Miss Nancy's
Early Learning Center
204 N. 18th St. • 247-2006

Miss Nancy's serves children from 6 weeks to 12 years of age with preschool, day care and after-school care.

Kids Kampus
600 N. 35th St. • 247-1866

Kids Kampus is designed for children from 5 to 12 years old in need of before- and after-school care.

Swansboro

Coastal Kiddie College
783 Corbett Ave. • (910) 326-3386

Coastal Kiddie College serves children

INSIDERS' TIP

The Beaufort Historical Association presents Harvest Days each fall, offering students from across the state a chance to step back in time. Demonstrations include cooking, spinning, bullet making and hunting.

from 6 weeks to 12 years of age with day care and before- and after-school care.

Hug A Bear Day Care
Mount Pleasant Rd. • (910) 326-7002

Hug A Bear cares for children from infancy to age 12.

Swansboro United Methodist Child Care and Preschool
N.C. Hwy. 24 • (910) 326-3711

This center accepts children from 6 weeks to 12 years of age and offers preschool and after-school programs.

Western Carteret County

Western Carteret County residents will find the larger child-care facilities in the community of Newport.

Miss Pat's Learning Center and Child Care
100 Fort Benjamin Rd. • 223-3432

Miss Pat's serves children from ages 3 to 12 with preschool and before-and-after-school programs.

Newport Child Care Center
51 Chatham St. • 223-3500

Newport Child Care Center serves children from 6 weeks to school age with a preschool program and offers before- and after-school programs.

Newport Kids Inc.
30 E. Chatham St. • 223-4303

This center offers before- and after-school care for school-age children as well as a summer program.

St. James Day Care and Preschool Center
1011 Orange St. • 223-3191

St. James offers day care for children from 6 weeks through 2nd grade. Before- and after-school programs for older children are provided.

Baby-sitting

Nancy's Nannies
P.O. Box 3375, Morehead City • 726-6575

Reliable sitters for children are available on the Crystal Coast. Nancy's Nannies is used widely and offers responsible adult sitters for children as well as the elderly for a day, night, weekend or longer.

This area will have one of the largest concentrations of marine scientists on the East Coast when the Center of Marine Sciences and Technology, being built on the west side of the Carteret Community College campus in Morehead City, is complete.

Higher Education and Research

Two higher educational institutions are accessible to Crystal Coast residents interested in pursuing additional education or seeking enrichment. The area is also home to many well-known and respected research laboratories.

Higher Education

Carteret Community College (CCC)
3505 Arendell St., Morehead City
• 247-6000

CCC is part of North Carolina's 58-campus community college system. The college has programs for traditional college students and for trade students seeking to upgrade their skills. The college offers associate degrees in a number of programs as well as courses in adult basic education and high school completion. Through East Carolina University in nearby Greenville, the college has transferable general education courses. CCC offers vocational courses, such as heating and cooling systems, auto mechanics, welding, computers, boat building and photography. CCC provides educational support and customized skills training to area businesses and industries. Day and evening classes are available, and there are several off-campus class sites throughout the county.

Coastal Carolina Community College
Admissions Office, 444 Western Blvd., Jacksonville 28546 • (910) 455-1221

This community college is also part of the state's community college system. Based in Jacksonville, it provides many of the same programs as Carteret Community College.

Carteret/Craven Community College East Carolina University Partnership Degree Program
115 Banks St., Morehead City • 726-7684

"This is a dream come true; I can finally finish my degree right here where I live and work." This is the reaction of many of the students enrolled in the Partnership Degree Program, an initiative of the state legislature aimed at extending the university system to more North Carolina residents. The pilot program encourages those who already have college credits to complete their bachelor's degree. Started in the fall of 1996, the partnership is geared to the lifestyles of its students, many of whom are working adults and, very often, parents. Classes are held in the evenings and all lectures, applications processing, college credit review and registration take place on the campuses of the two community colleges.

Partnership students receive their degrees from ECU in one of three major courses of study: information processing and adminis-

---

trative services, industrial technology, and middle grades education. Students learn via videoconferencing and can access the Internet from college computers to track class assignments, e-mail their homework, chat with other students, pose and answer questions and review class material. For more information contact John Connelly, Coordinator, Carteret/Craven Community College Partnership Degree Program at the phone number above.

Research Facilities

The Crystal Coast is home to numerous research facilities and will soon have one of the largest concentrations of marine scientists on the East Coast. That will come with the completion of the Center of Marine Sciences and Technology. In 1995 North Carolina State University received appropriations for this center from the General Assembly, and the center is being built on the west side of the Carteret Community College campus in Morehead City. The appropriation also provided for renovations to the existing Institute of Marine Sciences.

Most of the research facilities discussed here have something to do with the surrounding water and resources. They offer research, product development and personnel training for corporations around the world.

Area laboratories have been involved in developing many products. Contract research has included work with companies such as Strohs Brewery, W. R. Grace, Hercules Chemical, Biosponge Aquaculture Products, International Paint, Allied Chemical, Sunshine Makers, Aquanautics, Mann Bait Company, 3M Corporation and General Dynamics.

Duke University Marine Laboratory, 504-7503, was established by Duke University on Piver's Island near Beaufort in 1938. This interdepartmental facility has two objectives — research and teaching. The laboratory's large resident academic staff and innumerable visiting professors and researchers from throughout the United States and abroad have contributed to its worldwide reputation. The laboratory maintains a campus and two research vessels. The largest is the *R/V Cape Hatteras*, a 131-foot ship owned by the National Science Foundation. The ship is designed to carry out basic and applied research and education as required to meet national, state and private needs.

Also on Piver's Island is **Duke University Marine Biomedical Center**, 504-7508, supported by the National Institutes of Health. The center's research focuses on marine organisms and their relationship to humans and environmental health. This is one of four such centers in the nation.

The **University of North Carolina Institute of Marine Sciences**, 726-6841, has a facility in Morehead City with activities directed toward understanding basic aspects of the marine sciences. Established in 1947, this is the oldest state-supported marine research laboratory in North Carolina.

The National Oceanic and Atmospheric Administration (NOAA) operates the **Southeast Fisheries Center** on Piver's Island near Beaufort, 728-3595. Here, research is conducted on fish that are important to recreational and commercial fishing groups. This Beaufort laboratory is one of six labs operated as part of the Southeast Fisheries Center.

NOAA also operates a weather forecast center near Newport. The **NOAA National Weather Service Center**, 223-5122, provides state-of-the-art weather tracking and forecasting and includes a Doppler weather radar system with advanced weather capabilities.

The **North Carolina Division of Marine Fisheries**, 726-7021, has a large facility in Morehead City. Charged with stewardship of marine and estuarine resources in coastal creeks, bays, rivers, sounds and the ocean within 3 miles of land, this state agency is often in the midst of conflict between lawmakers, environmentalists and fishermen.

The **Rachel Carson component of the North Carolina National Estuarine Research Reserve** is just across Taylor's Creek from Beaufort. It may look like just an ordinary small island, but it is an active research and classroom site. Congress created the reserve sys-

Photo: NC Aquarium

The NC Aquarium and the NC Maritime Museum often offer educational trips on trawlers.

tem to maintain undisturbed estuaries for research on the natural and human processes that affect the coast, and the Rachel Carson island serves that purpose well. Educational trips are offered frequently. These Insiders recommend a visit; there are many fascinations to be observed while touring the island. For more information about the Rachel Carson component, call 728-2170 and also see our Attractions chapter. The other three components that make up the state Research Reserve are Masonboro Island and Zeke's Island near Wilmington and Currituck Banks on the Outer Banks.

P.O. BOX 825 • MOREHEAD CITY, NC 28557 • 919.726.7822 • 800.462.4252 • 919.726.4215 fax

Dear Carteret County Visitor,

Thank you for your interest in Carteret County. I hope you have an opportunity to visit the county and enjoy our unspoiled beaches, our great sportfishing and our historic sites. In addition to its wonderful quality of life, Carteret County offers many business advantages for companies considering an expansion or relocation to this area.

The state-owned and operated port in Morehead City is one of the deepest and most accessible ports on the east coast. PCS Phosphate and Weyerhaeuser are examples of companies which ship substantial cargoes through the Morehead City Port. Carteret County is also the only North Carolina county offering a direct port/rail/four-lane highway connection to the Global TransPark.

Carteret County excels in education at the primary, secondary, community college and post-graduate levels. Carteret Community College offers prospective employers free customized training programs. The marine science laboratories of Duke University, the University of North Carolina-Chapel Hill, N.C. State University, and the National Marine Fisheries Service have established Carteret County as a world-renowned research center, with excellent opportunities for business research and development.

Carteret County offers an abundant and proud labor force, supplemented with skilled labor from nearby military facilities at Cherry Point and Camp Lejeune. Developed acreage tracts are available for industrial, commercial and resort development opportunities. Carteret County Economic Development Council is available to provide you with confidential site assistance, local permit assistance, and labor needs. I hope that you will consider the business opportunities available in Carteret County... "where business is a pleasure."

Sincerely,

Donald A. Kirkman

Donald A. Kirkman
Executive Director

Commerce and Industry

Tourism and commercial fishing play lead roles in the area's economic picture, but a number of domestic and international companies call Carteret County home. The Carteret County Economic Development Council Inc., 726-7822 or (800) 462-4252, and the Carteret County Chamber Of Commerce, 726-6350, can provide detailed information about area businesses and industries. Below is a brief look at a few of the area's major businesses.

The **North Carolina Port at Morehead City** is the most visible industry in the county. Situated on the east end of Morehead City, the 116-acre main facility offers a foreign trade zone and one of the deepest channels and turning basins of any East Coast port. This is one of two state-owned ports; the other is in Wilmington.

The large piles of wood chips seen along the highway at the port are brought to Morehead City on trucks and train cars by **Weyerhaeuser** and **Canal Wood Corporation**. The chips, which are used for the production of fine quality paper, are exported via ships to Japan. **PCS Phosphate** (formerly Texasgulf) exports phosphate-based materials throughout the world and utilizes the Intracoastal Waterway to barge these materials from the company's Aurora mine to the port.

A new customer at the port is **Waterman Steamship Co.**, a barge line running to and from the Far East. Although this company handles a number of products, it is best known for importing rubber for Goodyear. Locally, much of the rubber is taken to the two North Carolina plants — one in Fayetteville and one in Reidsville.

The Port at Morehead City facility is the port of embarkation and debarkation for the Second Division of the **U.S. Marine Corps** at

Aquaculture Down East

A Down East agricultural tour would take you through fields of cabbage, collards, sweet potatoes, turnips and corn. But in Harkers Island there's a native crop grown on an unlikely farm you'd never notice.

The routines on this farm are the same as those on other farms: germinating, planting seedlings, harvesting, grading and shipping to market. However, it's different from the usual farm in that the farmers are scientists and inventors working in the water to merge the 20th and the 21st centuries in seafood production and meeting market demands. This farm's crop is clams and its field, Core Sound.

Carolina Cultured Shellfish is only seven years old. Among the first of North Carolina's commercial shellfish aquaculture ventures, its history from first planting in February 1990 to first harvest in 1993 is a story of approximation, experimentation, invention, trial and error.

"All the research for this was done out of state," said assistant manager Ken Brennan, "and successful conditions in Virginia or South Carolina don't necessarily apply in Core Sound."

In fact, conditions that result in significant differences in harvesting time vary within stone's throw distances in Core Sound or any tidal water. As Brennan summarized the trial-and-error nature of the shellfish aquaculture business: "If you haven't lost 900,000 (clams), you're just not doing it."

The order requisite to shellfish aquaculture has a lot of appeal. Beginning in the nursery, rows of cylinders contain the seed clams that grow from barely visible spats to around 4 millimeters. Nurtured by constantly circulating water from the sound, their growth is noted in byssal threads. At a size slightly larger than the holes in window-screen mesh they become recognizable as clams. Because the breeding stock is chosen for growth performance that shape characteristic growth patterns, about 75 percent of Carolina Cultured Shellfish clams are recognizable by their specific growth patterns.

"It's a tattoo, a brand of sorts," says Brennan. "Keeps the poachers away."

From the cylinders the thousands of growing mollusks, now the size of nail heads, go on to the raceways. Raceways are a resting place for the seedling clams to grow strong before bedding down in the Core Sound mud. They appear as happy as clams in the raceway's fuzz of filters, which are extended to grab invisible nutrients from the still circulating Core Sound water.

Next stop, Core Sound. Uniform north-south rows in beds measuring 10- by 25-feet are densely planted. It is here that a strong competitive streak is valued in a clam. There's food to compete for and predators to avoid in the real world of Core Sound mud.

Density, another trial-and-error factor, involves a balance between production necessities and survival factors.

"You plant as many clams as you can at a safe size and hope for the greatest survival rate," explained Brennan. "The more room you give them, the less competition they have for food and the greater the survival rate."

But that way fewer clams are produced. That is why the best competitors, the fittest survivors, the fastest growers are selected for breeding.

It requires an average of three years for a clam to grow from spat to harvest-size, which is one reason why everyone Down East isn't interested in shellfish aquaculture.

— continued on next page

Photo: Janis Williams

Seedling clams of this size are nurtured in raceways.
This handful will soon be an entire clambake.

Other retarding factors are the ever-tightening regulations governing commercial fishing and leases of bottom or water columns (surface to bottom) in public waters. But other factors that evade the traditional Down East farmer smile on the shellfish aquaculturist.

"Harvest responds to the market," explained Brennan. "As it is for other livestock, it's not like you can't leave the crop in the field. The money-size clam is about the size of a quarter. Harvested smaller, clams can be tossed back into the appropriate bed to finish growing or, at market size, to wait until the market calls. There is little waste in the efficiency of growth and harvest once the correct bed density/survival balance in the Core Sound lease is known."

The continuous efficiency refinements of Down East shellfish aquaculture has made the traditional commercial clammer a rare sight in 1997. Although the number of commercial aquaculture operations can be counted on one hand, they are meeting broad market demands. One reason aquaculture is becoming so popular is that the crop of clams is available year-round instead of seasonally.

"Our clams go to New Jersey, New York — the North and Midwest — Cleveland, Philadelphia . . .," Brennan said from the barge-like harvester custom-fashioned to this Core Sound farm's production requirements. From Atlantic City Clams Casino to the Cleveland Fire Department's annual clambake, the trained eye can recognize a Carolina Cultured Shellfish clam.

The untrained eye will definitely miss the farm. Haphazard stakes are the only evidence of this potentially large, but unobtrusive industry.

Photo: Scott Taylor

In Beaufort menhaden fishing is an industry that is passing into history.

Camp Lejeune, North Carolina. The port includes much of the land on Radio Island, which is the body of land on the southeast side of the Morehead City-Beaufort high-rise bridge.

Atlantic Veneer Corporation in Beaufort is the largest manufacturer of hardwood veneers in North America. With manufacturing facilities on three continents, the company also produces lumber, plywood and edgebanding. It exports about half of its products. With more than 500 employees, this corporation is the county's largest manufacturing employer.

Veneer Technologies in Newport employs about 100 people and manufactures a variety of products, including flexible veneer and endbands.

Bally Refrigerated Boxes Inc. is one of the Crystal Coast's newest manufacturing firms. Located off U.S. Highway 70 in Morehead City, Bally makes walk-in refrigerated units, coolers and freezers. The company employs more than 200 people.

Several apparel companies have their headquarters on the Crystal Coast, including **Cross Creek Apparel**, makers of Cross Creek Apparel and Russell Athletic Wear, and **Cre-** **ative Outlet Inc.**, producers of healthcare apparel.

Of Carteret County's 90,000 acres of farmland, 44,000 acres make up **Open Grounds Farm**. It is the largest farm east of the Mississippi River and produces corn, soybeans, beef cattle, wheat and cotton. Owned by the Ferruzzi Group, one of Italy's largest companies, the farm stretches from Merrimon Road outside Beaufort east to U.S. 70 near Sea Level. You can get a look at the farm by checking in at the main gate. Permission to enter is most often granted, although visits are not recommended on Sundays or during busy planting or harvesting times.

Beaufort Fisheries at the east end of Front Street opened in 1934 and is called the oldest existing industry in the area. Where there were once many, this is the only menhaden plant now operating in the state. Menhaden, an oily, high-protein fish, are caught by company vessels and brought to the docks along Taylor's Creek to be processed into fish meal, oil and solubles. Fish meal is used as a protein component in many animal feeds. Fish oil is used primarily in margarine, cosmetics and paints.

INSIDERS' TIP

Contact the Economic Development Council, 726-7822 or (800) 462-4252, for county business and economic information.

Fish solubles are high-protein liquid by-products also used in the feed market. During processing, a unique smell can travel through the seaside town. Locals, particularly the older folks who remember when fish plants were the biggest businesses in town, call it "the smell of money." Annual production at Beaufort Fisheries is estimated at 10,000 tons of meal and 300,000 to 450,000 gallons of oil.

Parker Marine Enterprises Inc. specializes in the construction of fiberglass fishing and pleasure boats. The company plant is on N.C. Highway 101 outside Beaufort. Boats are sold through authorized dealers.

Aquaculture and mariculture are exciting new forms of agriculture being promoted by the state. This production provides a dependable, year-round supply of seafood for wholesale and retail markets. **Carolina Cultured Shellfish** is one of the region's largest aquaculture operations and has facilities on Harkers Island.

There are also a number of large seafood dealers in the area. Two of the largest are **Luther Smith & Son Seafood** and **Clayton Fulcher Seafood**. Both of these family-owned and -operated businesses work from fish houses in the Down East community of Atlantic. Smith operates several steel-hulled trawlers in waters up and down the East Coast and has a second fish house in Beaufort. Fulcher buys seafood directly from independent commercial fishermen and has a second fish house on Harkers Island.

Home healthcare services help to bring people home earlier from surgeries, injuries and illnesses that have traditionally required hospital recoveries.

Healthcare

Routine and specialized medical care, diagnostic procedures, treatment and surgery are available and practiced routinely on the Crystal Coast. In cases requiring equipment or specializations not presently available here, referrals are usually to nearby New Bern or Greenville, which is no more than 2 hours away. In cases of emergency, residents and visitors receive medical attention on a walk-in basis at several locations around the county during weekday business hours. At other times Carteret General Hospital's emergency room is the best bet.

In almost every town or community throughout the county, there are clinics or specialized practices with one to a half-dozen doctors. It is not unusual, however, for routine appointments to be scheduled months in advance, although sickness and emergency cases are generally worked in. When moving to the Crystal Coast, it's best to arrive with a referral from your most recent doctor. Otherwise, as there is no medical referral service in Carteret County, ask a few Insiders for their recommendations and take the consensus.

Home healthcare services help to bring people home earlier from surgeries, injuries and illnesses that have traditionally required hospital recoveries. A six-unit kidney dialysis unit able to serve 24 patients opened in early 1997 in Morehead City. The availability of these services continues to meet the healthcare needs of Crystal Coast residents.

Alternative healthcare options available on the Crystal Coast mostly address the relief of pain and include massage therapies, yoga and herbal remedies.

Hospitals

Carteret General Hospital
3500 Arendell St., Morehead City
• 247-1616, 247-1540 emergency room

Carteret County's sole community hospital is Carteret General Hospital. The hospital's expanding medical staff includes 48 full-time physicians representing most medical specialties. The 117-bed facility offers 24-hour emergency services plus top-quality patient services including lithotripsy for kidney stone treatment, vascular surgery, cancer treatments and cardiac care that includes an outpatient rehabilitation program. The hospital's full service laboratory, imaging services and CT scanner provide state-of-the-art diagnostic services. The Raab Clinic provides outpatient chemotherapy and neurology services and other outpatient procedures. Construction of a new birthing environment and a new radiation therapy center for cancer patients is in progress with expected completion of both in 1997. The renovation of all patient care rooms was completed in 1996.

The hospital operates Carteret Home Health Care, formerly a function of the Department of Social Services, which provides a continuum of care for recovering and long-term care patients. Continual additions of facilities, services and equipment keep Carteret General Hospital abreast of the latest developments in medical diagnosis and treatment.

If other facilities are needed, the hospital makes arrangements to air-evacuate patients by helicopter to Pitt County Memorial Hospital in Greenville or to other larger city hospitals. This is sometimes necessary in the event of an extremely premature birth, severe burn or major head injury.

Craven Regional Medical Center
2300 Neuse Blvd., New Bern • 633-8111

This major medical facility includes 24-hour emergency room service, outpatient surgery, diagnostic services, critical care units, cardiac care services offering diagnostic catheterization and open-heart surgery and radiation oncology. Magnetic resonance imaging (MRI), CT scanning, home care, long-term care for older adults, speech and language therapy, rehabilitation, adult psychiatric services and women's health services are also offered. For more information, see the Healthcare section of the New Bern chapter.

Onslow Memorial Hospital
317 Western Blvd., Jacksonville • 577-2345

This hospital is used by some residents of western Carteret County because Jacksonville is only about 20 miles from Swansboro. The facility offers 24-hour emergency service and admissions, ambulatory surgery, an oncology clinic, private birthing suites and in-and-out treatment for minor illnesses, injuries or emergencies. Considerable remodelling has improved the hospital's efficiency by relocating outpatient and administrative services. The urgent care clinic provides non-emergency care services on an appointment or walk-in basis. The hospital houses its own poison control unit and has physicians on staff with a variety of specialties.

Pitt County Memorial Hospital
Stantonsburg Rd., Greenville • 551-4100

This large facility is affiliated with the East Carolina University School of Medicine and East Carolina Children's Hospital. It offers a wide spectrum of treatment, specialized staff and facilities that range from its well-known emergency room to a neonatal nursery used by smaller hospitals across the region. The

hospital also has an orthoscopic surgery clinic, and the new Leo W. Jenkins Comprehensive Cancer Center provides radiation therapy, chemotherapy and oncologic surgery.

Naval Hospitals
Camp Lejeune • 451-1113
Cherry Point • 466-5751

For active duty and retired military and their families, the Naval Regional Medical Center at Camp Lejeune, the U.S. Marine Corps Base at Jacksonville and the Cherry Point Naval Hospital at the U.S. Marine Corps Air Station at Cherry Point, Havelock provide in- and outpatient medical services.

Home Healthcare

Three home-healthcare businesses are available in Morehead City. These provide services to patients in the Crystal Coast area. Each offers nursing, rehabilitation therapies, medical social work, in-home aides, medical equipment and supplies.

Carteret Home Health Care
Carteret General Hospital, 3500 Arendell St., Morehead City • 247-1373

As a service of Carteret General Hospital, Carteret Home Health Care provides nursing-care services, recovery therapies, personal care and family aid services including bathing, meal preparation and light housekeeping. Special needs such as IV therapies, colostomy care, tube feedings and diabetic instruction are also available for patients departing the hospital and others requiring specialized care.

Comprehensive Home Health Care
3601 Bridges St., Ste. F, Morehead City • 247-4748

With offices that serve 40 counties in North and South Carolina, Comprehensive Home Health Care is a private business that offers an expanding range of home-care services that speed recoveries and offer health services that shorten hospital stays. Additional services

CARTERET GENERAL HOSPITAL

Offering Services
to meet Your Medical Needs

- New Birthing Center
- State-of-the-Art Critical Care Unit
- Nuclear Medicine/Ultrasound
- CAT Scanner/SPECT Scanner
- Cardiopulmonary Services
- Satelite Clinics - Family Practice
  - Cape Carteret · 393-6543
  - Sea Level · 225-1134
- Cancer Treatment Center
- Hospice

- 24 Hour Level II Emergency Room
  - Physician Staffed
- Surgical Services Include:
  - Same-Day Surgery
  - Laparoscopic Surgery
- Full Service Laboratory
- Sea Level Extended Care Facility
  - 108 Beds · 225-4611
- Home Health Services
- Wellness Program

24 Hours a Day
247-1616
FULLY JCAHO ACCREDITED

3500 Arendell Street • Morehead City, NC 28557

offered by this group include high-risk maternity care, pediatrics, pain management, chemotherapy, antibiotic therapy and comprehensive hospice care.

Home Technology Healthcare
3332 Makenzie Sq., Morehead City
• 726-9300   (800) 559-4800,
Care Focus 726-8746

Until recently known as Tarheel Home Health Care, Home Technology Healthcare is a private business that offers a full range of healthcare services for recoveries and care at home. Complete nursing services are offered in all infusion drug therapies and rehabilitation therapies plus 24-hour private duty and HIV/Aids case management. The CareFocus division extends assistance in living that ranges from companionship to skilled nursing.

Mental Health and Substance Abuse

Brynn Marr Behavioral Healthcare System
192 Village Dr., Jacksonville
• (910) 577-1400, (800) 822-9507 helpline counselor

Brynn Marr Hospital extends comprehensive services throughout eastern North Carolina in treatment of emotional and behavioral problems, mental illness, substance abuse and chemical dependencies for individuals of all ages. Designed to offer the least restrictive level of care needed by clients, Brynn Marr's Behavioral Healthcare System offers outpatient care, day treatment programs or full hospitalization for critical care needs. Brynn Marr's Helpline is a free crisis and referral service that offers round-the-clock telephone assistance with confidentiality in identifying needs and recommending an appropriate next step toward problem solution. One

may see a counselor at Helpline offices in the Crystal Coast area, in Jacksonville or in Hampstead for a no-cost evaluation. For senior citizens the hospital's New Beginnings day treatment programs address the specific mental health issues of elderly adults. Brynn Marr also offers numerous support services and outreach programs to the community, including no-cost professional workshops on mental health topics and free community education programs.

Neuse Center
500 N. 35th St., Morehead City • 726-0515

Neuse Center for Mental Health, Mental Retardation and Substance Abuse is a public outpatient facility that provides counseling and emergency services through Carteret General Hospital. It operates under state and county guidelines and accepts walk-in patients, doctor and emergency room referrals. Headquartered in New Bern, Neuse Center has offices in Morehead City.

Neuse Center operates Atlantic House, 1600 Arendell Street in Morehead City, a psychosocial rehabilitation clubhouse program fashioned on similar models that help members cope with long-term mental disabilities. Members help themselves avoid hospitalization by caring for themselves, the facility, working and preparing for work.

Urgent Care

Western Carteret Medical Center
N.C. Hwy. 24 E., Cape Carteret • 393-6543

The Western Carteret Medical Center, a subsidiary of Carteret General Hospital, is in the Cape Carteret shopping center. The clinic provides services by appointment with primary-care physicians as well as walk-in care for minor emergencies. Open weekdays from 8:30 AM until 5 PM, the clinic also offers blood pressure clinics and diabetic counseling.

INSIDERS' TIP

BCCCP, a cancer-screening program for breast and cervical cancers is offered through the Carteret County Health Department, 728-8550, for women with limited income and no health insurance.

The NC Aquarium at Pine Knoll Shores Turtle Release program
in May gives baby sea turtles a second chance to grow up.

Eastern Carteret Medical Center
U.S. Hwy. 70, Sea Level • 225-1134

Eastern Carteret Medical Center, also a subsidiary of Carteret General Hospital, offers the same services as the Western Carteret Medical Center. It was established to serve the eastern part of the county and is open from 8:30 AM until 5 PM weekdays.

Emerald Isle Primary Care
7901 Emerald Dr., Emerald Isle • 354-6500

Three medical doctors and a physician's assistant are available in Emerald Isle seven days a week for complete outpatient medical services. Offices are in Suite #7, Veranda Square. Services by appointment or on an emergency walk-in basis include internal medicine, pediatrics, gynecology, minor surgery and sports medicine.

Med Center One
Atlantic Beach Cswy., Atlantic Beach • 247-2464
69 Chatham St., Newport • 223-3011

Med Center One offers services on the Atlantic Beach Causeway, not far from the base of the high-rise bridge between Morehead City and Atlantic Beach, and in Newport. This privately owned facility has in-house X-ray services and a pharmacy. Med Center One provides emergency and other services on a walk-in basis. Hours are from 8 AM until 6 PM Monday through Friday, 9 AM to 6 PM Saturday and noon to 5 PM on Sunday. In addition to minor emergencies, the clinic schedules appointments and sees walk-in patients for general medical care.

Newport Family Practice Center
Howard Blvd., Newport • 223-5054

Since the nearest emergency room and hospital facilities are in Morehead City or New Bern, Newport Family Practice Center offers a needed service in the Newport community. This privately owned clinic is open from 8 AM to 5 PM weekdays and from 9 AM to noon on Saturday. The center prefers seeing patients who have made appointments in advance but will accept walk-ins in an emergency.

Carteret Urgentcare Center
Hestron Plaza, Ste. 101, Morehead City
• **247-0770**

Vacationers are welcome without an appointment at this privately owned urgent care practice in western Morehead City. On-site X-ray, lab work, EKG and pharmacy are available seven days a week. Hours are Monday through Friday 8 AM to 8 PM, Saturday 10 AM to 6 PM and Sunday 1 to 6 PM.

BeachCare
Urgent Medical Care Center
100 Morehead Ave., Atlantic Beach
• **808-3696**

Located at the main intersection of Atlantic Beach, BeachCare is staffed by emergency care and primary physicians for walk-in and scheduled medical services. Lab services, x-ray and pharmacy is on site. Immunizations, physicals and consultation services are available.

Support Groups and Services

In Carteret County there are a number of active support groups with concerns related to children and family difficulties, mental and physical health, lifestyle changes, challenges and substance abuse. Most support groups meet at the Neuse Center, Carteret General Hospital or at area churches, but that certainly doesn't cover all of them. Following are some of the many groups who meet regularly in the area. For information, call the contact numbers listed. If the list doesn't include a group related to your concern, contact the Neuse Center for Mental Health, 726-0515, or Helpline, 240-0540.

Alzheimer's Group, 726-0031

Battered Women Support Group, 728-3788

Better Breathers, 247-6000 ext. 169

Breast Cancer Support Group, 728-4533, 223-6336

Cancer Support Group, 247-3094 Ext.170

Cardiac Support Group, no contact number. Meets Thursdays, 6:30 P.M., at Carteret County Public Library in Beaufort.

Diabetes Support Group for Patients and Families, 726-7990

Divorce Support Group, 726-4840

Friends For Life, AIDS and HIV-positive support group for individuals and families, 240-2675

Hospice of Carteret County, 247-2808

Lifeline, 247-1530, provides a direct, electronic link between Carteret General Hospital and people needing emergency care

Multiple Sclerosis Support Group, 726-0515

Nervous Disorders Support Group, 728-5460

Neuse Center for Mental Health, Morehead City, 726-0515; New Bern, 633-4171

Overeaters Anonymous, 726-3295

Sexual Abuse Survivors, 240-0546

Alternative Healthcare

Alternative options in healthcare are somewhat limited in this area. Massage therapies are offered for stress reduction and pain relief. Rolfing is available for better posture and flexibility, recovery from surgery and accidents and relief of migraines, carpal tunnel and repetitive stress syndrome.

The Light Within
Morehead Plaza Shopping Center, Morehead City • 726-6500

As the area's holistic resource center, The Light Within offers holistic health counseling including herbal therapies, massage therapies and yoga designed for various ages and purposes. For the relief of back pain, yoga is instructed by Sherry Wells. A Feldenkrais workshop is led by Judi Clinton for the relief of pains associated with computer postures. Tai chi classes are also scheduled by The Light Within.

INSIDERS' TIP

A mixture of Avon's Skin So Soft and water is a soothing, good-smelling insect repellent for people and dogs.

Emergency Phone Numbers

Fire, Police or Rescue Squad — For any emergency, regardless of your location, dial 911.

Poison Control Center, (800) 848-6949

Crime Stoppers, 726-INFO

State Highway Patrol, 726-5766

Help Line, 247-3023

RAP Line for Teens, 726-3194

Neuse Center for Mental Health, 726-0515

Alcoholics Anonymous/Alanon, 726-8540

American Red Cross, 240-1002

Humane Society Animal Shelter, 247-7744

Crystal Coast Animal Protection League, 247-3341

Outer Banks Wildlife Shelter (OWLS), 240-1200

Volunteering brings satisfaction to many people's lives and gives them the chance to meet other people with common interests.

Volunteer Opportunities

Countless organizations on the Crystal Coast rely on volunteers of all ages to render their time, talents and services. Through a variety of volunteer opportunities residents give their time and talents in gardening, narrating historical tours, directing tourists, caretaking the lighthouse keepers quarters and greeting visitors at Cape Lookout, building houses, assisting hospital patients, and delivering food and presents to families at Christmas. Volunteering brings satisfaction to many people's lives and gives them the chance to meet other people with common interests.

People who like history, meeting the public or showing tourists around interesting historical restorations will enjoy channelling some spare time in the direction of the aquarium, museums and historic sites. If you'd enjoy lending a hand and hammer, you will be welcomed into the fold at Habitat For Humanity or Hammocks Beach State Park, who are always glad to see you help with inevitable repairs. All the public libraries employ volunteer help in children's programs, one-on-one assistance for patrons and outreach programs. To make a lasting contribution to the community, volunteer to help with reading or other programs in one of the schools.

Volunteers preferring the company of animals will be delighted with the opportunities at the Outer Banks Wildlife Shelter or at the Humane Society's animal shelter. The Hospital Auxiliary places volunteers in every area at Carteret General Hospital. Meals-on-Wheels and Hospice both depend on volunteered kindness to deliver meals or offer relief to caregivers. The Domestic Violence and Rape Crisis programs train volunteers who are interested in offering specific care in crisis situations. Helpline, the 24-hour crisis telephone line, is fully staffed by trained volunteers who are available to lend an ear and offer referral information. The Retired Senior Volunteer Program (RSVP) is very active and recognized for its matchmaking of retired volunteer expertise with appropriate recipients.

If you have some time to share, volunteering will open new doors. Consider the following organizations that always welcome and train new volunteers. You can learn something new or teach others something you do well. Your call will be welcomed and your experience broadened.

Public Sites and Parks

Beaufort Historical Association
138 Turner St., Beaufort • 728-5225
Training sessions for volunteers at the Beaufort Historic Site occur in March and April.

Volunteers guide tours of the Old Burying Grounds, six historic site buildings and Beaufort's historic district, and operate the Mattie King Davis art gallery and the thrift shop. Volunteers are needed as Warped Weavers and members of the Beaufort Herb Society or to specialize in costumes, special events and general administration.

Carteret County Public Library
210 Turner St., Beaufort • 728-2050

Volunteers work through the Friends of the Library to extend services through established library programs such as Storytime for kids. The Friends operate book sales through the year to keep the collections refreshed at the main branch, Bogue Banks and Newport public libraries and aboard the Bookmobile.

Core Sound Waterfowl Museum
Island Rd., Harkers Island
• 728-1500

Core Sound Waterfowl Museum depends on volunteer help for daily carving demonstrations during the summer months and on weekends during the rest of the year. The membership of the Decoy Carvers Guild needs lots of help in the early fall for the annual fish fry and pot luck supper for membership renewal. The annual Core Sound Decoy Festival each December relies on volunteers for help during the largest off-season event on the Crystal Coast.

Cape Lookout National Seashore
131 Charles St., Harkers Island • 728-2250

Volunteers are selected to staff the restored lighthouse keepers quarters at Cape Lookout during most of the year. Volunteers live at the Cape for a month at a time to greet and answer the questions of the visitors who arrive to see the natural history collection on display.

Carteret County Museum of History & Art
100 Wallace Dr., Morehead City • 247-7533

Staffing the museum gift shop is the daily work of volunteer members of the Carteret County Historical Society. The society's quarterly newsletter is the work of volunteers, as is

the museum's annual Christmas Bazaar during the Thanksgiving holidays.

Fort Macon State Park
E. Fort Macon Rd. (MP 1), Atlantic Beach
• 726-3775

Volunteers at Fort Macon are trained to help park rangers with special group tours and presentations. Volunteers are especially helpful with leading tours for school groups.

N.C. Aquarium at Pine Knoll Shores
Salter Path Rd. • 247-4004

Volunteering at the aquarium includes discussing animals in the touch tank, staffing discovery carts, leading tours, running projectors, greeting school groups and feeding baby sea turtles.

N.C. Maritime Museum
315 Front St., Beaufort
• 728-7317

Museum volunteers are always at the information desk. They provide tours and offer Discover Cart programs, build and restore boats in the Watercraft Center, help operate the Cape Lookout Studies Program, administer the Friends of the Museum and help with fund-raising, clerical work and mailings.

FYI

Unless otherwise noted, the area code for all phone numbers in this guide is 919.

Animal Care Services

Outer Banks Wildlife Shelter
5810 Arendell St., Morehead City
• 240-1200

This shelter for injured wildlife is entirely operated with volunteer help, including the help of licensed rehabilitators. Funding efforts include the Sand Sculpture Contest in August at the Atlantis Lodge, daily aluminum can recycling, an annual benefit dinner and contributions of visitors and rescuers of injured animals. Feeding and animal care is also volunteered.

Humane Society of Carteret County
Hibbs Rd., Morehead City • 247-7744

Members provide staffing for administration and animal care services, usually for dogs and cats that are in between homes.

"Whooo would like to volunteer at the Outer Banks Wildlife Shelter?"

Human Care Services

Big Brothers/Big Sisters of the Lower Neuse
201 Country Aire Suites., U.S. Hwy. 70, Morehead City • 240-2165

Volunteer mentors serve local children of single-parent families. Children range in age from six to 15 and are carefully matched with adult role models who spend three to five hours a week with the child. The purpose is to establish a real friendship that will enhance the child's feeling of self worth and to provide educational and other opportunities that may be missing in the child's life.

Carteret County Domestic Violence Program
402 Turner St., Beaufort • 728-3788

Volunteers contribute their time operating the Domestic Violence Program's upscale resale shop, Finders' Keepers, at 1300 Arendell Street in Morehead City. The shop collects households goods for women who are getting another start. Proceeds help fund the program's shelter.

Carteret County Hospital Auxiliary
Carteret General Hospital, Morehead City • 247-1532

Volunteers are scheduled and trained at Carteret General Hospital to assist patients and staff in every area of the hospital.

Carteret County Primary Reading Program
Carteret County Public Schools, 107 Safrit Dr., Beaufort • 728-4583

Volunteers willing to work with young children read one-on-one with selected students from kindergarten through third grade for 30 minutes, three days a week during the school year. Nine-hour training sessions occur in August.

Carteret Literacy Council
Cape Lookout High School, 1108 Bridges St., Morehead City • 808-2020

This program matches tutors who are trained in the Laubach method of reading instruction with students, usually adults, who need help with reading, writing or math. Sessions are arranged by the tutor-student team who meet, usually, twice a week for 1½ hours at a location convenient to both parties. Training is coordinated in the same way.

Crystal Coast Habitat For Humanity
312 Live Oak St., Beaufort • 728-5216

Habitat For Humanity provides volunteer labor to build or remodel homes for families qualified for the special loans that finance the home building efforts. A combined effort of Habitat labors and funding of Hope Mission at 1412 Bridges Street, Morehead City, are providing the needed facilities for Hope Mission as well as a permanent home for Habitat offices by 1997. Habitat's Fifty-Plus group built its first home single-handedly in 1996. The group formed an adjunct arm of Habitat to provide affordable repairs, especially for senior citizens.

Guardians ad Litem
402 Cedar St., Beaufort • 728-8574

After training, Guardians ad Litem are assigned by the juvenile court to investigate a case of child neglect or abuse and to report their findings to the court. This advocate for the child ensures that the child's interests are properly presented and represents the child's best interest to the judge.

Helpline
209 N. 35th St., Morehead City • 240-0540

Helpline is the county's 24-hour-a-day information, referral and crisis intervention line. Volunteers assist callers with varied problems and needs. Helpline volunteers refer emergency calls for the county's Rape Crisis Program. A Teentalk line is newly available for volunteers trained specifically to assist teens who call for help.

Hope Mission
1412 Bridges St., Morehead City • 240-2359

Hope Mission exists to meet immediate needs of people requiring help. At the mission's soup kitchen, volunteers assist in serving food provided by area churches.

Hospice of Carteret County
Webb Civic Center, Ninth and Evans sts., Morehead City • 247-2808

Hospice trains volunteers each year to help provide care and support for terminally ill patients and their families. The goal is to improve the quality of life for the patient and relieve physical and emotional pain in the last stages of life. Volunteers also assist with bereavement support, administrative and fundraising efforts of Hospice.

Foster Grandparent Program
17th and Fisher sts., Morehead City • 726-5219

The Foster Grandparents Program, administered by the Senior Citizens Center, provides a stipend for limited-income participants who have 20 hours a week for one-on-one extra assistance of a child in school or in the hospital. Volunteers must apply; contact Diane Williams at the number above.

Martha's Mission Cupboard
901 Bay St., Morehead City • 726-1717

This is an emergency food pantry for families in crisis in Carteret County. Every month, the mission provides food for 175 to 200 families, senior citizens and mentally and physically handicapped persons. Martha's Mission operates strictly on donations.

Meals-on-Wheels
Shirley Jackson, Coordinator • 726-9972, 247-5861

A solely volunteer program of participating area churches, Meals-on-Wheels provides services for an estimated 50 or more elderly or ill recipients who may or may not contribute to the cost. Program costs are aided by donations through churches and by donation of

INSIDERS' TIP

The summer Junior Volunteers at Harborview Health Care Center in Morehead City are preteens and teenagers. They give some of their vacation time to help room-bound residents by reading and writing, distributing food and ice, and transporting residents to activities. Volunteers are trained by the activity director; call 726-6855.

meals by the restaurant and retirement home kitchens that prepare them. The volunteers so vital to the program are the route drivers who deliver the meals daily and check on those who are served by the program.

Project Christmas Cheer
Daisy Hilbert • 726-5970

Project Christmas Cheer began in 1987 when a group of people volunteered their time to assist an overflow of families seeking assistance from the Department of Social Services. Volunteers take applications for six weeks in the fall and match the applicants with donors. Before Christmas each year, the donors make arrangements to deliver Christmas gifts such as food, toys, blankets, fuel oil and things that would really help during Christmas of a difficult year. Project Christmas Cheer assists more than 1,600 people each year.

Retired Senior Volunteer Program (RSVP)
17th and Fisher sts., Morehead City • 247-4366

Members of RSVP are age 55 and older and pledge to perform at least one hour of volunteer service each month. RSVP volunteers are matched with the tasks that suit their abilities and interests. They work with the Big Brother/Big Sister organization, drive to deliver meals and are substitute drivers. Some knit and crochet caps and scarfs for Project Christmas Cheer and help homebound seniors with shopping and errands.

Environmental Services

N.C. Big Sweep
N.C. Cooperative Extension Service, Beaufort • 728-8421

N.C. Big Sweep is a state-wide effort to clean the waterways of trash. It's a four-hour effort on a mid-September Saturday that is locally coordinated through the state Cooperative Extension Service office.

N.C. Coastal Federation
3609 Hwy. 24, Ocean • 393-8185

This coastal environmental protection organization works through education, information and legislative accountability and is funded through membership contributions. Volunteers are needed to help in the office and with an educational program that conducts field trips from May through October. Volunteers are vital to the organization's fund-raising efforts, and specific expertise is welcomed.

Rachael Carson Reserve
430-B West Beaufort Rd., Beaufort • 728-2170

Early in the year, the N.C. National Estuarine Research Reserve trains volunteers to lead field trips scheduled on the Rachael Carson Reserve in Beaufort during the spring and summer. Trips are conducted each week and special trips are also scheduled. Volunteers convey information on the islands' ecology and history.

WTEB 89.3 FM, broadcast on the campus of Craven Community College, is the area's National Public Radio station.

Media

Carteret County's media scene is somewhat limited but the options that are available are top quality. The county does not have a daily newspaper, but the *Carteret County News-Times* does a good job covering the news three days a week. Smaller weekly community newspapers cover specific areas of the county. The *Jacksonville Daily News* also covers some Carteret County news. Several radio stations are based in the area, and a few television stations are close by and cover local news. Time Warner Cable offer the full spectrum of cable channels.

Print

Carteret County News-Times
4034 Arendell St., Morehead City
• 726-7081

Carteret County has no daily newspaper, but the county's happenings are covered by the Carteret County News-Times, published Wednesday and Friday afternoons and Sunday mornings. The paper reports on news and features on the Crystal Coast and surrounding areas. State and national sports are included. *Carteret County News-Times* is published by Carteret Publishing Company, Morehead City.

NewsTalk 24 is a computerized phone service provided by the *News-Times*. Residents and visitors can dial 247-NEWS and then access from a number of information files. These files are advertised regularly in the newspaper and include information about area activities, schools, NASCAR and local businesses. For more information or a listing, call the NewsTalk 24 office, 726-7081.

Tideland News
101-2 Church St., Swansboro
• (910) 326-5066

Tideland News is published each Wednesday from its office in Swansboro. Owned by Carteret Publishing Company of Morehead City, the paper covers news and activities in the western part of the county — Swansboro, Cape Carteret, Cedar Point and Emerald Isle.

The Havelock Times
13 Park Ln., Havelock • 444-8210

Published each Wednesday, *The Havelock Times* covers news and features happening in and around Havelock and Newport. The paper is owned by Carteret Publishing Company of Morehead City and is based in Havelock.

Jacksonville Daily News
724 Bell Fork Rd., Jacksonville
• (910) 353-1171

The *Jacksonville Daily News*, a daily morning paper, includes state and national coverage and primarily covers Onslow County and the U.S. Marine Base at Camp Lejeune. The paper also covers Carteret County activities and county-wide issues.

The Mailboat
P.O. Box 3, Harkers Island • 728-4644

The Mailboat, published on Harkers Island, is a quarterly publication that includes anecdotes, recollections and stories about life as it used to be in Carteret County's Down East communities. Each publication is a treasured addition to local libraries. *The Mailboat* also puts out an annual booklet of Christmas recollections, which is included in the subscription price or may be purchased from area book stores.

Coaster Magazine
201 N. 17th St., Morehead City • 240-1811

Coaster is published seven times year with the majority of issues in the summer. About 210,000 magazines are printed annually and distributed at no charge to the public through 150 visitor locations on the Crystal Coast and out of the area. Now in its 15th year, Coaster provides details on local events and attractions, traditional culture and legends.

Crystal Coast Visitor's Guide
1724 Virginia Beach Blvd., Ste. 108, Virginia Beach • (800) 422-0742

Crystal Coast Visitor's Guide provides a variety of information for both the visitor and the resident. The magazine focuses on Crystal Coast entertainment and attractions, shopping, restaurants and real estate. It is published annually and free copies are available at many area establishments.

Television Stations

Time Warner Cable Channel 10
U.S. Hwy. 70, Newport • 223-5011

Time Warner Cable Channel 10 airs programming varying from school and health issues to sports and talk shows. Studio manager Marty Feurer focuses on community events and works hard to disseminate information about community projects and community-service activities. "Coastal Headline News" is shown twice an hour and "Do What?," a guide of local events for visitors and residents, is scheduled at various times.

UNC Center for Public Television
Research Triangle Park, Raleigh • 549-7000

Crystal Coast public television is broadcast locally on Channel 13. Viewers may chose from all the regular public TV programming as well as shows tailored to the interests of North Carolina residents.

WFXI-FOX
U.S. Hwy. 70, Newport • 240-0888

Television Channel 8 shows the regular Fox programming and offers a local news show at 10 PM.

WCTI
225 Glenburnie Dr., New Bern • 638-1212

Television Channel 12, the local ABC affiliate, provides comprehensive local coverage as well as ABC programming. The station offers local news coverage, sports and weather each weekday at 6 AM, noon, 5 , 6 and 11 PM.

A fish and game forecast is given during the news sports segment.

WITN
2002 S. Glenburnie Rd., New Bern • 636-2337

Television Channel 7 is the local NBC affiliate. Along with NBC programming, the station has area news coverage, including high school and college sportscasts.

WNCT
Hwy. 70 W., Newport • 247-2293

Television Channel 9, the local CBS affiliate, includes a morning local talk show and local news and sports shows along with its network programming.

Cable Television

FYI

Unless otherwise noted, the area code for all phone numbers in this guide is 919.

Time Warner Cable
500 Vision Cable Dr., Newport • 223-5011

Time Warner is the franchised cable provider for all of Carteret County. For hookup service, call the number above.

Radio Stations

WTKF 107.3 FM
U.S. Hwy. 70, Newport • 247-6343

North Carolina's first talk FM, WTKF carries news, talk, sports and NASCAR. "Wake Up Carolina", a local talk show, is featured each weekday from 8 to 9 AM. Rush Limbaugh, Alan Colmes and Bruce Williams entertain and inform while area hosts feature local news and newsmakers. The station also features a dozen local daily newscasts plus TV-12 weather twice an hour.

WBTB 1400 AM
205 Ocean St., Beaufort • 728-1635

WBTB features Christian talk from the Moody Bible Network. It has nondenominational programming with a Christian perspective on issues of the day. Call-in shows, news programs and children's programming make WBTB a well-rounded source for news and family entertainment.

Photo: Scott Taylor

Every few years, Frosty visits the Crystal Coast.

WMGV 103.3 FM
207 Glenburnie Dr., New Bern • 247-1033

V 103.3 offers a variety of adult contemporary music that appeals to all ages. The station offers news in the morning and weather at 10 minutes past the hour all day long.

WMBL 740 AM
5058 U.S. Hwy. 70 W., Morehead City • 240-0740

WMBL provides the best of 1940s, '50s and '60s. This easy listening station is very popular on the Crystal Coast. Morning host Jay Cobb often talks with community members from 7 to 9 AM and the show provides information about community projects and programs. Big Band music is featured each Sunday morning and Mary Alford's show titled "Reminisce" can be heard at 9:50 AM Monday through Friday. CNN news is featured at the top of the hour.

WRHT 96.3 FM
Little Nine Rd., Morehead City • 247-2002

WRHT, Sunny 96.3 FM, offers listeners top 40 and contemporary hits. It features "Charlie Byrd's Beach Music Show" each Sunday from 7 to 11 PM. The station's request line is 726-9600.

WTEB 89.3 FM
800 College Court, New Bern • 638-3434

This National Public Radio station is broadcast from studios on the Craven Community College campus. It offers "Morning Edition" weekdays from 6 to 9 AM and "Weekend Edition" from 8 to 10 AM Saturday and Sunday. The popular "All Things Considered" is aired weekdays from 4 to 6 PM. Classical music is featured during the week. On Saturday evenings, listeners enjoy ballroom music and on Sunday evenings WTEB plays jazz selections.

Many of the area's oldest churches are in Beaufort.

Worship

Residents, visitors and newcomers can choose from hundreds of worship centers on the Crystal Coast. Whether you're interested in attending a service, admiring architecture or learning about local history, the churches of the Crystal Coast have something to offer nearly everyone. Much of the area's social and community activities and volunteer efforts are spearheaded and organized by local houses of worship.

Churches are around every corner, but that's not unusual for an area many refer to as the "Southern Bible Belt." Baptist, Methodist and Pentecostal churches predominate. Episcopal, Presbyterian, Friends, Unitarian/Universalist and Catholic churches are also represented, along with many other denominations. Visitors who wish to worship at a synagogue may visit Temple B'Nai Sholem Synagogue, 505 Middle Street, New Bern.

Many of the oldest churches are in Beaufort. For the most part, these are wooden structures preserved to look just as they did hundreds of years ago. Each church in the area is distinct; some are modern structures, some are classic brick designs, others are weathered and vine-covered. Each has its own legends and stories held dear to members of its congregation.

It would be impractical to try to list the hundreds of worship centers scattered around the Crystal Coast. We have described a few of the most noted churches, whether that is because of the building's age, size of the congregation or convenient location.

For more information about other churches in the area, check the Yellow Pages.

Ann Street United Methodist Church, Ann and Craven streets, Beaufort, was built c. 1854. The church features curved wooden pews and beautiful stained-glass windows. An unusual feature is the handcarved rosettes in the ceiling. The steeple of the church, stretching high above the houses on the low coastal land, was shown on old mariners' charts as a point of reference, a beacon to aid those at sea. It is one of three churches surrounding the Old Burying Ground (see the Crystal Coast Attractions chapter). The church's modern educational building stands across the street and is used for community events.

Purvis Chapel AME Zion Church, 217 Craven Street, is Beaufort's oldest continuous-use church. Built in 1820, it stands on the same block as the Ann Street Church. Originally built by the Methodist Episcopal Church, Purvis Chapel was later deeded to the AME Zion congregation and is still owned by that group. The bell in the church was cast in Glasgow, Scotland, in 1797. The building is listed on the National Register of Historic Places.

The area's oldest Episcopal church is St. Paul's, c. 1857, located at 209 Ann Street, Beaufort. Local shipbuilders built the church building in two years. Visitors will notice that the interior of the sanctuary bears a striking resemblance to an upside-down ark. It is reported to be one of the 10 most acoustically perfect buildings in North Carolina. Holy Eucharist is on Sunday and a mid-week Eucharist is conducted each Wednesday.

St. Stephen's Congregational Church, Craven and Cedar Streets, Beaufort, was built in 1867 along with the neighboring two-story

Photo: Scott Taylor

Built in 1854, the Ann Street United Methodist Church features curved wooden pews and beautiful stained-glass windows.

school building that housed the Washburn Seminary. Records show the lot was purchased for $100 in 1867, and the seminary served as a school for many years.

Morehead City's First Baptist Church is one of the town's oldest churches. It is located at Ninth and Bridges streets. The congregation originally shared a small building near the waterfront with the town's Methodists. After the War Between the States, the congregation built the current new structure. The 18,000-square-foot family life center at First Baptist Church is available for community activities such as meetings and weddings. The center can handle such activities as basketball games, parties and dinners for as many as 800 people.

Glad Tidings Church
Maurice Phelps, Pastor

4621 Country Club Road
Morehead City, NC 28557
726-0160   726-0603

Morning Worship
9:00 & 10:30 a.m.

Children's Church
10:30 a.m.

Evening Worship
6:00 p.m.

Wednesday Family
Night
7:00 p.m.

Sunday School
9:00 a.m.

"Healing the Hurting"
In Carteret County & Around the World

A light and sound system allows for excellent quality concerts.

Standing on the corner of Ninth and Arendell streets in Morehead, the First United Methodist Church is home to one of the oldest Methodist congregations in eastern North Carolina. The church congregation's roots go back to Shepard's Point in 1797. The original chapel was built in 1879 and later was converted to a bakery by the Union Army in 1862. Today's sanctuary was dedicated in 1952.

St. Egbert's Catholic Church, located at 1612 Evans Street, had its start in Morehead in the early 1920s. The church now has its own school for students from kindergarten through 6th grade. In late 1991 it completed extensive renovations and additions to the church and parish house. Community service is emphasized, with support groups regularly meeting in church facilities. Parish services are offered Saturday and Sunday, and Mass is held on various weekdays.

The Unitarian Universalist Coastal Fellowship, at 1300 Evans Street, Morehead City, was organized in Carteret County in 1980. It has grown to a church with about 90 members. From May through September, services are held every Sunday at 10:30 AM in a renovated building that features a fellowship hall, kitchen and religious education rooms. In the off-season, services are held every other Sunday at 10:30 AM.

The Glad Tidings Pentecostal Holiness Church is located at 4729 Country Club Road, Morehead City. The family life center at Glad Tidings provides more than 10,000 square feet for activities. There is a large open area, 11 classrooms, a kitchen, storage areas and offices. This center is often available for weddings, conferences and meetings.

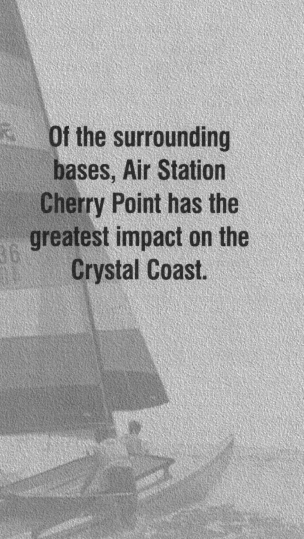

Of the surrounding bases, Air Station Cherry Point has the greatest impact on the Crystal Coast.

Military

Military bases and training facilities dot North Carolina's Crystal Coast, but they haven't spoiled its beauty. They have just added a few more people, a little noise, extra traffic every now and then and a lot of patriotism.

Occasionally residents express concern about low-flying aircraft, the noise a night training flight might cause or the increased traffic on two-lane roads, but overall the military bases are excellent neighbors. They provide employment and income and contribute to the community through uncountable volunteer hours. Military personnel often volunteer to tutor students, clear and construct school athletic fields, help non-profit groups with projects and raise funds for holiday programs. We're glad to have them in Carteret County.

Of the surrounding bases Air Station Cherry Point has the greatest impact on the Crystal Coast. Cherry Point, with its Naval Aviation Depot and the Marine Corps Air Station, is the leading military employer of Carteret County residents. About 2,000 civilian employees and 2,000 active-duty military employees and retired military reside in the county. In 1996, those workers earned approximately $110,000,000 out of a total Cherry Point payroll of $487,000,000. About 10,000 of Carteret County's 58,000 year-round residents are impacted by Cherry Point. That figure includes the employees, retired military, and military and civilian dependents.

The Port of Morehead City is the port of embarkation and debarkation for the Second Division of the U.S. Marine Corps at Camp Lejeune. This base is near Jacksonville and military troops often travel Highway 24 from Swansboro to Morehead City. Another area establishment is Seymour Johnson Air Force Base in Goldsboro, which is about a two-hour drive from the Crystal Coast.

What follows is information about some of the closest military establishments. For more about Marine Corps Air Station Cherry Point, see our Havelock chapter.

Marine Corps
Auxiliary Landing Field

Bogue Field, off N.C. Hwy. 24 • 393-2027

This 875-acre landing field fronts Bogue Sound. The field primarily is used for field carrier landing practice, and pilots perform many of these landings at night to simulate landing on an aircraft carrier.

Atlantic Outlying Field
and Piney Island (Marines)

These two facilities are in the Down East

This man is oystering on the intertidal flat of Rachael Carson
Reserve across Taylors Creek from Beaufort.

area of Carteret County. Atlantic Outlying Field is a 1,514-acre facility in the community of Atlantic. Piney Island, or BT-11 as the military refers to it, is a 10,000-or-so-acre electronic practice range at the eastern tip of Carteret County. As part of the Mid-Atlantic Electronic Warfare Range (MAEWR), Piney Island is used by various military groups, including active duty personnel and reservists. While planes actually do fly over the area, bombing simulations are recorded and scored electronically via computers to lessen the environmental impact.

Coast Guard Base Fort Macon
Fort Macon Rd., Atlantic Beach • 247-4598

Coast Guard Base Fort Macon is at the east end of Bogue Banks and is the home port of several large cutters and smaller vessels. The base is charged with patrolling the waters from Drum Inlet on Core Banks south to the North Carolina-South Carolina border. Coast Guard missions include search and rescue and law enforcement.

Coast Guard Station Swansboro
Station St., Emerald Isle • 354-2462

This station is at the west end of Bogue Banks in Emerald Isle. When the station was first established, Emerald Isle was not a town, so it was named after Swansboro, the town to the north. The name never changed. This station's vessels patrol an area from Marker 21 in Bogue Sound, which is in the area of Gales Creek community, south to the Surf City swing bridge in Pender County.

RAMADA INN
WATERFRONT & MARINA
NEW BERN, NORTH CAROLINA

- *Newly Renovated*
- *All Rooms Riverview*
- *In-room Coffeemakers*
- *Swimming Pool*
- *Minutes from Tryon Palace*
- *Marina with Slips Available*

Reservations (919) 636-3637
Off Hwy 70 East
(Across the River from Historic Downtown)

The Angus Steakhouse proudly features "CERTIFIED ANGUS BEEF" for the ultimate in Steaks and Prime Rib, plus fresh Select Seafood over a blazing hickory wood fire. We serve Breakfast, Lunch and Dinner in a casual waterfront setting. Sunday Brunch is served from 9:00am until 2:00pm every Sunday. Check out our Nightly Specials.

Waterfront Dining
Located at the
Ramada Inn
101 Howell Rd., New Bern

"Karaoke"
Wednesday & Saturday
Nights starting at 9:00 pm

New Bern

To really understand the New Bern of today, it's important to know its past. This river town maintains its heritage by standing guard over its Colonial, Georgian, Federal, Greek Revival and Victorian architectural styles. And, its citizens still maintain an attitude of friendliness and Southern gentility.

The town's Swiss look comes honestly. It was settled in 1710 by Swiss and German immigrants who named it after the Swiss capital of Bern. The town was officially founded by Swiss Baron Christoph deGraffenried. Just like any Swiss city, New Bern is distinguished by its red-brick clock tower above City Hall. The town emblem, as in old Bern, is a black bear, and the symbol appears frequently throughout the city.

New Bern has been fought over by Native Americans, Swiss, British, Colonials, Yankees and Rebels. After each skirmish, it pulled itself up by its boot straps and plodded onward. The result is a panoply of American history along tree-lined streets that have just the slightest look of old Switzerland. It's an odd mix that makes the town quite picturesque.

Historic markers point out the houses where the first elected assembly in the colonies met in defiance of the crown in 1774, where a signer of the U.S. Constitution lived and where George Washington slept — twice. Markers also show you where noted jurist William Gaston, the first chief justice of the state Supreme Court and composer of the state song, had his office.

The second-oldest city in North Carolina, New Bern is the site of many firsts. It was in New Bern that the first state printing press was set up and the first book and newspaper were published. The state's first public school opened here. The first official celebration of George Washington's birthday was held in New Bern, and it was here that the world's first practical torpedo was assembled and detonated. In the 1890s C. D. Bradham, a local pharmacist, invented Brad's Drink in New Bern. The drink later became known as Pepsi-Cola.

Photo: Swiss Bear

Middle Street in the 1800s ended in a working waterfront on the Trent River.

Without question, New Bern's center-piece is Tryon Palace, the lavish Georgian brick mansion named after William Tryon, the British Colonial governor who had it built in 1770. It is a sumptuous showplace inside and out. Twin rows of oaks leading up to the entrance provide a stately introduction, and the scenic backdrop is the wide and lovely Trent River. The palace is where delegates gathered for the first State Legislature meeting in 1777.

But even before all that, before the palace, the school and the white man's voice, the site captured the interest of the Tuscarora Indians. It is believed the Indians may have had hunting camps and villages here for thousands of years.

Downtown New Bern (see our map of New Bern's Historical District) sits on a point of land at the confluence of the Neuse and Trent rivers. Once the main hub, its downtown fell into great disrepair in the early 1970s due to the development of shopping malls and suburban housing outside the business district.

That all changed, however, in 1979 when local government gave Swiss Bear Inc., a nonprofit corporation composed of civic leaders, the authority and responsibility to revitalize the downtown area. Today, art galleries, specialty shops, antiques stores, restaurants and other businesses have resurrected downtown, turning it into a bustling hub of activity.

Progressive and exciting improvements are continuously underway. Built and dedicated in 1995, James Reed Lane is a lovely downtown mini-park and pedestrian walkthrough on Pollock Street across from Christ Church. The pleasant respite amid downtown activity was planned and funded through efforts of Swiss Bear Inc., in honor of the first rector of Christ Church. In October 1996 a

FYI

Unless otherwise noted, the area code for all phone numbers in this guide is 919.

downtown Welcome Center housing the Craven Convention and Visitors Bureau and the Greater New Bern Chamber of Commerce opened to visitors at the corner of Middle Street and Tryon Palace Drive. Swiss Bear Inc. and the City of New Bern are renovating the park at Union Point in several phases that began in 1996 with new bulkheading, railings and a riverside promenade. The entire 300 block of Middle Street is undergoing a face-lift inspired by the restored Kress Building at Middle and Pollock streets, and many of the building facades are returning their turn-of-the-century elegance. The Swiss Bear downtown revitalization initiative has been very visibly successful.

Just a few miles upstream from downtown, the Neuse River slows and quickly broadens into a mile-wide concourse. Joined by the Trent River, the Neuse takes a lumbering left turn and widens to 4 miles across, making it the widest river in the United States. The two rivers converge at downtown's Union Point Park, one of New Bern's best places for a picnic lunch.

This inviting link to the broad, shallow Pamlico Sound and the Atlantic Ocean helped shape New Bern's destiny. The town long thrived on the richness of its rivers and the fertile soil surrounding them. In Colonial times, West Indian and European vessels would dock here to trade cargos of merchandise. The river led inland to pitch, tar and tobacco and, of course, to local hospitality. Now the rivers serve as the focus of the area's recreational activities: water-skiing, sailing and fishing. Hotel-based marinas for modern-day skippers edge toward the Trent River channel from both banks between Union Point Park and the railroad trestle and also front the Neuse. New Bern's rivers are a tremendous source of area pride, and recent pollution symptoms in the Neuse

ENJOY
NEW BERN
IN COMFORT!

- Located on the Neuse River in Historic District
- Convenient to Tryon Palace, Civil War Museum, and all downtown shopping
- Whirlpool Suites/Fitness Center
- Waterfront Balconies
- Complimentary Deluxe Continental Breakfast
- Evening Guest Reception

Comfort Suites

Comfort Suites
Riverfront Park

218 East Front St.
New Bern, North Carolina 28560
(919) 636-0022
Reservations
800-228-5150

Photo: Janis Williams

New Bern is a gentle place, a place where one can still enjoy the passing scene. . . !!

have stirred tremendous state and local efforts in restoring its health.

New Bern's southeastern boundary is only a few miles from the Croatan National Forest, a 157,000-acre preserve that shelters deer, bears, alligators and the rare Venus's-flytraps. Canada geese and osprey are common sights along the rivers, as are the resident great blue herons. Given the right weather conditions and saltwater intrusion, the Neuse River has been known to hide 8- and 10-foot sharks.

New Bern has three historic districts with homes, stores and churches dating back to the early 18th century. Within easy walking distance of the waterfront are more than 200 homes and buildings listed on the National Register of Historic Places. Several bed and breakfast inns, most of the area's best restaurants, banks, antiques and specialty shops, Tryon Palace, city and county government complexes and many of the town's 2,000 crape myrtles are also nearby.

The crepe myrtle is New Bern's official flower, and it's no wonder. On those hot summer days when you feel like drooping, the crape myrtle seems to laugh with energy as it bursts forth in a profusion of blossoms. New Bern does its gardening quietly. Led by the example of the professionally pampered Tryon Palace gardens, the town's residents have a yen to make things grow. During the spring explosion of dogwoods and azaleas, a ride through the DeGraffenried neighborhood, about a mile from downtown, is breathtaking.

Gardens, both public and private, extend throughout the city and its suburbs. Summertime brings day lilies, dahlias, zinnias, black-eyed Susans and petunias. Home gardens produce tomatoes, chives, squash, corn and other favorites. In fall it seems everyone goes ga-ga for chrysanthemums. (See New Bern Annual Events for information about the fall Chrysanthemum Festival.) Flowering cabbage and pansies brighten the winter.

Besides the downtown historic district, New Bern also has the Ghent and Riverside neighborhoods, both of which carry official historic neighborhood designations. Ghent, across Trent Road from the DeGraffenried neighborhood, was the town's first suburb, and the dogwood-planted median on Spencer Avenue was once the bed of a trolley. The neighborhood displays an eclectic collection of architectural styles.

Riverside, developed at the turn of this century and across town from Ghent, runs between the Norfolk Southern railroad tracks and the Neuse River to Jack Smith Creek. It has a sort of baron-and-worker feel to it, with imposing mansions along National Avenue, giving way to the less sumptuous residences on neighboring streets.

Tucked between New Bern and the Trent River is Trent Woods, one of the wealthiest of North Carolina's incorporated towns. Here is the New Bern Golf and Country Club, the Eastern Carolina Yacht Club and some of the priciest real estate around. And Trent Woods' costly, pine-shaded real estate is more and more in similar company within New Bern's housing market. About 5 miles south of town off Highway 17 is River Bend, which began as a planned development but later incorporated. Like Trent Woods, it has its own country club, golf course, tennis club, marina and waterfront acreage along the Trent River and canals that lead to it.

Both River Bend and Fairfield Harbour, another planned community about 8 miles east of New Bern on the Neuse River, have attracted retirees primarily from the Northeast. Fairfield Harbour's amenities include a couple of golf courses, two swimming pools, tennis courts, a marina, a restaurant and lounge, miniature golf, horseshoes and walking and riding paths.

If all this sounds boringly nice, take heart. There are a few trouble spots. Insiders' brows furrow when they talk about the town's traffic lights and its lack of nightlife.

INSIDERS' TIP

"General George" is a longleaf pine in the Croatan that was a sapling in the Revolutionary War.

The Great Fire of 1922

Friday, December 1, 1922. It was the most tragic day in New Bern's modern history. The day after Thanksgiving. The morning was gray and overcast with a gale blowing out of the south. At 8 AM, the fire department was called just outside of town to the Rowland Lumber Company, the largest sawmill in North Carolina and the largest employer in town. Every piece of firefighting equipment and all personnel were required to fight the huge blaze that engulfed the mill.

Meanwhile in town, at the home of Henry and Hester Bryan on Kilmarnock Street, family members were gathered at the table for breakfast when someone called from the street that the chimney was on fire. Dr. Samuel Bryan was the youngest of the Bryan family at the table. He remembers, "Family members began immediately removing the furniture from the house. In the excitement of moving the furniture, it was discovered that I was still inside the house eating. A Mr. Chapman came in and took me from the table. Flame caught in the gable of our house, but men saved the house by beating out the flames. While houses burned all around, our house remained standing and served as a haven to several families . . ."

The December 2, 1922 issue of *The New Bernian* reported the sequence of events as follows:

"By an irony of fate it is very likely that had it not been for the fire at Rowland Mill an hour or so earlier the devastation of a portion of New Bern would not have occurred. But such was the fate and when, in answer to the alarm calling firemen to the new scene of the conflagration, the driver of the hose wagon found that there was no nozzle to be attached to the hose and it was necessary to rush back to headquarters after this. In the meantime the fire gained headway, burst beyond all bounds and the devastation of the city was consummated."

— continued on next page

Photo: George Multon Memories of New Bern by Emily Herring Wilson.

A tent city was erected in New Bern to house the victims of the devastating fire of 1922.

Fire was carried by the wind from house to house, easily igniting the wooden shingles that were typical in the area of town which is now Craven Terrace. Before the day ended, 3,200 people were homeless, nearly 1,000 buildings were destroyed, hundreds of jobs were lost and an area of forty blocks was destroyed in New Bern. That night, families were taken in all over town, but many slept with their salvaged belongings on open train cars and in Cedar Grove Cemetery.

In the days and months that followed, the town fed thousands of displaced fire victims at West Street School, and in the James City area of town a tent city was constructed as temporary housing. Because of the loss of jobs, many victims were forced to move away.

The fire changed the lives of all residents of New Bern in some way. As New Bern resident Dorcas Carter remembers it, "The big fire of December 1, 1922, caused me and my family to become scattered from our homes and my birthplace, church site and make new adjustments for another mode of life . . . To me, it seems as if I have been scattered from everyone ever since."

Personal recollections are based on interviews from the oral history *Memories of New Bern* by Emily Herring Wilson, published in 1995 by the New Bern Historical Society Foundation.

First, the traffic lights. Those approaching New Bern on the two-laned Highway 17 north of town, will find that New Bern's drawbridge and traffic lights offer a major hitch in the flow of your trip. As you follow signs through the downtown area, the small Colonial-sized city blocks, widely varying levels of traffic and ill-timed traffic lights give you a chance to pause and read the historic markers, whether you want to or not. If you're headed south, you can expect another bottleneck around the road's intersection with Highway 70. These traffic problems won't be the case much longer, however, because changes are looming over the Neuse.

Construction of a four-lane high-rise bridge began in October 1995. The bridge will span the Neuse River and go from Bridgeton on Highway 17 to James City on Highway 70. The new bridge will replace the John Lawson drawbridge now approaching New Bern from the north. Construction is expected to be complete in 1999.

That brings us to New Bern's nightlife. There are a few lounges, some live music, a few movie theaters and a bowling alley, but those with a hankering for more need to hit town at the right time. New Bern has good professional and amateur acting groups, a professional dance company, a subscription performance season and an annual jazz concert worth the wait.

The town also has wonderful festivals, shows and fun-for-all conventions — the Chrysanthemum Festival, the New Bern Preservation Foundation's Antique Show and the Clown Convention are among the favorites. Residents also gather for special occasions on the Trent River waterfront — on July 4th for the fireworks and in early December for the Christmas flotilla. But, otherwise, the town's social life takes place in private homes and social clubs and at various civic and charity functions that are staged on an annual basis.

To really get to know New Bern, you have to take it as it is. Think of the river city as a slow treasure hunt where gems are revealed as you walk its streets. It's there that you will discover the real New Bern. Visit its museums — the Bank of the Arts, Tryon Palace Historic Sites and Gardens, the New Bern Academy Museum, the Fireman's Museum and the Civil War Museum. Take time to read the historic markers and talk to the people in their gardens and on their porches.

You're likely to find a sailor from California, a cyclist from New Zealand, a city refugee from New York or a retired shop owner from Honolulu sharing your park bench. Ask them

ECIM

Urgent

Medical Care

Acute Illness/ Urgent Care
General Medical Care
Occupational/Industrial Health
Laboratory Service/Diagnostic Testing

Monday - Saturday
12:00 noon - 8:00 p.m.
Sunday
1:00 p.m. - 5:00 p.m.

919-636-1001
No Appointment Necessary

South Market Square
Glenburnie Road
New Bern, NC

Where Patients Come First

why they chose to live here. New Bernians like to talk about their town.

New Bern is a gentle place, a place where one can still enjoy the passing scene, where people know how to appreciate a pretty day. It's just that kind of town.

Getting Around

New Bern is growing in many ways. The number of retirees and new residents moving to the area is on the up and up, and the number of tourists coming here to explore the area's many treasures increases every year. No matter how they arrive — by land, air or sea — all routes lead to attractions that everyone will enjoy.

By Land

From the north, U.S. Highway 17 leads directly into the heart of New Bern. From the west, Interstate 95 leads to U.S. Highway 70, which continues straight into New Bern. From the north or south, U.S. 17 is the most direct route to the area. From the east, the drive here is along U.S. 70 from the Morehead City area.

Construction of a new bridge from the north side of New Bern to James City on the southeast side is underway and should be completed by 1999. This will allow travelers coming from the south or the north headed directly to the beaches to the bypass the heart of New Bern. The East Front Street Exit from U.S. Highway 70 W. into the downtown historic district or to U.S. Highway 17 N. is closed until March 1998 to accommodate the construction. Motorists arriving from the east should take Williams Road in James City to Howard Road, which enters U.S. 70 at the Ramada Inn. From the west, motorists must use the Pembroke Road/Trent Woods Exit. However, if you bypass New Bern on the way to the beach, make sure you include it in your return plans. There is much to see and do in

this city, and your visit to the area will not be complete without a stop here.

Bus and Taxi Service

Carolina Trailways serves New Bern and has a station at 504 Guion Street. Call 633-3100 for schedule and fare information. Connections to New Bern from all directions are made in Raleigh. New Bern's bus station schedule operates around departures and arrivals.

Taxis are franchise operations and operate 24 hours a day from the dispatcher at **Safeway Taxi Co.**, 633-2828.

Car Rental

You will need a car if you plan to see more of the area than downtown New Bern. A few car rental businesses are based at the airport.

Avis Rent A Car, Craven Regional Airport, 637-2130

Hertz Rent A Car, Craven Regional Airport, 637-3021

National Car Rental, Craven Regional Airport, 637-5241

By Air

Arriving by plane is as easy as flying into the **Craven County Regional Airport**, 638-8591. Situated about 2 miles southeast of downtown New Bern off U.S. 70, the airport offers daily flights on USAir Express for passengers coming or going to the large hub airport in Charlotte. Charter services are available with Carolina Air, 633-1400.

Michael J. Smith Field, 728-1777, is in Beaufort and offers charter air service. Beaufort Aviation is the fixed-base operator and handles all fueling, rental, flight instruction and charters. The other closest airport is **Albert Ellis Airport**, (910) 324-1100, in Jacksonville, about 30 miles south of New Bern. This airport offers commuter service to larger airports.

Photo: Kenny Barrow

The clock tower above city hall is the focal point of the downtown historic area.

Raleigh-Durham International Airport, 840-2123, is a major international airport that is about a 2½-hour drive from New Bern. This airport is a major hub for domestic and international travelers and is served by all major and several feeder carriers.

By Sea

Boaters arriving on the water come up the Intracoastal Waterway and then travel the Neuse River to New Bern. The Neuse River flows into the Pamlico Sound and has well-marked channels. New Bern also fronts the Trent River, which flows into the Neuse. A complete description of the rivers, bridge schedules and channel markers is offered in our section on Watersports and Fishing.

Once You're Here

If you arrive by air or water, a rental car would be a good investment if you are interested in truly exploring all New Bern has to offer. There is no public transportation in New Bern.

Bikes are another wonderful way to get around the downtown and waterfront areas. However, because of the narrow shoulders, bridge and interchange construction and increasingly heavy traffic, we wouldn't recommend biking along the highways that immediately lead to and from New Bern.

Walking is, actually, the most interesting way to travel in the downtown area, so park the car in any of the well-planned downtown parking areas and see New Bern at a slower pace.

Regardless of how you arrive, if you are a visitor contact the **Craven County Convention and Visitors Bureau** 314 Tryon Palace Drive, 637-9400. Maps, brochures and friendly staff make this a good place to get started. Ask about the narrated trolley trips. If you're overnighting at one of the downtown hotels, the tour trolley makes scheduled stops there.

If you are exploring the possibility of relocating to New Bern or the surrounding area, contact the **New Bern Area Chamber of Commerce**, 316 Tryon Palace Drive, 637-

INSIDERS' TIP

If you arrive in New Bern by boat or plane, it's a good idea to get a rental car to explore the area.

3111. There you will find maps, brochures and other specific information to help out.

Getting around New Bern is easy, so relax and enjoy your stay.

Restaurants

A delightful variety of dining options is available to New Bern residents and visitors. Restaurants feature culinary fare from around the world, and you'll find everything from traditional Southern home cooking to fine European cuisine. If you're looking for good seafood, you'll love dining out in New Bern. In fact, you would be hard-pressed to find a restaurant that does not offer some type of shellfish or other seafood.

The following guide alphabetically highlights some of the better-known restaurants and those we've found particularly tempting for reasons we've explained. We did not list the chain and fast food restaurants with which you are probably familiar. We encourage you also to ask locals for recommendations and to call ahead for hours of operation.

Price Code

The price codes we use in this section reflect the average price of a dinner for two that includes appetizers, entrees, desserts and coffee. Prices are also subject to change. Unless otherwise noted, all of these establishments accept credit cards.

$	Less than $20
$$	$21 to $35
$$$	$36 to $50
$$$$	More than $50

Annabelle's Restaurant & Pub
$$ • Twin Rivers Mall, U.S. 17 at U.S. 70 • 633-6401

Annabelle's offers a variety of foods in a relaxed atmosphere. The same menu is presented for lunch and dinner, and it includes something for everyone. Choose from a variety of beef, ribs, chicken and seafood entrees. The restaurant also has international selections, including Mexican fare. Annabelle's has a children's menu and early-bird specials Monday through Thursday. The

hot-fudge cake is a favorite dessert. The bar serves beer and wine and has all ABC permits. Lunch and dinner are served daily.

The Bagel Cottage
$ • 712 Pollock St. • 636-1775

Originally a take-out bagel shop, this is now a good stop for breakfast, lunch or daytime snacks. Behind Cherishables gift shop diagonally across from Tryon Palace, the shop offers a dozen varieties of fresh-baked bagels and almost as many homemade spreads, chicken salad, shrimp salad and homemade soups. There are special salads, quiches and muffins each day, along with tempting desserts and bagel chips for snacking. You can eat inside the small shop or take advantage of the outside tables overlooking the Tryon Palace Cutting Gardens. There are also a few rocking chairs at Cherishables' back porch entrance where you can make yourself comfortable.

The Berne Restaurant
$ • 2900 Neuse Blvd. • 638-5296

For hearty country-style cooking and seafood, the Berne Restaurant is the place to go. On the corner of one of New Bern's busiest intersections, this large establishment bears the telltale sign of good food to be found within: The parking lot is always full at meal times. A traditional country breakfast is featured daily, and a breakfast buffet is offered Saturday and Sunday. Home-style dinners are featured, from the regional specialty of pork barbecue to a rib-eye steak dinner. The Berne also has a large selection of seafood and shellfish including trout, flounder, oysters (in season) and shrimp served fried or broiled. There is a children's menu and banquet facilities that can accommodate more than 200 people.

Billy's Ham and Eggs
$ • 1300 S. Glenburnie Rd. • 633-5498

Open 24 hours a day, Billy's Ham and Eggs serves more than just that. Everything on the menu is home cookin' just like grandma used to make. Try ham and eggs, country-style fried potatoes, a Belgian waffle or a pork chop along with grits, pancakes or homemade biscuits. For hamburgers the way you remember them — before fast-food days — try Billy's Big Beef

Burger, a hefty helping of ground beef cooked to order and served on a sesame-seed bun with all the fixings. There are lots of home-style veggies on the menu. Seafood specialties include trout, shrimp, oysters, clam strips and crab cakes. Other selections include ham, chicken, meat loaf, hamburger steak, roast beef, spaghetti and pork chops. There is also a children's menu and plenty of homemade cakes and pies for dessert.

Captain Bordeaux's Bar and Grill
$$ • Fairfield Harbour, 104 Marina Dr. • 637-2244

This is a great place to end a day. Overlooking the Northwest Creek Marina at Fairfield Harbour, this hospitable establishment offers sunsets, refreshing beverages and casual dining on deck or inside. The menu offers a nice range of fare from light supper options such as burgers, salads, soups or a terrific Reuben to Cajun-style shrimp Creole, New York strip steak or Texas ribs. Board specials are announced nightly. A variety of sandwiches, soups and salads is also available for lunch. Reservations are not accepted.

Charburger
$ • 1906 Clarendon Blvd. • 633-4067

The Charburger is a good place to find a real hamburger served with hot, nongreasy fries in a no-nonsense setting. Before you place your order at the counter, check out the daily specials. Then take a seat in a booth and enjoy. Fried chicken, hot dogs, hamburgers, shrimp, trout and steak sandwiches are among the specialties. For dessert, try the apple turnover or an ice cream sundae. Charburger serves lunch and dinner.

The Chelsea —
A Restaurant and Publick House
$$$ • 325 Middle St. • 637-5469

You'll want to see the newly restored details of this 1912 building, which was a drug-

FYI

Unless otherwise noted, the area code for all phone numbers in this guide is 919.

store of pharmacist Caleb Bradham, the inventor of Pepsi-Cola. But come to The Chelsea for the delight of good food. The value of fine detail is apparent in every preparation from Chef Karl's kitchen. His training is traditional French, but in practice, the chef offers a fusion cuisine. Among the varied selection of appetizers try the Arroyo Rolls, a Southwestern egg roll stuffed with a blend of cheeses, roasted chicken, pico de gallo and black-bean salsa. For an exciting blend of tastes try the lunch sandwich combining smoked turkey, bacon, Monterey Jack cheese, lettuce and tomato in herbed pita bread and served with raspberry mayonnaise. It would be hard to find a burger or Monte Cristo better than the Chelsea's. Taste surprises are mixed with taste traditions on the menus that are nicely varied so anyone can be pleased. The Chelsea offers a wide selection of domestic or imported beers and wine and mixed drinks. This is a popular nightly gathering place (see the Nightlife section), and there is often live entertainment. The restaurant serves lunch and dinner.

Clancy O'Hara's
Restaurant and Lounge
$$ • 2000 S. Glenburnie Rd. • 637-2206

After a brief respite as Houston's, Clancy O'Hara's is back with enthusiasm and a people-pleasing menu. Customers are greeted in a sunny solarium that leads inside to a woody setting of rough-hewn timbers salvaged from old New Bern buildings. A model train runs overhead through the entire restaurant. Private booths or the open solarium provide comfortable seating. Weekday lunch buffets offer fresh vegetables and salads, soups and desserts. The Sunday lunch buffet adds carved roast beef, fried chicken and hot vegetables. The dinner menu offers Italian specialties and pastas, seafood, cuts of beef and chicken specialties.

INSIDERS' TIP

New Bern Insiders do business lunches at the Sheraton and fun lunches at the Chelsea.

The Flame
$$-$$$ • 2303 Neuse Blvd. • 633-0262

The unique Victorian decor, elegant meals and irreproachable service make dinner at The Flame a memorable event. For a special occasion, try The Flame's steak and lobster. You'll want to add one of the specialties of the house: the stuffed baked potato. Other specialties include grilled shrimp and teriyaki chicken. And don't pass up a trip to the gourmet salad and soup bar. Evening specials are offered on some weekdays and could include steak-and-lobster-for-two combos or a second steak at a fraction of the cost of the first. The restaurant has all ABC permits and specializes in fine wines.

Fred and Claire's
$$, no credit cards • 247 Craven St.
• 638-5426

This cozy little establishment in the downtown historic district offers a variety of intriguing and delicious dishes, all prepared fresh daily. Dishes include cheese and broccoli casserole, shepherd's pie or crab quiche served with fresh fruit, a muffin and sherbet. Lasagna, salads, soups, breads and desserts are all featured. Specialty sandwiches include spicy sausage subs, fillet of flounder on a French roll and homemade pimento cheese. You'll also find burgers and hot dogs. For weekday dinners, Fred and Claire's offers wonderful omelettes, seafood, and chicken livers and onions. Domestic or imported beer and wine are available to complement your meal.

Friday's 1890 Seafood
$$ • 2307 Neuse Blvd. • 637-2276

The decor of Friday's gives you the feeling of being below the deck of one of the many pirate and merchant ships that frequented the North Carolina coast in the 1800s. It's rustic, and the tables are tucked away for privacy. Friday's offers a varied menu that includes the all-time seafood favorites of shrimp, flounder, trout, lobster and crab legs served fried, boiled or broiled with all the traditional sides. In fact, all entrees come with a potato, hush puppies, coleslaw and a cup of clam chowder or a trip to the salad bar. Landlubbers' favorites include pork barbecue, rib eyes, hamburger steaks and chicken. Friday's serves lunch and dinner daily.

The Harvey Mansion
$$$ • 221 Tryon Palace Dr. • 638-3205

This restaurant and lounge are in a distinctive three-story building constructed by John Harvey in the 1790s. Through the years, the building served as a home, mercantile establishment, boarding house, military academy and even the early home of Craven Community College. The restaurant opened in 1979, and its award-winning Swiss chef, Beat Zuttel, has a devoted following.

New Bern has a long history of fine dining.

Diners at the Harvey Mansion are treated to a seasonally inspired dinner menu. Dinner might start with an appetizer of duck with pear and ginger compote or sauteed escargot. For your entree, consider one of the chef's Swiss specialties such as veal morsels with mushroom sauce and Swiss potato. A choice of fresh seafood is featured each night — grilled, poached or sauteed. Homemade desserts include Key lime and berry tartlettes, banana-nut-chocolate torte and yogurt moussecake. Insiders enjoy an early evening complete menu for one price. Downstairs, Harvey's Cellar Lounge offers an intimate atmosphere with a unique copper bar and frequently scheduled live entertainment (see our Nightlife section). The Cellar has private dining areas and offers a pasta, seafood and prime-rib bar menu. Guests can enjoy an extensive selection of wines, champagne by the bottle or glass, mixed drinks and domestic and imported beers.

Henderson House Restaurant
$$$$ • 216 Pollock St. • 637-4784

This award-winning restaurant in a restored, historic New Bern home features a collection of original art work and offers service in private party rooms. Henderson House offers an elegant candlelit atmosphere for dinner and requires appropriate dress. The menu includes dishes created with veal, duck, lamb and pheasant. Entrees offered might include tornadoes of beef with Béarnaise sauce, veal chop with chanterelles, pheasant in port wine, shrimp almandine or a delicious seafood casserole. There is an extensive wine list that favors French vintages but also includes wines from the world over. Mixed drinks are available. Dinner at the Henderson House is highly recommended and will certainly be a time to remember.

Jim Bob's
$-$$ • Town Square, 1908 S. Glenburnie Rd. • 637-4343, 637-6919

Come on in and bring your appetite, because Jim Bob's will take care of everything with hickory roasted ribs, chicken and barbecue. Here, you're also home on the range with Southwestern, Cajun and continental selections. It's a broad range, but Jim Bob's spans the planet with amazing ability. Beef or pork barbecue plates come with a choice of traditional side orders and rolls, as do the barbecued chicken selections and ribs cooked to order. Daily specials such as scallops Dijonaise, catfish Jambalya, Jamaican jerk chicken and roast Long Island duck are announced. Go figure, but it works at Jim Bob's. There have also been provisions set up for cigar nights. Jim Bob's goes the distance to please the entire crowd.

Kress Cafe
$ • 309 Middle St. • 633-9300

Kress Cafe is a delightfully authentic 1950s diner. Beautifully designed as the centerpiece of the Kress Building, a downtown mall undergoing renovations, the cafe is all chrome, neon and rock 'n' roll. You'll wish you had worn your poodle skirt. Jump in a booth for breakfast, lunch, dinner and Sunday brunch. Eggs any style, pancakes and omelettes are served in the morning. Lunch salads, sandwiches, burgers and dinner blue plate specials are tasty throughout the day. Try the meat loaf sandwich. The wait staff will tell you that the only two places for meat loaf are home and the Kress Cafe, and it's undeniable. Insiders will tell you that there's only one place for an ice cream soda, and that's the Kress Cafe. Live entertainment is frequent at night and always interesting (see our Nightlife section).

Latitude 35
$$$ • 1 Bicentennial Park, Sheraton Hotel and Marina • 638-3585

Although the elegant decor and menu at this hotel restaurant suggest strictly fine dining, don't be put off if you've just jumped off your boat. You can come as you are and enjoy the cuisine and the panoramic view of the Neuse River and hotel marina. Latitude 35's breakfast buffet, with its selection of egg dishes, grits, breakfast meats, French toast, waffles, muffins, wonderful biscuits, fresh fruit and cereals, is a favorite of locals and visitors. Weekday lunches offer sandwiches, soups and creative salads along with light plates featuring pasta, salad, seafood or meat. Attention turns to seafood in the evening. You'll find all types of fish and shellfish that can be broiled, baked, fried, grilled, peppered or blackened. The salad bar is included with each entree. For landlubbers, Latitude 35 offers pasta, chicken and beef, and there is an extensive children's menu. The Friday night seafood buffet is elaborate with fried, steamed, baked, broiled, Newburg and Jambalaya seafood preparations accompanied by about 15 vegetables.

Moore's Barbecue
$ • U.S. Hwy. 17 S. • 638-3937

Moore's specializes in eastern North Carolina chopped barbecued pork but offers more than that. Whether you eat in or take it out, the food at Moore's is good, home-style cooking. A meal of pork or chicken barbecue is served with coleslaw, french fries and hush puppies. There's also a seafood plate — shrimp, flounder and trout — and an honest shrimpburger. Moore's features both meals and bulk orders as take-outs. But before you decide what you want, check the specials. Moore's can cater small, large or huge events or put on a North Carolina-style pig pickin'.

Mustard's Last Stand
$ • Tryon Palace Dr. and E. Front St. • 638-1937

Mustard's Last Stand is a movable concession stand that offers the very best in hot dogs and Polish sausages on fresh-baked rolls. The hot dogs are better than those at the ballpark, and you don't have to fight for a parking space. The stand is next to the Exxon station at the corner of Tryon Palace Drive and Front Street and is the perfect place to stop while on a walking tour of New Bern. Mustard's also offers drinks, chips and more.

Nikola's
$$$ • 3515 Trent Rd. • 638-6061

Nikola's, a favorite among Crystal Coast restaurants, opened a second restaurant in New Bern this year in Trent Woods Plaza. Nikola's warm, Old World charm and Northern Italian cuisine make it a perfect place to take someone special or to gather with a group of close friends. Guests can enjoy three-course meals as well as à la carte selections. Meals include a choice of homemade soups or pasta, tossed green salad, two vegetables and entree. Exquisite entrees are chosen among veal selections, fresh seafood, prime beef cuts, chicken and made-from-scratch pastas, all prepared in Northern Italian styles. Our favorites are the numerous veal preparations, especially the simple and rich flavors of Veal Piccata sauteed with lemon and wine. Nikola's has all ABC permits and serves lunch and dinner daily.

Pollock Street Delicatessen and Restaurant
$-$$ • 208 Pollock St. • 637-2480

In an old house in New Bern's down-

INSIDERS' TIP

Calls between New Bern and Morehead City are extended local calls. So pick up the phone and make reservations for dinner. It's a small world after all.

town historic district, this restaurant serves wonderful New York-style cuisine for breakfast, lunch and dinner. Whether you eat downstairs, upstairs or on the patio, you can choose something as simple as a bagel with cream cheese or a homemade salad, or have a full meal with cheese-stuffed pasta shells, veal, chicken or sea scallops with pasta. The delicatessen offers an assortment of hot or cold sandwiches and sandwich platters. Daily specials are usually offered for lunch and dinner. Try the quiche or soup of the day served with fruit, a sub or a Reuben. Beer and wine are available. Homemade desserts include Key lime pie, cheesecake and chocolate mousse. Salads, deli-sliced meats and sandwiches can be ordered to go. Live music is often played, and the restaurant can accommodate special events. The Deli offers full-service catering.

Ragazzi's Italian Restaurant
$-$$ • 425 Hotel Dr. • 637-5090

At the U.S. 70 overpass at Clarendon Boulevard, Ragazzi's was welcomed to New Bern in 1996. Part of a chain of restaurants in eastern North Carolina, Ragazzi's features creative pasta combinations with a choice of pastas, toppings and sauces. Chicken, veal, seafood, steak and stuffed-pasta entrees are available in addition to the invincible pizzas and calzones. Light selections are available for those counting fat grams and calories, and all entrees are presented with fresh-baked bread and soup or salad. Special prices on selected menu items are offered during lunch hours, and everything is available for take out. Locals often call ahead and pick up dinner at Ragazzi's.

Ramada Inn's Angus Steak House
$$$ • 101 Howell Rd. • 636-3637

If you're looking for a good steak, try the certified Angus beef served at the Ramada. Each cut of meat is aged for tenderness and prepared with care by either slow roasting or cooking on a real hickory wood grill. You can order rib eyes, New York strips, tenderloin or prime rib. The Ramada offers steak Oscar and beef tips. Although the specialty is Angus beef, the Ramada also serves a variety of poultry and seafood selections. You'll find crab cakes prepared with jumbo lump crabmeat, shrimp, live Maine lobster and grilled catch of the day. The Ramada overlooks the Neuse River, and you can eat indoors or out on the deck. It's open for breakfast and dinner. The Sunday brunch buffet offers a wonderful selection of breakfast items, plus made-to-order omelettes. The Ramada Lounge also offers seafood and a light dinner menu.

Sandpiper Restaurant
$ • 2403 Neuse Blvd. • 633-0888

If you are looking for seafood at a reasonable price, Sandpiper is the place. The restaurant offers lunch and dinner from one menu and specializes in oyster stew and clam chowder, shrimp and oyster cocktails and steaks. Full meals include fried seafood platters with fish, shrimp, oysters, deviled crab and scallops. A typical house special might include fried trout fillets, fried shrimp, French fries and a hearty serving of coleslaw. One of the nice things about the Sandpiper is that each meal is preceded with hot hush puppies and butter.

Sarah Pocket Tea Room
$ • 303 Metcalf St. • 636-3055

Specializing in "doing lunch," this is a lovely stop for soup, salads, sandwiches or quiche in either the tea room or the adjacent sandwich shop. Civilized English teas and lace table linens encourage lingering for gingerbread or fruit pie desserts before continuing a tour of Colonial restorations or racing back to work.

Scalzo's
$$ • 415 Broad St. • 633-9898

Scalzo's is the absolute best for authentic Southern Italian cuisine. Founded by Chef Mario Scalzo, the restaurant insists on the freshest ingredients. For starters, try the sauteed shrimp or calamari, lamb meatballs, antipasto, roasted peppers or Italian bean salad. The variety of different pasta dishes is enormous, with 18-plus sauces that can be matched with one of eight homemade pastas. The pasta selec-

A keen sense of fashion goes a long way on the beach.

tion includes meat or cheese ravioli, gnocchi and capellini. The sauces range from the familiar marinara to an unusual black olive and capers creation. There is a mixed seafood sauce, red or white clam sauce and several vegetable or meat sauces. Create your own meal with pasta, sauce and veal, eggplant, beef or chicken. Veal Gorgonzola, a house specialty prepared with cheese, white wine and fresh tomatoes, is a favorite with Scalzo's loyal patrons. For dessert, choose from among several delicious Italian confections. Scalzo's has an extensive international wine list. The restaurant serves dinner only.

Sonny's Raw Bar & Grill
$$ • 235 Craven St. • 637-9000

A favorite downtown spot for lunch and dinner, Sonny's focuses on seafood but still serves a muy bueno enchilada, taco and burrito. Our lunch favorite is sauteed shrimp or scallops served with pasta and a vegetable of the day. The dinner menu shows seafood specialties such as stuffed fluke flounder served with vegetable, hush puppies and choice of potato, slaw or wild rice. Sauteed soft-shell crabs are offered with pasta. Sonny's raw bar steams shellfish from September through spring. The bar serves mixed drinks, wines and beers including a nice selection of Mexican beers.

Sweet Bears Pastry
$ • Pollock & Middle sts. • 635-5325

Freshly baked breads and pastries tempt even the most disciplined dieters from this corner bake shop. Just-baked breads range from yeasty traditionals to herby and adventurous varieties such as sun-dried tomato bread. The inventory of pastries, cookies and muffins is extensive, so be forewarned. Coffee choices are perfectly matched to any selection from the baked sweets, and the seating provides a comfortable vantage for watching New Bern's activity.

Trent River Coffee Company
$ • 208 Craven St. • 514-2030

This complete coffee bar and retail coffee shop is the social gathering place for downtown retailers on most weekday mornings for endless coffee and a selection of breakfast breads and pastries. This kind of coffee-break dropping in continues throughout the day, and it's a continuous flow of information. The most interesting vantage on New Bern has to be from behind the counter at the Trent River Coffee Company. On announced evenings this is the staging place for the Down East FolkArts Society live performances and George's Dinner Club, intimate alternative classic theater performances. Coffee, and a world of other things, is always brewing.

Yana's Restaurant
$ • 242 Middle St. • 636-5440

In late 1995, Yana's brought to downtown New Bern the same food and atmosphere that has long kept the population of Swansboro happy. Yana's serves breakfast and lunch faithfully every day, and real ice cream milk shakes, sundaes, splits and malts into the afternoon. Yana's opens with delicious fruit pancakes, omelette specialties and even low-fat breakfasts. Breakfast fades to lunch when burgers roll out among the 1950s Chevys that adorn the booth-and-lunch-counter setting. Yana's has brought a shrimpburger to downtown New Bern as well as a chicken-salad sandwich that continues to form lines for lunch in Swansboro. Don't forget that shake.

Nightlife

Although it isn't overrun with entertainment spots — a refreshing factor for a riverfront city — New Bern offers a nice variety of nightlife. Nighttime entertainment here revolves around smaller gathering places where friends meet to mix and mingle. Several lounges are on the waterfront so guests can relax inside or outside and watch the sunset over the river.

New Bern also has an active cultural arts scene. New Bern is home to a professional acting group, a professional dance troupe and a community theater organization. These groups stage a number of performances throughout the year, and there are several performances for children. The Craven Arts Council, 638-ARTS, has information about these groups. See our New Bern Arts section for more information.

As for the wander-in, sit-down-and-enjoy-yourself type of nightlife, New Bern has that to offer too. Although there are others, the nightspots that follow are among the more popular.

City Side Cafe
Sheraton Grand, 1 Bicentennial Park
• 638-3585

City Side is one of New Bern's most exciting gathering places. The atmosphere is lively and upbeat for those nights when you might want to stay up late. Entertainment varies and includes comedians, dance contests, pool tournaments and live bands playing beach, classic rock and Top-40 music. The City Side Cafe serves international food and imported beers and coffees and has all ABC permits. Favorite menu items include the top-your-own pizzas and burgers.

Oar House Lounge
1 Marina Rd., River Bend • 633-2006

If you're looking to party and have lots of fun, head to the Oar House. On the Trent River in River Bend, the Oar House can be reached by car or boat — just dock at a slip beside the lounge. Inside you'll find a large dance floor, a bar serving mixed drinks, bar snacks and plenty of fun. Sunday afternoons are for beach music and the T-Bird Shag Party. (The shag is the indigenous dance of the coastal Carolinas and is danced to a type of music called beach music.) Other nights you'll find a jukebox or a DJ.

Ramada Lounge
101 Howell Rd. • 636-1998

This is a spot that might be comfortably peaceful one night and buzzing with activity the next. Attracting a mixture of locals and visitors, the lounge offers guests lots of windows from which to view the river and downtown New Bern. Live entertainment is offered some weekends; a DJ spins tunes on weeknights; karaoke is featured on Wednesday and Saturday; and there is a jukebox on other nights.

Little Did Caleb Bradham Know . . .

Could a would-be pharmacist ever have believed that a drink concocted in the back room of a drugstore in the 1890s would, more than 100 years later, be advertised by legendary crooner Ray Charles, singing, "You got the right one, baby, uh-huh"? Probably not.

Today, Caleb Bradham's syrupy concoction is known around the world as Pepsi-Cola. The location of his first drugstore, where the original mix was first brewed, is marked by a historical marker at the corner of Middle and Pollock streets in downtown New Bern.

Caleb Bradham had aspirations to be a pharmacist, but was forced to leave school and return home when his father's business failed. In his drugstore, sometime during the 1890s, he concocted a new soda fountain drink he called Brad's Drink. He advertised it as "exhilarating, invigorating and aids digestion." By 1898, young Bradham had given the new carbonate the name Pepsi-Cola.

Bradham began his cola operation on an organized basis in 1903. The company, headquartered in the back room of the drugstore, packaged the syrup for sale to other soda fountains. The bottling process was on the rise but still in second place to over-the-counter sales at soda fountains.

Business boomed until right after the war years, 1917-18, when sugar jumped from 5.5¢ a pound to 22.5¢ a pound. For Pepsi-Cola, which was retailing at a nickel per bottle, it spelled disaster.

After collapsing into bankruptcy, the company changed hands four times before winding up in 1931 as a subsidiary of Loft, the parent of the internationally known Pepsi of today.

Today, the only extant buildings with a direct link to Caleb Bradham are his home on

Photo: Benner's Studio

Bradham's state-of-the-art Broad Street drugstore was the birthplace of Pepsi.

— continued on next page

the corner of Johnson and E. Front streets and a building on the corner of Broad and Middle streets that was leased by the Bradham Drug Company. It was known as the Broad Street Store. Mr. Bradham's attorneys had their offices upstairs and Bradham's state-of-the-art pharmacy was on the street level. The building is now the Chelsea Restaurant, which houses a wall mural depicting the Pepsi Cola story.

Pro Sail Club
Sheraton Grand, 1 Bicentennial Park • 638-3585

Named after a professional sailing competition series, the Pro Sail is the place to enjoy casual relaxation in a sailor's haven. The club features a long, irregular-shaped bar, comfortable seating and lots of windows overlooking the harbor. There is also an outside deck. Live entertainment is offered on most weekends, and there is a large-screen television.

The Chelsea
335 Middle St. • 637-5469

The Chelsea is a popular downtown gathering place for those interested in mingling with friends or soon-to-be friends. The bar is in the restaurant area (see the New Bern Restaurants chapter) and serves mixed drinks, beers and wine. The building and the decor are interesting in themselves, with lots of Pepsi memorabilia.

Kress Cafe
309 Middle St. • 633-9300

If you're into '50s rock 'n' roll, be sure to stop by the Kress Cafe in the historic Kress Building now undergoing restoration. On Friday and Saturday nights until about 1 AM, Kress entertains with live music, and patrons are invited to dance the night away. The cafe's atmosphere is — you guessed it — 1950s diner-style, and it's carried off with quite a flair. The Kress Cafe has all ABC permits and features daily drink specials. Food (our favorite is Kress' homemade meat loaf) is served until 9:30 PM. For more about the cafe's menu and food service see our New Bern Restaurants chapter.

Harvey's Cellar Lounge
221 Tryon Palace Dr. • 638-3205

As the name implies, this lounge is in the cellar of the Harvey Mansion, which offers patrons an upstairs restaurant serving lunch and dinner (see the New Bern Restaurants chapter). This intimate lounge features a small, unique copper bar and offers a bar menu and mixed drinks. Call ahead; there is often live entertainment that might include music or scenes from a play.

Annabelle's Pub
U.S. Hwy. 17, Twin Rivers Mall • 633-6401

The Pub is part of Annabelle's restaurant and offers a casual, relaxed atmosphere. The bar serves beer, wine and mixed drinks and features at least one drink special each day. For information about the restaurant, see the New Bern Restaurants chapter.

Clancy O'Hara's
2000 S. Glenburnie Rd. • 637-2206

Except for a few months in 1996, this popular restaurant and lounge has been owned by the Nicodeme family for 19 years. Brothers Victor and Michael oversee the operation to make sure customers enjoy themselves. Clancy O'Hara's is a large place, but the lounge, with its half-moon shaped bar, is comfortable and cozy. It's visually separated from the restaurant and a good place to wind down. Drop in after work — from 5 to 7 PM you can take advantage of the daily drink specials and on-the-house chicken and shrimp hors d'oeuvres. On weekend afternoons watch sports on the lounge's big-screen TV, and on Friday and Saturday nights listen and dance to music on the juke box. Clancy O'Hara's has a big dance floor and often has

INSIDERS' TIP

According to North Carolina law, a person is legally impaired when his or her blood-alcohol level is .08 or higher. If you've had your limit, call Safeway Taxi Co., 633-2828, which operates 24 hours a day.

Photo: Swiss Bear

Middle Street at the turn of this century was part of
New Bern's bustling commercial waterfront.

karaoke. Consult our New Bern Restaurants
chapter for more information.

Movie Theaters

New Bern's movie houses offer discounts
for children and at matinees. For what's showing, call the theater or check the daily listings
in *The Sun Journal*.

Cinema Triple, 2500 Neuse Boulevard in
New Bern, 633-4620

Southgate Cinema 6, 2806 Trent Road,
New Bern, 638-1820

Liquor Laws
and ABC Stores

ABC stores are the only establishments in
the state allowed to sell liquor by the bottle.
Beer and wine are sold in grocery and convenience stores and in specialty food shops
throughout the area. All ABC stores are open
Monday through Saturday, but the hours vary.
No personal checks are accepted, and only
those 21 years old or older are allowed in the
stores.

ABC Store No. 1, 318 Tryon Palace Drive,
637-3623

ABC Store No. 4, 1407 Neuse Boulevard,
637-9744

ABC Store No. 5, 2005 Glenburnie Road,
638-4847

Accommodations

Overnight lodgings in New Bern become
more numerous each year, and the river city
now has several major hotels silhouetting its
skyline. There are also a number of excellent
bed and breakfast inns, at least one of which
is said to be inhabited by a friendly spirit. However, those seeking less spiritual digs may
choose from a nice variety of options.

Hotels positioned along the city's picturesque waterfront offer lovely views of the
Trent and Neuse rivers, and a number of
economy and budget motels are near the
downtown or outlying commercial areas.
Cozy and architecturally interesting bed and
breakfast inns are sprinkled throughout the
historic district. The listing here is alphabetical and not intended to recommend one
place over another.

Price Code

Room prices fluctuate with the seasons, but for the purpose of reflecting rate information, we have shown high-season rates for double occupancy. Winter rates may be substantially lower. Rates are subject to change, therefore we urge you to verify rate information when making your reservations. All hotels and bed and breakfasts accept most major credit cards.

$	$35 to $59
$$	$60 to $79
$$$	$80 to $124
$$$$	More than $125

The Aerie
$$$ • 509 Pollock St. • 636-5553, (800) 849-5553

Just one block from Tryon Palace, this bed and breakfast inn is in a Victorian-style home that was built in the 1880s. It is furnished with fine antiques and reproductions, and a player piano graces a downstairs sitting room. Each of the seven guest rooms comes with either twin, queen or king beds, a private bath and cable television. The inn provides complimentary wine, beer, soft drinks, light refreshments, afternoon English tea, a wealth of games, reading materials and books of local lore. A choice of three full country breakfasts is offered each morning and served in the dining room.

The Tea Room at The Aerie is open Wednesday through Saturday serving teas, coffees, cocoa, scones with cream and jam, tarts and an assortment of tea cakes. Even if you're not staying the night, you're invited to enjoy afternoon tea at The Aerie.

Comfort Suites Riverfront Park
$$-$$$ • 218 E. Front St. • 636-0022

This new hotel has a Colonial look and a warm, friendly atmosphere. It features 100 suites, many with waterfront balconies that of-

fer beautiful views of the mile-wide Neuse River. All suites have refrigerators, microwaves and coffee makers; whirlpool suites are also available. Other amenities include free local calls, complimentary continental breakfasts, an outdoor pool with a waterfront courtyard, an outdoor heated whirlpool, a fitness center, a guest laundry room, a board room and meeting facilities. Room service is available with dinners prepared by the kitchen of the Harvey Mansion. Vouchers for golf privileges are available, and special golf packages can be arranged. Boat and Jet Ski rentals by Shorebird are available right at the marina. The hotel is within walking distance of New Bern's downtown area and historic sites.

Days Inn
$ • 925 Broad St. • 636-0150, (800)325-2525

Recently refurbished, New Bern's 110-room Days Inn offers guests tastefully appointed units, an outside pool and a continental breakfast. On site is the delightful Aberdeen oriental restaurant and lounge. The inn is only two blocks from Tryon Palace and New Bern's historic downtown district. A large banquet room can accommodate 300 guests, and smaller conference facilities are available to accommodate conventions, workshops or family functions. Laundry service, free local calls, and historic walking tours are offered to guests.

Fairfield Harbour
$ • 750 Broad Creek Rd. • 638-8011

Any of Fairfield Harbour's 237 timeshare units is available for rent. Rental rates shown here are based on four people sharing a two-bedroom condo in a summer week. Units range in size from a small condominium for two to a two- or three-story house that can accommodate eight guests. Units can be reserved on a weekly basis through area real estate offices or on a monthly basis at the onsite Fairfield Realty office. Renting guests are offered a full range of recreational ameni-

---

INSIDERS' TIP

The New Bern Trolley Tours can conduct historic district tours in Spanish, German or French.

ties. Fairfield Harbour features two golf courses, a country club with an outdoor pool, nine tennis courts, a recreation center with indoor and outdoor pools, an exercise room, a game room, video rental and a miniature golf course. For those activities requiring a fee, Fairfield guests receive a reduced rate.

Hampton Inn
$-$$ • 200 Hotel Dr. • 637-2111, (800) 448-8288

Off U.S. Highway 17 at the U.S. Highway 70 bypass, this modern 101-room hotel opened in May 1993. Tastefully furnished like other hotels in its chain, it is equipped with a pool, a Jacuzzi, an exercise room and meeting facilities. It also offers free local calls and free in-room movies; 75 percent of its rooms are designated for non-smoking guests. A free continental breakfast is offered, or guests may dine at one of many nearby restaurants. Twin Rivers Shopping Mall is just across the highway. Golf packages and tour packages of New Bern's historic district, which is about 3 miles from the hotel, can be

arranged by the hotel staff. Government discount rates are offered, and the hotel has a special third-and-fourth-adults-stay-free plan. Children stay free with their parents.

Harmony House Inn
$$$-$$$$ • 215 Pollock St. • 636-3810, (800) 636-3113

The rocking chairs and swing on the long front porch and the two front doors (you'll see what we mean) distinguish this Greek Revival-style bed and breakfast in the downtown historic district. The original part of the house was built sometime before 1809. Additions and porches were added and, around the turn of this century, the house was sawed in half and the west side was moved 9 feet to accommodate a new hallway and staircase. The inn now has nine guest rooms and one romantic suite, all furnished with antiques and reproductions. All rooms have private baths and decorative fireplaces. A full breakfast, which may include house specialties such as orange French toast, stuffed pancakes, egg and bacon casserole and fresh-baked coffeecake, is served each morning in the dining room. A social hour is hosted each evening by Ed and Sooki Kirkpatrick, who offer their guests a selection of beverages and interesting conversation. Before bed, a glass of sherry or port is available.

Holiday Inn Express
$$ • U.S. Hwy. 17 S. at Glenburnie Rd. • 638-8266

Newly opened in New Bern, Holiday Inn Express offers the comfort standards of Holiday Inn at a no-frills price for the absence of such amenities as an on-site restaurant. However, the motel is in an area with bountiful restaurant options and, it offers guests a morning breakfast bar, use of the pool and a fitness room. The Holiday Inn Express is within easy access from U.S. 70, at the U.S. 17 South Exit, on Clarendon Boulevard where there are also numerous shopping opportunities. Transportation is necessary to see New Bern's attraction sites.

King's Arms Inn
$$$ • 212 Pollock St. • 638-4409, (800) 872-9306

Built in 1847, the King's Arms Inn was a private residence until 1980 when it was established as an inn, New Bern's first bed and breakfast. Named for a New Bern tavern said to have hosted members of the First Continental Congress, King's Arms has eight guest rooms, each with television, telephone, private bath and antique and reproduction furniture. A housetop suite offers a beautiful river view. Breakfast, served in-room or on the back porch with the morning paper, includes cinnamon coffee, specialty teas, juice and home-baked breads, muffins and fresh fruit. Complimentary soft drinks and home-baked treats are always on hand, and the hosts happily make arrangements and reservations for their guests to enjoy the best of New Bern.

FYI

Unless otherwise noted, the area code for all phone numbers in this guide is 919.

The Magnolia House
$$$ • 315 George St. • 633-9488, (800) 601-9488

Formerly the Margaret M. Hanff House, c. 1870-80, this Charleston-pink bed and breakfast inn is just a stone's throw from Tryon Palace and within walking distance of the town's center and waterfront. Hosts John and Kim Trudo offer three cozy guest rooms, each with its own decor including one room decorated with pieces from the East Lake period when the house was built. Rooms are fully heated and cooled and have private baths. House furnishings include family treasures, locally gathered antiques, estate pieces and local art. An onsite gift shop makes antique finds available to guests or anyone who catches the antiques bug while in New Bern. Guests are welcomed each morning with fresh-baked breads and muffins, seasonal fruits and fresh-ground coffees. A full breakfast is also offered. Afternoon tea with scones, tarts and finger sandwiches is served at 4 PM.

New Berne House Inn
$$$ • 709 Broad St. • 636-2250, (800) 842-7688

This Colonial Revival-style bed and breakfast is about a block from the Tryon Palace Complex. Among the furnishings in the seven guest rooms is a notorious brass bed said to have been rescued from a burning brothel in 1897. All rooms are air-conditioned and have private baths and telephones. Rooms accommodate two people and are furnished with either twin, queen or king beds. Lounging in the front porch swing is encouraged. Refreshments and beverages are served, and guests are treated to a full, home-cooked breakfast. The house library is always open, and a tandem bicycle is available for those who enjoy leisurely cycling around town. The inn also conducts monthly mystery weekends, full of intrigue and wonderful food at one price per couple.

INSIDERS' TIP

River dwellers know to plant beans and squash when the moon waxes and that the best fishing is on a northeast wind.

Palace Motel
$ • Hwy. 17 S. • 638-1151

Long a mainstay for New Bern travelers, the 66-room economy Palace Motel has a pool and a full-service restaurant that features homestyle Southern cooking and banquet facilities. All rooms have telephones and cable television. Guests will need transportation to see area attractions.

Ramada Inn
Waterfront and Marina
$$$ • 101 Howell Rd. • 636-3637, (800) 228-2828

One of the newer hotels in New Bern, the 112-room Ramada is across the Trent River from the city's downtown area. All rooms, offered with numerous discounts, have water views, in-room coffee makers and complimentary fruit baskets. The Ramada also offers four suites with Jacuzzis. The hotel's Angus Steakhouse specializes in certified Angus beef. For a more casual atmosphere, the Ramada Lounge offers light dinners and appetizers overlooking the water or service on the expansive, covered outdoor deck. Both eateries provide lovely waterfront views. Guests may also enjoy the hotel's swimming pool. Although it's just a short walk to the historic district, the way is heavily trafficked and guests will need transportation to see the area.

The Sheraton Grand
New Bern Hotel and Marina
$$$-$$$$ • 1 Bicentennial Park • 638-3585, (800) 326-3745

One of the attractions of this downtown hotel is that all 100 guest rooms overlook the Trent River and the hotel's marina. An additional inn has 72 guest rooms, suites and mini-suites in the style of grand Southern inns. The inn is attached to the hotel via a covered walkway and offers guests both waterfront and city-side views. The inn has an executive level made up entirely of suites. To serve the hotel and inn, two restaurants and two lounges offer opportunities for dining and relaxing. Latitude 35 overlooks the marina and features full breakfast,

Photo: Chip Henderson

New Bern's location on the Neuse River offers plenty of boating opportunities.

lunch and dinner menus spotlighting the chef's signature entrees. The City Side Cafe offers casual dining and a lighter menu and features live entertainment. (See our Restaurants section.) The Pro Sail Lounge is a great place for a relaxed day's end, and the Quarterdeck Gazebo & Bar extends the night under the stars with outdoor entertainment. The Sheraton has ample meeting facilities, a swimming pool, an exercise room, and boat and bike rentals. Golf and tennis privileges at area clubs can be included in your stay. Group rates are available.

INSIDERS' TIP

Don't feel embarrassed to wander residential streets or stop and gaze at any of the houses in the historic district. Everyone appreciates your admiration.

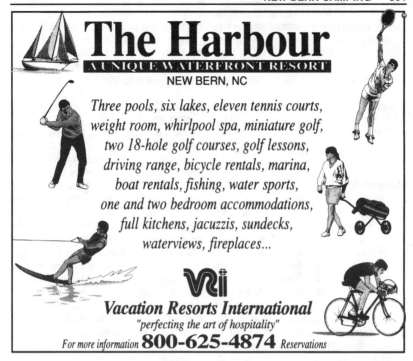
Vacation Resorts International
$ • Broad Creek Rd. • 633-1151

A professional management company since 1964, Vacation Resorts International manages properties in the Fairfield Harbour community offering fully furnished one- to three-bedroom condominiums on a daily, weekly or monthly basis. Rental rates shown are based on four people sharing a two-bedroom unit during the summer. All units at Fairfield Harbour will accommodate six to eight people and are on one of the two 18-hole golf courses in the development. Guests are extended all development amenities including the 300-slip marina, rental boats, country club with restaurant, three swimming pools and two golf courses. For rentals on a daily basis, a minimum of three days is required.

Ziegler Motel
$ • 1914 Trent Blvd. • 637-4498

Set amid a virtual forest of dogwoods and azaleas one block off Highway 17 S., this neat, clean, 11-room, family-run motel offers mod-est accommodations. Two cottages are also available. It is in a primarily residential section of town, and transportation will be necessary to visit area attractions.

Camping

If you enjoy communing with nature by camping, you're in for a treat when you visit the New Bern area. Nature enthusiasts can either rough it or not, depending on their predilections. You'll find commercial campgrounds ready to provide a number of services and primitive camping sites and hiking trails well off the beaten path that are part of the Croatan National Forest. The forest rangers allow primitive camping anywhere in the Croatan, except in picnic areas and parking lots. Reservations are not accepted for any recreation area in the Croatan. For a complete discussion of this magnificent forest, see our Crystal Coast Attractions chapter.

The camping facilities in the Croatan National Forest have been upgraded recently, and most can now accommodate any size recreational vehicle. The forest has several camping areas with various kinds of facilities. For detailed camping information, call forest headquarters, 638-5628, or stop in and pick up maps at the Ranger Office, 141 E. Fisher Avenue, 9 miles south of New Bern off Highway 70 E. Office hours are 8 AM to 4:30 PM, Monday through Friday. A map machine is available outside the office 24 hours a day.

Neuse River Campground
U.S. Hwy. 17 N., Bridgeton • 638-2556

This privately owned campground, about 3 miles north of New Bern, is the kind of place you can't miss. The back side of the park, which has 83 spaces for visitors, is on the Neuse River. Some campsites are specially designed for tents, while others have full RV hookups. The campground provides a comfort station, a laundry room, a dump station, an outdoor theater, a pizza and sub shop, an indoor arcade, a dance floor and juke box, a boat ramp and a swimming pool. A man-made swimming lake, surrounded by a white sandy beach and filled with treated water, awaits your leisure. It is open year round. Nightly fees vary according to site.

Fishers Landing
Croatan National Forest, U.S. Hwy. 70 E., Riverdale • 638-5628

Perched on a bluff above the Neuse River about 8 miles south of New Bern, you can reach Fishers Landing by turning left across U.S. 70 E. at the Riverdale Mini-Mart. This recreation area offers only the barest of man-made amenities, but what it lacks in creature comforts is more than compensated for by the chance to be among some unusual creatures. Take an early morning walk along the crescent-shaped sandy beach, accessible by wooden stairs set into the cliff, and you'll see ospreys, egrets, sea gulls and herons. Between the small parking lot and the bluff is a wide, grassy area, backed by a row of trees. You can swim in the Neuse here, but we suggest shoes for protection against rocks and tree stumps on the bot-

tom. The site offers unimproved walk-in camping and picnicking, non-flush toilets, grills, drinking water and picnic tables. Fishers Landing is open year round, and undeveloped trails for exploring wind through the thick surrounding forest.

Neuse River (Flanners Beach) Campground
Croatan National Forest, U.S. Hwy. 70 E.
• 638-5628

Locals call this campground Flanners Beach. You will find it 10 miles south of New Bern off Highway 70 along the Neuse River. The site has 24 units, flush toilets, warm showers, drinking water and a dumping station. Nightly fees are charged for campsites. The swimming area has flush toilets and cold showers, and the picnic spot has 44 tables, flush toilets and drinking fountains. These facilities are free. A real treat is the short walk across a swamp, through a hardwood forest and along the sandy beach. The site is open April through October, subject to weather conditions, so it's a good idea to call before arriving.

Pinecliff
Croatan National Forest, Havelock
• 638-5628

Visitors can indulge in day-use activities such as picnicking, hiking and fishing at this Neuse River-based recreation area. Chemical toilets, well water and trailhead parking for the Neusiok Trail (see the hiking section of this chapter) are also provided. Pinecliff operates from 8 AM to 8 PM, April through October. Walk-in use is allowed for trail access November through March.

Shopping

New Bern offers a variety of shopping opportunities from large department stores to specialty shops and boutiques.

Twin Rivers Mall, 633-2800, has about 50 stores, making it New Bern's largest collection of stores under one roof. At the junction of U.S. Highway 17 and U.S. Highway 70, the mall is anchored by **Belk**, **JCPenney** and **Kmart**. Nearby are Rivertowne Square with **Wal-Mart** as the anchor, and Berne Square with **Roses** and **Kerr Drug** as anchors.

discover
New Bern

Hearne's Jewelers

(Wal-Mart Shopping Center)

"The Store That Combines Courtesy With Integrity"

Services Offered:

- Loose Diamonds & Colored Stones
- Expert Jewelry Repair Done on Premises
- Engraving
- Appraisals
- Free Gift Wrapping
- All Major Credit Cards
- Hearne's Charge Card

Hearne's Jewelers

22 Rivertowne Square • New Bern, NC
(919) 637-2784

Scattered among the streets that comprise New Bern's Historic Downtown (see our map), you'll discover a selection of shops that make anyone's must-shop list. The pleasant meander along Middle, Pollock, Hancock and Craven streets and Tryon Palace Drive is an experience known as The Governor's Walk. We've highlighted a few of the shops on the walk and a few others in the area. These shops are certainly not the totality of the New Bern shopping experience, but they'll whet your shopping appetite. Antiques shops are featured at the end of this section.

Don't be put off by the name — **Captain Ratty's**, 202 Middle Street, is anything but. It's named in honor of Ratty the Water Rat of *Wind in the Willows* fame. If you're looking for a particularly memorable gift for someone who is into sailing, this is the place to shop. They have marvelous seagoing gifts, unusual souvenirs from New Bern, marine clocks, lanterns and instruments, antique charts and prints. Captain Ratty's also carries foul-weather gear, embroidered clothing and nautical and local books. This is also the place to pick up Sunday editions of out-of-town newspapers.

Book lovers should visit Toba Weiss' **Middle Street Book Store**, 215 Middle Street. Her shop is the home of a large collection of used books and some new ones with subject matter ranging from adventure and romance to cooking, health and mystery novels. She stocks lots of good kids' books too. Sit in the shop's comfortable chairs and sip a cup of coffee while you peruse the books.

Jeth Lindsey's **Art of the Wild etc.**, 218 Middle Street, is a magical mix of local and imported art objects. The art is predominantly animals in the wild and sculpted and carved in wood, marble resin, water buffalo horns, driftwood and tree roots. Fish and birds abound. Jeth's work, as well as the work of his sons, Arden and Bol, and other local artists, is rep-

resented here. You'll also find drawings and prints, framed and unframed.

Hill's, 219 Middle Street, was established in 1910 and is a quality men's haberdashery and ladies' specialty shop. Hill's offers the finest in men's and ladies' styling from the traditional to the fashionable.

Carolina Creations, 226 Middle Street, combines many irresistible things and is a favorite store of many Insiders. Where else could you find a weaving studio, knit shop, art studio and gallery all under one roof? Weavers, spinners and knitters will find looms, spinning wheels and a wonderful selection of fibers that includes silk, cotton, linen, rayon and wool. Available, too, are spun yarn ready for use and cross-stitch supplies and patterns. Shoppers may choose from North Carolina pottery, beautiful stained-glass creations, baskets of all types, and watercolors depicting New Bern and surrounding areas. All items are handmade, some by the shop's four owners, who are artists in their own right. The shop represents mostly North Carolina artists. The staff will put together a sensational gift basket for you.

Crafter's Emporium, 230 Middle Street, housed in an old foundry, offers a wonderful collection of work by area artists and craftsmen. The shop appears small from the outside; however, one step inside reveals otherwise. Shoppers will find nautical and wood crafts, ceramics, needlework, paintings, American Indian art, photographs, carvings, notecards, baskets, clothing items, jewelry and many supplies. The Emporium also offers bird houses, garden items, flags and craft supplies.

The Four C's, 252 Middle Street, is a trail and nature shop offering gifts and active outdoor wear for women and men. It carries Atlantis clothing and Teva sandals. You'll find New Bern T-shirts, books, cards, kites, jewelry and a nice selection of duffle bags and totes.

FYI

Unless otherwise noted, the area code for all phone numbers in this guide is 919.

INSIDERS' TIP

In the Croatan National Forest, don't camp around boat ramps or in parking lots. The Park Service wants to keep these areas easily accessible for motor vehicles and for fishing and boating.

Saints' Creations, 809 Pollock Street, is in the beautiful old All Saints Chapel. Volunteers from the New Bern Historical Society run the shop. It features original handcrafted gifts by area artisans. There are paintings, prints, notecards, gifts and sometimes a decoy or two.

Tryon Palace Gift and Garden Shops, 600 Pollock Street, has two separate stores, one featuring New Bern and Colonial memorabilia and gift items, and the other devoted totally to garden things. The gift shop faces Pollock Street, and the garden shop is on the palace grounds. Insider gardeners visit the Garden Shop every spring to get old-time plants and herbs that are hard to find elsewhere.

Branch's of New Bern, 309 Pollock Street, is really much more than the office supply store it appears to be. Among the fine gift items on display are David Winter cottages, Baldwin brass and Tom Clark figurines. You will also discover a wonderful selection of bird feeders and lawn and garden ornaments. Branch's has a sister store in Morehead City.

New Bern is the only officially designated daughter city of Bern, Switzerland. **Bern Bear Gifts**, 303 Pollock Street, reflects that relationship. The store carries Swiss, German, Austrian, North Carolina and New Bern gifts and novelties. There are also flags from New Bern and the state, Swiss music boxes, German clocks and steins, Swiss Army knives and Swiss chocolates.

Backyard Bears, 718 Pollock Street, is the perfect shop for a teddy bear lover. Inside you will find teddy bears for all ages along with limited editions, collectibles and gifts. Plus, the gourmet country fudge is sure to please everyone. The shop also features 3-D windsocks, greeting cards and more.

In the old City Hall building, **Favorite Things**, 3601 Trent Road, features unusual gifts and decorative accessories. Patrons will discover lovely lawn and garden accessories, bird feeders and supplies, children's items, educational books, gourmet food items and tasteful seasonal decorations.

Mitchell Hardware — Since 1898, 215 Craven Street, is a place you have to experience. The window display is like a historic showing of farm and garden equipment. Step inside to find an eclectic offering of traditional hardware items in a turn-of-the-century setting. Mitchell's carries a complete line of hardware, garden and yard equipment, practical gifts, cast-iron and enamel ware, garden seeds and bulbs. There is also a large country store section with everything from country hams to crockery and pottery.

Walk into **Southern Pleasures**, 220 Craven Street (recently relocated from Broad Street), and you will marvel at the myriad offerings of salsas, jams and jellies, marinades, mustards and salad dressings. Helpful staff will advise you on what is hot, not-so-hot, mild and meek. If you're shopping on a cool fall or winter day, linger in front the huge gas-burning fireplace while you contemplate what to choose from the store's extensive selection of wines and domestic and imported beers.

The **Farmer's Market**, 421 Tryon Palace Drive, 633-0043, housed in a new building, is the place to go for fresh vegetables and fruits, seafood, flowers and crafts. The market is between Middle Street and Tryon Palace. Hours vary depending on the season, so call ahead.

Both **Peacock's Plume** and **A Step Up** are at 22 Tryon Palace Drive. Peacock's Plume carries upscale clothing and accessories for women. The shop offers beautifully designed shirts, blouses and skirts and handsome costume jewelry for every occasion. A Step Up, housed within Peacock's Plume, is a trendy women's shoe store. Besides the great selection of shoes, take a look at owner Sandy

Slaughter's many attractive handbags and belts. Both shops have an excellent sales staff, ready to help you in any way.

Cooks & Connoisseurs, 3310 Trent Road, is a wonderful specialty food store that offers gourmet and international foods from around the world. A variety of coffees and cheeses, necessary cooking tools and gadgets, and an extensive selection of wines and beers are for sale. Gift baskets can be prepared for that special friend, and fresh bread, croissants, muffins and cookies are prepared daily. A cooking school is also offered.

Hearne's Jewelers, Rivertowne Square, offers quality men's and women's jewelry and is a trusted, well-established company. Founded in 1972 by Mickey Hearne and now run by his son, Mike, the business combines courtesy with integrity. Hearne's offers exquisite rings, earrings, necklaces and bracelets, as well as a fine line of watches including those made by Seiko and Citizen. This is also the place to go for jewelry repairs, remounts and watch repairs.

Antiques

New Bern offers plenty of antiques shops to nose around in and discover lost treasures. We've included a few to get you started. The New Bern Preservation Foundation hosts an antiques show in February that features invited dealers. For more information, contact the New Bern Preservation Foundation, P.O. Box 207, New Bern 28563, 633-6448.

Seaport Antique Market of New Bern, 504 Tryon Palace Drive, is a multi-dealer shop specializing in quality antiques and collectibles. The antique market is a great place to browse and look at all the treasures.

Will Gorges Antiques and Civil War Items, 308 Simmons Street, has just about everything in the way of memorabilia and collectibles from the Civil War. The shop is run by Will Gorges, a Civil War buff himself. There

are all kinds of authentic Civil War memorabilia, including muskets, pistols, uniforms, books and other items. Will Gorges also operates the Civil War Museum on Metcalf Street.

Visit **Middle Street Flea Market**, 329 Middle Street, and you'll find dealers that offer lots of great stuff. The market features antiques, collectibles, furniture, silver, china, some jewelry and lots more. The market also buys items.

Poor Charlie's Flea Market and Antiques, 206 Hancock Street, features 17 dealers with booths offering just about everything a nostalgia buff could imagine. The old warehouse that houses the booths evokes the feeling of long-ago places, complete with dimly lit interior and that alluring smell of old, stored-in-the-attic stuff. Patrons will find lamps, crockery, doll furniture, kid-sized furniture, books, baskets, wooden chests and really neat junk.

As the name implies, **Tom's Coins and Antiques**, 244 Middle Street, offers coins and antiques of all types and much more. The shop has beautiful antique and reproduction furniture, estate jewelry, stamps and sports cards. There are lots of nostalgic items and collectibles.

The **Antique Depot**, 626 Hancock Street, offers household items, antique and reproduction furniture, old jewelry, china and glassware on consignment.

Jane Sugg Antiques, 228 Middle Street, offers period and reproduction furniture, lamps, silver, crystal and an assortment of boxes.

Attractions

The importance of New Bern's history cannot be overemphasized. What exists today is attributable to a history that predates the founding of America by Europeans. Shortly after its settlement in 1710, New Bern was nearly wiped out by Tuscarora Indians. Gradually settlers forced the Indians to move inland, and the city of New Bern, with its ideal location at the confluence of the Neuse and Trent rivers, began to flourish as a farming and shipping community.

INSIDERS' TIP

You'll feel like you stepped back in time when you visit Mitchell Hardware on Craven Street. This old "feed and seed" store carries plenty of the basics, plus some extras.

Photo: Janis Williams

The tulip gardens at Tryon Palace are resplendent during
New Bern's Spring Historic Homes and Gardens Tour.

The city soon became an important port, exporting naval stores and later, tobacco and cotton. The captains of the ships that hauled these high-demand products used the spires of New Bern's churches to guide them up the Neuse River that at the time had few navigational aids or other landmarks. Several of the older homes have widows' walks projecting above the roofs, where wives would watch for their husbands' ships returning from long sea voyages.

Pirates also found the dark coves and creeks along the rivers ideal for subversive activities and, of course, for hiding treasures. Blackbeard is supposed to have stayed in a huge house by the Neuse, where he planned his raids on oceangoing ships carrying rich cargo between the American colonies, England and the West Indies.

New Bern can credit its gentility to the once-thriving area plantations that produced exportable products to be shipped around the world. The plantations themselves often became small cities, but today little remains of the beautiful estates that depended on the dark waters of the Neuse and Trent rivers for livelihoods. What does remain are the moss-hung oak and cypress trees guarding the many creeks and sloughs along the winding Trent and broad

Neuse. Like other cities, New Bern endured the pangs of growth and change, eventually developing a character all its own. It did not, however, forget its past.

History taught New Bern many hard lessons, one of which was to value its heritage. To that end, a great number of old homes and churches have been restored, and, in cases of potential loss, relocated, thanks to groups such as the New Bern Preservation Foundation. Salvaged structures now number more than 150, and restoration efforts are continuous.

While the historical museums, homes and buildings are the focal point of New Bern, there are additional attractions in the river city and surrounding area. A growing community of reputable artists grace New Bern with their work, which is often exhibited at the Bank of the Arts, the public library, ART Gallery Ltd., Carolina Creations, City Art Works and in the town's public buildings.

New Bern is known for its cultural activities. Fine antique and art shops have opened in recent years and browsers are always welcome. Not listed in any guidebooks (except this one) but known to New Bernians are its churches, each distinctive and worthy of a sightseeing visit.

Of the area's seven historic houses of worship, it is perhaps **Christ Episcopal Church** on Pollock Street that has the most interesting lore. Included in the church's regalia is a silver communion service donated by King George II. The service survived two fires and reconstruction but, according to local history, was stolen in the 1960s or '70s. The thief, so goes the tale, fenced it with a man who recognized it for what it was and returned it to the church.

In addition to the official sights of New Bern, walking tours of the historic district are very popular. Attractions open to the public primarily center on the town's history; however, many of the historic homes are private residences and are closed to the public. Nonetheless, walking the streets and viewing the architecture and landscapes of these grand old homes will truly give you the feel of the city's Colonial heritage.

Most of the attractions are within walking distance of each other, and we have listed a number of the sites here. For a detailed walking map and description of the more than 100 historic locations, let your first stop be the new **Craven County Convention and Visitors Bureau**, 314 Tryon Palace Drive, 637-9400 or (800) 437-5767. Everyone there is very helpful with orienting you to their town. Hours are 8 AM to 5 PM Monday through Friday, 10 AM to 5 PM on Saturday and 1 to 4 PM on Sunday.

For those who enjoy the woodlands as well as the city, nearby **Croatan National Forest** provides a close-up look at coastal marshes, estuaries and maritime forests. The 157,000-acre preserve is home to insectivorous plants, uncommon wildflowers, marsh and shorebirds and a variety of forest animals such as black bears, alligators, deer and wild turkeys. Forest hiking trails and overnight campsites are popular with nature lovers. For a detailed discussion, see our Crystal Coast Attractions chapter.

Tryon Palace
Historic Sites and Gardens
Pollock and George sts. • 514-4900, (800) 767-1560

Tryon Palace, built in 1770 by Colonial Gov. William Tryon, was known at the time as one of the most beautiful buildings in America. The elegant, Georgian-style mansion is mostly a reconstruction of the original building that stood at the same site. After its use both as a colonial and state capitol, the palace fell into disrepair. When reconstruction was undertaken in the 1950s, only one wing — the stables — remained standing. The palace now houses an outstanding collection of antiques and art, and the grounds are devoted to extensive landscaping, ranging from English formal gardens and a kitchen garden to wilderness garden areas.

Included as part of the main palace complex are the John Wright Stanly House (1783) on George Street and the Dixon-Stevenson House (1828) on Pollock Street. The Stanly home, which was originally on New Street and moved to its present location in the early 1960s, was built by a Revolutionary War patriot who entertained George Washington on two occasions. The Dixon-Stevenson House is a prominent Federal-style home noted for its rare neoclassical antiques. The 1810 Robert Hay House on Eden Street across from the palace is a new addition to the historical complex. Its restoration, which should be complete in late 1997, will accurately reflect the lifestyle technology of its time. The palace also has dominion of the New Bern Academy Museum at New and Hancock streets.

Daily palace and garden tours are guided with special tours added during summer and the Christmas seasons. A new self-guided interior tour offered in 1997, A Servant's Life, focuses on the behind-the-scenes tasks necessary to an 18th-century palace. Historical re-enactments supplement the tours during special times in the summer months. Annual events include the colorful Christmas Celebration tours in December, Decorative Arts Symposium in March, Gardener's Weekend during New Bern's Historic Homes and Gardens Tour in April, King George III's Birthday and Festival of Colonial Life in June, the July Independence Day Celebration and the Chrysanthemum Festival in October. The monthly Garden Lecture series is offered year round. Cooking, blacksmithing and weaving are among regular craft demonstrations. The palace gift shop in the Daves House and the crafts and garden shop behind the palace east wing are open daily. An audiovisual orientation program is shown at the visitors center for all guests.

The palace is open year round from 9:30 AM to 4 PM Monday through Saturday and from 1:30 to 4 PM on Sunday. The last tour begins at 4 PM. The palace is closed on Thanksgiving Day, December 24 through 26 and New Year's Day. A number of tour options are available including two-day and annual passes, and group discounts are extended to pre-arranged groups of 20 or more. For current price information or group reservations, call 514-4900 or (800) 767-1560. The historic sites and gardens are partially equipped for handicapped visitors.

John Wright Stanly House
307 George St. • 514-4900, (800) 767-1560

On his Southern tour in 1791, President George Washington dined and danced at Tryon Palace, but his two nights in New Bern were spent at the nearby home of John Wright Stanly. Washington described his overnight accommodation as "exceeding good lodgings."

During the Revolutionary War, Stanly's merchant ships plied the waters as privateers, capturing British ships to aid the American cause. The elegance of Stanly's house, built in the early 1780s, reflects the wealth of its owner. Distinctive American furniture of the period complements the elegant interior woodwork, and Stanly family history provides a fascinating chronicle of father and son, epidemic and duel, war and wealth. Admission is charged as part of the Tryon Palace Complex admission.

Dixon-Stevenson House
609 Pollock St. • 514-4900, (800) 767-1560

Erected in 1828 on a lot that was originally a part of Tryon Palace's garden, the Dixon-Stevenson House epitomizes New Bern's lifestyle in the first half of the 19th century, when the town was a prosperous port and one of the state's largest cities.

The house, built for a New Bern mayor, is a fine example of neoclassical architecture. Its furnishings, reflecting the Federal period, reveal the changing tastes of early America. At the rear of the house is a garden with seasonal flowers, all in white. When Union troops occupied New Bern during the Civil War, the house was converted to a regimental hospital. Admission is charged as part of the Tryon Palace Complex admission.

Attmore-Oliver House
511 Broad St. (parking entrance on Pollock St.) • 638-8558

Built in 1790 by prominent New Bernian Samuel Chapman, the Attmore-Oliver House today is the home of the New Bern Historical Society and the New Bern Preservation Foundation. It was enlarged to its present size in 1834 and houses 18th- and 19th-century antiques, a doll collection and Civil War memorabilia. Of particular interest is the fine Greek Revival portico and two-story porches at the rear of the house. It is open seasonally Tuesday through Friday from 1 to 4:30 PM and closes from mid-December until the Spring Homes and Gardens Tour weekend in early April. Otherwise, it is shown by appointment. The house may be reserved for private functions and is not handicapped accessible.

Walking Tour Attractions

As we mentioned earlier, a number of New Bern's historic homes are private residences; however, a leisurely stroll along river walks through the historic district will allow you to observe the landscapes, architecture and gardens of these vintage homes. Walking will give you a real sense of the many Old World customs that characterize this Colonial town. Self-guiding brochures are available at the Craven County Convention and Visitors Bureau, 314 Tryon Palace Drive. Guided walking tours, organized by **New Bern Tours**, 637-7316, for

INSIDERS' TIP

Weyerhauser's donation of 95.6 acres of its Taberna Community to the Croatan National Forest plus cooperative donations of MCAS Cherry Point, North Carolina Wildlife and the Forest Foundation will allow the national forest to complete it's Brice's Creek canoe trail by the year 2000.

Photo: Kenny Barrow

Fire Wagon Number One is displayed at New Bern's Fireman's Museum.

six or more people, depart from the Commission House across from the Tryon Palace gate. A few of the more noted residences and buildings are listed here.

The **John Horner Hill House**, 713 Pollock Street, is a Georgian period dwelling built between 1770 and 1780. It is noted for its rare nine-over-nine sash at the first-floor windows.

The **Henry H. Harris House**, 718 Pollock Street, was built in 1800 and is a well-preserved example of vernacular Federal period architecture.

The **Anne Green Lane House**, 804 Pollock Street, is a transitional late Georgian-early Federal house built between 1790 and 1800. It was remodeled during the Victorian period.

The **All Saints Chapel**, 809 Pollock Street, is a good example of Gothic-style architecture. It was built c. 1895 as a mission chapel by Christ Episcopal Church.

The **John H. Jones House**, 819 Pollock Street, is a small Federal house with an unusual central chimney. Its original separate kitchen remains at the rear.

The **White House** at 422 Johnson Street is a simple sidehall Federal house built c.1820-30. It is noted for its two end chimneys with a small closet in between.

The **Cutting-Allen House**, 518 New Street,

is a transitional late Georgian-early Federal sidehall house built in 1793. It is considered unusual because of its flanking wings and large rear ballroom. It was saved from demolition in 1980 and moved to its present location.

The **Hawks House** at New and Metcalf streets offers a side-by-side comparison of styles. Dating from the 1760s, the western part of the house is Georgian, and the eastern section is Federal, added by Francis Hawks, son of John Hawks, architect of Tryon Palace.

The **Clark-Taylor House**, 419 Metcalf Street, was built between 1795 and 1804. It is one of several gambrel-roofed houses in the historic district.

The **Attmore-Wadsworth House**, 515 Broad Street, is an unusual one-story Italianate-style house built c. 1855. Several Italianate-style homes are part of the city's historic architecture.

The **McLin-Hancock House**, 507 Middle Street, is unique for its strict symmetry and diminutive scale.

The **W.B. Blades House**, 602 Middle Street, was built in 1903 and is noted for its elaborate Queen Anne design.

The **Jerkins-Duffy House**, 301 Johnson Street, was built c. 1830 and is unusual because of its exterior Federal design and interior Greek Revival elements. It is also noted for its captain's walk and exposed-face chimneys.

The **George Slover House**, 209 Johnson Street, was built c. 1890 and is an eclectic combination of Queen Anne and shingle-style architectures.

The **Charles Slover House**, 201 Johnson Street, is a stately brick townhouse built in 1847 that was selected as headquarters by Gen. Ambrose Burnside during the Civil War. C. D. Bradham, inventor of Brad's Drink (now known as Pepsi-Cola) purchased the house in 1908.

The **Eli Smallwood House**, 524 E. Front Street, is one of the finest of New Bern's Federal brick sidehall houses, built c. 1810. It is noted for its handsome portico and elegant interior woodwork.

The **Dawson-Clarke House**, 519 E. Front Street, was built c. 1808 and is one of several historic homes exhibiting the use of double porches, a popular style in the coastal region.

The **Coor-Gaston House**, 421 Craven Street, is a Georgian home (c. 1770) built by architect, builder and patriot-statesman James Coor. It was purchased in 1818 by Judge William Gaston and was the scene of the founding of St. Paul's Roman Catholic Church. Gaston was a brilliant orator, lawyer, member of Congress, State Justice and author of the state song.

The **David F. Jarvis House**, 220 Pollock Street, is a good example of neoclassical revival architecture.

The **Edward R. Stanly House and Dependency**, 502 Pollock Street, was built c. 1849 in Renaissance Revival style. The cast-iron grills over its windows are unique in New Bern.

The **Wade House**, 214 Tryon Palace Drive, was built in 1843 and remodeled before 1885 in the Second Empire style. The cast-iron crest on the mansard roof and the iron fence are notable surviving features.

Christ Episcopal Church
320 Pollock St. • 633-2109

Having celebrated its 250th anniversary in 1991, Christ Episcopal Church is the oldest in New Bern and one of the oldest in North Carolina. This is actually the third church building to stand in this area. The first was completed in 1750 and was later destroyed by fire. The foundation of that first church is on the current church grounds. The second church was completed in 1824 and destroyed by fire in 1871. The church you see today was completed in 1875; it is a Gothic Revival building that incorporates surviving walls of that second church. The steeple, with its four-faced clock, is one of the identifying marks of the downtown skyline. Among the treasures on display are a 1752 Book of Common Prayer, a huge 1717 Bible and a five-piece silver communion service given to Christ Church by King George II. Each bears the royal coat-of-arms. Those interested in touring the building should enter the side door weekdays between 9 AM and 5 PM.

Centenary United Methodist Church
309 New St. • 637-4181

First organized as a congregation in 1772, the current Centenary United Methodist Church was designed by Herbert Woodley Simpson and completed in 1904. Its rounded walls and turrets have an almost Moorish look. Visitors can tour the building between 9 AM and 4 PM weekdays.

First Presbyterian Church
418 New St. • 637-3270

The oldest continually used church building in New Bern, First Presbyterian was built in 1819-22 by local architect and builder Uriah Sandy. The congregation was established in 1817. The Federal-style church is similar to many built around the same time in New England but is unusual in North Carolina. Like

---

INSIDERS' TIP

A taped walking tour of the residential streets in the historic district and along the waterfront is available for visitors at the Craven County Convention & Visitors Bureau, 314 Tryon Palace Drive.

that of Christ Church, the steeple on First Presbyterian is a point of reference on the skyline. The church was used as a Union hospital and lookout post during the Civil War, and the initials of soldiers on duty in the belfry can still be seen carved in the walls. Visitors are welcome to tour the church between 9 AM and 2 PM weekdays.

Temple B'Nai Sholem Synagogue
505 Middle St. • 638-4228

The stucco, Neoclassical Revival synagogue is a beautiful, uncommon specimen of architecture in the area. A Herbert Woodley Simpson-designed structure, the synagogue was built in 1908 by the congregation that was organized about 1824.

The New Bern Academy Museum
New and Hancock sts. • 514-4900,
(800) 767-1560

Founded in 1764 and built in 1809, New Bern Academy is the oldest public school in North Carolina and one of the oldest in America. It was used as a school recently enough to still be remembered by a number of New Bern's residents. After it closed, it sat vacant for several decades. In the 1980s, it was purchased and renovated by Tryon Palace and today houses exhibits illustrating the 300-year history of New Bern and eastern North Carolina. The Academy Museum is open daily for self-guided touring. Admission is charged as part of the Tryon Palace Complex admission.

Bellair Plantation and Restoration
1100 Washington Post Rd. • 637-3913

The last and largest brick plantation country house of the 18th century in North Carolina, the Bellair Plantation (c. 1734) is a majestic three-story brick building approached from Highway 43 N. by two long driveways, one lined by lavish old cedars. Georgian handcrafted woodwork greets visitors at the imposing eight-panelled door and continues through the main rooms. Original family furnishings are still in the house, probably because Bellair was specifically guarded from harm during the occupation of Federal Forces during the Civil War by order of Gen. Ambrose Burnside. The writ-

ten order, dated March 20, 1862, still hangs on the wall at Bellair. The basement holds the cooking fireplaces with crane, tools and ironworks of the period. One-hour tours of the historic site are offered hourly from 1 to 5 PM Saturdays and Sundays. The last tour each day begins at 5 PM.

The Civil War Museum
301 Metcalf St. • 633-2818

Opened in 1990, the New Bern Civil War Museum houses one of the finest in-depth private collections of Civil War memorabilia and weapons in the United States. Included are rare uniforms, battlefield artifacts, knives and swords — one inscribed "Yankee Slayer" — and typical soldiers' gear. One collection is devoted to lives of confederate women. Articles from the museum have been featured in Time-Life Books, *Mid-Atlantic* magazine and numerous other periodicals. In 1992, a display from the museum won Best in Show at the Old North State Civil War Exhibition. History buffs and Civil War scholars say it is a site not to be missed. John Lonergan, museum manager and host, is known to suit up in complete Confederate uniform to lead visiting groups through the museum's collection.

Less than a block from Tryon Palace, the museum is open from April 1 to September 30 from 10 AM to 4 PM Tuesday through Saturday. From October 1 to March 31, it is open weekends only from 11 AM to 4 PM and by appointment. Admission is $2.50 for adults and $1.50 for students. The museum has a gift shop and access for people with handicaps.

Bank of the Arts
317 Middle St. • 638-2787

A former bank built in 1912, the interesting granite structure now serves as headquarters for the Craven Arts Council and Gallery. The classical facade of the building features Ionic columns leading into the open, two-story gallery. Detailed pilasters and Corinthian columns have been highlighted by colors in the beaux-arts motif. Changing exhibits of various media — painting, sculpture, photography, pottery, fiber art and other art forms — showcase the work of local and Southeastern artists. Many special events, such as concerts, lectures and receptions, are offered here throughout the year.

The Bank of the Arts does not charge an admission fee and visitors are welcome to browse. It is open Monday through Saturday from 10 AM to 5 PM. The arts building is handicapped accessible.

Farmer's Market
421 Tryon Palace Dr. • 633-0043

Bringing fresh local produce to downtown New Bern throughout the year, the Farmer's Market is a town treasure operated by the Co-operative Extension Service. From fruits to flowers and through the range of baked, canned and prepared goods, the Farmer's Market is a favorite stop, but you have to keep the days and hours in mind. From June 15 through September 15, days of operation are Tuesday, Thursday and Saturday from 6 AM to 1 PM. After September 15 and before June 15, the Farmer's Market is open Saturdays only, 6 AM to 1 PM.

Fireman's Museum
408 Hancock St. • 636-4087

The New Bern fire company is one of the oldest in the country operating under its original charter. The restored museum is just behind the fire department's Broad Street headquarters and houses steam pumpers and an extensive collection of other early fire-fighting equipment. Also on exhibit are rare photos, Civil War relics and even the mounted head of the faithful old fire horse, Fred, who, according to stories told by fire fighters, died in his tracks while answering an alarm. Retired New Bern firemen are regularly at the museum to tell fire-fighting stories.

Museum hours are Monday through Saturday from 10 AM to 4:30 PM, and on Sunday from 1 to 5 PM. The museum is open year round, except for a week around the Fourth of July and a week around Christmas. Admission is $2 for adults and $1 for children. The museum is handicapped accessible.

Cedar Grove Cemetery
Queen and George sts.

If you're one of those people who loves wandering through old graveyards, you'll not want to miss this one. Statuary and monuments beneath Spanish moss-draped trees mark burial traditions from the earliest days of our nation. One smallish obelisk lists the names of nine children in one family who all died within a two-year time span. The city's monument to its Confederate dead and the graves of 70 soldiers are also here. The cemetery's main gate features a shell motif, with an accompanying legend that says if water drips on you as you enter, you will be the next to arrive by hearse.

New Bern Trolley Tours
Tryon Palace, Pollock St. • 637-7316, (800) 849-7316

Touring the town by trolley is a comfortable and interesting alternative to a walking tour if you've arrived without your sneakers. Narrated 1½-hour tours depart Tryon Palace between April 1 and December 31 at 11 AM and 2 PM on most weekdays and at 2 PM on Sundays. Tours or charters for special groups or occasions may also be arranged. Professional guides narrate the tours with attention to historical and architectural interests and spice the narrative with folklore and local knowledge. Trolley tours are $10 for adults and $5 for children 12 and younger. A 30-minute "Get Acquainted Tour" of the Historic District departs Comfort Suites, 218 E. Front Street, twice a day. Fares are $5 for adults, $2 for children. Tickets are purchased on the trolley car and are available at Cherishables Gift Shop, 712 Pollock Street, near Tryon Palace.

Union Point Park
Tryon and E. Front sts. • 636-4660

This lovely waterfront park is often the site of outdoor activities and offers a welcome respite for weary visitors who want to take a load off their feet. Music is sometimes fea-

INSIDERS' TIP

"Bern" is a German word meaning "bear," which explains a lot of bear-related symbols, statues and names of sports teams in both Bern, Switzerland and New Bern, North Carolina.

tured here. It is an excellent place to simply sit and watch the world float by. There are lovely river views, and the site is particularly pleasant for evening sunset viewing. On-site facilities accommodate picnicking, boat launching and other outdoor activities.

Extensive renovations of Union Point Park are taking place in phases. Bulkheading and the construction of a waterfront promenade with railings will be completed in 1997. The City of New Bern and private donations are financing the renovations.

Croatan National Forest
141 E. Fisher Ave. • 638-5628

Croatan National Forest is an expansive nature preserve bordered by New Bern, Morehead City and Cape Carteret. It is headquartered on Fisher Avenue, which is approximately 9 miles south of New Bern just off Highway 70 E. Well-placed road signs make the office easy to find. Within the forest's boundaries are endangered animals and rare plants. Black bears, otters, deer, raptors and other forest creatures live in this coastal woodland. Insectivorous plants such as the Venus's-flytrap, butterworts, pitcher plants, sundews and bladderworts find the forest an ideal habitat and are protected by law. The forest is also well-known for its beautiful wildflowers. Pamphlets on the wildflowers and insectivorous plants are available at the Fisher Avenue headquarters. Because of the forest's coastal location, many unique features can be found here. Some of the ecosystems present include pocosins, longleaf and loblolly pine and bottomland and upland hardwoods. Sprinkled throughout the Croatan are 40 miles of streams and 4,300 acres of wild lakes.

The forest areas are excellent for hiking, swimming, boating, hunting, fishing and picnicking. Miles and miles of unpaved roads lace through the woodland, providing easy if sometimes roundabout access to its wilderness. Recreation areas are available for a

day's outing or for longer visits. Camp fees vary, so call headquarters, 638-5628, for season rates.

Because the Croatan is so expansive and undeveloped, it is best to stop in at headquarters on Fisher Avenue and pick up a forest map before heading out. The best times for venturing into coastal woodlands are fall, winter or early spring. Summer can be very hot and buggy, so prepare yourself with insect repellent. Some forest areas are closed November through March. For more information on the Croatan National Forest, see the Crystal Coast Attractions chapter.

Kidstuff

Once upon a time, there was a beautiful place at a point where two rivers met. It was such a beautiful place that even the first person who ever saw it, a Tuscarora Indian, wanted to live there. In fact, the entire tribe decided it was the best place to live. And it was. There were lots of fish in the two rivers, and there was a big forest with many trees that the Indians could use to build all the things they needed, such as boats.

One day, some other people arrived in the beautiful place. Their leader was from a faraway place called Bern, Switzerland. The people saw that the two rivers came together here and saw the big forest with wood they needed to build things. They also decided that this was the best place in the New World to live. They called the place New Bern to remind them of their old city. Except for once or twice, the people of New Bern got along pretty well with the Tuscarora Indians, but that's another story.

The people of New Bern built quite a fine town with pretty houses, and their town became a capital where the king sent a governor to rule the whole land. The people built a palace in New Bern for the governor. Everyone loved the palace, and people came from all over the land to enjoy it. Even pirates came up

---

INSIDERS' TIP

Fort Totten Park and Union Point Park have playgrounds with swings. There's a baseball diamond at Fort Totten; picnic tables, ducks and public restrooms at Union Point.

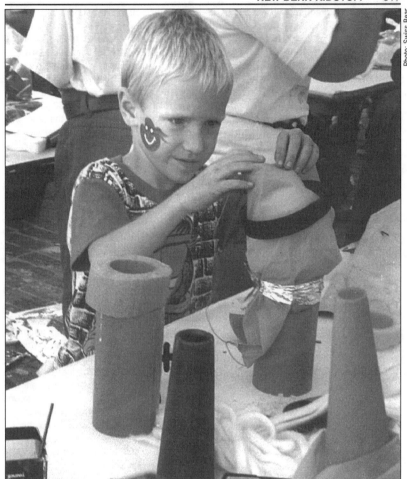

Photo: Swiss Bear

Children's activities are part of most area festivals.

the river from the sea to enjoy the town with the palace. And because it was always a beautiful place to live, people kept coming to New Bern.

Over the years, the people of New Bern got together to build a fort for their children to play in, and a Cow Cafe where their children have parties and eat ice cream. Today, they help their children put on plays that everyone enjoys and they bring wonderful performers from far away to teach and entertain the kids. They even have an arts camp in the summer and craft classes before Christmas and a fish-

ing contest in the rivers for the kids in the summer.

And while the people of New Bern continue to live happily ever after, people still come from near and far to New Bern to enjoy the town with their kids. And this is hardly The End. Read on for the details.

A Series of Smiles
Craven Arts Council, 317 Middle St.
• 638-2577

The delightful Children's Performing Arts Series, held each spring for preschool and school-aged children, is sponsored by the Craven Arts Council (see our New Bern Arts chapter). The series offers three programs from February through April, each staged at Orringer Auditorium on the Craven Community College campus. In 1997 A Series of Smiles featured puppet theater, Dr. I. Wonder's Science Circus and David Parker, "Pied Piper of sign," who combined sign and song in a wonderful interaction with the audience. The cost for the entire series is $10.50. Individual performances are $4 at the door and group rates are offered.

The Cow Cafe
301 Ave. C • 638-1131

Treat yourself and take a kid to the Cow Cafe at the Maola Milk and Ice Cream Company's processing plant. Inside is a window on the world of milk processing. Everything looks like a cow, from the cafe seats to the toilets to the unimaginable range of gifts. Snacks and lunches — no burgers! — include Cow Coney hot dogs, Save-A-Cow barbecue and Uncle Mooford's old fashioned milk shakes and malts. If you're limited to only one selection, take the Death By Chocolate. It's our choice of execution.

The Fireman's Museum
410 Hancock St. • 636-4087

The Fireman's Museum houses steam pumpers and other early fire-fighting equipment that was used by the New Bern Fire Department, one of the country's oldest fire departments. Rare photos, Civil War relics and the mounted head of Fred, the faithful fire horse who died while answering an alarm, are part of the collection. The museum is open Tuesday through Saturday from 10 AM to 4:30 PM and Sunday from 1 to 5 PM. See our New Bern Attractions chapter for further information.

Kidsville Playground
1225 Pine Tree Dr. • 636-4061

Kidsville is a beautifully planned active and interactive fort-like play environment that captivates both children and adults. Next to the West New Bern Recreation Center on Pine Tree Drive near the intersection of U.S. Highway 70 and N.C. Highway 17, Kidsville is the product of the fund-raising efforts of two mothers and a town with enough heart to contribute all that was needed to make it real. Efforts in 1994 raised $100,000 for the necessary materials, and all the labor and the location were donated. With or without a kid, Kidsville merits a visit. Whether you choose to slide, climb or clamber through its interesting maze or you spend your time taking note of the plaques naming the many contributors, Kidsville will wow you. You may arrange for large group visits by contacting the New Bern Parks and Recreation Department.

Summer Arts Camp
Craven Arts Council and Gallery
• 638-2577

Sponsored by the Craven Arts Council and Gallery, the Summer Arts Camp for children ages 4 to 13 is a one-week arts program designed to be fun and educational. Day campers strengthen their creativity in process-oriented activities in arts disciplines such as creative drama, music, creative movement and visual arts. Classes for particular age groups are limited in size, so early registration is a good idea. Activities occur at J.T. Barber Elementary School. Transportation is provided from central pick-up locations and fees are $45 for arts council members, $50 for nonmembers.

YMCA Youth Sports and Services
Twin Rivers YMCA, 100 YMCA Ln.
• 638-8799

With the emphasis on fair play, participation and fun, the YMCA offers year-round sports activities for all age groups in gymnastics and competitive swimming and seasonal basketball, T-ball and girls softball. Whiffle ball preschool T-ball is organized for ages 3 to 5 years too. Swimming in-

INSIDERS' TIP

The Attmore-Oliver House has a beautiful doll collection on display at 510 Pollock Street.

struction is a specialty from beginning lessons to Water Safety Instructor certification. Summer Day Camp programs offer a terrific range of sports activities for all age groups. The Youth Center for ages 6 to 18 years provides supervised gaming such as bumper pool and table tennis. Babysitting services are available for parents using the YMCA facilities.

Craven County Recreation and Parks Dept.
406 Craven St. • 636-6606

The county recreation and parks department offers programs and classes for preschool and school-age kids throughout the school year and in summer day camp programs. Swimming lessons in summer months are instructed for ages 3 and older. Gymnastics and karate lessons are instructed year round for ages 5 and older. Tennis lessons, girl's softball, T-ball, coach pitch baseball and little league, soccer, Pop Warner football, basketball for girls and boys is all organized and supervised seasonally.

Kids' Fishing Day
Croatan National Forest Service
• 638-5628

Kids' Fishing Day in June is organized by the Croatan National Forest Service for kids of all ages. Participants range from ages 1½ to 15. Local businesses and organizations sponsor prizes for the largest, smallest and most fish caught.

New Bern-Craven County Public Library Children's Programming
400 Johnson St. • 638-7815

The children's library at the New Bern-Craven County Public Library is well-organized for preschoolers to teens to enjoy selecting from the collection of books, video and audio tapes and compact discs. Help is plentiful. Weekday programs for children are planned each week. Time Out For Toddlers on Friday mornings is a program of stories, songs and finger plays for children younger than 3. Preschool Storysteps for ages 3 to 5 occurs three times on Tuesday mornings, offering stories, puppet plays, music and other fun. For kids between the ages of 5 and 9, the Children's Story Hour is held on Thursday afternoons. It involves storytelling, movies and age-specific activities. For kids 10 and older, the Storytelling Club meets on the second and fourth Wednesdays of the month after school. The club is a membership activity with goal-oriented projects that involve learning techniques of storytelling, puppetry and drama. Call Children's Librarian Pam Machle at the number above for further information.

Putt-Putt Golf & Games
4172 Hwy. 17 S. • 635-1570

When you have a day to spend with the kids, invite a few more and take a carload to the 18-hole miniature Putt-Putt Golf & Games on Highway 17. There are some interesting holes to play, even for the seasoned golfer. A game room and facilities are available for 19th-hole hot dogs and ice cream, picnics and birthday parties. Daily specials and group rates are offered.

Snapdragon Specialty Toys
214 Middle St. • 514-6770

If you have a child with you while you're shopping the historic downtown district, reward both of you with a stop at the Snapdragon. New to Middle Street, this is the stop for a play break that everyone enjoys. There are wooden play stations with a train for older kids and a motion maze for the younger ones to enjoy while you shop among the inviting selection of learning toys, books and toys for fun and cuddling. Snapdragon has an interesting selection of scientific projects and art supplies.

INSIDERS' TIP

A favorite summer destination for a day with the kids is Flanners Beach, a Croatan National Forest recreation area on the Neuse River. It's 10 miles south of New Bern off Highway 70 E. on Flanner's Beach Road.

The Arts

For the first three decades of the 20th century, New Bern was known as the "Athens of North Carolina" because of its many artistic and educational endeavors. While the Great Depression put a halt to much of the activity, a rebirth occurred in the 1970s, and today locals enjoy performances and exhibits from an ever-increasing number of area and touring artists.

The **Craven Arts Council and Gallery**, located in the Bank of the Arts on Middle Street, supports and features all art disciplines and is a ticket outlet and information center for almost any art event taking place in Craven County. The council sponsors the popular New Bern Sunday Jazz Showcase, the Children's Performing Arts and Craven Concerts series and many other visual and performing arts events throughout the year.

The **New Bern-Craven County Public Library** at the corner of Johnson and Middle streets, 638-7800, selects an artist of the month and displays his or her work in its attractive buildings. Photographers and other visual artists are featured each month.

The evidence that activity in the arts is treasured in New Bern is most visual on a walk through New Bern's historic downtown. Galleries are proliferating in renovated buildings, and teaching studios are active in and above shops and galleries. Murals on the walls of public buildings reflect the work of varied artists interpreting New Bern's history. Local artist Doug Alvord, who is involved in projects that preserve the area's maritime history in paintings, says there is a lot of activity in the arts scene in New Bern. Art activity attracts artists, and the activity in New Bern is, simply, visible.

Among those artists to whom New Bern "just feels right" is stained-glass artist Michaele Rose. She and her husband relocated to New Bern from Florida, bought a Middle Street building and renovated the downstairs as a retail gallery and studio. New Bern had the right composite of ingredients: proximity to water, an active arts community and affordable real estate. She is active in instruction, with commissions for renovations and in the retail aspect of her business. She says her story of relocation is one she hears others repeat frequently.

New Bern is also home to an active community theater group, the **New Bern Civic Theater**, which has its own performing hall, the Saax Bradbury Playhouse, a former movie theater on Pollock Street. The group stages a number of productions annually. Alternative and repertory theater groups are also active in town as are numerous musical groups and dancers including historical dancers. **Atlantic Dance Theater**, professional touring dancers, gives a number of performances throughout each year in the public schools and also gives a public performance.

Here, we've described our arts organizations. If a group doesn't have a street address or regular office, we have given the contact person's name and phone number.

Visual Arts

Craven Arts Council and Gallery
317 Middle St. • 638-2577

Besides nurturing local artists, this organization provides exhibition space for local, regional and national artists in the Bank of the Arts, a reclaimed 1912 bank building that also houses the arts council's administrative offices. The large, open main gallery is the staging area for nine exhibits each year. Popular traveling exhibits are often featured, and overall works include a variety of media, ranging from traditional to contemporary. At Christmas, the gallery becomes a huge gift shop for the sale of art works, cards, fine crafts and other original creations. As part of its continuous sup-

---

INSIDERS' TIP

Take your chair or blanket down by the river and enjoy the Saturday evening Sounds of Summer outdoor concert series sponsored by the town and county recreation departments and the arts council at Union Point Park.

port of the arts, the council organizes and runs Arts in Education, an outreach program of performances and artists' presentations designed to enrich and integrate the arts through an educational curriculum. The program includes the acclaimed Day at the Improv workshop designed for 4th and 5th grade students. The workshop uses creative drama to strengthen communication and cooperative skills. Evening workshops are also free and open to the public. The energetic support of the Craven Arts Council and Gallery in integrating arts activity throughout the county and region is recognizably effective in its explosive growth. The council publishes a monthly newsletter, *Luminary*, that informs of upcoming arts events. Classes in oil, watercolors and other art forms are often taught at the Bank of the Arts.

Twin Rivers Art Association
Kathy Pickett • 636-3422

The Twin Rivers Art Association sponsors two shows each year. Work is limited to two-dimensional paintings in any medium, including multimedia. Group shows are staged in the spring and late fall; however, members exhibit paintings throughout the year at various locations in New Bern and surrounding counties. Membership is $15 per year; show fees are $15 per show. Meetings are held at 7:30 PM on the first Wednesday of each month, except in July and August, at PJR Studio on

Shoreline Drive in River Bend. The group exhibits its work at River Bend Town Hall, Bank of the Arts and Twin Rivers Mall.

Theater

New Bern Civic Theater
414 Pollock St. • 633-0567

A community group, the civic theater relies on a bevy of part-time performers and behind-the-scenes technicians and assistants to produce a variety of performances at the Saax Bradbury Playhouse. The group's theatrical productions range from serious drama to lively musicals, including original works. Plans for 1997 include productions of *Right Bed, Wrong Husband; Blithe Spirit;* and *Fiddler on the Roof.* It's children's performing group, StageHands, stages entirely unique performances simultaneously in sign and spoken language.

George's Dinner Club
Bill Hand • 635-1293

This group involves a repertory core of actors who are joined for particular performances by actors from other theatrical groups to stage daring, interesting productions. George is George Bernard Shaw, whose work inspired the group's production of classics, old and modern, in settings that are close to and involve the audience. It's intimate theater for a thinking audience, according to the director and founder of the theater group. In settings like Trent River Coffee Company, Harvey Mansion and The Chelsea, George's Dinner Theater has performed Moliere's *Imaginary Invalid*, Sartre's *No Exit*, Shaw's *Mrs. Warren's Profession* and one-act plays by August Strindberg and Eugene Ionesco. Dinner theater productions make especially interesting evenings, by George.

Dance

Atlantic Dance Theater
Elizabeth Pope • 636-1760

A professional touring dance troupe, the company's dancers come from across the United States to put together dance programs for students in public schools. For school performances, the company performs traditional ballet as well as other dance styles to give young audiences a broad view of dance as an art form. One concert performance each year is given to the general public.

Craven Historical Dancers
Paige Whitley-Bauguess • 633-9622

Now totaling about 15 members of all ages, this unique dance troupe performs 18th-century social dances in costume. Their dances include reels, country dances, minuets, cotillions and jigs. They entertain at holiday and fund-raising madrigal dinners, where they perform 16th-century dances. Craven Historical Dancers often participate in Tryon Palace's holiday festivities. They have danced at the Hope Plantation in Edenton and traveled as far as New York to dance at a Baroque music festival. The group meets weekly, and new members do not need previous dance experience to join.

Down East Dance
2500 Trent Rd. • 633-9622

This dance studio involves students of all ages in an impressive range of dance

instruction. Under the direction of Paige Whitley-Bauguess, the ballet faculty and students annually perform *The Nutcracker* with guest artist Thomas Baird and participating members of the Craven Historical Dancers.

Music

Fairfield Harbour Chorus
Pat Rivett • 638-8470

This chorus began with 24 enthusiastic members in 1984. Today, membership totals approximately 60 vocalists. The group performs about 15 concerts each year, featuring all types of music, including show tunes, gospel, Broadway hits, holiday arrangements, pop and contemporary. It has given numerous performances in area churches, rest homes and retirement homes and has combined its talents to perform with other choruses at Cherry Point and Craven Community College. Members must be residents of Fairfield Harbour. Rehearsals are conducted on Monday evenings at 7 PM at the Fairfield Community Center. Rehearsals begin the first Monday after Labor Day and continue until mid-May. The group is subsidized by a grassroots grant from the Craven Arts Council.

Craven Concerts
Gene Fegely • 636-5935

This organization schedules five musical concerts each year, staged at Grover C. Fields Middle School auditorium on Clarendon Boulevard. Attendance is by subscription membership only, with membership fees of $35 for adults and $5 for students. Productions include a variety of performances and always include one concert by the North Carolina Symphony. A membership campaign is conducted each spring, and membership forms and information are available at the Craven Arts Council and Gallery on Middle Street.

INSIDERS' TIP

Among New Bern's favorite community bands is the Crisis Band, a group of doctors and lawyers in their mid-life crisis years. They can usually be counted on for a performance during Mumfest in October.

Craven Community Chorus
Philip Evancho • 638-7357

This large choral group has 70 members and performs locally, as well as in surrounding counties and out of state. There are no auditions, and membership is open to anyone who can carry a tune and enjoys singing. The group likes to include musicians whenever possible and usually plans its shows around a theme. Performances have featured Dixieland standards, Old West favorites, Big Band hits and classic '50s rock 'n' roll. The singers also perform folk songs, patriotic compositions, spirituals, swing, pop, some classical works and holiday favorites.

Pro Musica of New Bern
Pat Rowett • 638-5144

This a cappella singing group, formed in the late 1970s, is a local favorite that performs a variety of music from opera to pop, but its specialty is madrigals. Composed of about 12 members, Pro Musica is most frequently heard at occasional madrigal dinners, which occur in New Bern churches. Biannually, the group performs a progressive Christmas concert.

Voci Allegri Vocal Ensemble
Lorraine Hale • 638-5295

These four or five women form a very flexible and professional a cappella vocalist group that has performed together for around five years. Voci Allegri schedules a Friday Refresher Concert Series between the fall and spring months of the year featuring four late-afternoon concerts at the Bank of the Arts. The ensemble performs a variety of music: Gilbert and Sullivan, folk songs, Broadway tunes, madrigals, opera, music of the Italian Renaissance. Undaunted by any musical challenge, they obviously enjoy themselves.

Commercial Galleries

Art and Accessories
230 Middle St. • 633-2209

Offering original paintings by local artists, this is an interesting stop for decorative arts for the home.

ART Gallery Ltd.
502 Pollock St. • 636-2120

On the second floor of the Edward Stanly house, this gallery offers fine works in contemporary North Carolina arts including paintings, limited-edition prints, glass, sculpture, jewelry, stoneware, porcelain and tapestry.

Art Materials
220 Middle St. • 514-2787

An exhibiting artist is frequently at work in this downtown hub of arts activities. Active artists find all necessary supplies here and studio classes are on going.

Benners Studio
206 Middle St. • 636-2373

A portrait photography studio, Benners also does copy and restoration work with photographs and has a processing lab for black-and-white and color photography.

Carolina Creations
226 Middle St. • 633-4369

An art studio and gallery, Carolina Creations offers exclusively North Carolina arts including pottery, stained glass and jewelry. This is also an active studio for fabric arts, and knitting supplies and weaving classes are offered.

City Art Works Gallery
225 Middle St. • 636-3434

Representing works of fine contemporary artists of the southeastern United States, this gallery reliably shows an interesting variety of original paintings in watercolors, oils and pastels as well as jewelry, pottery and sculpture.

Crystal Lady
217 Middle St. • 637-9880

This is an interesting, active spot for custom stained-glass and gemstone designs. An active studio offering a variety of classes, Crystal Lady also offers supplies for artists in beads, stones and stained glass.

Classicist on the River

What could be better than reading of Neuse River life in local author Janet Lembke's essays? How about having her personally guide you through her river world on the lower Neuse? On one spring and one fall day each year, the classical scholar and naturalist leads field trips (scheduled by the N.C. Maritime Museum) down by the riverside and into her cultural and natural experience of Great Neck Point, an impossible place to find without a bread-crumb trail.

Close-up

Directions to Great Neck Point by road are, cumulatively, an essay that starts from familiar highways, travels past colorful landmarks (some that require stops, such as the field with the skeletal tree bearing an osprey nest) to a homecoming at the end. Along the way, you have to watch for state road signs, count the unpaved turns and read messages on trees. It's much easier to visualize the location by water: south of Minnesott, southwest of Oriental, east of the Pamlico Sound at the mouth of the Neuse. It is in the context of the riverbanks here, of the finger creeks and surrounding woodsy wetlands, that Lembke's books *Looking For Eagles*, *Dangerous Birds*, *River Time* and *Shake Them 'Simmons Down* are set.

There is comfortable order within the structure of her essays; in the mythological parallels she shows us in natural life cycles and in revelations disguised in Latin scientific names of marsh grasses, land crabs and parasites. Any other order at Great Neck Point is out of the question. Motley is the operative word in the neighborhood. Initially, it's a bit confusing. Lembke herself is the picture-perfect classicist-in-nature wearing a Neuse River Foundation tee-shirt, baseball cap and a welcoming smile that correctly forms her greeting as she meets the museum's minivan. Most of us passengers are strangers to her, but we all know her intimately — her husband, Chief,

Photo: Janis Williams

Janet Lembke points toward one of her favorite places just off the Neuse River — Courts Creek.

— continued on next page

her dog, Sally — from her essays. Chief, in his overalls, raises his bottled beer in greeting as we come to a stop in front of the mobile home.

Adjusted now, we're off across the neighbor's lawn and into a hedge where Lembke raises a finger to signal the proximity of a bird we should be sighting.

"Carolina wren buzzing."

She walks on and we follow, all looking up instead of ahead.

"*Pizza, pizza, pizza.*"

She's calling an Acadian flycatcher. We're looking everywhere for it; she's hearing it. We stop for a winged sumac, then a netted chain fern.

"The most wonderful collection of weeds and wildflowers is along here," says Lembke as the woods thicken and vines begin to form a web from canopy to forest floor.

"Pish, psh, psh, psh." The subject has changed back to birds. Everybody's pishing now. The sound is a universal distress call and birds come to see what's wrong. It really works. "This is a magical place. It's the only place I've seen a worm-eating warbler," says Lembke. Expectations for the remarkable are rising.

The opening ahead is Courts Creek. As we approach a rickety pier amid the marsh grass, Lembke tells us that something always happens on Courts Creek. She demonstrates, pointing and exclaiming: "Blue heron. Osprey. Turtle nose!"

Between bird and turtle sightings, the silence is underscored by a constant clicking. "It's fish snapping, the river talking . . .," she says.

In her *River Time* essays Lembke speaks of conversations between river and shore, their different languages. And here it is, the sounds on quiet water.

"I've seen extraordinary things on the Neuse this year," Lembke responds to a query concerning the woeful state of the Neuse River. "More oysters live in our part of the Neuse than ever before. They must like the increased nutrient. We've had runs of black drum — bazillions of them. That indicates more salt water."

"Is it safe to eat them?" someone asks.

"We do all the time. I don't feel that way about fish caught up river, though. I have noticed changes in the blue crabs. Their normal weight has been 1.45 to 1.6 ounces. Last summer, crabs were averaging 1.1 ounces. I keep notebooks."

No doubt about that. Vigilant stewardship is a full-time job. It's vigilance that reveals the magic in places along the Neuse like Great Neck Point.

To arrange for a tour with Janet Lembke, call the N.C. Maritime Museum in Beaufort at 728-7317

Annual Events

"The Athens of North Carolina" has been New Bern's fond and familiar epithet since Colonial times, and living up to it, the town does an Olympian job of entertaining and educating throughout the year. Tryon Palace hosts a variety of special events, and the Craven Arts Council and Gallery sponsors art exhibitions, music and dance performances year round. Sailing regattas take place all year, and the city has been known to throw itself a party at the drop of a hat.

Each year, New Bern hosts the Craven Concerts Series including an annual concert by the North Carolina Symphony, solo artists and dancers. Performance dates change with each year's calendar. The New Bern Civic Theater schedules a variety of dramatic presentations year round, as do neighborhood dramatic groups. Numerous musical and art organizations annually schedule shows and perform at city functions and festivities. The New Bern Farmer's Market hosts dance bands for the public at various times during the year and interesting things are always brewing at Tryon Palace. Current calendar information may be obtained through the Craven Arts Council, 638-2577, and the Craven County Convention & Visitors Bureau, 637-9400 or (800) 437-5767.

January

Garden Lecture Series
Tryon Palace • 514-4900, (800) 767-1560

Tryon Palace tries to accommodate local green thumbs with a Garden Lecture Series beginning in mid-January. The lectures combine a historical perspective on the art of gardening with practical advice on timely topics throughout the year. One-hour garden lectures in 1997 occur on the second Saturday of each month. Horticulturists and various other experts discuss garden photography, attracting and identifying birds, historic varieties of tulips, English gardens, botanical medicines, holiday greenery and Victorian gardens. Garden lectures are conducted in the Tryon Palace Visitor Center auditorium at 10 AM. Admission is by purchase of a $4 garden ticket or annual pass. No advance reservations are necessary.

Shrine Winter Ceremonial
Sudan Temple, 403 Front St. • 637-5197

The Shrine Winter Ceremonial occurs annually during the third week of January, bringing Shriners to New Bern from all over North Carolina for events centered at the Sudan Temple. Shrine parades, wherever performed, are fun, funny and as festive as a fez. The state's Nobles put on the most colorful parade possible on Saturday of ceremonial week in downtown New Bern.

February

Sunday Jazz Showcase
Sheraton Grand • 638-2577

The town goes cosmopolitan in early February for two performances of some of the finest jazz you'll hear anywhere. The New Bern Sunday Jazz Showcase, sponsored by the Craven Arts Council and Gallery, takes place at the Sheraton Grand Hotel. The annual jazz showcase assembles some of the most recognized names in modern jazz. Both afternoon and evening performances are always a sellout so reservations are a must. Performances are at 1:30 and 7:30 PM.

New Bern Preservation Foundation Antique Show
Sudan Temple • 633-6448

Antiques also take the stage in mid-February when the New Bern Preservation Foundation sponsors its annual two-day Antique Show and Sale at the Sudan Temple on E. Front Street. The show hosts as many as 30 dealers who sell, demonstrate, instruct and exhibit 18th- and 19th-century American antiques. Proceeds benefit the Preservation Foundation's restoration projects, particularly the city's historic Union Station, which is now underway. Tickets are $3.50 in advance and $4 at the door.

March

Decorative Arts Symposium
Tryon Palace • 328-6143, (800) 767-9111

In addition to their gardens, New Bernians are proud of the authenticity of their vintage belongings. Here again, Tryon Palace fills the bill with its annual Decorative Arts Symposium in mid-March, illustrating regional styles in decorations. Cosponsored by the East Carolina University Division of Continuing Education, the event includes nationally recognized speakers as well as meals, social events and special tours. A registration fee is required, and a brochure is printed each year outlining the events.

Model Train Show
New Bern High School • 637-4026

Late March brings the annual weekend Model Train Show of the Carolina Coastal Railroaders. The interesting collection of miniatures and model trains shown in the New Bern High School auditorium is a great stop for kids younger than age 12 who are admitted free with an adult.

INSIDERS' TIP

Gardeners who visit Tryon Palace during the Spring Historic Homes and Gardens tour enjoy shopping for plants and herbs sold at the palace Gardens Shop.

Photo: Swiss Bear

There is fun for all ages at the Chrysanthemum Festival.

April

Spring Historic Homes and Gardens Tour
Attmore-Oliver House, 510 Pollock St.
• 638-8558

Many people enjoy visiting New Bern in early April for the New Bern Spring Homes and Gardens Tour. The event is cosponsored by the Historical Society and the New Bern

Preservation Foundation, and the town puts on its prettiest face to welcome visitors. The tour includes private homes, gardens and churches in the historic district, with guides and location maps provided. The tour can best be enjoyed on foot and is an ideal opportunity to explore selected homes and landmarks in the river city. During the two-day event, Tryon Palace opens its gardens for tours at no extra charge and offers palace tour tickets at a discount to tour ticket holders. Homes and Gardens Tour tickets may be purchased on tour days at the headquarters for both sponsoring organizations, the Attmore-Oliver House. Tickets can also be ordered by mail in advance.

Gardeners' Weekend
Tryon Palace • 514-4900, (800) 767-1560

The weekend of the New Bern Spring Historic Homes and Gardens Tour is the same as Gardeners' Weekend at Tryon Palace. Palace gardens are open free throughout the weekend, and walking tours of the gardens are guided by horticultural staff members on Sunday. Thousands of gloriously colored tulips are in bloom, along with expansive plantings of blazing daffodils and pansies. All of this is on a luxurious background of azaleas and dogwoods. It's quite a sight to walk through.

Two-Man Classic Invitational Golf Tournament
The Emerald Golf Club, Carolina Pines • 637-3111

If golf is your game, sign on for the annual Two-Man Classic Invitational Tournament in early April. Sponsored by the New Bern Area Chamber of Commerce and the Greater Havelock Chamber of Commerce, tournament play is held simultaneously at The Emerald Golf Club and at Carolina Pines.

May

Cinco de Mayo
El Cerro Grande Restaurant, Havelock • 638-2577

In early May, the Craven Arts Council stages a two-day Cinco de Mayo Fiesta in the parking lot of the El Cerro Grande Restaurant in Havelock. The free festival is in celebration of the Mexican holiday and features arts of the Hispanic culture including music, food, crafts, piñatas, dancing and other entertainment.

School children are bused in to enjoy the traditional celebration, and the public is welcome both Friday and Saturday.

Colonial Clown Convention
Sheraton Grand Hotel • 638-9110

Late May in New Bern brings in the clowns for the annual Colonial Clown Convention. That's right. It's a three-day weekend with more than 200 clowns about town. Clowns in training are taught how to walk the walk by the pros. Wannabes can develop an entire personality through costuming, makeup, walking, talking and acting. Slapstick, juggling, puppetry, magic, gospel routines, the difference between circus and town clowning, it's all there, so take it away! Performances are frequent, and audiences are vital to training clowns. Everyone is invited into the "prop room" at the Sheraton Grand to get into the act. A theater performance is presented on Saturday evening. Whether as clown or a member of the audience, it's a good time to be in New Bern.

Drama Tours
Tryon Palace • 514-4900, (800) 767-1560

Beginning the last weekend in May, Tryon Palace's Drama Tours are daily living history presentations by characters who enact a typical day in the palace in the year 1771. The tours continue through mid-August. During Memorial Day Weekend, the gardens of Tryon Palace are open free of charge, and a regimental encampment occurs on the palace grounds.

June

King George III's Birthday: Festival of Colonial Life
Tryon Palace • 514-4900, (800) 767-1560

Visitors are invited to a Colonial America celebration of King George III's Birthday: Fes-

---

INSIDERS' TIP

The annual spring concert performance of the 40-voice Southern Gentlemen Barbershop Chorus at the Grover C. Fields Middle School in June gets New Bern ready for the good old summertime.

tival of Colonial Life in mid-June at Tryon Palace. The palace grounds and gardens buzz with activity of 18th-century life including a regimental encampment, entertainment, craft demonstrations and activities for all ages free of charge. Interior and Drama Tours of the palace historic sites are offered at the regular fee.

July

Fourth of July
Various locations • 637-9400, (800) 437-5767

As one of America's first towns to have a Fourth of July celebration, New Bern still enjoys a well-turned-out celebration full of traditional hot dogs and fireworks. The fireworks display takes place at Lawson Creek Park on First Street near downtown. Spectators can watch the sky light up at Lawson Creek, or from even better vantage points at either Union Point Park or Bicentennial Park. Military bands have traditionally performed patriotic music to complement the event. Additional holiday activities take place at Tryon Palace, where gardens are open free to the public and entertainment and activities occur throughout the historic site.

August

Rotary Cup Regatta
Sheraton Grand Hotel • 633-9463, 444-2349

Sailors from all over the Southeast converge on New Bern for the annual Rotary Cup Regatta each Labor Day weekend. Formerly the Michelob Cup Regatta, the Rotary Regatta is a leisurely, fun sailing competition for cruising class boats beginning in Oriental and finishing in New Bern, a distance of about 12 miles on the Neuse River. Festivities begin on the eve of the race in Oriental and continue at the Sheraton Marina following the competition. The New Bern Rotary Club sponsors the event, and everyone can join the fun that usually involves dances, a road race and seafood feasts.

September

River Homes Tour
New Bern Preservation Foundation • 633-6448

Every other year, the New Bern Preservation Foundation sponsors a River Homes Tour weekend in mid-September. This tour, unlike the Spring Homes and Gardens tour that features historic restorations, focuses on contemporary homes on the Trent and Neuse rivers. Featured homes are designed for "architectural immortality," taking advantage of sites and river views while accommodating the lifestyles of their owners. The next autumn weekend River Homes Tour will be in September 1998.

Curtis Strange Shrine Classic
The Emerald Golf Club • 633-4440

The Curtis Strange Shrine Classic is a one-day golf exhibition occurring annually in mid-September at The Emerald Golf Club for the benefit of the Shriner's 22 hospitals. Celebrity golfers scheduled to play in the eighth annual exhibition classic in 1997 feature Ben Crenshaw, Billy Ray Brown and Stewart Clink. The event has raised $625,000 for the Shrine Hospitals during the seven years it has been played.

Treasure Doll Club Show and Sale
Sudan Temple • 633-5157, 637-5953

From the latest Barbies to antique cloth teddies, all the dolls gather for the Tryon Treasures Doll Club's annual one-day show and sale in mid-September. Collectors and chil-

---

INSIDERS' TIP

On the corner of Pollock and Middle streets is a cannon buried muzzle down. The cannon was taken from the Revolutionary British ship-of-war *Lady Blessington* following an engagement with a privateer owned by New Bern patriot, John Wright Stanley.

dren enjoy the full show of antique, modern, reproduction and cloth dolls as well as teddy bears, doll furniture, supplies and clothing at the Sudan Temple. Admission is charged, and a portion of the show's proceeds are donated to local organizations concerned with women and children.

Neuse River Day
Union Point Park • 637-7972

In late May, the Neuse River Foundation sponsors Neuse River Day, a Saturday festival to celebrate and save a valuable natural resource. The day's activities take place at Union Point on the Trent and Neuse rivers and include boat rides, a ski show, a yacht parade, a fish fry, food booths, sailboat races, the annual Ducky Cup Regatta in which any age participant may sponsor the fastest plastic duck in the river race. There are also amusement rides and informational exhibits, speakers and demonstrations that increase awareness of the impact we have on the delicate balance of river ecology. Proceeds from the event help to fund the River Keeper program that employs a full-time professional and provides numerous volunteers to monitor the health of the Neuse River and its tributaries.

October

Mumfest
Downtown New Bern • 638-5781

Swiss Bear Downtown Revitalization group, in cooperation with Tryon Palace and the city of New Bern, hosts one of eastern North Carolina's major annual events, the Chrysanthemum Festival, in early October. The colorful three-day weekend festival is a celebration of gorgeous autumn weather, colorful flowers and an inviting downtown full of interesting activities. Spread along the downtown streets and waterfront are booths of food, crafts, paintings and antiques, a clas-

sic car show and musical performances both in the street and on stages in various locations. Festival activities include sporting events and a bass fishing tournament, traditional and changing events for the entire family each year. Tryon Palace grounds, highlighted with thousands of mums in bloom, are open without admission charge, and military encampments provide diversions on the wide back lawn. Craft demonstrations, entertainment and other activities attract a grand turnout year after year.

Ratty's Regatta
Sheraton Grand Marina • 633-2088

Ratty's Regatta was first raced in 1996 and promises to annually bring out classic craft for the mid-October rowing event, which starts from the Sheraton Grand Marina docks. Organized and sponsored by Captain Ratty's, the full day of races and demonstrations shows off the advantages of hull designs and crew skills in competitive events that are fun to watch.

Oktoberfest
Farmer's Market • 636-1640

Oktoberfest, a celebration that usually signals the beginning of October, is celebrated late in the month in 1997. Oktoberfest gathers New Bernians with European roots for a Saturday evening celebration that's an annual event at the Farmer's Market on Tryon Palace Drive. The Little German Band and Dancers of Raleigh are usually there to provide the music and entertainment.

New Bern at Night Ghost Walk
Attmore-Oliver House, 510 Pollock St.
• 638-8558

In late October, the New Bern Historical Society conducts its New Bern at Night Ghost Walk, complete with ghosts from New Bern's past. Walking tours take place from 5 to 9 PM on two weekend nights and feature his-

---

INSIDERS' TIP

Cedar Grove Cemetery's weeping arch entrance of coquina shells holds moisture, and it is local superstition that if water drips on you as you pass under the arch, you will be the next to arrive at the cemetery — by hearse.

toric homes, churches and the Cedar Grove Cemetery. Ghost Walks focus on historic events particular to New Bern, and ghosts from historic occasions are present in homes and historic buildings on the tour to tell how the times affected them. Banners, T-shirts and books are available as souvenirs of a truly chilling experience. Tickets are available at retail locations and the historical society's headquarters, the Attmore-Oliver House.

November

Decorating for the Holidays
Tryon Palace • 514-4900, (800) 787-1560

Residents and visitors from surrounding counties look forward to Tryon Palace's two-part Decorating for the Holidays workshop in mid-November. The workshops teach participants how to make innovative and natural holiday decorations. Subjects covered often include wreaths and wreath-making, garland-making using Christmas greenery, kissing balls and spectacular centerpieces using fresh fruits and natural greenery. Admission to the workshops is by purchase of a $4 garden ticket or advance purchase of a Christmas Celebration Tour ticket. Workshop times and locations vary.

December

Coastal Christmas Flotilla
Bicentennial Park • 637-4827

It's traditional in New Bern that the city's Coastal Christmas Celebration begins the first weekend in December with a festive flotilla bringing Santa to Bicentennial Park. Now in its 12th year, the Coastal Christmas Flotilla is truly a celebration bringing Santa to town aboard a Hatteras yacht. The flotilla proceeds down the Trent River and passes Union Point, giving spectators a long, lingering look at the boats festooned with sparkling lights, diving dolphins and red-nosed reindeer.

Tryon Palace
Christmas Celebration
Tryon Palace • 514-4900, (800) 767-1560

Staff and volunteers prepare for weeks for the Tryon Palace Christmas Celebration. By early December the palace looks much as it did during the holidays in 1770 when Governor William Tryon hosted a "very grand and noble Entertainment and Ball" to celebrate the grand opening of his sumptuous home and the Royal capitol. The palace is lighted and adorned with fresh fruit and fragrant greenery. Cooks are busy in the kitchen preparing confections and delicacies, and the air is filled with holiday aromas. Christmas Insider Tours take place through mid-December focusing on decorations and food in Tryon Palace and other historic sites from the 18th to 20th centuries. Through mid-December, palace horticulture staffers lead visitors on Winter Garden Tours focused on evergreens and exterior decorations. Two weekends are reserved for evening Christmas Candlelight Tours featuring 800 candles burning throughout the palace. Carolers, dancers and musical entertainment are continuous during the spectacular evening tours.

Handel's Messiah
Centenary United Methodist Church, Middle and New sts. • 638-2577

An annual production of Handel's *Messiah* is a tradition in its 17th year at Centenary United Methodist Church. Performances in early December combine 150 community voices and North Carolina Symphony musicians with conductor James Ogle. Two concert performances and one afternoon practice are quickly sold out when tickets become available around Thanksgiving at the Bank of the Arts.

Coastal Christmas Celebration
Various locations • 637-9400, (800) 437-5767

Other annual events of New Bern's Coastal Christmas Celebration include the Craven County Arts Council's annual Holiday Showcase show and sale at the Bank of the Arts, the Down East Dance performance of *The Nutcracker*, community caroling along the waterfront and lighting of the community Christmas tree in the yard of Christ Episcopal Church at Pollock and Middle streets each December. You can easily catch the spirit of the season in New Bern.

On the Water

Because of New Bern's location, it's not surprising that New Bernians take to the water like, well, ducks. The weather is mild enough year round to entice the locals into sailing, skiing, fishing or relaxing on or around the rivers.

Waterways

Boaters, fishers and lovers of the outdoors in the New Bern area have two waterways to explore: the expansive Neuse River that flows into Pamlico Sound or the slow, meandering Trent River that flows into the Neuse.

The Neuse River is ideal for cruising by sail or power, with miles of sandy beaches, clearly marked channels, easy access via the Intracoastal Waterway (ICW) and Pamlico Sound and many marinas and protected anchorages. The Trent River is deep, has a marked channel and is navigable by small boat. Its lower reaches are fine for uncrowded water-skiing. Brices Creek, a tributary of the Trent, winds far into the forest and offers excellent fishing and wildlife observation.

Rotating bridges at New Bern open on demand daily except from 6:30 to 7:30 AM and 4:30 to 5:30 PM. On weekends and holidays between May 24 and September 8, the bridges are closed between 2 and 7 PM, with openings at 4 and 6 PM. The remainder of the year, the daily schedule is in effect seven days a week. The bridge tender monitors channel 13 VHF. The railroad bridges upriver from New Bern are always open except when in use. National Oceanic and Atmospheric Administration (NOAA) stations in the area are New Bern and Beaufort, WX-2 (162.475 MHz) and Hatteras, WX-3 (162.40 MHz).

A clearly marked channel up the Neuse from the ICW will bring you into historic New Bern. The natural channel depths generally run between 8 and 12 feet, with little noticeable tidal effect. A strong easterly or northerly wind will raise the level, while a sustained westerly breeze, say 25 knots, can lower this level by as much as 2 feet. Also noteworthy to boat-ers are the sapling stakes dotting the river, strung with nets in the early spring and late fall. The nets are usually buoyed by corks or plastic bottles or marked by white flags.

The Neuse is a very wide river, which invites sailing in addition to motor-cruising and water-skiing. The many wandering tributaries promise scenic canoeing and exciting fishing. Much of the Neuse River's shoreline south of New Bern forms one of the boundaries of the vast 157,000-acre Croatan National Forest. Here locals and visitors enjoy public recreation areas, with swimming and picnic facilities near the Minnesott ferry terminal and at Flanner's Beach south of New Bern.

Fishing

Expect to hook bass, bream, flounder and many more fish in local waters. Bass fishing tournaments are popular competitions often scheduled during the year as fund-raising events by area organizations. Swiss Bear Inc. usually schedules a bass-fishing competition during Mumfest each October. The Neuse River is also home to many crabs, the catching of which provides tasty and profitable rewards for many locals.

FYI

Unless otherwise noted, the area code for all phone numbers in this guide is 919.

Nearby Croatan National Forest permits fresh- and saltwater fishing; however, fishing in the forest's freshwater lakes is poor because of the acidity of the water. But along its river shoreline, oystering, crabbing and flounder gigging can be worthwhile efforts. For the best fishing spots, talk to a ranger at the ranger office on Fisher Avenue, 9 miles south of New Bern just off U.S. Highway 70 E. The office is open from 7:30 AM to 4:30 PM.

If you just like to cruise backwoods waters, several forest locations have fishing piers and boat ramps, including Brices Creek, Cahooque Creek, Catfish Lake, Great Lake and Haywood Landing. Some of these sites are deep in the Croatan National Forest, so it's best to check with a ranger for specific directions. Better yet, stop by the ranger office and pick up a forest map. (For more information on places to fish in the

What's Biting?

The Croatan National Forest permits fresh- and saltwater fishing in its many waterways. Here's what you might be lucky enough to catch:

Catfish and Great Lakes: Yellow bullheads, fliers, yellow perch and black crappie

Brices Creek: Catfish, bluegills, redbreast sunfish, largemouth bass, black crappie, yellow perch, bowfin and gar.

Photo: Scott Taylor

There can be some good fishing in the Croatan, but you better go early as you won't be alone.

White Oak River and Hadnot Creek: Striped mullet, pumpkinseed, chain pickerel, largemouth bass, flounder, redbreast sunfish, spot (seasonal), croaker (seasonal) and gar.

Neuse River: Striped bass, redbreast sunfish, largemouth bass, crappie, bluegill, flounder, gar.

Source: Croatan National Park

park, see our New Bern Recreation and Parks chapter.)

For fresh bait, stop by **Neuse River Seafood**, 638-1891, or **Tripp's Seafood**, 637-7700.

Boating

Marinas

Boats of all sizes can find berthing space in downtown New Bern and nearby marinas. Whether you're just cruising around or wish to launch your boat at one of the many local ramps, most locations have similar facilities. In the downtown area especially, it is not unusual for leisure yachters or sailors to arrive for what they thought would be a short visit only to find themselves living aboard their vessels, staying weeks, sometimes months, even years. If you're traveling to New Bern from some distance, it is wise to call ahead to assure docking space

availability, especially during the warmer months.

Sheraton Marina
1 Bicentennial Park • 638-3585

Part of the Sheraton Grand hotel complex, this marina is on the Trent River and has a floating breakwater/dock that can serve larger yachts. The marina is open year round, and it docks sail and power vessels up to 300 feet in its 200 slips, 25 of which are transient berths. The marina also has a marked entry channel and approach, a dockside depth of 12 feet, gas and diesel fuel, a pump-out station, ice, electricity, showers and a restaurant. All floating docks and finger piers were recently rebuilt. Telephone service is available, and cable TV is free.

Ramada Marina
101 Howell Rd. • 637-7372

The Ramada Marina is across the Trent River from the Sheraton Marina. Damaged by storms last summer, it was been rebuilt and opened in June 1997. The Ramada Marina is open year round and serves sail and power vessels up to 125 feet. It has 125 floating concrete slips, 15 of which are transient berths, a marked entry channel with 12-foot approach depth and a dockside depth of 8 to 16 feet. Amenities include a pump-out station, ice, electricity, showers, laundry facilities, patio and grills, a restaurant and a snack bar. Cable TV hookups are also available

River Bend Yacht Club & Marina
1 Marina Dr. • 633-2006

River Bend is reached by boat via an entry channel south of the Trent River bridge. It is about 5 miles upstream from downtown New Bern. A private club, the marina is open year round and serves sail and power vessels up to 40 feet. It has 75 slips, six of which are transient berths, a marked entry channel, launching ramp, gas, electricity and an approach and dockside depth of 6 feet. It offers propeller and hull repair services and stocks marine supplies, groceries and ice. In addition to dock space, which can be rented short- or long-term, guest memberships to the town's golf course, tennis courts and swimming pool can also be purchased. The Oar House Restaurant and Lounge is on site for food and libations.

Northwest Creek Marina
104 Marina Dr. in Fairfield Harbour
• 638-4133

Northwest Creek Marina has become the center of action for the Fairfield Harbor resort development. It is on the north side of the Neuse River, is open year round and serves sail and power vessels up to 60 feet. Larger boats are accommodated by special arrangements. It has 235 slips, 15 of which are transient berths, a marked entry channel with 7 feet of water depth, dockside depth of 12 feet, gas and diesel fuel, a pump-out station, a launching ramp, electricity, showers, a weight and sauna room and laundry facilities. The Harbour Breeze General Store can help provision your boat for the day or an extended cruise with groceries, supplies, clothing and fishing gear. Marina patrons have full use of all the resort's amenities including two 18-hole golf courses, indoor

and outdoor pools and lighted tennis courts. For dining Captain Bordeaux Bar & Grill at dockside features an upstairs bar and lounge and casual fine dining in the downstairs restaurant. Transportation will be needed to visit New Bern's attractions.

Duck Creek Marina
Sandy Point Rd., Bridgeton • 638-1702

At the head of Duck Creek on the north side of the Neuse, this marina is open year round and serves sail and power vessels up to 46 feet. It has 55 slips, a marked entry channel with approach depth of 6 feet, dockside depth of 8 feet, railway and 35-ton lift, storage yard for repair work, marine supplies, electricity and showers. Because the marina is across the river from New Bern, you will need transportation for shopping or to visit the city's attractions.

Union Point Park
Tryon and E. Front sts. • 636-4060

Union Point Park serves as a city park and public docks. Boaters often anchor here to orient themselves to the area and locate more permanent mooring. The park features a boat ramp and public facilities; however, a city ordinance prohibits overnight dockage.

Tidewater Marina Co. Inc.
300 Madame Moore Ln., 637-3347

On the Trent River, Tidewater Marina Co. is open year round and serves sail and power vessels up to 40 feet. It has 16 slips, three transient slips, a marked entry channel with controlling depth of 21 feet, 15 feet at dockside, railway and lift, a launching ramp, gas and diesel fuel, supplies and electricity. It also offers repairs on propellers and hulls. Because it is away from New Bern's hub, you will need transportation to see the sights.

Nearby Marinas

Nearby marinas at Clubfoot Creek, Minnesott Beach and Oriental, all on the Neuse River, are destinations for enjoyable day sails or cruising trips from New Bern. See our Oriental chapter for details on the marinas there. In addition, there are many marinas along the Crystal Coast, which is easily accessible from New Bern via the Neuse River and the ICW. See our Crystal Coast Marinas chapter for listings. For the convenience of boaters, we are including an alphabetical list of some of the marinas near New Bern that you can call on as you make your way up and down the Neuse River or toward Pamlico Sound.

Clubfoot Creek, on the south side of the river near Havelock, provides anchorage for water traffic. The riverside community of **Minnesott Beach** on the north side of the Neuse also offers safe mooring. The quaint village of **Oriental**, on the ICW on the north bank of the Neuse, is called "the sailing capital of North Carolina," but many power and pleasure vessels find safe harbor at area docks as well. (For more information about this town read our separate chapter on Oriental.)

Matthews Point Marina, RFD 1, Havelock, 444-1805, is off the beaten track on Clubfoot Creek on the south side of the Neuse River, 10 miles east of Cherry Point. Nestled comfortably in a safe harbor, the marina is open year round and serves sail and power vessels up to 45 feet. It has 106 slips, six of which are transient berths, a marked entry channel, approach depth of 7 feet, dockside depth of 6 feet, gas and diesel fuel, a launching ramp, electricity, a pump-out station, showers and ice. A clubhouse, cookout area and upper deck lounge are also available to boaters.

Minnesott Beach Yacht Basin, Bennett Road, Arapahoe, 249-1424, is on the north side of the Neuse River. It is open year round and serves sail and power vessels up to 50 feet. It has 150 slips, five of which are transient berths, a marked entry channel, approach depth of 8.5 feet, dockside depth of 10 feet, gas and diesel fuel, a 60-ton lift, electricity, a pump-out station, supplies, ice, limited groceries, showers, laundry facilities and a pool. Propeller and hull repairs are available for both gas and diesel vessels. The marina has a lounge with a TV and fireplace and is close to the country club golf course. Transportation to a nearby restaurant can also be arranged.

Boat Rentals and Charters

Shorebird Boat Rentals Inc.
Three locations • 670-2514, (800) 948-3524

A popular boat rental operation is Shorebird, which offers rentals at the Sheraton Hotel and Marina downtown, the Northwest Creek Marina in Fairfield Harbor and the Tidewater Marina on the Trent River. You can rent anything from a 17-foot power boat to a 24-foot pontoon as well as canoes, Waverunners, sailboats and jet boats. Shorebird has a 26-foot cabin cruiser that you can rent for overnight trips. Guided fishing tours and tow service are available.

Nautical Adventures Sailing Charters
4416 Riverside Dr. • 633-1871

Nautical specializes in the "total sailing experience" for those who want to sail the Neuse. Captain John Hill will take you on a river ride for a morning or an afternoon of pleasurable cruising. His 21-foot San Juan sailboat comfortably accommodates two or three, and John will give novices get-acquainted-with-sailing lessons. Charters set sail from Riverside Drive in New Bern.

On The Wind Sailing School and Charter Service
Northwest Creek Marina • 633-0032

This school and charter service offers a variety of charters, including day and evening sails. All cruises depart from Northwest Creek Marina at Fairfield Harbour.

Sailing

For sailors the premier event is the annual **Rotary Cup**, which is detailed in our New Bern Annual Events section. Other sailing competitions take place throughout the year. For more

---

INSIDERS' TIP

Boaters love to plunder Goldman Metals in New Bern for bargains in stainless steel discarded by Hatteras Yachts.

information call **Blackbeard's Sailing Club**, 633-3990, or **On The Wind Sailing School and Charter Service** at Fairfield Harbour, 633-0032.

Several yacht clubs are active in the New Bern area, including **Eastern Carolina Yacht Club**, which meets in Trent Woods at 4005 Trent Pines Drive, and the **New Bern Yacht Club**, which meets at the Sheraton Grand Hotel and Marina downtown.

Canoeing

If you want to explore some interesting places by canoe, try these two open-water lakes in the Croatan. Both Great Lake, 2,809 acres, and Catfish Lake, 962 acres, are home to osprey, alligators and black bears. They are unusual bodies of water because they are surrounded by pocosin, the Indian name for "swamp on a hill." Pocosin is an impenetrable jungle of pond pine, titi, zenobia and greenbriars, but it supports fragile ecosystems that add to the beauty and wildness of the Croatan.

If you prefer to canoe in enclosed waters, take your canoe to the smaller creeks: Brices, Hadnot, Hancock, Cahooque, Hunters and Holston. In these waters, you can observe a rich variety of plants and wildlife. Want to canoe in moving waters? Then paddle in the White Oak, Neuse and Newport rivers. Here many varieties of shore birds show themselves. Watching them in their natural habitat is a fascinating experience.

Recreation and Parks

New Bern is surrounded by water and great open spaces, making it an excellent location for all kinds of recreational activities. There are numerous places for adults and children to exercise and take part in sporting programs. Walking is one favorite form of exercise in New Bern. Some call it strolling and use that time to check on the progress of neighbors, their children or area businesses.

For those who seek more athletic pursuits, New Bern and Craven County offer active, year-round recreation programs and public areas for tennis, power walking, running, baseball, basketball, softball and soccer. Both the county and city maintain public boat ramps and fishing piers.

Recreation and Fitness Centers

Craven County Recreation and Parks Department
406 Craven St., New Bern • 636-6606

Craven County's recreation facilities are connected to the county's public schools. Facilities offered to the public include tennis courts (Craven County Community College has several lighted tennis courts) and ballfields. Youth programs are plentiful: karate, gymnastics, soccer leagues and camps, baseball, swimming, saltwater fishing classes, tennis lessons and a six-week summer day camp. In June and July, kids can learn to swim or enhance their swimming skills at the Carolina Pines pool. Adults can take part in such activities as softball, basketball, exercise and line-dance classes. The recreation department organizes the Special Olympics for mentally handicapped individuals ages 3 and up. Competition is held in track and field, tennis, power lifting, basketball, bowling and aquatics.

The department also sponsors the area's Senior Games, which awards gold, silver and bronze medals for events such as archery, basketball, billiards, croquet, golf, horseshoes and much more; the Pizza Hut Classic Tennis Tournament for amateur tennis players; and the Annual Rotary Cup Road Race, a 5K race that winds through Historic New Bern on Labor Day weekend.

Since many events and activities can vary ac-

INSIDERS' TIP

For water-skiing enthusiasts, a choice spot is along the Trent River, with its usually calm waters, from Lawson Creek Park to Trent Woods.

cording to season and available resources, you might want to visit the department. Office hours are 8 AM to 5 PM, Monday through Friday.

New Bern Recreation and Parks Department
Administrative Offices, Pine Tree Dr.
• 636-4060

The New Bern Recreation and Parks Department operates the bulk of its programs from two centers — the Stanley White Center on Chapman Street, 636-4061, and the West New Bern Recreation Center, 1225 Pine Tree Drive, 636-4061. The programs vary at each center and with each season. Programming includes youth lessons in swimming and tennis, summer day camps, youth ceramic classes and football. T-ball and baseball are offered to youth between the ages of 6 and 12. Babe Ruth baseball is played by youths 13 through 18.

Twin Rivers YMCA
100 YMCA Ln. • 638-8799

At the intersection of Fifth and Sixth streets is a 45,000-square-foot athletic facility that houses a 25-yard, six-lane heated indoor swimming pool, a regulation-size gymnasium with an upstairs track, a gym, a youth activity center, racquetball courts, a free-weight room and a wellness center with step machines, a treadmill and bicycles. The staff will analyze patrons' fitness levels and help develop a personalized activity program, if needed. There is a CAM II Center with Nautilus equipment and a fitness center with a sauna and a whirlpool. Classes are taught regularly in swimming, gymnastics, aqua aerobics, arthritis aquatics, water safety instructor training, junior lifesaving, basic lifeguard training, scuba and cardiopulmonary resuscitation.

The Y also offers programs in aerobics, fitness for people older than 40, racquetball, volleyball and weights. Competitions are conducted in a variety of activities. Youth programs are offered in gymnastics, basketball, volleyball, softball and T-ball, and transportation is provided from several schools for after-school programs. The Y sponsors day camps during Easter and Christmas vacations. Babysitting services are available, and the Y will host children's birthday parties.

Courts Plus
2911 Brunswick Ave. • 633-2221

Courts Plus of New Bern is a membership racquetball facility with four indoor courts. The facility offers swimming and aqua aerobics in its indoor and outdoor pools. At Courts Plus, you can participate in organized karate, basketball, volleyball and aerobics. There is Nautilus workout equipment, and for winding down, try the saunas, steamroom or whirlpool for soothing relaxation. Lockers, towels and a tanning booth are also available. The pro shop offers apparel, equipment and accessories for your fitness needs. Courts Plus has several racquetball leagues and serves as site host for a number of regional racquetball tournaments. The lounge offers refreshments and light snacks. Child care and special programs for children are also offered. Courts Plus does not have trial memberships, but visitors may avail themselves of a one-month, temporary membership.

Bowling

B & R Lanes
1309 Tatum Dr. • 633-3424

This 15-lane alley hosts adult and senior leagues and is equipped with video games and a snack bar. Reduced rates are available for groups. Manager Cassie Buck and her staff will help novices learn how to bowl. During the summer, B & R Lanes closes on Wednesday and Sunday.

Hiking

Island Creek Forest Walk
Croatan National Forest, New Bern
• 638-5628

This one-half mile trail is perfect for a morning or an afternoon hike. As you traverse it, you will see a virgin-like stand of upland hardwoods, picturesque Island Creek with bottomland hardwoods, and a managed stand of loblolly pines. Before setting out, stop at the Ranger Office on Fisher Avenue and pick up the Island Creek Forest Walk brochure. The brochure contains a self-guided tour that identifies trees and other trail features. It also gives a map and directions to the trail.

Neusiok Trail
Croatan National Forest • 638-5628

This area is strictly for those who enjoy roughing it. No camping facilities exist along the trail, but you may primitive camp if you pack out your garbage. You'll need to bring along drinking water and wear boots to cross wet areas. The trailhead starts on the Newport River and ends on the Neuse River at Pinecliff Recreation Area. It passes through a cypress-lined sandy beach, hardwood forests and thick pocosin with pond pines to the estuary at Oyster Point. The length of the trail is 21 miles, and it crosses several paved and unpaved roads. Because of biting, stinging and zinging insects, fall, winter and early spring are best for camping and hiking. Catfish Lake and Great Lake also have additional primitive camping. Boat ramps are available at Brices Creek, Cahooque Creek and Haywood Landing. Locals favor these spots for their natural beauty and handy access to water; however, insects can be prolific in the summer months. For directions, call forest headquarters, 638-5628, or stop by the Ranger Office on Fisher Avenue.

Parks

The city of New Bern has lots of parks that are great places to go for outdoor enjoyment. For details about seasonal programs, call the New Bern Recreation and Parks Department, 636-4061 or 636-4061, and ask for brochures or visit one of the two recreation centers. Each is staffed by a center supervisor, an athletic supervisor and program directors. They will be happy to answer your questions.

INSIDERS' TIP

Union Point Park is a great place to pause for a break after exploring the New Bern waterfront.

Glenburnie Park
N. Glenburnie Rd.

In the Glenburnie Gardens residential area off Oaks Road, this park is shaded by a grove of old pine trees. It fronts the Neuse River and has boat launching ramps, four picnic shelters with tables and grills, fishing piers, a playground and public restrooms.

George Street Park
George St.

Next to the United Senior Services building, this park offers two tennis courts, a youth baseball field and the Kafer Park ballfield, which was once home to New Bern's professional baseball team.

Lawson Creek Park
Country Club Rd.

Off Pembroke Avenue and fronting the Trent River, this park has six boat-launching ramps and is a major attraction for water enthusiasts. Lawson Creek Park has something for everyone — two soccer fields, six fishing piers and a picnic area called Jack's Island. Besides all this, you can walk the park's fitness and exercise trail, which meanders through the marsh land that makes up much of the park.

Union Point Park
E. Front St. and Tryon Palace Dr.

This park is downtown where the Trent River joins the Neuse. It is a great place to sit and watch the river traffic. For those who love being outdoors, Union Point offers many activities — two boat-lunching ramps, boat docks and fishing piers. The park's other amenities include a stage, where Sunday summer afternoon concerts are often performed, picnic tables and public restrooms.

Fort Totten Park
**Intersection of Trent Rd.
and Fort Totten Dr.**

This small park has a ballfield, children's play area, a picnic shelter and public restrooms.

D. E. Henderson Park
Chapman St.

This park offers a playground, two ball fields, two lighted outdoor basketball courts and a picnic shelter. In addition, you'll find the Stanley White Recreation Center and public restrooms.

Seth West Parrott Park
1225 Pine Tree Dr.

This is a major park for recreation and attractions for kids. The West New Bern Recreation Center is here as well as the Kidsville Playground (see New Bern Kidstuff chapter). In addition, you'll find two lighted tennis courts, a lighted outdoor basketball court, two youth baseball fields and the Heath and Cutler and Babe Ruth Fields.

Golf

Golf courses are abundant in the New Bern area. Many have won acclaim from amateurs and professionals alike and host a number of large golf tournaments. Golfing residents and visitors are fortunate: Popular courses are easily accessible, and the normally mild climate allows for year-round play.

What follows is a list of the courses in the immediate vicinity. Most also offer tennis courts and swimming pools. For information about nearby golf courses, see our Crystal Coast Golf chapter, which includes information on Bogue Banks Country Club in Pine Knoll Shores; Star Hill Golf and Country Club in Cape

Photo: NC Travel and Tourism

New Bern is a paradise for golf lovers.

Carteret; Brandywine Bay Golf Club near Morehead City; and Silver Creek Golf Club on Highway 58 near Cape Carteret.

The Emerald Golf Club
5000 Clubhouse Dr. • 633-4440

Rees Jones designed The Emerald, creating the 7,000-yard course to be a challenge to golfers at all levels of skill. Jones used various grasses to give each hole a totally different feel and appearance, and sculptured the 18-hole course to create variety. Most holes have four or five pin locations. The fourth tee, for example, features four locations that hit across the water and one high land route. Carts are available. The golf course and tennis courts are open to the public; tee times should be arranged for two days in advance. While only residents of the Greenbrier community can be permanent members of the golf club, there are social memberships that entitle members to tennis, swimming pool and club facilities as well as golfing privileges. The Emerald is home to the Curtis Strange Golf Classic, played annually to raise money for the Shriners' Hospitals. Golfers can take advantage of a fully stocked pro shop, a driving range and lessons by pro Jerry Briele.

Fairfield Harbor Country Club
100 Pelican Dr. • 541-0050

Fairfield Harbour is a resort community, with timeshare accommodations plus several large residential developments. To get there, cross the Neuse River on Highway 17. Turn right on Highway 55, continue about a mile to the traffic light and turn right onto Broad Creek Road. Signs will direct you from there. Fairfield Harbour has two 18-hole, championship courses. One is the Shoreline Course, with bermudagrass greens; the other is the Harbour Pointe Golf Links, with bentgrass greens and similar in layout to the golf courses of Scotland. Both courses are open to the public. The club also has several tennis courts, a pro shop, swimming pool, driving range and restaurant. Golf lessons are available from Fairfield's PGA pro, Sam Maraffi.

River Bend Golf and Country Club
94 Shoreline Dr., River Bend • 638-2819

River Bend Golf and Country Club, an 18-hole course with a 71 par, is a semiprivate course allowing greens fee play. The course is open every day. All you need to do is call and set your tee time. Ron Anderson is the club's PGA professional. River

INSIDERS' TIP

Check with area hotels about golf packages that include rooms, green fees, meals and more.

Bend offers a well-stocked pro shop, driving range, tennis courts and an Olympic-size swimming pool. This is truly one of the area's nicest courses.

Carolina Pines Golf and Country Club
Carolina Pines Blvd. • 444-1000

On the Neuse River just west of Havelock, this is a challenging 18-hole, par 72 course with a pro shop, driving range and target greens. Tim Dupre is the club pro, and he will arrange lessons for those who are interested. Golfers will also find tennis courts, a pool and a club house with a lounge and patio overlooking freshwater lakes and golf links.

Neighborhoods and Real Estate

Just a few years ago Craven County was listed as the fifth fastest-growing county in the state, and North Carolina, the fifth fastest-grow-

ing state in the nation. That growth continues as Craven County and New Bern attract new residents from across the state and country. Many factors are affecting the area's growth. These include the tide of retirees flowing into the greater New Bern area, and the demand for housing from nearby Cherry Point military base. It's not surprising then that New Bern's housing market has expanded substantially to meet the influx of new homeowners.

The city is in the midst of a vibrant community renaissance. In New Bern's three historic neighborhoods, you will still see some structures in need of repair among the beautifully restored buildings, but this is changing at a handsome pace. Unrestored Georgian, Federal and Victorian edifices are being purchased and restored, adding considerably to the city's Colonial charm.

Another big plus for the city is its location near water. Positioned where waters of the Neuse and Trent Rivers come together, New Bern is less than an hour's drive from the ocean. Its moderate climate, nearby recreational waterways and challenging golf courses are added pluses in making New Bern a popular vacation, relocation and retirement spot for people from all walks of life.

With this in mind, New Bern's expanding homes market offers newcomers a wide choice of neighborhoods and housing in styles and prices sure to appeal to any taste or income bracket. Choices include historic homes, contemporary structures, bungalows, ranch-style residences, riverfront condominiums, townhouses and building lots in ever-increasing new developments.

Because both waterfront and nonwaterfront homes and lots are often within the same district, real estate values can vary widely within the same neighborhood. Prices for lots and houses quoted here are approximations and, of course, are subject to change. Our descriptions of neighborhoods will help orient you to the personality, price range and availability of New Bern housing.

If you are interested in New Bern neighborhoods, a helpful guide is *Real Estate Magazine: New Bern, Craven and Pamlico Counties*, published monthly by the *Sun Journal*. It contains descriptions and pictures of properties currently on the market. It's free and you can get copies at restaurants, hotels, supermarkets, real estate firms and scores of local businesses.

Another good source of information is the Road-Street Map of Craven County (including New Bern, Havelock and surrounding towns), which shows streets and major subdivisions (printed in red) of the New Bern area. It's free and available at the Craven County Convention and Visitors Bureau, 316 Tryon Palace Drive, the Greater Havelock Area Chamber of Commerce on Main Street and the Crystal Coast Visitor Center on Arendell Street in Morehead City.

Neighborhoods

Downtown Historic District

New Bern's Downtown Historic District is a 56-square block area that for two centuries grew along the point of land jutting into the confluence of the Neuse and Trent Rivers and extending west to Queen Street. The district was officially entered into the National Register of Historic Places in 1973. This is the mecca for those who desire to live in the town's oldest and most distinguished homes. It contains buildings and landscape elements that chronicle New Bern's growth — from its days as the Colonial capital of the Carolinas from 1766 until 1778, to its status as an important mercantile center in the mid-18th and early 19th centuries, to its period of prosperity fueled by the lumber industry in the late-19th and early 20th centuries.

The New Bern Preservation Foundation, in the years since its organization in 1972, has bought, stabilized and sold more than 50 structures of historical or architectural significance in New Bern's historic downtown. Once it sells the structure, the Foundation then serves as a source of expert advice to the new owners who restore the dwellings. The foundation's work has provided the impetus for many other property owners to follow suit, resulting in the restoration of more than 150 residences. A few of these date from the mid-1700s, built shortly after New Bern was founded in 1710 by Swiss nobleman Christoph deGraffenried.

The focal point of downtown is Tryon Palace on Pollock Street. The former home of the Carolinas' British governor, William Tryon, its gardens and associated buildings have been beautifully reconstructed or restored. This North Carolina historic site draws thousands of visitors each year. (For information on Tryon Palace, see our New Bern Attractions chapter.) In the surrounding neighborhood, professional offices, businesses and bed and breakfast inns occupy tastefully renovated old homes. The city has an astonishing number of landmarks listed in the National Register of Historic Places, and most of these are found in the downtown district.

Facing the Neuse River north of the U.S. Highway 17 bridge are approximately a dozen square blocks of pedigreed houses dating from the 18th, 19th and 20th centuries. Most of the elegantly restored homes have two or three-stories, and occasionally one is for sale. Fully restored historic houses are going for $200,000 and can run to more than $500,000. Smaller home restorations away from the river in this neighborhood are available in the

The Blades House is one of New Bern's fine old homes.

$100,000 range. As you move farther away from the Neuse, blocks become more transitional and prices get lower.

The cost of homes throughout the entire downtown district varies enormously, depending upon location and the degree of restoration. Sometimes, homes along the fringes are offered in the $50,000 to $70,000 range, but you can bet they require a tremendous amount of work and TLC.

Interest is also keen in preserving downtown commercial buildings. Preservation has stimulated demand for smaller residential spaces in the shopping area of New Bern's historic downtown. New living quarters in the upper floors of these buildings are now becoming available. Two-bedroom condominiums, complete with "stamped tin" ceilings, skylights and hardwood floors can be found in the beautifully restored Kress Building on Middle Street. These units range from 1,600 to 2,000 square feet and are priced from

$140,000 to $150,000. Development of condominiums is also underway in the building next door to the Kress.

Middle Street East condominiums are in a new building, three blocks from Tryon Palace. These are two-bedroom, two-bath units, just under 1400 square feet, and sell for $140,000 to $165,000.

Queen's Point is a new, upscale townhome project on the Neuse River at East Front and Queen streets. Construction is underway and finished residences will have two or three bedrooms and two-car garages. Boat slips, elevators and a security gate are also features at Queen's Point. Prices for phase one range from $240,000 to $300,000. Prices for the second-phase units will run in the mid-$200,000s. Sales are handled by any of New Bern's real estate firms (see the Real Estate section of this chapter).

Riverside Historic District

Riverside is also on the National Register of Historic Places. It comprises National Avenue and the section east of the avenue to the Neuse River. Development began in the late 1890s in response to the lumber industry, which flourished along the Neuse. Riverside was originally a mixed-use community of residential buildings and commercial enterprises. People wanted to live where they worked. Regrettably, as lumber ceased to be economically important, Riverside fell into disrepair. The result is a neighborhood where beautifully refurbished homes and rundown buildings stand side-by-side. But fortunately for New Bernians, both the city and the Preservation Foundation are taking measures to restore this once-handsome community to its original function as home to a number of businesses and private residences.

Many of Riverside's larger homes were built between 1896 and World War II, so there is a pleasant mix of architectural styles in the neighborhood. On National Avenue, high-peaked, two-story Victorian structures with wraparound porches and plenty of shade trees are situated well back from the road. On the cross streets perpendicular to National Avenue and the Neuse are rows of tidy bungalows.

Homes along the River Drive waterfront are of an entirely different character. Here, you will find pretty brick ranch dwellings on small lots with plenty of trees and meticulous landscaping. Real estate values vary widely, with some of the older bungalows offered in the $30,000 to $50,000 range. Renovated historic dwellings here start at about $125,000, with ranch-style houses along the shore selling for a bit more.

Ghent Historic District

This is the newest of New Bern's three historic districts; admission to the National Register occurred in 1983. Ghent contains private homes dating from 1913 to World War II. The area encompasses Spencer, Rhem and parts of Park Avenues. It began as a trolley car suburb in the days when working folks wanted homes away from the hustle and bustle of downtown New Bern. Today, Spencer Avenue is considered one of the prettiest streets in New Bern, with old-fashioned street lamps along a landscaped median separating two lanes of traffic. Large flowering fruit trees are breathtakingly beautiful in April.

Ghent is an energetic, people-oriented neighborhood where residents take to the sidewalks whenever the weather permits, which is often in the mild New Bern climate. In recent years, it has become a highly desirable section for homeowners and has undergone a lot of sprucing up. Bungalows and cottage-style homes with neat lawns make up a large part of the neighborhood. Some residences feature antebellum column fronts, and many have open or screened porches for those warm summer evenings.

The neighborhood is close to one of the area's nicest amenities, the new YMCA, which includes a Jr. Olympic-size swimming pool, a gymnasium, weight rooms and a racquetball court. The "Y" also offers day care and exercise classes. Ghent is also fortunate to be situated between Fort Totten Park, which has a baseball field and bleachers, and the larger Lawson Creek Park, a popular fishing spot with nature trails, boat launches and picnic tables. Homes here are larger than in many of the new housing developments surrounding New Bern, but many still require remodeling and renovation. Prices range from $65,000 to $120,000.

DeGraffenried Park

This distinguished neighborhood lies between Trent and Neuse boulevards directly north of the Ghent Historical District. Homes here are generally large and well-placed on spacious, beautifully landscaped lots. Sidewalks invite neighborhood walks, and streets carry names such as Queen Ann Lane and Lucerne Way.

Many of the more notable residences are stately, two-story brick dwellings with dignified Federal features. Brick walls and wrought-iron fences embellish many of the houses in the district. You can expect to pay between $100,000 to $200,000 for these homes.

Trent Woods

This large, mature development lies between New Bern and the Trent River. It has been incorporated to give residents better control over their neighborhoods, and there is virtually no commercial development within its borders. Over the years Trent Woods has spread out from the central New Bern Golf and Country Club. Now its winding lanes contain some of the ritziest neighborhoods and poshest dwellings in the area.

Trent Woods is composed of several subdivisions, some of which are primarily waterfront property. Manning Park, Holly Hills, Chelsea, Trent Shores and Ward Point are on the Trent River. Others, such as Creeks End and Edgewood, are along Wilson's Creek. Lakeview Estates and Cypress Shores are on

Cypress Lake, and the three Haywood subdivisions line the banks of Haywood's Creek.

Most of the residences tend toward conservative rather than contemporary architectural styles and are constructed of wood, brick or stucco. Homes are large, with two and three stories, and usually have attached or separate two-car garages. Lots are spacious, wooded and impeccably landscaped, often with Spanish moss draped in towering trees. If you take a drive through Trent Woods in the spring, you'll be greeted by a stunning display of flowering trees and shrubs.

In addition to the country club, the area boasts other amenities such as the Eastern Carolina Yacht Club. The average price for a home in Trent Woods starts around $100,000; building lots are priced from the mid-$70,000s; and waterfront houses begin in the $300,000 range.

Olde Towne Harbour

This is one of the nicest subdivisions in New Bern, just east of Trent Woods and south of Highway 70. Though just minutes from the downtown district and the shopping malls on Highway 17, Olde Towne Harbour offers quiet seclusion in a lovely, natural setting. Here, you can find some of the most lavish, custom-built contemporary homes and condominiums in New Bern. The largest of these sprawl along the shores of the Trent River and Olde Towne Lake, (actually a river inlet). This is a strictly residential, built-in development, and it appears no expense has been spared by those who have recently purchased and built on these choice, waterfront lots. Lots here begin at about $45,000, condos at $175,000 and homes at $150,000. Waterfront homes, again, are another story, ranging upward into the $500,000 category.

Taberna

Taberna is one of the newer communities in the area. Under development by Weyerhaeuser, this community is about 5 miles

INSIDERS' TIP

This year marks the 25th anniversary of New Bern Preservation Foundation. Programs and activities in honor of the birthday will be held throughout the month.

east of downtown New Bern on U.S. 70 east. Taberna means "place of hospitality" and was actually the original name of Bern, Switzerland, New Bern's sister city. Residences at the planned 1,100-acre golfing community will include single-family homes, patio homes and townhouses, with golf villas scattered throughout. Approximately 750 to 800 homesites will be available when all phases are complete. The focal point will be the championship 18-hole golf course. Features of the community include rolling hills, dense foliage, lakes, streams and wetlands, along with pedestrian trails, a canoe dock and a canoe trail system.

River Bend

The 1,200-acre town of River Bend lies along a winding inlet on the north shore of the Trent River, also about 5 miles east of New Bern. This location allows many of the homesites to have water frontage and private boat slips. The land was originally owned by the Odd Fellows, a fraternal group of black tenant farmers raising tobacco. During the recession of 1914, they were forced to sell their land to the "company store" for supplies and debts. During the first half of the century, a wealthy family owned the land and continued to have it farmed for tobacco. In 1965, real estate speculator J. Frank Efird recognized the area's potential as a retirement development for people moving south from the northeast. He organized The Efird Company to acquire and develop the old Odd Fellows farm.

True to Efird's vision, large numbers of retirees now live in River Bend, although a number of young families live there too. The community has its own country club to service its 18-hole golf course. The club includes a well-stocked pro shop, a small sandwich shop, an outdoor swimming pool and four lighted tennis courts.

River Bend was incorporated in 1980 in order to maintain roads and provide other services. The municipal building, finished in 1986,

has a 99-seat meeting hall and is adjacent to a small park with a children's play area, baseball field and small dock. The development consists mainly of single-family dwellings, all with attached or detached one- and two-car garages. In recent years, clusters of townhouses and duplexes have been added to the community. Houses here begin a little below $100,000 for a nonwaterfront location. Townhouse prices depend on the subdivision, but the range is between $60,000 and $150,000. In several of the subdivisions, homesites start at $22,000. River Bend is near New Bern Quinn Elementary and New Bern High School.

Fairfield Harbour

This expansive community is across the Neuse River off Highway 55 and 6 miles down Broad Creek Road. It is a 3,000-acre resort development featuring a large canal system that gives many homes water access at their back doors.

The development is unusual in that it is a combination of mostly single-family homes, with some condominiums, townhouses and timeshare condos added for good measure. In general, you can expect homes to start in the $80,000 range and continue on up into many thousands of dollars, depending upon proximity to the water.

Lots may be wooded, fronting one of two 18-hole golf courses, or on a canal where a private boat can be docked. Several hundred lots are available, with prices ranging from approximately $8,000 for an interior lot, $15,000 for a golf course lot, and from $44,000 to more than $100,000 for waterfront lots. Some waterfront sites have natural frontage, while others have bulkheads.

Condominiums and townhouses at Fairfield Harbour are arranged around small man-made lakes. Winding paths and roads connect all locations, and the combination of layout and landscaping gives a feeling of privacy, even with neighbors only a few feet away. The condos were built at different times in different styles, and they have varying levels of modern ameni-

---

INSIDERS' TIP

In 1894, New Bern adopted the armorial bearings and colors including the red and black bears of its namesake city, Bern, Switzerland. Since then New Bern's athletic teams have been "Bears" or "Bruins."

ties. Jacuzzis and Jenn-Aire ranges are common in most, as are balconies, decks and screened porches. Most have two or three bedrooms. Developers have shown careful respect for the trees that were on the lots first. It is not unusual to see decks cut to accommodate a tree. Prices start in the $60,000 range for these maintenance-free homes.

The Harbour's combination of year-round residents and vacationers requires that a wide variety of activities be readily available. Established community activities are too numerous to list but include such interests as men's and women's golf associations, a chorus, quilting, weaving, swimnastics and garden, drama, book, bridge, RV, tennis and yacht clubs. The community features two 18-hole golf courses, one indoor and two outdoor pools, nine tennis courts, four of which are lighted, a country club with a restaurant, two pro shops and two marinas on the premises. Boat rentals and cruises are available year round.

Brice's Creek

The Brice's Creek region lies southwest of New Bern and James City and south of the Trent River. A number of subdivisions exist in this area, including the Lake Clermont subdivision, Snug Harbor, Oakview, Deer Run and River Trace. Some of these are fully built up, while others are in the beginning stages. Many homes are on interior lots, but the more elegant residences face the waterfront and are set well away from the road on large, wooded lots. They tend to be brick or stucco in contemporary styles. Homes on the waterfront generally sell in the $200,000 to $400,000 range depending on their water frontage. Houses away from the creek sell in the $90,000 to $175,000 range. The Craven County Airport, which only serves small aircraft, is just east of Brice's Creek.

Green Springs

Huge, contemporary dwellings on large, wooded lots grace the western banks of the Neuse River on Greensprings Road just off Highway 70 E. between New Bern and Havelock. Waterfront homes start around $350,000, with lots in the price range of $125,000.

Farther east along Rivershore Drive, you can find older frame houses and large cottages tucked into the river bluffs. Prices here vary greatly because of age, size and lot space. Just across the street and facing the water, though not on it, is a small development of brand-new, one-story contemporary homes on half-acre lots. Prices of these homes start at about $85,000, but the value is increasing rapidly.

River Bluffs

This subdivision is off U.S. 70 E. just outside of New Bern. It has half-acre interior lots and wooded waterfront lots on the Neuse River. It also has an inland lake. Lot prices range from $19,000 to $150,000. This developing neighborhood is well-suited for retirees and young families with children.

Carolina Pines

About 11 miles east of New Bern off Highway 70 on Carolina Pines Boulevard, Carolina Pines is a large, well-established residential resort golf community along the Neuse River. It offers a blend of quiet countryside living combined with country club flair and neighborhood charm. Housing varies and includes modest patio homes, ranch styles and elegant two-story showplaces. A typical quarter to one-third acre wooded homesite can be purchased for about $20,000. New and resale houses, including lots, often sell in the $100,000 to $160,000 price range.

A challenging 18-hole golf course, a golf pro, a pro shop, tennis courts, a pool, a clubhouse with a restaurant and lounge and a patio overlooking freshwater lakes and the links are some of the available amenities. An added bonus is the adjacent Croatan National Forest, where residents can enjoy camping, hiking and horseback riding. Homes and home sites are marketed by the Carolina Pines Real Estate Company, located in the development.

West New Bern

This area is bounded by Neuse Boulevard on the northeast, Clarendon Boulevard on the southeast, Highway 70 on the southwest and Glenburnie Road on the northwest. Homes in this attractive neighborhood are large, brick ranch and two-story dwellings on generous lots. This part of New Bern is wooded, and there is plenty of undeveloped pine forest bordering many lots. Most of the homes have numerous large trees in the yards. Prices here begin at about $80,000 and go up to $100,000. These homes are very convenient to the West New Bern Recreation Center that offers tennis courts, baseball fields, a basketball court and a supervised game room with pool tables. Trent Park Elementary School and Fields Middle School are also here.

Colony Estates

Homes in this completed development are approximately 10 to 20 years old. They are one-story brick and wood houses, with many attractive, contemporary features. The lots are about a quarter-acre. Yards are nicely landscaped, and the neighborhood is very neat and clean. There is some variety in architectural design of homes here, although they tend to be three-bedroom ranch dwellings with attached garages.

Derby Park

Farther west, the newer Derby Park subdivision has one-story homes with three or four different floor plans. The builders here varied the exterior designs with combinations of wood, brick and vinyl siding in light pastels. Houses have nice-size backyards but are squeezed closely together. Most have at least three bedrooms, and all have attached garages. Homes in both developments range in price between $65,000 and $85,000.

Greenbrier

Greenbrier is a distinguished 700-acre subdivision right in the middle of New Bern. It is off S. Glenburnie Road and is a neighborhood well-suited for families with young children and for retirees. Lots range from an eighth of an acre to more than a full acre, and excellent architectural planning has effectively blended a variety of home styles into a delightful community. Many homes are of contemporary brick designs, and all utilities are underground. Lot prices begin in the low $40,000s and go up to

$100,000 for lakefront property. Homes on spacious lots begin at about $150,000. The entire development surrounds an 18-hole championship golf course managed by The Emerald Golf Club and designed by Rees Jones.

The clubhouse at The Emerald Golf Club at Greenbrier is often the chosen location for major local charity events. It contains an Olympic-size, Z-shaped pool and four lighted tennis courts. Golf club members can sharpen their skills on one of the finest new practice complexes in the state. (For more information about The Emerald Golf Club, see our chapter on New Bern Golf.)

From Greenbrier's front gate, you are within 2 minutes of major shopping, 5 minutes from the local schools and hospital, and adjacent to the campus of Craven Community College. The development phase at Greenbrier is nearly completed, and resales are handled by area real estate companies.

Real Estate Companies

Many good real estate agencies do business in New Bern, and we have listed in alphabetical order some of those that come recommended. If you have questions about area real estate companies, consult the New Bern Board of Realtors, 636-5364. For questions about building contractors, contact Jean Overby of the New Bern-Craven County Home Builders Association at 636-3707.

Carolina Pines
Real Estate Company Inc.
390 Carolina Pines Blvd. • 447-8000, (800) 654-5610

This two-agent company specializes in new construction, resales, lots and acreage throughout Havelock and New Bern, particularly in the Carolina Pines subdivision south of New Bern off Highway 70 E. The Carolina Pines subdivision contains 270 homes and has numerous lots for sale. The company is a member of the Multiple Listing Service.

Century 21 Action Associates
1916 S. Glenburnie Rd. • 633-0075, (800) 521-2780

This company is the oldest Century 21 franchise in New Bern and has more than 1,000

listings throughout the area. In addition to working with sellers, the company also offers a buyer's service, meaning it negotiates price and terms in the best interest of the buyer. Its agents pride themselves on providing good follow-up and personal care for their clients. The firm also offers property management and rental services.

Century 21 Zaytoun-Raines
1307 S. Glenburnie Rd. • 633-3069, (800) 548-3122
302 Tryon Palace Dr. • 636-1184, (800) 548-3122

George Zaytoun began building homes in 1964, and Marvin Raines began a real estate career in 1971. In 1986, they combined their expertise to create what has become one of the area's most successful real estate companies. The firm has been awarded Century 21's most distinguished award, the Centurion Award, presented to only eight of Century 21's 176 offices throughout North and South Carolina. It's impossible to drive through New Bern and not see Zaytoun-Raines "For Sale" or "For Rent" signs. The services of about 20 agents are available to handle residential, commercial and investment properties as well as acreage and property management services.

Coastal Homes Real Estate
**3300 Hwy. 70 E. P.O. Box 628 • Weekdays 637-4081, (800) 533-5751;
Weekends 633-3843, (800) 663-3843**

Coastal Homes does it all. It specializes in new-home construction and sales of existing homes and building lots throughout the New Bern area, including Craven, Jones and Pamlico counties. Coastal also sells and leases businesses and commercial properties. Owner-broker Jeff Vaughn is both a North Carolina-licensed home inspector and a builder. Joan LoCascio, broker-manager, is an experienced agent who offers "none better" service as a buyer's agent. All of Coastal Homes' agents and staff strive to serve the community with integrity and dedication.

Coldwell Banker
Willis-Smith Company
115 Middle St. • 638-3500, (800) 334-0792

With more than 20 agents and a good reputation, this reliable firm's offices are downtown near the New Bern waterfront. The company operates as a seller's and buyer's agency, offering a full range of services that includes residential brokerage and development and referrals to and from its national network. Its well-trained and experienced agents are knowledgeable about available housing in all of New Bern's long-established neighborhoods and about homes on the market in many of the area's new developments and subdivisions. Coldwell Banker also handles some rental properties in the New Bern area.

D. Seiple Land Marketing Inc.
119 Randomwood La., River Bend
• 633-4520

Farms, acreage, building lots and commercial properties are the specialties of this company. Clients in pursuit of business or industry locations often rely on Dick Seiple to provide currently marketed property appropriate to their purposes.

Eastern Shore Realty Inc.
3317-E Hwy. 70 E. • 636-3050

Eastern Shore Realty is the agent for the Eastern Shore townhouses in Bridgeton, which include both a garage and a boat slip for each condominium. The firm also can help you find acreage or homes in other areas of the county. Call Sandra Haddock with your residential or commercial real estate needs.

Fairfield Harbour Realty
750 Broad Creek Rd. • 638-8011,
(800) 317-3303

Fairfield Harbour Realty operates in the Fairfield Harbour planned community. Its staff handles the sales of building lots, single-family homes, condominiums and timeshare condominiums. They also offer property management services.

Heritage Real Estate
309 Metcalf St. • 638-4663, (800) 728-4670

Heritage Real Estate is a growing and diversified agent-owned firm with offices in the historic district, just around the corner from Tryon Palace. The agency handles residential and commercial sales and rentals, and offers property management services. Its agents specialize in relocation and work extensively with retirees. Call ahead or stop by for an informative relocation packet, a brief orientation tour or an opportunity to have your questions answered. Heritage Real Estate's experienced agents are an excellent source of local knowledge about neighborhoods and homes throughout the New Bern area.

Kelso-Wheeler & Associates Inc. Better Homes and Gardens
1404 Neuse Blvd. • 633-3043, (800) 471-6899
48 Shoreline Dr., River Bend • 633-2434, (800) 846-0740

In business since 1962, the company's staff of more than 20 handles this nationally connected firm. It is a full-service real estate and insurance agency, and New Bern natives Chris Kelso and Gray Wheeler have an in-depth knowledge of homes and properties available throughout the area. The company handles both residential and commercial sales and has an in-house appraiser and builder.

Lupton Associates Inc.
2002 S. Glenburnie Rd. • 637-6120, (800) 833-5671

Lupton Associates Inc. is a full-service real estate agency and a well-known construction company that handles properties throughout New Bern, Craven County and surrounding areas. It is a family-run business that has been doing well for more than 10 years. One of its specialties is the handling of lots in Deerfield near River Bend.

Nancy Hollows Real Estate
624 Hancock St. • 636-3177

A one-woman dynamo, Nancy Hollows specializes in knowing everything there is to know about New Bern's historic homes. She has a good understanding of ordinances that govern historic district properties; however, she handles sales of all types of property throughout New Bern. Her forte is one-of-a-kind purchases, and she enjoys helping customers who are looking for unique waterfront locations. In addition, she has assisted buyers in acquiring bed and breakfast inns and marinas. Her office is in a historic building that also houses her antiques shop, The Antique Depot.

Neuse Realty
601 Broad Creek Rd. • 633-4888, (800) 343-0186

Serving New Bern since 1977, this second-generation, family-owned firm focuses on relocation and total service, from the initial information-gathering process through site purchase, construction planning or resale services. Upscale and waterfront locations and Fairfield Harbor properties are their specialties. The firm is nationally affiliated with RELO, the largest intercity relocation service and is a member of the New Bern and Havelock Board of Realtors, the Employee Relocation Council and the Craven County Committee of 100. Neuse handles a broad selection of rental properties.

New Beginnings Realty Inc.
50 Shoreline Drive • 636-5858, (800) 331-8982

In business for 11 years, this company specializes in waterfront and golf areas for newcomers looking for retirement and relocation sites. It handles new residential homes, lots and resale of established homes. The firm has three agents who are happy to provide no pressure, relaxed tours of available homesites in the area. A free cassette tape that describes New Bern properties is available to those interested in relocating.

New Bern Real Estate Inc.
1315 S. Glenburnie Rd. • 636-2200, (800) 636-2992

This independently owned-and-operated full-service agency opened in 1985 and specializes in locating homes for retirees and local residents. Free brochures and newcomer packages are available to inquiring home seekers. Six knowledgeable and experienced agents conduct between two and five comprehensive home-finding tours per week, covering 48 miles in about 3½ hours. Clients

are provided with a free map and video tape, and the tour includes a complimentary lunch.

Resort Homes of the Carolinas Inc.
530 Hwy. 55 E. • 637-8080, (800) 892-8901

Resort Homes of the Carolinas is a full-service real estate company with a construction division as part of its operation. It handles sales of building lots, homes, condominiums, timeshare properties and manages rental properties. The company specializes in Fairfield Harbour resales and also offers new homes in River Bend and Lakemere. A home model is erected in Fairfield Harbour on Pelican Drive.

Tryon Realty
233 Middle St. • 637-3115

In business for more than 32 years, Tryon is a small company that specializes in building and development. It is the main developer of Olde Towne subdivision on the Trent River. Contact Tryon Realty with your residential and commercial real estate needs or for property management information.

Tyson and Hooks Realty
2402 Clarendon Blvd. • 633-5766, (800) 284-6844

This firm has been in business since 1972. It offers general real estate services including commercial and residential lots and acreage, along with property management services and rental properties.

Weyerhaeuser
Real Estate Company
101 Middle St. • 633-6100, (800) 622-6297

Weyerhaeuser Real Estate Company is a subsidiary of Weyerhaeuser Company, the international wood and pulp giant. It offers an extensive inventory of homesites in New Bern and elsewhere in eastern North Carolina. Taberna is a Weyerhaeuser community; see the description in our Neighborhoods section above.

In New Bern, the company established Greenbrier community development, a 700-acre, upscale residential neighborhood surrounding the championship golf course, The

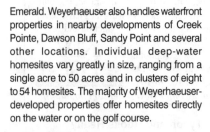
Emerald. Weyerhaeuser also handles waterfront properties in nearby developments of Creek Pointe, Dawson Bluff, Sandy Point and several other locations. Individual deep-water homesites vary greatly in size, ranging from a single acre to 50 acres and in clusters of eight to 54 homesites. The majority of Weyerhaeuser-developed properties offer homesites directly on the water or on the golf course.

Utility Services

The **City of New Bern** provides water service to customers living within the city limits. The city Public Works Department is at 300 Pollock Street, 636-4025. **First Craven Sanitary District**, 633-6500, and **Craven County Water and Sewer**, 636-6615, provide water and sewer services for those residents and business customers living outside the New Bern city limits.

For electricity **Carolina Power & Light,** 1433 S. Glenburnie Road, 633-5688, serves residential and business customers in the areas surrounding New Bern. The City of New Bern, 249 Craven Street, 636-4000, provides electrical service to customers living within the city limits of New Bern and in Trent Woods.

Sprint serves the entire area for telephone service. Dial their toll-free number, 633-9011.

Education and Child Care

New Bern residents have several excellent education opportunities. Adults have access to a state-supported university, college-level classes and a first-rate community college. Parents have the option of sending their children to the Craven County public schools or one of the many private schools in New Bern. There are also several trustworthy child-care options available for children who are too young for school.

Colleges and Universities

Those interested in furthering their education may choose from two-year associate's degrees, bachelor's degrees in partnership with East Carolina University, accelerated four-year degree programs and continuing education classes.

Craven Community College
800 College Ct., New Bern • 638-4131

Craven Community College offers two-year degrees and adult continuing education. Two-year associate's degree programs in the arts and sciences and more than 30 technical and vocational programs are available. The college offers basic adult education programs, two-year technical and transfer programs, one-year vocational programs and extension programs in occupational, practical and vocational courses of study. Craven Community College is part of North Carolina's 59-campus community college system.

Carteret/Craven Community College Partnership Degree Program
115 Banks St., Morehead City
• 726-7684, (800) 398-9275

This program is designed for those who have earned college credits and seek to complete a four-year bachelor's degree. It is conducted in partnership with East Carolina University. Full details are given in our Crystal Coast chapter on Higher Education and Research.

East Carolina University
Office of Undergraduate Admissions,
Greenville 27858 • 328-6640

A little more than an hour's drive from New Bern, East Carolina University in Greenville is a state-supported university that offers a wide range of study areas for bachelor's, master's and doctoral degrees. The university has an enrollment of about 17,000 students. Two popular curriculum areas are education and health sciences. Many working adult students pursue degrees by commuting to the Greenville campus. Craven Medical Center in New Bern is a clinical site for students enrolled in the ECU School of Nursing.

Mount Olive College
New Bern Center
2131 S. Glenburnie Rd., Ste. 6
• 633-4464, (800) 868-8479

"Finish what you started" is the motto of Mount Olive's accelerated degree completion program. Responding to the increasing demand to help adults complete a 4-year degree, in 1993 Mount Olive opened its New Bern campus with that goal in mind. The college offers two bachelor of science degrees — Business Administration and Criminal Justice — for working adults who have earned 60 college credits. Students benefit from a special format that permits them to earn a degree in about 55 weeks, while continuing to work full time. Class modules begin throughout the year and meet once a week for a 4-hour session

either in the evenings or on Saturday mornings. Currently, Mount Olive's New Bern campus is serving more than 250 students who are in various stages of program completion.

Schools

Public

Craven County Schools

The **Craven County School System**, 300 Trent Road, New Bern, 514-6300, serves more than 14,600 city and county students. The schools are fully accredited by the Southern Association of Colleges and Schools and the N.C. Department of Public Instruction. The system employs about 1,050 teaching professionals and about 675 support personnel. These employees staff the county's 14 elementary schools (kindergarten through 5th), four middle schools (6th through 8th) and three high schools. The system's average teacher-student ratio is 1 to 26.

The school system offers a comprehensive curriculum based on the North Carolina Standard Course of Study. In addition to the traditional academic courses, the education program includes music, foreign languages, art, dance, theater, athletics, computer classes and advanced placement courses.

The high schools focus on positive school climate and the identification and prevention of problems that may lead to an unsuccessful high school career. All high schools are on block scheduling, which allows students to take four courses each semester in 90-minute class periods versus the traditional 55-minute classes. Instead of the maximum six courses per year, students are able to take as many as eight courses — four per semester. Among several advantages, block scheduling gives students the flexibility of enrolling in more electives without giving up required academic classes.

To prepare students for the workplace, Craven County Schools has implemented a developmental program that helps students entering high school choose and focus on a career path. Students may select from four career pathways: engineering, industrial, and manufacturing technology; business and marketing; health and human services; and liberal and fine arts. A student's choice of career pathway is aided by the development of a four-year educational plan and supplemented by career guidance that helps her or him make a smooth transition into the work force, or an associate or bachelor's degree program.

Middle schools emphasize educational experiences that bridge learning between elementary school and high school. All four middle schools operate on a team concept. Two to five teachers collaborate to develop plans and strategies to deal with the instructional, social and emotional needs and interests of students. Along with the core curriculum, students are exposed to critical thinking and problem solving, health and fitness, cooperative learning, and exploratory courses such as foreign languages, vocational education and visual arts.

Elementary education in Craven County encourages kids to meet academic objectives through developmentally appropriate activities. Hands-on experiences and problem-solving strategies are designed to harmonize with the natural characteristics of children's developmental stages. Besides the core curriculum of communication skills, science, math and social studies, students and teachers are involved in enrichment programs such as art, physical education, computers, music and drama.

The Craven County School System offers many support services: comprehensive testing, programs for exceptional and academically gifted students, dropout prevention and drug education programs, library/media skills programs and the services of school psychologists, social workers and nurses. In addition, numerous services are available for students with visual, hearing, speech, orthopedic and other health impairments as well as for the mentally handicapped, learning disabled and homebound. Contact Barbara Richardson, Director of Exceptional Children's' Programs, 514-6355, for more information.

The Craven County School System has an excellent free information portfolio that includes a countywide activities calendar, descriptions of and directions to all 21 schools, a discussion of the system's educational curriculums, and a central services directory with the names and phone numbers of all support staff. The school system encourages requests for information; write or call the Craven County Board of Education, Marie Lansche, Director of Community Schools, 3600 Trent Road, New Bern 28562; 514-6300.

Private Schools

New Bern offers a number of private schools, and another is about 40 miles west in Kinston. Additionally, the Yellow Pages section of the phone book lists a number of day camps and day schools for young children.

Ruth's Chapel Free Will Baptist Church School
2709 Oaks Rd. • 638-1297, 638-8161

This school serves about 250 students in kindergarten through 12th grade and an additional 35 students in day care and before- and after-school programs. A structured program is also offered to 3 and 4 year olds.

St. Paul's Education Center
3007 Country Club Rd. • 633-0100

St. Paul's has about 300 students from preschool through 8th grade. The school provides after-school care for its students and is affiliated with St. Paul's Catholic Church.

Arendell Parrott Academy
1901 Dobbs Farm Rd., Kinston • 522-4222

Arendell Parrott offers nonsectarian instruction for students in prekindergarten through 12th grade and has a total enrollment of 600 students. The school offers transportation to out-of-town students. About 30 percent of the students come from New Bern.

Child Care

As is the case across the nation, the need for quality day care in New Bern continues to grow.

INSIDERS' TIP

Contact the New Bern-Craven County Public Library, 638-7800, for a list of programs especially for kids.

We have listed here, in alphabetical order, some of the day-care facilities in and around New Bern. Craven County and the State of North Carolina regulate day-care homes and day-care centers through the issuance of registrations and licenses. Regulations call for all such facilities to meet health and safety standards. In the case of nonsectarian child-care institutions, standards for children's learning and play programs must be met. For a complete list of regulated day-care homes and licensed day-care centers, call Pinkie Moore, Day Care Coordinator, Craven County Department of Social Services, 636-4900.

All About Children Day Care & Preschool Inc.
2610 Neuse Blvd. • 633-2505

This day care accepts children from 6 weeks to 12 years old and offers before- and after-school care. Transportation to and from school is also provided.

Cobb's Child Care Center
603 Gaston Blvd. • 638-8175

Cobb's takes care of children from 6 weeks to 12 years old. The facility separates children into age groups and has its own kindergarten classes. Before- and after-school care and transportation to and from local schools are also available.

Colony Day Care and Child Care Center
1108 Brunswick Ave. • 633-2787

Colony cares for children from ages 1 year to 12 years and has a van service to and from local schools. Before- and after-school care is also available.

Kid's Korner
403 Ninth St. • 638-2957
3705 Old Cherry Point Rd. • 636-3791

Kid's Korner accepts children from 6 weeks to 12 years. These two facilities offer before- and after-school care. The Ninth Street Kid's Korner also provides transportation to and from area schools.

Horizon's Academy Day School
704 Newman Rd. • 633-1050

This nonsectarian school has been operating for 10 years, and currently has an enroll-

ment of 140 children. It accepts 3-year olds for the prekindergarten program and teaches grades 1 through 4. Horizon's Academy has before- and after-school care for its students and for kids enrolled in public schools.

Retirement

New Bern's popularity as a delightful retirement location is evident in its relocation statistics. Nearly 2,000 retired couples move to New Bern each year, an average of about six per day. New Bern's combination of mild climate, relatively low-cost living, beautiful surroundings and friendly people seems too good to pass up. Activities such as fishing, golfing, sailing, hiking and boating are possible within a stone's throw of river city living. The colonial setting of the city itself is inviting, and a wide range of social, cultural and recreational activities enhances the attractiveness of living in New Bern.

New residents find the city's excellent regional hospital, doctors' offices, shopping centers, golfing and sports facilities, quality restaurants and numerous religious denominations important factors in making a decision about changing their location. Those who decide to take the plunge and move to New Bern are seldom disappointed.

As more retirees settle in the area, a growing number of services and programs are being developed and tailored to meet their needs and interests. Agencies and public service organizations are expanding their offerings, and retirement communities are being designed to create stress-free environments. Housing options vary according to the needs of individuals, and agencies offer a variety of services aimed at assisting new and retired residents.

Agencies and Services

A number of agencies and organizations in New Bern are equipped to deal with the needs or problems that may confront older people.

United Senior Services Inc.
811 George St. • 638-3800

Handling most of the city's services geared toward senior citizens, this agency offers a variety of programs and activities and serves a daily meal at its Senior Citizens Center on George Street. United Senior Services also operates centers in the communities of Havelock, Harlowe, Vanceboro, Dover and Trenton. Popular center pastimes include quilting, crafts, exercise programs, self-help and supportive services, health screenings and various enrichment classes in cooperation with Craven Community College. The center operates several programs: the Senior Companion Program through which seniors help seniors; the Silver Crime Advocacy Program for persons older than 60 who are victims of crime; the Silver Friends, an inter-generational program involving youths and seniors; the Elder Employment Program, which provides employment for eligible persons older than 60; the Hastings Security Program, an in-home security service for seniors and the disabled; the Elder Care Program, which meets special needs of seniors; the N.C. Tar Heel Discount Program, which provides shopping discounts at cooperating merchants; and the city's Meals on Wheels program.

United Senior Services also operates the Craven County Information Line, 636-6614, a service that covers topics and requests of interest to seniors and the public at large, including phone numbers and referrals. The service conducts annual events such as Senior Awareness Day, Founder's Day, Volunteer Recognition Day and activities and celebrations on all major holidays. Tours, picnics, a grandparents' celebration, holiday dinners and birthday parties are also part of the regular activity schedule.

Craven County Department of Social Services
2818 Neuse Blvd. • 636-4900

The Department of Social Services offers information and assistance to seniors concerning health, Medicare and rest-home and nursing-home facilities. The department operates an in-home aide program, a transportation program and an Adult Home Specialist Service. It also refers clients to other agencies and organizations for help with special situations.

Social Security Office
2822 Neuse Blvd. • 637-1703

Administering the Social Security and Supplemental Security programs, this office is open weekdays to provide information concerning Social Security guidelines and requirements and to answer other consumer questions. Clients are seen by appointment, and for those in Jacksonville or Morehead City, appointments can be made by calling (800) 772-1213.

Home Health Hospice Services
Craven County Health Dept., 2818 Neuse Blvd. • 636-4930

Serving homebound clients and those authorized for care by physicians, this organization provides in-home services, nursing, home health aid, nutritional care and physical, occupational and speech therapy. It also offers hospice care for the terminally ill and their families.

Area Agency on Aging (AAA)
Neuse River Council of Governments, O'Marks Sq., 233 Middle St. • 638-3185

The state of North Carolina designated this agency to address the concerns and needs of the elder segment of the local population (estimated at 15 percent) as mandated through the Older Americans Act. The AAA is integrally tied to local area governments whose representatives make up the regional council policy board. The agency is responsible for direct contracting with local providers for priority services such as transportation, nutrition, in-home care, case management, housing, legal and other services. It also provides technical assistance involving training, grant preparation, community coordination efforts, needs assessments and resource inventories. It carries out regional ombudsman assistance to county-appointed nursing home and domiciliary home community advisory committees. The agency oversees development and implementation of aging programs, assists in the development of multipurpose senior centers and designates community focal point facilities for delivering services to the older population.

Home Care Services
1918 Clarendon Blvd. • 633-8182

A division of Craven Regional Medical Center, the facility offers care for clients who have been authorized for services by their physicians. Home Care can provide skilled nurses, physical and speech therapy and home health aides. The organization is certified for Medicare.

Gold Care
Craven Regional Medical Ctr. • 633-8902

This program, developed by Craven Regional Medical Center, is for adults 55 and older. Membership offers monthly healthcare seminars, a physician referral service, consultation to arrange home healthcare services, support groups, a Medicare hotline to assist with insurance and benefit matters, a quarterly newsletter and other activities. Annual membership is $15 for a couple or $10 for singles.

Professional Nursing Service
1425 S. Glenburnie Rd. • 636-2388

This service has licensed LPNs and RNs to assist with healthcare. It can provide sitter companions, certified nursing assistance, private duty nurses and supplementary staffing.

Housing Options and Facilities

Berne Village Retirement Community
2701 Amhurst Blvd. • 633-1779, (800) 634-7318

This 15-acre retirement and assisted living complex is near U.S. 70 off Glenburnie Road. The village is a series of single-story apartment and service buildings set in a landscaped park environment.

The central building houses 60 rest-home beds and is also the site of the community dining room, recreation facilities, library, barber and beauty shops. Facilities are available for memory impaired patients, respite care and adult day-care services. In addition, the village has one- and two-bedroom, unfurnished apartments for independent living. Three financial arrangements are available: a rental plan, a year's lease or a buy-in deposit. All three arrangements cover utilities, weekly cleaning, insurance, maintenance, transportation, 24-hour security, one meal a day in the dining room and a personal emergency alert system in each bedroom and bathroom. Apartment residents are required to pay for their own cable TV and telephone services.

Christian Care Center Retirement Home
104 Efird Blvd. • 633-3455

This facility is just off U.S. 17 S. at the entrance to River Bend. Each of the facility's one- and two-bedroom apartments has a stove, refrigerator and hookups for washers and dryers. Independent living apartments are available, and a rest home is on site. A residents' council works with staff to plan activities, and the center staff maintains the apartments and grounds. One month's rent plus a month's rent in advance is required for admission. Residents are responsible for their own electricity and phone charges, but water, sewer and garbage fees are included in the rent.

Nursing and Rest Homes

Twin Rivers Nursing Center
1303 Health Dr. • 633-8000

Owned and operated by Craven Regional Medical Center, this new facility offers the advantage of being next door to the hospital should an emergency arise. The nursing center offers recuperative therapies and long-term care.

Britthaven of New Bern Nursing Home
2600 Old Cherry Point Rd. • 637-4730

Britthaven is equipped with rest-home and nursing-home beds. Additional nursing-home beds have been added to a recently completed skilled Medicare unit. A special feature of the facility is its specially designed wing that accommodates Alzheimer's patients. The new wing has a well-equipped activities room and dining room as well as two enclosed patios and a large hallway to allow patients to walk about without the dangers of becoming lost or injuring themselves. Requirements for persons entering the Alzheimer's program are that they be at least partially ambulatory, able to control their bladders and bowels and able to feed themselves.

Guardian Care of New Bern
836 Hospital Dr. • 638-6001

This nursing bed facility is adjacent to Craven Regional Medical Center. Permanent staff includes a full-time dietician, social worker and activities director. Physical, speech and occupational therapies are available. Activity programs for residents include daily scheduled events, holiday parties and seasonal entertainment. Community groups often visit to provide entertainment and social interaction with residents.

Charles McDaniel Rest Home
2915 Brunswick Ave. • 638-4680

With both private and semiprivate rooms, the facility provides basic rest home or custodial care. They also provide transportation to the doctor and community events. A full-time activities director is on staff.

Healthcare

The availability of quality healthcare is a primary consideration for newcomers and residents of any area, and New Bern is particularly fortunate to have a wide range of topnotch professional services. The quality of life and the presence of an excellent medical center have attracted many physicians and specialized health professionals to the area.

With the continuous relocation of retirees to the New Bern area, additional healthcare services, such as home care professionals, cardiac rehabilitation services and geriatric care, are expanding in New Bern. These services are not often available in a town of similar size. The Craven Regional Medical Center has an open-heart surgery unit that makes it the nearest hospital in North Carolina's central coastal region to offer the procedure. In addition, the medical center offers state-of-the-art diagnostic equipment and services at its New Bern Diagnostic Center, same-day surgery at New Bern Outpatient Surgery Center, a comprehensive medical rehabilitation center and a mental health unit.

Craven Regional Medical Center
2000 Neuse Blvd. • 633-8111

Since it opened in 1962, Craven Regional Medical Center has worked to keep up to date with equipment and services. Community leaders boast that the center is widely recognized as a leading medical facility serving eastern North Carolina and was the first in this part of the state to perform radiation therapy. The center is acutely attuned to quality medical care and implements a total quality management program.

The 314-bed facility offers a comprehensive range of services not often found outside larger urban areas. At least partly because of that, it has been named a primary health provider for a number of area counties and, most recently, for Defense Department beneficiaries in eastern North Carolina. An outstanding medical staff of more than 120 physicians, a dedicated professional and support staff of more than 1,100 and a progressive administration and board strive to combine the best of medical care with empathy for patients.

All the major specialties are represented by the medical center's physicians and staff. Cardiac care is a focal point, with the area's most advanced services for diagnosing and treating heart disease including interventional cardiology and cardiac surgery. It was the first eastern North Carolina hospital to offer cardiac rehabilitation on an outpatient basis. Its modern cardiac surgery suite includes surgical, recovery and intensive care rooms. Likewise, the medical center's oncology services lead the area in chemotherapy and radiation therapy on an inpatient or outpatient basis including support services.

INSIDERS' TIP

The nine-county Area Agency on Aging (AAA) represents the fastest-growing segment of our population, the 15 percent older than age 60. Contact the agency about its ombudsman programs for the elderly, 638-3185.

The medical center's outpatient services include the New Bern Diagnostic Center, offering state-of-the-art diagnostic imaging equipment, mammography, ultrasound, nuclear medicine, X-ray and EKGs in a comfortable private setting. You can arrange same-day surgery at the New Bern Outpatient Surgery Center, which includes procedures for cataracts, hernias and an ever-expanding list of surgical treatments. The Women's Center offers comprehensive gynecological care including outpatient procedures and laser surgical techniques, and the Family Birth Place stresses family involvement in childbirth.

Specialty units include Crossroads, a 24-bed facility specializing in group-based care of adult mental-health disorders, and the Coastal Rehabilitation Center, a 20-bed unit designed to help victims of stroke, orthopedic and neurological disorders return to independent living and health as soon as possible.

Extended patient support services of Craven Regional Medical Center include home care and referral services, assuring that medical needs are met and services are provided.

Craven County Health Department
2818 Neuse Blvd. • 636-4920

Housed with other county services including the Department of Social Services in the Human Services Complex on Neuse Boulevard, the health department provides assistance and referrals in family planning, maternity care, child inoculation, adult and child healthcare, dental care, home health and health education.

Neuse Center for Mental Health
800 Cardinal Rd. • 636-1510

Neuse Center for Mental Health, Mental Retardation and Substance Abuse is a public outpatient facility that operates under state and county guidelines. It provides services in developmental disabilities, mental retardation and

substance abuse including court and family services. Neuse Center provides counseling, emergency and support services and accepts walk-in patients, doctor and emergency room referrals. Group homes operated by Neuse Center and rehabilitative enterprises are in Craven, Carteret and Jones counties. Neuse Center is headquartered in New Bern.

Home Healthcare

Many patient services provided by hospitals during long-term recoveries and illnesses are available at home with the assistance of monitoring and therapies of home health services. Home healthcare is an alternative to institutional or hospital care that fosters patient independence and family care. All services offer nursing, rehabilitation therapies, medical social work, in-home aides, medical equipment and supplies.

Craven Regional Medical Center Home Care Services
Craven Regional Medical Center, 1918 Clarendon Blvd. • 633-8182, 633-8817

Craven Regional Medical Center can provide continued recovery services at home for departing hospital patients. Professional nursing care is offered 24 hours a day, seven days a week. Other services provided include physical, speech and nutritional therapies.

Home Health-Hospice Services of Craven County Health Dept.
2818 Neuse Blvd. • 636-4920, 636-4930

The county health department provides home health and hospice services including 24-hour nursing care, physical, occupational, nutritional and speech therapies.

Home Technology Healthcare
US Hwy. 17 S., Pollocksville • 224-1012, (800) 559-4800

Until recently known as Tarheel Home

Health Care, Home Technology Healthcare is a private business that offers a full range of healthcare services for recoveries and care at home. Complete nursing services are offered in all infusion drug therapies and rehabilitation therapies plus 24-hour private duty and HIV/Aids case management.

Private Practices

Eastern Carolina Internal Medicine Urgent Medical Care
South Market Sq., Stes. 9 and 10, Glenburnie Ave. and Trent Rd. • 636-1001

This urgent-care center provides treatment for minor emergencies and family medical needs after usual office hours. Hours of operation are from noon until 8 PM Monday through Saturday and 1 until 5 PM Sunday. No appointment is necessary. General practice and internal medicine physicians of the Eastern Carolina Internal Medicine group staff this urgent care facility and others located in Havelock and Pollocksville.

Eastern Carolina Internal Medicine
New Bern Medical Arts Ctr., 1917 Trent Blvd. • 638-4023, (800) 676-8221

Eastern Carolina Internal Medicine is a large group practice with offices also in Havelock and Pollocksville. A team of four physicians specializing in general and sub-specialty internal medicine provides care for infectious diseases, cardiology disorders, lung diseases, arthritis, digestive disorders, cancer diagnosis and treatment, and hematology. The practice also specializes in aviation medicine. Its radiology department includes diagnosis and treatments involving ultrasound, CT and nuclear medicine.

New Bern Internal Medicine and Cardiology
702 Newman Rd. • 633-5333

Eight physicians with internal medicine specialties provide a complete range of diagnostic and therapeutic medical care for nonsurgical adult health problems involving cardiac and pulmonary medicine, respiratory allergies, digestive disorders and cancer diagnosis and treatment. All physicians are certified by the American Board of Internal Medicine. Patients are seen by appointment, and office hours are 8:30 AM to 5 PM, Monday through Friday.

New Bern Surgical Associates
701 Newman Rd. • 633-2081, (800) 682-0276 ext. 8419

The New Bern Surgical Associates practice involves five physicians specializing in laparoscopic procedures, general, vascular and pediatric surgery. Patients are seen by referral and by appointment during office hours — 9 AM to 5 PM Monday through Friday. Emergency calls are received at 633-3557 at all other times.

Coastal Eye Clinic
802 McCarthy Blvd. • 633-4183, (800) 252-6763

The Coastal Eye Clinic provides comprehensive medical, surgical and neuro-opthalmology services for patients with vision disorders. Five physicians and surgeons specialize in cataract surgery with lens implants, laser surgical techniques, glaucoma surgery and treatment, vitreous, retina and macular diseases, cosmetic surgery, pediatric ophthalmology and general eye examinations. Optical services allow for on-site selection of eyeglasses and contact lenses. The Coastal Eye Clinic also has offices in Morehead City.

Alternative Healthcare

The encouragement to wellness is approached by individual practitioners and

---

INSIDERS' TIP

With just one volunteered hour per month, each Meals On Wheels volunteer helps 10 people to maintain their independence at home.

groups that have assembled to spiritually support each other in coping with recurrent disease. Naturopathic wellness is also a practicing philosophical approach to health and wellness available in New Bern.

Naturopathic Wellness Center and Herbal Apothecary
2303 Clarendon Blvd. • 636-3008

Nurturing the healing forces natural to human beings is a philosophy as old as civilization. Recognizing the interconnection of mind and body, naturopathic wellness involves identifying underlying causes of disease in an individual and assistance toward disease prevention and wellness. Herbal therapies are used to enhance innate healing forces. Naturopathic practitioner and herbalist David Janson also makes recommendations concerning diet and nutrition, psychological orientations, lifestyle modifications and exercise to evoke the strength of natural healing forces. The Naturopathic Wellness Center is a division of Toktela Institute in New Bern.

Emergency and Important Numbers

For any emergency (police, sheriff, fire and rescue service) dial **911** regardless of your location.

Crisis Line, 638-5995
Craven County Alanon, 633-4441
Alcoholics Anonymous, 633-3716
Craven-Pamlico Animal Services Center, 673-4606
Craven-Pamlico American Red Cross, 637-3405
Craven County Health Department, 636-4920
Craven County Department of Social Services, 636-4900
Craven Regional Medical Center, 633-8111
Drug and Alcohol Dependency Problem Hotline, 637-7000

Photo: Scott Taylor

This rare sighting of a pointy headed, pencil-necked,
slim shank has local ornithologists atwitter.

Volunteer Opportunities

Many of New Bern's public service agencies and nonprofit organizations rely heavily on the services and talents of volunteers. Some simply could not operate without reliable volunteer assistance. New Bern has a number of spare-time opportunities, and new ones are popping up all the time. We've included several here, and you will find that volunteering with one organization often leads to developing interests in others. All organizations and agencies listed provide volunteer training.

New Bern Historical Society
510 Pollock St. • 638-8558

The historical society relies on volunteers for most of its vital functions. Volunteers make up the society's membership, education, marketing and program committees, serve as tour guides, staff the gift shop, or- ganize and carry out fund-raisers, put together the *Historical Society Journal* and newsletter, help maintain historical buildings and grounds, and coordinate special projects. Volunteers are in great demand during the city's Spring Homes and Gardens Tour and the New Bern at Night Ghost Walk. If you enjoy history and its preservation, you will find a niche here.

New Bern Preservation Foundation
510 Pollock St. • 633-6448

Like the historical society, the preservation foundation counts on volunteers and uses their skills to operate its organization. Most volunteers are young retirees, and the foundation could not function without them. Docents serve as hosts or hostesses for home tours, help in the office, work to produce the foundation's newsletter, help with the foundation's annual Antique Show and Sale in February, cater meals and assist with property cleanup and maintenance of historical buildings and grounds. They are also called upon to do archival work and help with special events.

Tryon Palace
610 Pollock St. • 514-4900

The paid staff manages most of the year-round palace duties; however, during the Christmas season, when thousands of visitors and residents descend on the Colonial capital for day and candlelight tours, volunteer forces are called into action. Decking the palace halls with natural, handmade decorations requires the help of many, as does the making of confections and beverages in the palace kitchen. It is a very festive time, and volunteers seem to thoroughly enjoy their work.

Craven County Arts Council and Gallery
317 Middle St. • 638-2577

Like any county-based arts organization, the Craven County Arts Council relies on volunteers to keep its wheels moving. Council volunteers serve as hosts in the main gallery, help in the office, assist with mass mailings, conduct programs such as the popular Jazz Sunday Showcase in February and Arts in the Schools, work on a variety of committees and assist with city-wide art projects, programs and fund-raising events throughout the year. If you have an affinity for art and organization, this is your kind of place.

Craven County Convention & Visitors Bureau
314 Tryon Palace Dr. • 637-9400

This is a wonderful place to contribute some time and help acquaint visitors with the places they should see in New Bern. Volunteers are warm, enthusiastic and truly seem to love sharing the city of New Bern. It's also a great place to learn about New Bern if you are newly relocated and have volunteer time to offer.

American National Red Cross
1916 S. Glenburnie Rd. • 637-3405

This well-known organization uses volunteers to assist with bloodmobile clinics, serve as instructors for first aid and CPR, aid in disaster situations and help out in the office. When necessary, the Red Cross provides training for specific volunteer positions.

Craven Regional Medical Center
2000 Neuse Blvd. • 633-8111

Officials here will tell you that the hospital would not run as well or as smoothly without its faithful volunteers. The center uses its 470-strong volunteer corps for everything from delivering mail to running the gift shop and snack bar. There is a junior volunteer group especially for 14- to 18-year-olds and a volunteer chaplaincy program for ordained ministers. Volunteers also help in the library, newborn nursery, emergency department and critical care waiting area. They operate the book cart and humor cart in the hospital, work in the office, assist in the nursing center and help with physical therapy and lifeline programs. The Gray Ladies and Gray Lads are perhaps the most active group, assisting with a variety of hospital-related duties. There's also an auxiliary group that coordinates activities in 25 different areas. If you have time and energy to spare, the center can put them to good use.

Craven County School System
3600 Trent Rd. • 514-6300

The school system welcomes volunteers to aid teachers and students in a variety of ways. Perhaps most in demand is assistance for children having problems in particular subjects, such as reading, English or math. Volunteers are also needed on field trips and in the library. Fund-raising is always going on, and the parent-teacher organization is

INSIDERS' TIP

Swiss Bear Downtown Revitalization Corporation always needs volunteer assistance with its fund-raising projects, especially with the Chrysanthemum Festival weekend events. To let them know you're available to help, call 638-5781.

pleased to have volunteers help with special programs and projects to benefit the schools and students.

Craven County Emergency Services
406 Craven St. • 636-6608

The right arm of the county government, this agency relies on an all-volunteer staff to oversee and operate 15 fire-fighting units and seven rescue squads. The service responds to emergency and non-emergency calls, hazardous materials cleanup standby, search and rescue, fire and many other immediate-action situations.

Meals On Wheels
811 George St. • 638-3800

This program, administered by United Senior Services, serves more than 60 meals a day with the help of its volunteers who deliver the meals and check on the recipients. The program requires eight volunteers five days a week for delivery and help with day-to-day operations.

New Bern-Craven County Public Library
400 Johnson St. • 638-7800

The library seeks volunteers to provide library services to hospitals by circulating books and magazines to patients. Its Friends of the Library group helps with fund-raising and programs, and area artists volunteer to exhibit work in the library's Artist of the Month display. If you enjoy books and literature, you may find this organization worth exploring.

Guardian Ad Litem
406 Craven St. • 633-0023

This organization trains volunteers to advocate for children involved in neglect or abuse court cases. The volunteer is assigned to investigate the home situation, meet with the child and adults involved and report to the court. The information gathered is of particular assistance to the caseworker and can speed up the disposition of the case.

Media Information

Newspapers

The Sun Journal, 638-8101, provides coverage of Craven, Pamlico and Jones counties. This daily newspaper also reports on state and national events.

Television

New Bern is home to ABC affiliate WCTI-TV 12, 638-1212. The station covers New Bern and the surrounding area with news and weather reports. Other television stations close by include WNCT-TV 9, 355-8500, the local CBS affiliate; and WITN-TV 7, 636-2337, the local NBC affiliate. Daily television listings are printed in *The Sun Journal*.

Cable television service is available through Multi-Media Cable Vision of New Bern, 638-3121.

Radio

Besides a good selection of rock 'n' roll, nostalgia and easy-listening stations, New Bern is home to WTEB, 89.3 FM, 638-3434, a Public Broadcasting Service station at Craven Community College.

Other radio stations based in the area include WNBR Bear 94.1 FM, 633-9401; and WSFL 106.5 FM, 633-1065 or 633-2406.

INSIDERS' TIP

For Storm and Hurricane Information call Craven County Emergency Services Office, 636-6608, which is charged with the responsibility of assessing storms and damage. Hurricanes should be taken seriously when predicted.

Commerce and Industry

Commerce and industry in New Bern are broad-based and receive strong support from the presence of Cherry Point Marine Corps Air Station and its affiliated Naval Aviation Depot (NADEP) in Havelock.

NADEP is one of the largest aeronautical maintenance, engineering and logistics support facilities in the Navy and is one of the largest civilian employers in eastern North Carolina. Managed by Marine officers, the facility has a work force of about 4,000 employees, most of whom are civilian. That number continues to grow.

The depot refurbishes a variety of military aircraft and provides emergency repair and field modification teams to do repair work on aircraft unable to return to the depot. For more information about NADEP, see the Havelock chapter of this book.

Industries with large work forces in New Bern include Weyerhaeuser, Hatteras Yachts, S-B Power Tool Company, Moën, Amital Spinning Corporation, Sprint Carolina Telephone and Maola Milk.

Weyerhaeuser grows and harvests timber and processes it in a huge pulp mill just outside New Bern. The company employs about 700 people and owns more than 500,000 acres in eastern North Carolina.

Hatteras Yachts builds luxury watercraft in its New Bern plant and employs about 750 people. S-B Power Tool has about 350 workers. A producer of plumbing fixtures, Moën has about 600 employees. Maola Milk and Ice Cream has about 170 workers, and Amital Spinning employs about 300 people. In early 1997, EBS Home Appliance (part of the Bosch-Seimens company) opened a factory that manufacturers dishwashers; they employ about 60 people.

Large non-industry employers include New Bern-Craven County Schools, county govern-ment, Craven Regional Medical Center and the City of New Bern.

Several New Bern groups are organized to encourage new businesses and facilitate economic growth. The New Bern Area Chamber of Commerce, 316 Tryon Palace Drive, 637-3111, represents the interests of the local business community in the local, state and national government arenas. It also offers numerous programs and events designed to promote the businesses of its members. Swiss Bear Downtown Redevelopment Inc., 233 Middle Street, Suite 105, 638-5781, is a nonprofit corporation that locates funding for private enterprises willing to revitalize the downtown area. Benefits to the community as a result of Swiss Bear's efforts include the renovation of more than 50 buildings and the creation of more than 250 new jobs.

The Committee of 100, a private group formed by area business leaders, and the Craven County Economic Development Commission are responsible for encouraging manufacturing and development. The Committee owns the 519-acre Craven County Industrial Park that straddles Highway 70 about 5 miles west of New Bern. The park is about 30 percent developed and features an incubator facility that offers free office and manufacturing space to new manufacturers. The Committee of 100 and the Economic Development Commission are constantly looking for new businesses to move into the industrial park or into the county. Contact the Committee of 100, 100 Industrial Drive, 28562, 633-5300.

The Small Business Assistance Center at Craven Community College offers workshops, seminars and group study sessions addressing the needs of small business owners. Also provided is one-on-one counseling and specialized employee training. For more information, contact the Director, Business & Industry, Craven Community College, P.O. Box 885, New Bern, 28560; 638-4131.

INSIDERS' TIP

The City of New Bern and Swiss Bear Inc. adopted an urban design plan in 1990 that is guiding the development of the downtown area and its waterfront for the next decade.

Worship

New Bern has a number of historic churches that are open to residents and visitors who would like to tour or attend services. In addition to the distinctive architectural styles seen in many of the downtown churches, several churches have features that stand out above the rest, such as the pipe organ at First Presbyterian Church on New Street, the stained-glass windows in Centenary United Methodist Church at Middle and New streets, the gifts from King George II displayed at Christ Episcopal Church on Pollock Street and the graceful white arches in First Baptist Church on Middle Street. All these churches are within three blocks of one another.

In New Bern, church-sponsored events attract community-wide interest. During the Christmas celebration, many churches conduct special concerts. Another staple of the town's Christmas celebration is a full performance of Handel's *Messiah* by a combined church choir of hundreds of voices and soloists at Centenary United Methodist Church. Musicians for the performance are members of the North Carolina Symphony.

All major Protestant religions as well as Catholics and Jews have long-established churches in New Bern. Check in the Yellow Pages for a complete list of other options. New Bern's oldest churches are wonderful places to learn about the area's history, and you can explore most of them while walking in the downtown area. (See our Attractions section for more details.)

Having celebrated its 250th anniversary in 1991, the parish of Christ Episcopal Church is the oldest in New Bern and one of the oldest in North Carolina. Today, the church has about 900 members.

First organized as a congregation in 1772, the current Centenary United Methodist Church was designed by Herbert Woodley Simpson and completed in 1904. Its rounded walls and turrets have an almost Moorish look. Standing at the corner of New and Middle streets, Centenary has about 800 members.

Organized in 1809, the narrow Gothic Revival First Baptist church was built in 1847. The church property adjoins McClellans and O. Mark Square. The main sanctuary is strikingly simple and peaceful in its design. The Sunday service is televised by WCTI-TV 12.

The oldest continually used church building in New Bern, First Presbyterian was built in 1819-22 by local architect and builder Uriah Sandy. The congregation was established in 1817. The church has about 1,200 members today.

With its new church constructed about 10 years ago, St. Paul's Catholic Church is the oldest Catholic parish in North Carolina. Members built their first New Bern church on Middle Street in 1840. That building is open to the public during daylight hours. The new church features strikingly modern architecture and is in a large, parklike setting. Sharing the land is St. Paul's Education Center, a private school.

The stucco, Neoclassical Revival Temple B'Nai Sholem Synagogue is a beautiful, uncommon specimen of architecture in the area. A Herbert Woodley Simpson-designed structure, the synagogue was built in 1908 by the congregation organized about 1824.

Working harder than
ever with our
customers and local
businesses
in providing the best
available cable service
at a reasonable cost.

**TIMEWARNER
CABLE**

*Proudly bringing Carteret, Onslow &
Craven Counties
into the 21st Century.*

Cherry Point (919) 447-7101
Newport (919) 223-5011
Jacksonville   (910) 353-3500
Wilmington   (910) 763-4638

Havelock

Welcome to the city of Havelock. Best known as the home to Marine Corps Air Station Cherry Point, the largest Marine Corps Air Station in the world, Havelock is a diverse city with much to offer visitors and residents.

The city and the military base have a population of about 20,500, making it the largest city in Craven County and the 23rd largest in North Carolina. This is a far cry from the 100 residents recorded in 1950. Admittedly, Havelock gained a few residents when the base was annexed, but it is still one of the fastest-growing urban areas in the state. More and more people are choosing to locate in the city because of its proximity to the coast.

Havelock was named for Gen. Henry Havelock, a British general best remembered for his courageous rescues of hostages during a bloody uprising in India in the mid-1800s. A marble bust of Gen. Havelock stands in the Havelock City Hall.

First called Havelock Station, the community saw action during the Civil War when troops from the Rhode Island Heavy Artillery came ashore in 1862 near what is now the base Officer's Club. From that point, Union troops captured New Bern and Fort Macon on Bogue Banks.

At one time, the production of tar and turpentine had more economic impact on Havelock than farming, but once steam engines began replacing wooden ships as transporters of goods, the market for tar and turpentine fell.

Because of its proximity to local waters and forests, Havelock gained notoriety in the late 1800s and early 1930s for its fishing and hunting opportunities. Area historians and artifact collectors value pictures of baseball great Babe Ruth, who often spent time in the area pursuing outdoor sports.

Today's residents and visitors to the Havelock area can enjoy being outdoors in the Croatan National Forest. This 157,000-acre forest spreads in a triangle between Morehead City, Cape Carteret and New Bern, and borders Havelock on three sides. The Croatan features many ecosystems, endangered animals, plant species and wildflowers. For more information about the Croatan National Forest, see the Crystal Coast Attractions chapter of this book.

Because of its continued growth Havelock is experiencing more and more traffic, and the city has responded to its increased traffic needs. Streets were widened, turn lanes created and traffic lights synchronized. Additionally, a new back gate to the base was created a few years ago.

A bypass is also planned to guide traffic off the existing U.S. Highway 70 just west of Havelock to take that traffic south of Havelock and reconnect it to Highway 70 at the Craven County-Carteret County line on the east side of Havelock. This bypass will be connected to the city in several areas as it loops the city. Construction of portions of the thoroughfare will begin in 1998 and continue over the next several years.

It will come as no surprise that the community shares in the pride and traditions of the Marine Corps. The most striking example of that pride is the Harrier monument in the center of town. Visitors and residents are re-

---

INSIDERS' TIP

Did you know? Cherry Point Marine Corps Air Station is an alternative landing site for the Space Shuttle. In case they are ever needed, specially trained teams of marines are always on the ready to recover the shuttle and the astronauts.

minded of their dependency on the military when a Harrier or an Intruder flies overhead. A sign in front of the base says it best: Pardon Our Noise — It's The Sound Of Freedom.

Havelock is often referred to as the "Gateway to Cherry Point." With more than 14,000 sailors, marines and civilians housed at the air station, Cherry Point is the largest Marine Corps Air Station in the world, and it ranks as the No. 1 industry for many of the surrounding counties.

The air station was first authorized by Congress in 1941. The arduous task of clearing the original 8,000 acres of swamp, farm and timberland began in August 1941, with actual construction beginning just 17 days before the attack on Pearl Harbor.

The air station was commissioned on May 20, 1942, as Cunningham Field, in honor of the Marine Corps' first aviator, Lt. Alfred A. Cunningham. In August 1942, the first troops arrived at the air station, and the Marine Aircraft Wing was officially formed in November 1942.

Although rumors abound on how the base took the name Cherry Point, it is believed to have been adopted from an old post office established in the area years before. The post office, used by the Blades Lumber workers, was closed in 1935. The original "point" was just east of Hancock Creek, and "cherry" came from the cherry trees that once grew there. The airfield itself, consisting of the runways and tower, is still technically named Cunningham Field.

In April 1946, the 2nd Marine Air Wing found a home at Cherry Point and was integral in training thousands of Marines for the Korean Conflict, Vietnam and the Persian Gulf War. Now, the 2nd Marine Air Wing has elements permanently stationed at MCAS Cherry Point, MCAS New River, North Carolina, and MCAS Beaufort, South Carolina. It is equipped with helicopters, fighters and attack and refueler/transport aircraft.

Over the years, Cherry Point has grown from a small airfield to one of the Marine Corps' most important air stations. The original 8,000-acre area has been expanded continuously and now encompasses more than 11,000 acres at Cherry Point and an additional 15,000 acres in assorted support locations. Built in 1941 at a cost of $14.9 million, the plant value of the base is now more than a staggering $1.6 billion.

Approximately 7,800 marines and sailors stationed at Cherry Point earn an annual payroll of about $215 million. Combined with the station's nearly 6,000 civilian employees, more than $480 million is pumped into the local economy every year from Cherry Point. These salaries, plus local expenditures for supplies and capital improvements, have an economic impact of more than $618 million annually on the state of North Carolina.

One stop at the Havelock Chamber of Commerce, 494 Westbrooke Shopping Center, 447-1101, will certainly help visitors or new residents. The friendly staff provides maps and lots of information. The Havelock Chamber serves as a visitors center in addition to providing services for its more than 400 member-businesses. Chamber officials sponsor numerous events such as educational seminars, community services, social and business meetings, ribbon cuttings and workshops.

Havelock has a lot to offer, but don't just view the city from Highway 70. Take a turn here or there. Stop at a few businesses — you might be surprised at what you find.

Here we offer a quick look at the city of Havelock. One note about the addresses: Main Street is actually Highway 70. So, if an address is on E. Main Street, it would be on the town's eastern end of Highway 70. West Main Street is on the New Bern side of the intersection of N.C. Highway 101 and Highway 70.

Below, we have listed some general information about Havelock businesses, events and services. You'll find a listing of restaurants, accommodations, shopping, attractions, annual events, golf courses and real estate agencies. These sections are by no means comprehensive. Information about area industry and military services follows.

Restaurants

From fast-food to family dining, Havelock eateries are sure to satisfy whatever yen you may experience.

The restaurants listed alphabetically below represent only a small portion of the establishments in town. Ask locals for other recommendations or stop by the Havelock Chamber of Commerce.

Price Code

The price code noted below the restaurant name will give you a general idea of the cost of dinner for two, excluding alcoholic beverages, tax and tip. Because entrees generally come in a wide range of prices, the code reflects an average meal — not the most or least expensive items. Of course, lunch would cost less. The price code used in the reviews is as follows:

$	Less than $20
$$	$21 to $35

Chop Sticks
$ • 500 Miller Blvd. • 447-1521

Chop Sticks serves wonderful Japanese cuisine and draws diners from all around. In a small building beside a Jim Dandy Food Store, Chop Sticks could easily be missed. But if you skip over this restaurant, you'll be sorry. Open for lunch and dinner, Chop Sticks serves a variety of Japanese dishes featuring seafood, beef, chicken and pork.

Blue Sky Bistro
$-$$ • 424 W. Main St. • 447-4669

There's a new pub in town — one that's sure to delight the appetites and sensibilities of all the folks in Havelock and the surrounding areas. Owners Vincent and Debra Scialo have purchased the former Mama Angela's Cafe and have changed its ambiance to candlelit booths and wood-grain paneling. They've even added an espresso bar. The Scialos want the Blue Sky Bistro to be the hometown pub of Havelock, and they're well on their way to reaching that goal. Patrons may choose from moderately priced, homemade entrees of pasta, grilled chicken, quiches, steaks and vegetable dishes. Especially mouth-watering are Debra's desserts — German chocolate cake, cranberry-walnut pie, truffle cake and ice cream pie. Everything is made fresh in the kitchen. The bistro serves imported beer and has all ABC permits.

El Cerro Grande
$ • 405 W. Main St. • 444-5701

El Cerro Grande offers Mexican food at its best and is a popular lunch and dinner spot.

Photo: Sgt. Anthony G. Sousa

An AV-8B Harrier prepares for flight.

Appetizers include guacamole salad and dip, chili with cheese or nacho chicken. Entrees vary from combination plates with a choice of chicken, cheese, beef, potato or spinach fillings to special dinner platters that offer tostadas, burritos, steak ranchero and fajitas. The vegetarian menu features a wonderful potato burrito and spinach enchilada. Desserts turn to such favorites as sopapillas and fried ice cream. The restaurant serves several Mexican beers, wine and mixed drinks, including fabulous Margaritas.

Winstead's Family Restaurant
$-$$ • 1222 E. Main St. • 447-2036

Winstead's is a family dining establishment with a casual atmosphere. This restaurant is very popular with locals as well as visitors.

Opened in 1987 by the Winstead family, the restaurant offers a fabulous lunch and dinner buffet. The buffet features a multitude of seafood entrees and chicken, beef and pork entrees along with fresh hot vegetables, a salad bar, a number of extras and dessert. The all-you-can-eat crab legs and the prime rib dinner are favorites. Winstead's recently expanded and is available for parties and banquets with seating for 175. The restaurant is open for lunch and dinner every day except Saturday, when only dinner is served.

Accommodations

Visitors to Havelock will be pleasantly surprised by the diverse accommodations offered. For years, only two motels served Havelock, with the majority of their clientele limited to traveling members of the armed services. With the increased popularity of nearby beaches and a local effort to attract industry to the area, new establishments have sprung up in recent years. We have only described a few in the section below.

Best Western Havelock Inn
$ • 310 E. Main St. • 444-1414

Best Western has 63 rooms offering a selection of sleeping arrangements. From a standard double to the presidential and honeymoon suites, there is a size and style to fit any traveler. The inn offers rooms with kitchenettes, balconies and Jacuzzis. A restaurant, lounge and outdoor pool are on site.

Comfort Inn
$$ • 1013 U.S. Hwy. 70 E. • 444-8444, (800) 228-5151

Comfort Inn offers a total of 58 rooms. Rooms are designed in various configurations including standard king- and double-bed rooms and presidential and executive suites. All suites offer microwaves, refrigerators and whirlpool tubs. Guests can enjoy an outdoor pool during the summer and an indoor exercise room year round. A free deluxe continental breakfast is served, and the inn is within walking distance of restaurants. A conference room is offered that can accommodate 40 people.

Days Inn
$ • U.S. Hwy. 70 E. • 447-1122

Beside Winstead's Family Restaurant, Days Inn offers 73 rooms that open to an interior hallway. The hotel offers the comfortable and clean rooms people have come to expect from the Days Inn chain. The inn also has an outdoor swimming pool, and special rooms are available for those traveling with pets.

Holiday Inn
$$ • 400 U.S. Hwy. 70 W. • 444-1111, (800) HOLIDAY

This 103-room establishment offers room service during restaurant hours. Rooms vary in size and furnishings from a standard room to the executive suite, which features a small conference room and two adjacent bedrooms. Conference and banquet facilities for as many as 350 people are available. A restaurant and lounge are accessible from the inn's main lobby, and an outside pool is open during the summer months.

Hostess House
$ • 449 McCotter Blvd. • 447-3689

This unique motel might just revolutionize the way travelers think of hotels. Hostess House offers 85 units in several configurations, and 75 are completely equipped kitchenettes for longer-staying guests. An on-site laundry facility is an added feature. Hostess House is behind Food Lion grocery store at the east end of town. A Hostess House is also in Newport (see the Crystal Coast Accommodations chapter).

Sherwood Motel
$ • U.S. Hwy. 70 W. • 447-3184

The Sherwood Motel is well-established, having been in business for many years. Guests will find a clean, quiet motel offering 89 rooms complete with cable TV, HBO and

INSIDERS' TIP

The Naval Aviation Depot at Cherry Point is one of the largest civilian employers in eastern North Carolina, with a current civilian work force of more than 4,000.

all the expected comforts. Refrigerators and microwaves are available, and an outdoor swimming pool is open in the summer.

Shopping

Shopping opportunities continue to grow in Havelock. There are no shopping malls or major retail chain stores, but there is plenty of variety. Additionally, many Havelock residents shop in nearby Morehead City and New Bern, and military families have the opportunity to shop at the base exchange. Many of the shops in Havelock are service oriented, i.e., video outlets, hairstyling salons and laundry facilities. You'll also find a number of furniture stores, pawn shops and military surplus outlets. Below, we have chosen to highlight a few of our favorite shops. Antiques shops and flea markets are listed at the end of this section.

Bob Clark's Pharmacy
233 W. Main St. • 447-8102

This pharmacy offers the usual items you would expect plus a wide selection of gift items. The store also has North Carolina souvenirs such as mugs, thimbles, spoons, bells etc., which are perfect for gifts for out-of-state or out-of-country friends.

Bike Depot
Century Plaza, U.S. Hwy. 70 W. • 447-0834

The Bike Depot offers Cannondale, Trek and Giant bicycles and makes repairs on all types. The store carries clothing, accessories, helmets and used bicycles. It's in the Century Plaza at the west end of town.

Dolls Galore
314 U.S. Hwy. 70 W. • 447-4147

This shop offers all kinds of collector and better play dolls. Shoppers will find lovely Madame Alexander dolls and collector Barbies.

Michael's Frame & Art
& Country Store
Westbrooke Plz., U.S. Hwy. 70 • 447-3582

Michael's offers complete framing services and some artwork. Its specialty is cross-stitch supplies, and it's the largest cross-stitch shop in eastern North Carolina.

Palate Pleasers
Maxway Shopping Ctr., U.S. 70 W.
• 447-2577

This gourmet shop is a tempting place to browse. You'll find a good selection of gourmet foods, wines, cheeses, coffees and teas. Palate Pleasers also offers wonderful gift items or can prepare a gift basket for you.

Antiques/Flea Markets

Heirloom Shop
502 E. Main St. • 447-3154

Lamps, lamps and more lamps. The Heirloom Shop can make a lamp from just about anything — a decoy, bottle, carving — then fit it with a lampshade made of silk, cotton, muslin, linen or other materials. This shop also sells table linens.

Plaza Trade Center Flea Market
Cherry Plaza, U.S. Hwy. 70 E. • 447-0314

This place offers a new concept in flea-market retailing. With about 85 dealers and room for more, the Flea Market offers rental booths. Each item is marked with the vendor's number. When a sale is made, whether the vendor is there or not, the market's cashier handles the transaction and credits the vendor's account. The Flea Market carries new and used items.

Annual Events

Havelock hosts a number of events each year that are enjoyed by both residents of the city and visitors. We have listed a few of the larger and most popular events.

Cherry Point Air Show
MCAS Cherry Point • 466-4241

This is one of the largest events in the area, with more than 60,000 people attending when the air station opens its gates to the public. The free air show features a variety of aerial displays from military and civilian aircraft. The numerous static displays allow visitors to get an up-close look at many of the military's high-tech aircraft. Cars are parked on the runways, so wear comfortable shoes as you may have to walk a slight distance. The show is conducted on a weekend each April and alternates location from one year to the next between Cherry Point and New River Air Station in Jacksonville. In 1998 the air show will be held in Jacksonville.

Easter Egg Hunt
U.S. Hwy. 70 E., Havelock City Park
• 444-6429

All children younger than 9 are invited to the park to hunt for eggs stuffed with gift certificates, money and toys. The day of the event changes each year, depending on when Easter falls, so call ahead. Children need to bring a basket.

Craven County Two-Man Classic Invitational Golf Tournament
Area courses • 447-1101

The Two-Man Golf Tournament is sponsored by the Havelock and New Bern chambers of commerce and draws a field of about 300 players. Held in mid-April, tournament play is simultaneous at The Emerald in New Bern and Carolina Pines in Havelock.

Flounder Jubilee Golf Tournament
Carolina Pines Golf and Country Club, Carolina Pines Blvd. • 444-1000

The competition is sponsored by the Men's Golf Association of Carolina Pines each June. There is no deadline for entering, but early entrants are given first consideration. The event is a two-person superball competition.

Old Fashioned Fourth of July
Walter B. Jones Park, U.S. Hwy. 70 E.
• 444-6429

As the name says, this is the city's Fourth of July celebration. It is the prelude to the fireworks display later that evening. In prior years, crowds have enjoyed a variety of entertainment including musical groups, clowns and games. Food is available.

U.S. Marine Corps Battle Color Ceremony
MCAS Cherry Point • 466-4241

This ceremony is held every year, usually the second Monday in September. The whole family — from little kids to grandfolks — will enjoy this inspiring event. The ceremony aims to demonstrate the qualities the title "Marine" embodies — pride, discipline, esprit de corps, teamwork. Featured are the Battle Colors, containing myriad streamers and silver bands representing every battle and campaign the Corps has participated in; the U.S. Marine Drum and Bugle Corps, known as the Commandant's Own, a superbly disciplined marching band; and the Silent Drill Platoon, which performs an inspiring exhibition of precision drill without any verbal command. There are two performances — one at noon on the base and one in the evening in Havelock.

North Carolina Chili Cook-Off Championship
Walter B. Jones Park, U.S. Hwy. 70 E.
• 447-1101

Havelock hosts the state Chili Cook-Off Championships, and it really is a big deal. Folks come from all over to compete for prizes and to eat some of the best chili around. So, if you like chili, Havelock is where you need to be each October. Havelock plays host to 50 of the state's premier chili chefs, each vying for the title of state champion and the right to compete in the national cook-off contest. The festival also attracts cooking teams that travel the region. This is one event not to be missed, whether you like chili hot, mild or not at all. In addition to chili, music, crafts and other displays keep everyone busy. A number of local charities benefit from the profits.

Christmas Parade
U.S. Hwy. 70 • 447-1101

Like most area towns, Havelock hosts a Christmas parade on a weekend in early December. Decorated floats and a visit from Santa Claus are part of the events. Holiday music is provided by the members of the Marine Corps 2nd Marine Air Wing Band as well as other area bands.

Christmas In The Park
Havelock City Park, U.S. Hwy. 70 E.
• 444-6429

This is one of the area's favorite Christmas celebrations. It is usually held each year on a

Thursday before Christmas. The event consists of a Christmas carol sing-along and a live nativity scene.

Christmas Fair
Downtown Havelock • 447-1101

Sponsored by the Havelock Chamber of Commerce, this all-day family event takes place in mid-November. It features business and craft vendors, pork and chicken barbecue, holiday music and Santa Claus. The fair benefits the Equal program, which splits the proceeds equally among Havelock's public schools.

Attractions

Although there are few bona fide attractions in and around Havelock other than Croatan National Forest, the ones listed here are must-sees for anyone traveling in the area.

Cherry Point Base Tours
MCAS Cherry Point
• 466-4241

It is possible to tour Marine Corps Air Station Cherry Point and see unclassified points of interest. The tours were first started in 1984 as a way to promote understanding between the air station and the surrounding community, and they continue today. Tours are offered every Thursday of the month from June through August. From September to May, tours are offered on the first and third Thursday of each month. Those interested in taking a tour should meet the tour guide at the Welcome Center at the station's main gate. Tours leave promptly at 9 AM. Reservations are needed for groups of 10 or more, and school groups are welcome. Tours vary depending on activities but could include a look at the weather and radar facilities, the military working dogs, the tower or a squadron and last about two hours. For exact times, reservations and details, call the Joint Public Affairs Office at the number above.

Harrier Monument
Hwy. 70 and Cunningham Blvd.

An AV-8A Harrier jump jet looms at the intersection of Highway 70 and Cunningham

Boulevard. Mounted on a pedestal and encircled by flags, the AV-8A is a symbol of the past. Although Cherry Point is home to the largest number of Harriers in the world, the jet was taken out of service during the mid-1980s and replaced by the new AV-8B. The most noticeable difference between the two jets is that the landing gear on the A was located on the wing tips, while the B landing gear is closer to the center of the wings. This mounted jet was the second AV-8A military officials gave to civilians for display purposes. The first is on display at the Smithsonian in Washington, D.C.

Aircraft Viewing

The sound and sight of aircraft in flight is a regular occurrence for locals. However, it is often the very thing a visitor wants to experience. Although there is no designated or best spot for prime viewing, a good vantage point is along Highway 101 near the main gate. Runway 5 ends here and, if the winds are right, it is often used by Harriers, Intruders and C-130 cargo planes. The sound can be deafening, so a few words of caution: Brace yourself, warn your children and protect infants' ears from the noise.

Croatan National Forest
Ranger's Office, 141 E. Fisher Ave., New Bern • 638-5628

This 157,000-acre national forest borders Havelock on three sides and offers visitors and residents a wide range of activities. Outdoor recreational activities include camping, picnicking, boating, hiking, hunting and salt- or freshwater fishing. For more information about the Croatan National Forest, see the Crystal Coast Attractions section.

Golf

Unless you have access to the golf course on the air station, you will end up traveling out of town to play. Numerous courses are on the Crystal Coast and in New Bern. The closest course to Havelock is described below.

Carolina Pines
Golf and Country Club
Carolina Pines Blvd. • 444-1000

Between Havelock and New Bern, this 18-hole, par 72 course is open year round. Carolina Pines is a residential resort development, and unlike most courses that get you in touch with nature, this course also gets you in touch with the neighbors. Residential homes dot the areas along the beautifully designed and challenging course.

Marinas

Those boaters with access to the air station also have access to a number of launching facilities. Two boat ramps will get you into either Slocum or Hancock creeks. Two other marinas, one on the Neuse River and the other on Slocum Creek, provide boat rentals and docking facilities. Without base access, your choices of marinas and ramps near Havelock are limited. Check the marina listings in the Crystal Coast and New Bern sections for nearby facilities. Below are a few of the closest choices.

Matthews Point Marina
Temples Point Rd. • 444-1805

At the mouth of Clubfoot Creek, this is a membership marina, but often boaters are able to use an available wetslip overnight. A clearly marked entry channel is provided with facilities to accommodate both sail and power boats. The approach depth is 8 feet. Open year round, the marina has ice, gas and diesel fuel available. Finding the marina by land is more difficult than by water. Seekers should follow Highway 101 toward Beaufort. Just a few miles out of Havelock, a church marks the corner of the highway and Temples Point Road. The marina is at the very end of Temples Point Road.

Cahoogue Creek
Cahoogue Creek Rd., off Hwy. 101

The National Forest Service offers a boat ramp at Cahoogue Creek, which actually allows boats to access Hancock Creek and the

Neuse River. In addition to the ramp, the facility provides a grill, a picnic table and a small dock designed primarily to aid boarding. There are no bathroom facilities. When driving on N.C. 101, there aren't really any landmarks to look for, so slow down and look for the road sign.

Real Estate

Residential housing is abundant, with prices ranging from around $35,000 to $250,000. The majority of homes in Havelock and surrounding areas are less than 10 years old. Many planned communities have popped up in the surrounding areas and appeal to a wide range of individuals. Lured by the mild climate, low tax rate and relatively low cost of living, many retirees, both military and civilian, are finding a home in the Havelock area. Some of today's primary growth areas are the waterfront developments along the Neuse River and large creeks.

Because of the number of military entering and exiting the Havelock area, renting a place here for a period of time is a lot easier than in most areas. Rentals are abundant and come in many forms, including houses, apartments or mobile homes. Rental prices vary according to the type of accommodation and could range from $225 to $750 per month. Many storage units are also available and vary in size.

Carolina Pines
Real Estate Company
390 Carolina Blvd., New Bern • 447-2000, (800) 654-5610

This company markets new homes, resales, lots and acreage throughout Havelock and New Bern. Carolina Pines handles the Carolina Pines subdivision.

Century 21 Home Realty
of Havelock
Westbrooke Shopping Ctr. • 447-2100, (800) 858-4663

One of two Century 21 offices in Havelock, Home Realty offers sales in residential and

INSIDERS' TIP

Taking a tour of Cherry Point Air Station is a thrill for the entire family. Tour information is available by calling the Joint Public Affairs Office, 466-4241.

commercial property and handles residential rentals. This is the place to find someone with extensive knowledge of the area and access to property in the surrounding four counties with multiple listings service.

Century 21 Town & Country
406 W. Main St. • 447-8188, (800) 334-0320

Town & Country is a good place to start looking for a home in or around Havelock. This is the oldest franchise real estate company in the city. Town & Country is an independently owned, full-service agency with a large market share of new and existing homes, residential and commercial rentals and investment properties for sale.

Coldwell Banker First Realty
102 Roosevelt Blvd. • 444-3333, (800) 396-7772

This agency is a good place to start your search for that special house or commercial property. Let owner-broker Gwen Schultz show you properties in Craven and Carteret counties. The Company also has a full property management department.

First Carolina Realtors - Better Homes & Gardens
101 W. Main St. • 447-7900, (800) 336-5610

The office is easy to spot in an attractive two-story, homelike structure at the junction of highways 70 and 101. Stop by First Carolina Realtors for information about residential and commercial property for sale in the area.

The Property Shoppe
957 E. Main St. • 447-1031

The Property Shoppe offers a wide range of services. Carol DeGennaro is the owner-broker and has been in the real estate business since 1977. The Property Shoppe is a well-established firm that handles sales of residential and commercial property in both Carteret and Craven counties, as well as rental property management.

Media

Havelock Times
13 Park Ln. • 444-8210

Published each Wednesday, the *Havelock Times* covers news and features in the Have-

lock and Newport areas. The paper is owned by Carteret Publishing Company of Morehead City, and it is based in Havelock.

Havelock News
230 Stonebridge Sq. • 444-1999

This paper is distributed every Wednesday and covers any news having to do with the town of Havelock. Readership is both military and civilian. *Havelock News* covers city schools, government and news of Havelock residents. The paper is published by the Ellis Publishing Co., which also publishes *Windsock*.

Windsock
MCAS Cherry Point • 466-4241

The *Windsock* is published weekly and distributed on Marine Corps Air Station Cherry Point. The newspaper features messages from the Commanding General, Marine news, Squadron spotlights and information from the Naval Aviation Depot. The paper also includes "Socksports," a sports section, recreation listings and classified advertisements.

Commerce and Industry

The number of manufacturing companies in Havelock continues to grow. Through the years, a number of private firms have popped up and are helping to diversify the economic base of the city. This growth is in part thanks to the efforts of the Craven County Economic Development Commission (EDC) and Craven County's Committee of 100, 633-5300. The county has two incubator facilities and an industrial park. Here, we have highlighted a few of the largest industrial/manufacturing influences on Havelock's economy. Although it is not a private company, we have listed first the Naval Aviation Depot (NADEP) at Cherry Point because of its tremendous economic impact on the area.

Naval Aviation Depot
MCAS Cherry Point • 466-7999

NADEP is one of the largest civilian employers in eastern North Carolina. Managed by Marine officers, the facility currently has a work force of more than 4,000.

NADEP was originally established in 1943 as the Assembly and Repair Department at the air station. Since then, the facil-

ity has grown into one of the finest aeronautical maintenance, engineering and logistics support facilities in the Navy. Its depot refurbishes a variety of military aircraft including the AV-8 Harrier, C-130 Hercules, H-46 Sea Knight helicopter, F-4 Phantom, A-4 Skyhawk, CH-53E Super Stallion and MH-53E Sea Dragon. NADEP also has extensive facilities designed to test and repair a number of different engine types, including the T58-400, which is used in the VH-3 presidential-executive helicopters. The depot also provides emergency repair and field modification teams to do repair work on aircraft unable to return to the depot. At a moment's notice, these field teams can be sent to any location around the world. Depot personnel were sent to various locations in the United States and overseas during the Persian Gulf War to perform such services.

Jasper Textiles Inc.
103 Outer Banks Dr. • 444-3400

Jasper Textiles was the charter member of the Havelock Industrial Park off Highway 101. The company manufactures men's sports shirts under the "Outer Banks" label. Jasper Textiles opened the Havelock plant in 1991 and employs about 170 people.

United Parcel Service
201 Belltown Rd. • (800)742-5877

UPS offers express letter and parcel delivery, and the Havelock facility is a regional terminal. Opened in 1986, this facility currently employs about 50 people.

Military

The military plays a large part in the lives of all Havelock residents. Nearly 14,000 marines, sailors and civilians work at the air station.

Military Organizations

Marine Corps Air Station, Cherry Point includes 13,164 acres on the air station proper, with an additional 15,756 acres of auxiliary activities, including marine Corps Auxiliary Landing Field Bogue, along Bogue Sound in Carteret County.

The largest command at Cherry Point is the 2nd Marine Aircraft Wing, as well as Marine Aircraft Group 14, Marine Wing Support Group 27 and Marine Air Control 28. Other 2nd MAW units include helicopter squadrons MCAS New River, N.C., and F/A-18 Hornet squadrons at MCAS Beaufort, S.C.

Marine Aircraft Group 14's flying squadrons include three AV-8B Harrier squadrons, four EA-6B Prowler squadrons and one KC-130 Hercules refueling squadron. The Marine Corps' only Harrier training squadron and Hercules training squadron are also located at the air station.

Marine Wing Support Group 27 provides logistical support for the wing with marine Wing Support Squadron 274 located at the air station and Marine Wing Support Squadron 271 providing support for the Bogue landing field.

Marine Air Control Group 28 employs some of the most advanced equipment for command of tactical air operations. The marines who control the air war are defended by a battalion of marines who employ the Stinger anti-aircraft missile system to control the skies overhead.

Services

A number of services are available to the military and their dependents ranging from housing to recreational facilities. All military personnel are entitled to live in base housing if they desire and if space is available. Often there is a wait to get housing. More than 2,700 housing units are available for married personnel, ranging from apartments to houses. Three housing areas for noncommissioned officers are along the perimeter of the base and are accessible from Havelock. Thousands of barrack rooms are available for single personnel.

Military personnel are also able to utilize the three-story Naval Hospital Cherry Point, which was dedicated in memory of Pharmacist Mate Second Class William D. Halyburton, a North Carolina native. The $34 million, 201,806-square-foot hospital houses the most modern technology to support its 23 medical/surgery beds, two operating rooms, three birthing rooms and two labor and delivery rooms. Additionally, the hospital provides for the primary medical needs of our community.

Other facilities aboard the base are designed to afford military personnel a wide variety of conveniences and recreation. The Marine Corps Exchange offers a department store, grocery store, flower shop, liquor store and a number of small shops. There are also a child development center, a bank, dry cleaning and laundry facilities and a service center with a convenience store.

Recreational activities are also available and are geared to Marines and their dependents. These include a large gymnasium, fitness center, three pools, an 18-hole golf course, a bowling center and a number of marinas.

Although the base offers many services for convenience and fun, the Marine Corps stresses the importance of improving one's education. The Marvel Training and Education Center provides a wide range of educational services. Offices are operated by Craven Community College, Southern Illinois University, Boston College and Park College. The center provides services such as admissions testing, independent study course catalogs, counseling and a basic skills education program. The base has one of the most comprehensive libraries in the area with everything from reference materials to children's books.

Many more services and facilities are on base. MCAS Cherry Point is a community in itself. For more information, call Base Information, 466-2811, or the Joint Public Affairs Office, 466-4261.

Service Directory

Tax Rates

The Craven County 1996-97 tax rate and the municipal tax rates are based on $100 valuation and are subject to change at the end of the fiscal year. Craven County's rate is 60¢ and Havelock's rate is 39¢.

Utilities

Utility service is provided by a number of companies. Here we have listed a few of the larger providers.

Cable Television

Time Warner Cable (for MCAS Cherry Point), 223-5011

Time Warner Cable (for service in Havelock), 447-7902

Electric

Carteret-Craven Electric Membership Corporation, 247-3107

Carolina Power & Light, 633-5688

Telephone

Carolina Telephone, 633-9011

Water

Havelock City Water and Sewer, 444-6404

Trash Collection

Waste Management, 633-6330

Oriental is a sailors' haven. That fact is apparent by the number of sail makers and the number of chandleries offering marine supplies, equipment and repairs.

Oriental

Sitting on the banks of the Neuse River, Oriental is a tucked-away sort of place. Quiet, pretty and filled with genuinely friendly people, this small village is a haven for those needing a bit of tranquility in their lives. You can get to nearly every place in Oriental by foot or bicycle. But while not fast-paced, this riverside town is certainly not boring. There's plenty to do — if you should you care to do anything at all.

Oriental is in Pamlico County, on the northern banks of the Neuse River directly across from Carteret County. It is only a 20-minute ferry ride from the Crystal Coast (or a short drive from New Bern). The free **Cherry Branch-Minnesott Beach Ferry** leaves from outside Havelock (see our Getting Around chapter), crosses the Neuse and docks in Minnesott Beach. From there, Oriental is a short 10 miles away — just follow the road signs.

The town is situated amid six creeks: Smith Creek, Camp Creek, Raccoon Creek, Green Creek, Whittaker Creek and Pierce Creek. A 10-foot channel connects Oriental with the Intracoastal Waterway. Boat people are crazy about Oriental, which is known as the "Sailing Capital of North Carolina." Because it's on the Intracoastal Waterway, Oriental is a convenient and popular year-round port for sailing vessels. In winter when ships from the North are southbound, they stop for a couple of days; in spring, headed back North again, they linger longer. An estimated 5,000 to 6,000 ICW travelers visit every year.

Unlike many other coastal communities that are experiencing new-found popularity and increased demands for housing and services, Oriental is enjoying a relaxed time. In 1910 the town's population was 2,500. Today, year-round residents number about 850. In recent years, some new neighborhoods and marinas have sprung up around the town, offering waterfront lots, boat ramps and recreational areas.

Oriental is named after the *USS Oriental*, a Yankee cargo ship that sank in stormy seas off the Outer Banks in 1862. Some years later, Rebecca Midyette, wife of Oriental's founder Louis Midyette, came across the ship's nameboard hanging on the wall of a private residence in Manteo, North Carolina. Mrs. Midyette liked the name, and after talking it over, the residents of Smith's Creek (the original name of the town) renamed their village Oriental. In 1899 Oriental was incorporated and the first post office was established with Louis Midyette as the first postmaster.

Oriental is a sailors' haven. That fact is apparent by the number of sail makers and the number of chandleries offering marine supplies, equipment and repairs. In the last few years several art studios and craft shops have opened. In our view, Oriental is the perfect getaway for relaxing, browsing, dining and enjoying the water.

It's a good idea, but not essential, to get a town map before you start to explore Oriental. Free street maps and other information are available at most of the real estate companies and outside the Oriental Motel and Restaurant on Hodges Street. Helpful staff at Oriental's Town Hall, Broad Street, 249-0555, will also supply you with free information. The Town Hall's mailing address is P.O. Box 472, 28571.

INSIDERS' TIP

The Oriental Rotary Club tags tarpon so that information can be collected about the life habits of this fish. In 1996 a tarpon tagged in Oriental's 1994 tarpon tournament was caught in Havana, Cuba — a journey of over 1,000 miles.

Things to Do and See in Oriental

theater to school kids through their Puppet Division. Tickets are for sale at the theater door. For more information, call Carole Boris, 249-2090.

Sailing

For those who want the true Oriental experience, chartering a sailboat is the thing to do. Call or write **Carolina Sailing Unlimited**, P.O. Box 796, Oriental, 28571, 249-0850, (800) 372-WIND. Or you can visit owner and Captain Reginald Fidoe, who is from London by way of Detroit, at 502 Church Street. For the past seven years, Captain Reg has been taking up to six passengers on charter cruises aboard his 33-foot ketch *Puffin* for a half day, a full day or overnight. Two-hour evening cruises conclude with wine.

Carolina Sailing Unlimited also teaches sailing. Stressing safety above all, the school tailors lessons to individual needs and enthusiasms. You can select from a half-day personal course on your own boat or a day, weekend or week-long course on the school's boats.

Another option for learning how to sail is **Oriental's School of Sailing**, Lupton Drive, 249-0960. This 16-year old school offers its program two ways: five consecutive days, with a new class beginning every Monday, or Saturday and Sunday over three consecutive weekends. Lessons begin in April and go through the last week of October. Instructors emphasize safety and hands-on experience.

Performing Arts

Pelican Players is the community's performance company. Organized in 1983, this nonprofit volunteer organization is affiliated with both the Pamlico and the North Carolina Arts Councils. The group stages four productions a year, with performances at the **Pamlico County Civic and Culture Center** on Broad Street (across from the Town Hall). Dramas, broadway and dinner theater hits and original reviews make up their repertoire. The players also take their productions on the road around Pamlico and Craven counties and they bring

FYI

Unless otherwise noted, the area code for all phone numbers in this guide is 919.

Events

Oriental's popularity soars on the Fourth of July weekend when thousands of visitors arrive for the annual **Croaker Festival**. The event honors the croaker, a tasty fish found only in Southern waters that's very vocal when caught. If you've never heard a croaker's croak, you need to spend more time on North Carolina waters. But the more customary traditions of the Fourth are not neglected. The festival weekend concludes with a patriotic fireworks display that inevitably elicits breathless ooohs and aaahs from the holiday crowd.

For over 30 years, Oriental has commemorated New Year's Eve in its own special way. Every December 31, the community stages its annual **Running of the Dragon**. A huge golden Chinese dragon, with about 40 or 50 pairs of feet, appears twice during the evening beside the harbor. When it shows itself, New Year's Eve revelers pursue the dragon as it winds in and out of the town's streets. How many feet propel the dragon body depends on how many folks don't mind running around in the dark under a blanket. Needless to say, Oriental's Dragon Run attracts lots of visitors. Kids can see the dragon at 8 PM and grown-ups can stay up for the 11 PM run.

The **Annual Oriental Rotary Tarpon Tournament** is held in August. In case you didn't know, a tarpon is a big bony, silvery sport fish that averages 80 pounds and some 6 feet in length. (Tarpons have been known to weigh in at 200 pounds.) The fish winter in Florida's coastal waters and in the summer swim up the Atlantic, right into Pamlico Sound and the Neuse River. During July and August, tarpon abound in Oriental's waters. They are an excellent sport fishers' fish, often fighting for 10 minutes to as long as an hour.

The tournament, sponsored by the Oriental Rotary Club as a fund-raiser for the club's scholarship program, is a catch-and-release

Photo: C. Doyle

Ships anchored in the Neuse River sit idle before another day on the water.

affair. Volunteer observers accompany the fishing boats to record official scores. The winning vessel is the one that catches and releases the most tarpon. Prizes are cash, and typically about 70 boats enter the tournament for a fee of $200. This three-day event includes a Saturday night pig picking barbecue and a Sunday afternoon award ceremony. For more information, call Alan Probst at Mariner's Realty, 249-1014.

Shopping

Some people might call the **Ol' Store** on S. Water Street a curiosity shop; others might call it a junk shop. Regardless of what it is, it's really worth a look. The place is jam-packed and filled to the brim with stuff. You never know what you'll find inside or outside on the porch. Best of all though, is Lucille Truitt, owner and local artist. If you visit the Ol' Store on a chilly day, you'll find Lucille (with her very little, very watchful, personal guard dog, Coco Puffs) sitting in front of the wood stove surrounded by visitors — all of whom are comfortably relaxed in overstuffed chairs. Lucille will call out to you: "Come in; welcome!" She will invite you to sit. And you can't resist her.

Lucille paints pictures of long-ago Oriental, using either her memory or old photographs as reminders. You can buy her original work or prints at the Ol' Store or at other Oriental shops and galleries. When you leave, Lucille and her visitors will wish you well, encourage you to return and thank you sincerely for your visit.

The **Inland Waterway Treasure Company** is on Hodges Street. It carries marine hardware, charts, foul-weather gear, nautical books and charts, gifts, T-shirts and nautical clothing. The company also rents bikes.

Croakertown Shop on Broad Street is a complete gift store. It carries a good collection of nautical books, prints and photographs of local scenes by local artists, an extensive choice of cards and a variety of gourmet coffees, mustards, sauces and jams and jellies. The Croakertown is also known as a fireplace shop because it sells wood and gas

INSIDERS' TIP

Croakers are so plentiful in the waters around Oriental that the town is known to many as "Croakertown."

stoves along with the appropriate accessories.

Across the street is **Circle 10 Art Gallery**, operated by Oriental's artists' cooperative. Art lovers can view and purchase original creations in a variety of media: acrylics, oils, watercolors, pastels, basketry, raku, glasswork, fiber art and jewelry. Circle 10 is open Thursday through Sunday from April to December. During the winter, it's open on weekends or by appointment. The gallery regularly features art shows for local artists in its front room. For more information about what's being scheduled call 249-0298.

At the corner of Broad and Hodges streets is a turn-of-the-century hotel that has been converted into shops and businesses. The **Old Hotel Gallery** offers one-of-a-kind ceramics and sculpture. Many pieces have a nautical theme. **Caldwell Creek Gallery**, also in the converted hotel, is a fine-art photography studio.

Restaurants

The **Trawl Door**, New Street, 249-1232, is at the foot of the bridge leading into Oriental. The building was constructed around 1915 and operated as a hardware and grocery business until the early 1970s. In 1978, the building reopened as an eatery and today it's the best-known restaurant and nightspot in town.

The large attractive lounge serves micro brews and has a bar menu that offers many kinds of nibblers as well as big, fat sandwiches, baskets of shrimp or oysters, soups and salads, and new this year — pizza with 14 different toppings. Live entertainment is usually available in the lounge on weekends. In the dining room, patrons will find various steamed shellfish and local softshell crabs. An excellent prime rib is featured on weekends. The Trawl Door has all ABC permits and offers banquet rooms for private parties.

Village Restaurant, Broad Street, 249-1700, is a popular spot. Among the breakfast items is a savory vegetable omelet accompanied by tender, homemade biscuits. The lunch salad bar and clam chowder are local favorites, along with the freshmade hamburgers, trout and chicken sandwiches and shrimp burgers. For dinner, you can choose from rib-eye steak and fried or broiled seafood platters. Oriental residents are particularly fond of the Saturday night seafood buffet. The Village has all ABC permits.

Oriental Marina Restaurant, Hodges Street, 249-1818, overlooks the harbor. It serves lunch and dinner inside a lovely dining room. Menu items include seafood, steaks, sandwiches, soups, salads and creative pasta dishes. The Topside Lounge upstairs is a popular spot for enjoying a drink and live entertainment on Saturday nights during the summer months. The restaurant has a full bar and patrons can call ahead to order take-out food.

M&M's Cafe, 205 S. Water Street, 249-9000, is in a former residence and has the ambience of a warm and friendly old inn. The food is delicious and imaginative and the service is excellent. For lunch, try the grilled vegetable salad, which comes with seared sweet peppers, potatoes, onions, summer or winter squash, feta cheese and pita bread. M&M's specials change daily. The cafe offers pasta dishes, lamb, veal, fish and homemade desserts (let the pumpkin cheesecake tempt you).

During cold snaps, M&M's patrons can dine on the glassed-in porch and enjoy the comfort of a gas-log fire while admiring the winter-flowering quince and views of the river. In summer and autumn, the glass is replaced with screens for al fresco supping and enjoyment of the river breezes. If you prefer, you can relax with a drink at the outdoor bar. M&M's Cafe has full ABC permits. It is open for lunch and dinner every day except Tuesday.

Accommodations

Accommodations can be found in motels and bed and breakfast inns. **Oriental Marina and Restaurant**, Hodges Street, 249-1818, is on the downtown harbor. Guests of this motel are privy to beautiful views of the river. The Oriental has 18 rooms decorated in a tropical island motif. Each room has a private bath and cable TV. A large deck and swimming pool, complete with a Tiki bar, are in the back. The marina accommodates 14 deep-water rental slips with water and 30- and 50-amp electrical

hookups. The Oriental is handicapped accessible and accepts major credit cards. Kids are welcomed, but pets are not allowed.

River Neuse Motel at the corner of S. Neuse Drive and Mildred Street, 249-1404, is a two-story motel in a quiet residential area beside the Neuse River. This motel offers 16 rooms with private baths, cable TV and in-room telephones. A private fishing pier and water-skiing are available for guests.

At the **Cartwright House**, British hosts Tina and Glyn Dykins will feed you incomparable breakfasts, cosset you and ensure that your stay in their bed and breakfast inn is unforgettable. Located at 301 Free Mason Street, 249-1337, this Victorian inn is warm and welcoming. Embraced by a large wraparound porch, where guests sit or swing as they watch the sailboats pass by, the Cartwright House takes you back in time, when life was slower and people stopped awhile to chat. Each of the inn's five bedrooms has a unique personality (and a private bath and cable TV). The wood-paneled Garret Room is hidden at the top of the house and is gotten to by its own private staircase. It was once the design studio of the former owner, solo racing and yacht designer Jerry Cartwright. The Victorian Suite is just right for celebrating a very special occasion. It has a fireplace, a double jacuzzi and a king-size bed. If you request, Tina and Glyn will welcome you to the suite with champagne, hors d'oeuvres and a rose or two.

Every morning the Dykins serve coffee on the landings of the three floors so that guests can have a cup without having to dress for breakfast first. But when you do arrive in the large, sunny dining room, Tina will have something divine for you to eat. You might be served scones made with golden raisins or blueberries or cranberries and slathered with clotted cream; or perhaps Tina will bake a crab or shrimp quiche or a cheese strata. Maybe there will be sausage and ham and crepes with cream cheese and fresh-picked raspberries. Whatever the dish, you can be certain that your dietary preferences will be taken into consideration and you can be sure that the breakfast table will always have fresh fruit, tea, milk and juice available.

Weekenders are treated to a Friday evening social hour where guests may mingle, sip complimentary wine or soft drinks and partake of Tina's hors d'oeuvres. The Dykins accept Visa and Mastercard, personal and travelers' checks. The inn is open all year and mid-week AARP discounts are available. Glyn will help you arrange golf outings and sailing charters. Ask him about the inn's bicycles, which are available gratis to all guests.

The **Tar Heel Inn Bed and Breakfast**, 205 Church Street, 249-1078, is open year round. Innkeepers Shawna and Robert Hyde offer

Drop by Lucille Truitt's Ol' Store to feel like an Oriental Insider.

eight bedrooms with private baths. Each room is individually decorated in Laura Ashley prints and each has either a four poster or a canopy bed. All rooms are nonsmoking. A brick patio, a courtyard and gardens entice guests to relax and luxuriate in the peacefulness of Oriental. Guests are treated to delicious breakfasts that appeal to every appetite — house specialties such as cheese blintzes with blueberry sauce, French toast in cinnamon syrup, vegetable quiches and baked omelets. Coffee, tea, juice and homemade muffins and breads are available every morning.

Marinas

Oriental Marina
Hodges Street, Oriental • 249-1818

This marina is just off the ICW. It is open year round and serves sail and power vessels up to 80 feet. It has 15 slips, 10 of which

are transient, an 8-foot entry channel, dockside depth of 6 feet, gas and diesel fuel, electricity, groceries, ice, showers, laundry facilities, a restaurant and an 18-room motel. Gas and diesel fuel are available as are some repairs.

Sea Harbour Marina
Harbour Way, Oriental • 249-0808

Sea Harbour Marina is on Pierce Creek about a mile from town. It is open year round, has 90 slips, serves sail and power vessels up to 45 feet, has gas and diesel fuel, a pump-out station, electricity, water hookups, a pool and restrooms.

Whittaker Creek Yacht Harbor
Whittaker Point Rd., Oriental • 249-0666, 249-1020

Whittaker Creek Yacht Harbor is about a half-mile from town on Whittaker Creek. It is open year round, has 160 slips including 20

INSIDERS' TIP

Local lore has it that the last eggs of a firebreathing Chinese dragon were aboard the shipwrecked *USS Oriental*. One survived and each year it appears on December 31 at the New Year's Eve Dragon Run.

transient slips, serves power and sailing vessels of up to 120 feet and has a marked entry channel with 8 feet of water on approach and at dockside. Gas and diesel fuel are available, as are a pump-out station, electricity, supplies, a ship's store, ice, laundry facilities and restrooms. The marina offers repairs and a courtesy car. A pool and restaurant are on-site.

Real Estate Companies

If you are interested in property or housing in Oriental, either to buy or rent, several firms can help you.

Coldwell Banker Harbor Realty, Hodges Street, 249-1000 or (800) 326-3748, can help you locate a residential or commercial prop-erty to suit your needs. It also offers a limited number of rentals.

Mariner Realty Inc., Broad Street, 249-1014, handles residential and commercial property sales and vacation and long-term rentals. Mariner also appraises and manages property.

Sail/Loft Realty Inc., Broad Street, 249-1787 or (800) 327-4189, handles sales of residential and commercial property, vacation and long-term rentals along with property management services, appraisals and storage units.

Village Realty, Broad Street, 249-0509 or (800) 326-3317, handles sales of residential homes and lots and commercial property. Village also handles vacation and long-term rentals.

The small, historic hamlet of Bath is North Carolina's oldest town.

Daytrips

Daytrips are the ideal way to see and enjoy more of North Carolina's coast, so we've provided this quick guide to some of our favorite getaway spots. These places are close by and are Insiders' favorites for various reasons — the relaxed atmosphere, scenic beauty, rich history, delicious restaurant fare or quiet evenings. After getting a taste of and learning more about these places, you might want to plan a longer visit.

The North Carolina Travel and Tourism Division of the Department of Commerce, Raleigh 27611, 733-4171 or (800) VISIT NC, offers information about sights throughout the state. And the North Carolina Department of Transportation, P.O. Box 25201, Raleigh, 27611, can provide the latest state maps, featuring travel information and details about state bicycle paths. Also, you should check out other books in the Insiders' Guide® series, such as *The Insiders' Guide® to North Carolina's Outer Banks* and *The Insiders' Guide® to Wilmington and North Carolina's Southern Coast*. An order form is provided at the back of this book.

Ocracoke Island

Visitors to Ocracoke love the leisurely, easy pace of this tiny island. From the time you arrive until the time you leave, you will be on Ocracoke Time — so slow down and enjoy the relaxed life.

The fact that you can get to Ocracoke only by water or air has something to do with the carefree pace. Most visitors and residents travel to and from the island via state operated ferries, so there is no need to hurry — you can

only come and go when the ferry does. The island's airstrip is about 1 mile from the village.

From the Crystal Coast, daytrippers take the Cedar Island-Ocracoke Ferry. This 2-hour and 15-minute ride ends in the heart of Ocracoke Village. Many people bring their cars to the island, but some passengers prefer to leave their cars on Cedar Island and walk or bike onto the ferry since there is no parking fee at the ferry terminal. Once in Ocracoke, visitors can walk or bike to just about any location on the island. Bike rentals are available on the island, as are rentals of fishing equipment, sailboats and boards, beach umbrellas and chairs, and camping and hunting supplies.

Ocracoke was established as a port by the colony of North Carolina in 1715. Early maps refer to the settlement as Pilot Town, because it was home to the men who were responsible for piloting ships safely into the harbor. About that same time, Edward "Blackbeard" Teach discovered the Outer Banks. The pirate and his crew robbed ships, murdered crews and terrorized island residents until 1718, when Lt. Robert Maynard of the Royal Navy and his crew ended Blackbeard's reign. Blackbeard was killed at a spot off Ocracoke now known as Teach's Hole. Legend has it that the pirate's head was mounted on Maynard's ship's bowsprit. Blackbeard's body was thrown overboard, where it reportedly swam around the ship seven times before it sank.

The island's solid white lighthouse was built in 1823 to replace the 1798 lighthouse that

---

INSIDERS' TIP

An estimated 35,000 tundra swan winter at Lake Mattamuskeet National Wildlife Refuge. Their arrival is celebrated with Swan Days, an annual November weekend festival sponsored by the Swan Quarter Service Group, at the lake.

was just inside Ocracoke Inlet and remained in operation until 1818 when it was damaged in a storm. This is the oldest and shortest of the Outer Banks' lighthouses, measuring only 65 feet in height, or 75 feet including the lantern. A keeper manned the light until 1929 when it was given electrical power. It is now operated by the Coast Guard. The lighthouse isn't open for tours or climbing, but sometimes volunteers offer historical talks and answer questions. Ask about staffing times at the visitors center or National Park Service offices.

Ocracoke Village is nestled on the edge of Silver Lake on the southern end and the broadest part of the small island. There are docks for pleasure and commercial fishing boats, inns, gift shops, private homes, historic graveyards, seafood wholesale and retail businesses, restaurants and marsh lands surrounding the water. Some homes date to the late 1800s, and many were built with timber from shipwrecks. As more visitors discover the island hideaway, more homes and lodgings are being built, and the face of the village is changing.

N.C. Highway 12, the island's main road, stretches the entire 16 miles of the island, from the Hatteras-Ocracoke ferry terminal on one end to the Cedar Island-Ocracoke ferry terminal at the other end. But much of the beauty of Ocracoke lies on the side streets. Howard Street is the most noted of the village's side streets. It was probably named for William Howard, who supposedly purchased Ocracoke Island in 1759 and is said to have served as Blackbeard's quartermaster.

Thirteen miles of undisturbed area stretch between Ocracoke Village and the Hatteras-Ocracoke Ferry terminal. On one side of the road is marsh leading to the sound and on the other is the Atlantic Ocean. This is the southern tip of Cape Hatteras National Seashore. This quiet area is the perfect spot for shelling, fishing, sunbathing and ocean sports.

Because of the town's small size, many of Ocracoke's businesses do double duty. Restaurants are also nightspots, inns feature restaurants and restaurants offer gifts. Ocracoke has a surprising number of businesses. The more you explore the village, the more places you will find tucked away.

There are all types of accommodation choices on the island, including inns, motels, bed and breakfasts and rental cottages. While not all the places remain open year round, those that do offer some inviting winter rates. Here is a small sampling of the shops, restaurants and accommodations you will find on Ocracoke.

The village is dotted with arts, crafts, gift and apparel shops. **Island Ragpicker**, N.C. 12, and **Village Craftsmen** on Howard Street are two favorites that sell handmade crafts. On the road leading to the British Cemetery, you'll find **Over the Moon**, 928-3555, a wonderful shop filled with celestial gifts. Down the road is **Island Artworks**. It's a great place for gift-shopping for things like blown-glass balls, painted boxes and unique jewelry. Just a stone's throw away is **The Village Bake Shop**, where early morning treats and coffee really hit the spot.

The Back Porch, 1324 Country Road, 928-6401, offers relaxed dining on its screened porch or in its dining room. The restaurant is an island favorite with such offerings as smoked bluefish, crab beignets, pastas, salads, seafood prepared in creative ways, prime meats, secret sauces and freshly ground coffees. Unfortunately, it is closed in the winter.

Island Inn and Dining Room, N.C. 12, 928-7821, is the oldest inn and restaurant on the Outer Banks. Guests are offered 16 traditional rooms in the 1901 country inn and 19 more modern rooms in another wing that fronts the island's only heated pool. The dining room is generally open for breakfast and dinner.

INSIDERS' TIP

While visiting Bath, ask to see the hoof prints of Jesse Elliott's race horse. The town legend tells of the 19th-century resident's challenge by the devil and the race "to win or to hell." Elliot was killed and his challenger disappeared, but the horses' hoof prints have remained clear to this day.

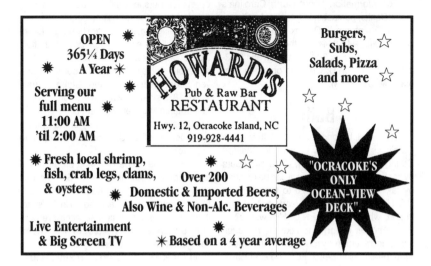

Howard's Pub & Raw Bar, N.C. 12, 928-4441, is the home of the Ocracoke Oyster Shooter — a raw oyster covered with Texas Pete or Tabasco, a shot of beer and black pepper. Try it! Howard's is also the best place to go on Ocracoke for good food and a good time. Enjoy local seafood, burgers, subs, salads, soup or any of the many menu choices and appetizers inside or on the large screened porch. Howard's doesn't close for hurricanes, holidays or winter, so you'll find the place open from 11 AM until 2 AM every day of the year.

Cafe Atlantic, N.C. 12, 928-4861, is in a traditional beach-style building but features innovative, nontraditional fare. Views from the dining room look out across marsh grass and dunes. The food, featuring seafood and a range of chicken, beef and pasta, is fantastic. And you've got to leave room for dessert. The restaurant has a nice selection of beer and wine and has a children's menu.

Silver Lake Motel, N.C. 12, 928-5721, overlooks Silver Lake and offers one wing with 20 rooms facing a shared porch. A newer wing has 12 suites with private balconies and some extras, such as huge whirlpools. The rustic inn is open all year, and dock space is available for guests with boats.

Anchorage Inn, N.C. 12, 928-1101, offers accommodations fronting Silver Lake Harbor.

Chairs are scattered around the porches. The five-story inn stands high above the traditional island structures, and its brick exterior is atypical of the local architecture. Guests are offered a pool, a boat ramp and docks, and rental sports equipment.

Pony Island Motel & Restaurant, N.C. 12, 928-4411, offers rooms, efficiency units and cottages. This reasonably priced motel has offered accommodations for more than 30 years. New additions include large bedroom suites with wet bars and refrigerators. The adjoining restaurant is open for a hearty breakfast and for dinner.

For more information about Ocracoke, stop by the Ocracoke Museum and Visitors Center, which is in the two-story yellow house across from the ferry terminal, or call the Ocracoke Civic Club, 928-6711.

If you venture a little farther north than Ocracoke, you will discover all of North Carolina's Outer Banks. Of course, once you leave Ocracoke on the Ocracoke-Hatteras Inlet Ferry, you really aren't daytripping anymore — you're traveling. The Hatteras Inlet Ferry, a 30-minute trip, actually puts passengers off at Hatteras Village. From there, N.C. 12 strings along the narrow islands all the way up to Corolla at the northern tip of North Carolina's Outer Banks.

For information about North Carolina's Outer Banks, contact the Outer Banks Chamber of Commerce, P.O. Box 1757, Kill Devil Hills 27949, 441-8144, or the Dare County Tourist Bureau, Box 399, Manteo 27954, 473-2138, which is on U.S. 64 and operates from 8:30 AM to 5:00 PM.

Bath

The small, historic hamlet of Bath is North Carolina's oldest town. Located in Beaufort County, this coastal village is about two hours by car from the Crystal Coast. It can be reached by taking U.S. Highway 70 to New Bern to U.S. Highway 17, which will lead you to Washington, where you take N.C. Highway 92 to Bath. Another option is to take the more leisurely and scenic ferry route. Board the Cherry Branch-Minnesott Beach Ferry outside Havelock (see our Getting Around chapter), which will take you to the north side of the Neuse River on N.C. Highway 306. Drive along N.C. 306 to the Aurora-Bayview Ferry, which will deposit you on the north side of the Pamlico River. You will soon reach N.C. 92, which you follow for a few short miles into Bath.

Incorporated in 1705, Bath remains almost entirely within the boundaries of the original town plan designed by John Lawson, surveyor general to the crown of England. Today's residents are proud of their heritage, and the restoration of the town's significant 18th- and early 19th-century buildings began around 1970. Seeing the historic sites can easily be done on foot. Before heading out on your own, stop by the visitors center on Carteret Street and view the orientation film *A Town Called Bath* as background for your walking tour. Although Bath is a small village, it has a number of historic sites well worth exploring.

Out the back door of the visitors center is a path leading to the **Van Der Veer House** (c. 1790). The structure was relocated from the waterfront on the north edge of town. Continuing along the oyster-shell walkway, you will come to the **Palmer-Marsh House** (c. 1740), with its large double chimney. The building is an excellent example of a large house from the Colonial period and its architecture and history were the basis for its being designated a National Historic Landmark. The house

opens for tours in April, and admission is by ticket obtained at the visitors center.

Crossing Water Street to **Harding's Landing** you will find a public boat dock that offers a picturesque view of the town shoreline. Heading south on Main Street to the corner at Craven Street leads you to the **Glebe House**. This c.1835 structure was the residence of several notable 19th-century Bath citizens. It has been restored and is property of the Episcopal Diocese of East Carolina. It is not open to the public.

Behind the Glebe House is probably the town's greatest landmark, the **St. Thomas Church**. The church was built between 1734-62 and remains the oldest church in the state. It has been restored, and services are conducted each Sunday. Visitors are welcome for self-guided tours. Continuing one block on Main Street will lead you to the **Bonner House** (c. 1830). The house was the home of the Bonner family, one of the distinguished families in Beaufort County history. It is an excellent example of North Carolina coastal architecture, which is characterized by large porches at the front and rear. Main Street in Bath is characterized by late 19th- and early 20th-century homes and commercial structures. **Swindell's Store**, a late-19th-century brick commercial structure, is still in operation as a general store. Notice the ballast stones used for walls and building foundations of many of the town's structures. They are reminders of Bath's rich maritime heritage.

Admission and guided tours of historic homes and buildings are by ticket that can be obtained at the visitors center. The historic town's visitors center hours are Monday through Saturday from 9 AM to 5 PM and on Sundays from 1 to 5 PM. For information before you go, call the visitors center at 923-3971.

Belhaven

If you've ventured as far as Bath, you'll be doing yourself a great disservice if you don't drive the few extra miles to scenic Belhaven. The riverside village is on the shores of the Pungo River and has a population of about 2,500. The river provides many opportunities for swimming, sailing and water-skiing and is a favorite fishing spot because of crabs and a wide variety of fish. The area is well-known among hunters of white-tailed deer, geese and ducks.

Located on the Intracoastal Waterway, the town is accessible by boat or car. From the Crystal Coast, you can get to Belhaven on four wheels by taking the Cherry Branch-Minnesott Beach Ferry and the Aurora-Bayview Ferry. By boat, simply follow the Intracoastal Waterway north.

The main industries in Belhaven are fishing, farming, phosphates, forestry and garment manufacturing. The county is the state's largest crab meat processing center and soybean and pulpwood producer.

Belhaven has been celebrating the **Fourth of July** for more than 80 years with a parade, fish fry, ski show, art show, dances and concerts. The day of excitement ends with a fireworks display over the Pungo River.

Belhaven's **Memorial Museum** is one of the 14 sites on the Historic Albemarle Tour. The City Hall, which houses the museum, is included in the National Register of Historic Places. The museum, open from 1 to 5 PM every day of the week except Wednesday, has a unique collection of items depicting the area's cultural and natural history. The town also has an interesting art gallery, **EEii's**, 315 Pamlico Street, that displays a wide range of paintings, sculpture and artwork. The hospitable **Chamber of Commerce Welcome Center**, 101 W. Main Street, is nearby. Tours for groups can be arranged through the chamber to see any of the town's points of interest. Many visitors enjoy Belhaven in mid-April when the **Dutch Festival** in nearby Terra Ceia celebrates the fields of tulips and gladiolas grown there.

One of the most popular places in Belhaven, reachable by land and sea, is the **River Forest Manor**, 600 E. Main Street, 943-2151 or (800) 346-2151, a rambling riverfront home that offers guest accommodations. Rooms are filled with antiques, and guest amenities include a hot tub, a swimming pool

and a full-service marina. The inn is famous for its wonderful Southern cuisine and lavish smorgasbord spread nightly. The original owner, John Aaron Wilkinson, president of a lumber company and vice president of Norfolk and Southern Railroad Construction, began construction of the Victorian mansion in 1899. Italian craftsmen were called in to carve the ornate ceilings, and by 1904 the mansion was completed. Carved oak mantels surround each of the 11 fireplaces, cut glass is leaded into windows, and crystal chandeliers and mahogany features garnish the house. Two of the baths include oversize tubs for two. In 1947 the house was purchased by Axson Smith of Belhaven and the inn was opened. Mr. Smith's family continues to offer its signature Southern hospitality.

For more information about Belhaven or group tour assistance, contact the Belhaven Community Chamber of Commerce, P.O. Box 147, Belhaven 27810, 943-3770.

Lake Mattamuskeet National Wildlife Refuge

OK, so a trip to Lake Mattamuskeet might require a bit more than a day. We have included it in the Daytrips chapter because it seems like an appropriate side journey if you make the jaunt to Oriental, Bath or Belhaven. The expansive wildlife refuge is on U.S. Highway 264. Well-placed road signs make it easy to find.

Lake Mattamuskeet National Wildlife Refuge stretches from Englehard on the east to Swan Quarter on the west. The refuge's 50,000 acres of water, marsh, timber and croplands are managed by the U.S. Fish and Wildlife Service. This beautiful area lies in the middle of the Atlantic Flyway. From October to March, the shallow 40,000-acre lake, which is said to be no deeper than a swan's neck, is a winter refuge for many migrating birds. Waterfowl populations are at their peak from December through February, and so are bird-watchers.

INSIDERS' TIP

The River Forest Manor is a delightful daytrip destination in Belhaven. Be sure to allow several hours to enjoy the buffet.

Photo: Scott Taylor

One of North Carolina's most picturesque lighthouses is in Ocracoke Village.

According to refuge information, 35,000 tundra swan winter at Mattamuskeet, and more than 150,000 birds gather at the lake between October and March. Thousands of snow and Canada geese and 22 species of ducks are seasonal inhabitants. The refuge provides habitat for osprey, red-tailed hawks, coots, blue herons, green-winged teals, black and ruddy ducks, cormorants, widgeons, mergansers, loons and many other birds. The refuge is also home to otters, bobcats, deer and black bears. Several endangered bird species, such as the peregrine falcon and the bald eagle, seek refuge around the lake. The refuge provides public hunting of swans, ducks and coots in season. For information on hunting dates and procedures, contact the refuge manager.

The 18-mile long and 5- to 6-mile wide lake is the state's largest natural lake, making it and its adjacent canals a popular spot for boating and sport fishing. Largemouth bass, striped bass, catfish, bream and other species can be taken from March 1 to November 1. Fishing is excellent in the canals and along the lake shore in spring and fall.

Herring dipping and blue crab fishing at the water control structures are very popular sports enjoyed by all ages. Herring dipping is permitted from March 1 to May 15, and crabbing is permitted year round from the water control structures. All fishing activities must be conducted in accordance with state regulations. Bow-fishing for carp and other rough fish is permitted during the fishing season.

Prohibited activities in the refuge include camping, littering, swimming, molesting wildlife and collecting plants, flowers, nuts or berries. Fires and firearms are also prohibited without special authorization. The speed limit on refuge roads is 25 miles per hour, and no vehicles, such as overland vehicles or trail bikes, are allowed outside regularly used roads and trails. Boats may not be left on the refuge overnight without a special use permit.

The **Lake Mattamuskeet Lodge** is the former pumping plant constructed in the early 1900s in an investment effort to convert the lake bottom to agricultural land and model community patterned after similar projects in Holland. The bankruptcy of one company after another in this effort led to its eventual abandonment, and the land was acquired by the U.S. Government in 1934 for the establishment of a waterfowl sanctuary. The pumping station was converted to a lodge for visitors and hunters and operated until 1974. It is now a National Historic Site of architectural and historic interest.

Nearby accommodations can be found in Englehard, Fairfield, Swan Quarter and Belhaven. For additional information about area accommodations and restaurants, write or call Hyde County Chamber of Commerce, P.O. Box 178, Swan Quarter 27885, 925-5201.

For information about Mattamuskeet National Wildlife Refuge, contact the refuge headquarters, Route 1, Box N-2, Swan Quarter 27855, 926-4021.

Wilmington

A visit to Wilmington will probably require more than a day if you want to do more than drive into town, walk the waterfront and return to the Crystal Coast. This upscale but laid-back river city is about 45 miles south of Jacksonville on U.S. Highway 17, about a two-hour drive from the Crystal Coast area. It's a good jumping-off point to explore several nearby beaches and attractions.

There is much to discover about this delightful city and its nearby attractions. For a complete guide to accommodations, restaurants, shopping, sightseeing and beaches, pick up a copy of *The Insiders' Guide® to Wilmington and North Carolina's Southern Coast.* (Or call (800) 995-1860 to order a copy.)The telephone area code for all numbers in the Wilmington area is 910.

There are two plantations that make for interesting sidetrips while in the Wilmington area. **Poplar Grove Historic Plantation**, 686-9989, is an estate at Scotts Hill, 9 miles north of Wilmington on U.S. 17. The 628-acre plantation, restaurant and country store are open to the public February through December. Poplar Grove Plantation is listed on the National Register of Historic Places.

Orton Plantation and Gardens, just south of the city and a few miles off U.S. 17, features a tour of the outbuildings, gardens of brilliant azaleas, Luola's Chapel, built in 1915, and an exterior view of Orton House, built in 1735. The house is one of the region's oldest historically significant residences in continuous use. The plantation gardens and outbuildings are open March through November. For information call 371-6851.

Several nearby beaches and attractions are a few minutes drive from downtown Wilmington. Fifteen minutes from the town hub lies **Wrightsville Beach**, which is primarily a family beach and small island community that features a number of quality hotels, motels, apartments, cottages, condominium develop-

INSIDERS' TIP

Visiting the Outer Banks in the fall and winter is a good way to avoid the flock of summer vacationers.

ments and many marvelous seafood restaurants.

Down U.S. Highway 421 is **Carolina Beach**, best known for its wide, uncrowded shore, swimming, surfing, pier fishing and deep-water charter boat fishing. Its shops, water slides, boardwalk and family amusement park offer something for everyone. **Carolina Beach State Park**, on the Intracoastal Waterway at Carolina Beach, is known for its collection of diverse plants, including the endangered Venus's flytrap. The state park has 1,773 acres with a marina, picnicking spots, hiking areas and a camping area. Call 458-8206 for general information or 458-7770 for the marina.

Continuing down U.S. 421 is **Kure Beach**, a site convenient to several attractions. It is adjacent to Historic Fort Fisher and is less than 2 miles from the N.C. Aquarium. The **Fort Fisher Historic Site** on U.S. 421 is near the mouth of the Cape Fear River and includes the remains of the old fort, a visitors center, a museum with items salvaged from blockade runners and a reconstructed gun battery. Guided tours of the old earthwork fortifications are available, and the site's 287 acres offer 4 miles of recreational beach, fishing and swimming areas, nature trails, boat ramps, picnic areas and refreshment facilities.

Nearby, the **N.C. Aquarium at Fort Fisher** houses display tanks, the largest shark tank in the state, a hands-on touch tank and changing displays and exhibits. One of the state's three aquariums, it is open year round and activities include films, talks, lectures, field trips, workshops and educational programs. For information call 458-8257.

Back to the river city of Wilmington. This historic town is home to one of the East Coast's fastest-growing deep-water ports. During the Revolutionary War, Wilmington gained importance as a point of entry, and its port was the last one on the Atlantic coast open to blockade runners during the Civil War. Continuous restoration and preservation make the town a history buff's delight. Its fast-growing population includes many students who attend the state university, UNC-Wilmington.

Almost everyone who visits Wilmington includes a tour of the **Battleship North Carolina**, 350-1817, on the Wilmington riverfront just off U.S. 17. Commissioned in 1941, the 44,800-ton warship wielded nine 16-inch turreted guns among its arsenal and carries nickel steel hull armor 16 to 18 inches thick. It was this platform that helped her survive at least one direct torpedo hit in 1942. The battleship came to its present home across the river from the downtown area in 1961. Recently repainted and redecked, Battleship *North Carolina* is open for tours every day of the year from 8 AM to sunset. Choose between two self-guided tours, both of which begin with a 10-minute orientation film. Tours cost $6 or $3 for children ages 6 to 11. Keep a lookout for old Charlie, the alligator who makes his home near the ship at the river's edge.

Another must-see in Wilmington is **St. John's Museum of Art**, 763-0281, at 114 Orange Street in the historic district. Housed in three restored buildings dating from 1804, the museum exhibits one of the world's major collections of romantic color prints by renowned 19th-century American artist Mary Cassatt.

The **Bellamy Mansion Museum of Design Arts**, 503 Market Street, 251-3700, is a classic Victorian example of Greek Revival and Italianate architecture. The mansion currently houses a museum of the design arts, embracing regional architecture completed in 1861, landscape architecture, preservation and decorative arts.

Another point of interest is **Brunswick Town** on N.C. Highway 133 just off U.S. 17, the site of the first successful European colony in the region. There are excavated ruins of the Colonial port town founded in 1726 and burned by the British in 1776. Displays include **St. Philip's Church**; **Russellborough**, the home of two royal governors; and the earthen mounds of the **Confederate Fort Anderson**.

Cape Fear Museum, 814 Market Street, (910) 341-4350, is a must for history buffs. The long-term exhibition "Waves and Currents: The Lower Cape Fear Story," follows the progress of the Lower Cape Fear from settlement to the 20th century and presents an expansive picture of southeastern North Carolina's heritage. Scenes come alive with life-size figures and miniature re-creations of Wilmington's waterfront, c. 1863, and the Fort Fisher Battle paints a picture of antebellum and Civil War times. Interactive children's ac-

Photo: Scott Taylor

This drum was taken from the surf at Ocracoke.

tivities, videos, changing exhibitions and special events add vitality to this learning experience.

Thalian Hall, 310 Chestnut Street, (910) 343-3664 or (800) 523-2820, is a historic center for performing arts. The hall regularly hosts dramatic and musical performances, many featuring national stars.

For shopping, Wilmington's downtown streets are lined with unique stores and restaurants. Be sure to check out the **Cotton Exchange**, 321 N. Front Street, 343-9896. Housed in eight restored 19th-century buildings on the waterfront, it features distinctive shops and several good restaurants. **Independence Mall** at Oleander Drive and Independence Boulevard, 392-1776, is home to more than 90 stores.

For an overnight stay, Wilmington has a number of fine chain hotels, and delightful bed and breakfasts are bountiful in the downtown historic district. **The Inn at St. Thomas Court**, 101 S. Second Street, 343-1800; the **Worth House**, 412 S. Third Street, 762-8562; the **Graystone Inn**, 100 S. Third Street, 763-2000, and **The Curran House**, 312 S. Third Street, 763-6603, are several noteworthy examples.

The river city abounds with fine restaurants offering delectable food. Some that come highly recommended are **Elijah's** in Chandler's Wharf, 343-1448; **The Pilot House** in Chandler's Wharf, 343-0200; **Caffe Phoenix**, 9 S. Front Street, 343-1395; **Szechuan 132**, 419 College Road, 799-1426; and **Crooks By The River**, 138 S. Front Street, 762-8898. But these are just a few of the many wonderful eateries available.

In mid-April, Wilmington's annual **Azalea Festival** draws visitors from miles around. Hundreds of lovely, old Southern homes on lots filled with huge trees draped with Spanish moss are surrounded by blooming azaleas. The entire community gets in on the act, with parades, contests and citywide celebrations. For information about the festival, call (910) 763-0905.

Stop downtown at the **Cape Fear Coast Convention & Visitors Bureau**, 24 N. Third Street, 341-4030 or (800) 222-4757, for answers to specific questions while you're in the Cape Fear area.

Index of Advertisers

Index

Going Somewhere?

Insiders' Publishing Inc. presents 40 current and upcoming titles to popular destinations all over the country (including the titles below) — and we're planning on adding many more. To order a title, go to your local bookstore or call (800) 955-1860.

Atlanta, GA	Maine's Mid-Coast
Boca Raton and the Palm Beaches, FL	Minneapolis/St. Paul, MN
Boulder, CO, and Rocky Mountain National Park	Mississippi
Bradenton/Sarasota, FL	Myrtle Beach, SC
Branson, MO, and the Ozark Mountains	North Carolina's Central Coast and New Bern
Cape Cod, Nantucket and Martha's Vineyard, MA	North Carolina's Mountains
Charleston, SC	Outer Banks of North Carolina
Cincinnati, OH	The Pocono Mountains
Civil War Sites in the Eastern Theater	Relocation
Denver, CO	Richmond, VA
Florida Keys and Key West	Southwestern Utah
Florida's Great Northwest	Tampa/St. Petersburg, FL
Golf in the Carolinas	Virginia's Blue Ridge
Indianapolis, IN	Virginia's Chesapeake Bay
The Lake Superior Region	Washington, D.C.
Lexington, KY	Wichita, KS
Louisville, KY	Williamsburg, VA
	Wilmington, NC

Insiders' Publishing Inc. • P.O. Box 2057 • Manteo, NC 27954
Phone (919) 473-6100 • Fax (919) 473-5869 • INTERNET address: http://www.insiders.com